HORSEWOMANSHIP
IN 19TH-CENTURY AMERICA

HORSEWOMANSHIP
IN 19TH-CENTURY AMERICA

WORKS FROM
Thomas Craige
Elizabeth Karr
Theodore H. Mead
C. De Hurst

EDITED WITH AN INTRODUCTION BY
Ellie Woznica

WHITLOCK PUBLISHING
Alfred, NY

A Conversation Between a Lady and Her Horse by Thomas Craige
first published in 1851.

The American Horsewoman by Elizabeth Karr
first published in 1884.

Horsemanship for Women by Theodore H. Mead
first published in 1887.

How Women Should Ride by C. De Hurst
first published in 1892.

First Whitlock Publishing edition 2017

Whitlock Publishing
Alfred, NY

ISBN: 978-1-943115-26-6

This book was set in Adobe Garamond Pro on 55# acid-free paper that
meets ANSI standards for archival quality.

ACKNOWLEDGEMENTS

A huge thank you to Dr. Allen Grove for his support
and for teaching me "how paper works."

A special thanks to my good friend, Haley Ruffner,
for her feedback on the many drafts of the introduction.

This anthology is dedicated to
my mother, Joyce, and my little sister, Lauren.

NOTE ON THE TEXT

The pieces found within this anthology are based on nineteenth century editions. Archaic spellings and phrasings were preserved in order to maintain the authenticity of the literature. However, obvious typographical errors have been corrected.

CONTENTS

INTRODUCTION

FROM BEING STONED to death and eaten on the steppes of Asia and Europe, to pulling plows faster than the ox and carrying warriors into battles, horses have played a significant role in history, allowing mankind to achieve things otherwise impossible with their own two legs. As men became more aware of the horse's athletic potential, the species moved from a staple food source and work animal to a means of enjoyment and exercise for men, accompanying them on long distance travels and the traditional fox hunt. But what about women? Compiled here for the first time are the works of Thomas Craige, Elizabeth Karr, Theodore H. Mead, and C. De Hurst, in an effort to see what it meant to be a horsewoman in nineteenth-century America. Exploring the acceptable ways for women to ride, dress, and interact with men while riding, these works expose social constraints on women in the horse industry.

These texts work together to present the reader with both the obvious and subtle differences between horsemanship and horsewomanship during the century. Looking specifically at the creation of the sidesaddle and the significance of the habit, the reader can see how women were alienated from the equestrian world that horsemen occupied, bound up in constricting clothing and made to balance on horseback in an unnatural, compromising position. Regressing from the basic freedoms developed by the earliest horsewomen, American women of the nineteenth century adopted these sexist expectations and a role that rendered them male-dependent, even on the back of an extremely powerful animal often celebrated for its ability to liberate its rider.

The Sidesaddle

Based on art depicting the warrior women of the Amazon, historians assume that women originally rode astride, riding horses for work, play, and even galloping into battles. Following Anne of Bohemia's introduction of the sidesaddle in 1382, women slowly stopped riding astride and gave up the convenience of the straddling position. Anne of Bohemia's model undeniably turned women into passengers—not riders—with its chair-like design that made it physically impossible for a woman to mount from the ground without assistance, let alone control or steer her own horse. This sidesaddle's design required a handler to lead the horse as the rider had absolutely no ability to manage her horse's pace or direction. During this time and for centuries thereafter, a façade of poise and beauty took precedence over effectiveness and comfort in riding for female equestrians and their mounts. De Hurst argues that riding astride "is impracticable, since they cannot sit down in the saddle and grip with their knees as they should, owing to the fact that their thighs are rounded, instead of flat like a man's. It might be possible for a lean and muscular woman to acquire a secure seat, but not for the average one." He sums up by saying, "Aside from any physical reasons, the [astride] position for a woman is, in my opinion, most ungraceful and undignified."

However, women did manage to evolve within their inhibiting space in the horse industry. During the first half of the nineteenth century, M. Pellier, Sr. invented the iconic sidesaddle that is still in use today. Though women were still forced to sit lopsided, this new model enabled them to face forward and steer their own horse, thus regaining some power and independence in riding. Pellier's sidesaddle offered women the means to take more control of their riding while still conforming to society's ideals of horsewomen as attractive and graceful; but, it still did not allow women to demonstrate the same level of capability as would be possible riding astride like their male counterparts.

Royal women around the world adopted the sidesaddle, and common women emulated them, relishing their chance to ride in the regal style of queens. Sidesaddle enthusiasts viewed those who did not adapt to the trend as unrefined and unladylike. For example, in the General Prologue of Geoffrey Chaucer's *The Canterbury Tales*, the Wife of Bath is not characterized as an ideal, virtuous woman; rather she is described as crass:

> She was a worthy womman al hir lyve:
> Housbondes at chirche dore she hadde fyve,
> Withouten oother compaignye in youthe,—
> But therof nedeth nat to speke as nowthe.

The Wife of Bath is a woman unbecoming of a sidesaddle. Even in the mid-twentieth century Lida Fleitmann Bloodgood wrote in her book, *The Saddle of Queens: The Story of the Side-saddle* that those "bemoaning the fact that women rode like men with a leg on each side of the horse, implied that they were no better than indecent hussies." Popular belief stated women could not ride astride while still looking the part of a proper lady.

THE HABIT

Though there were customary garments for men to wear while horseback (specifically while participating in a fox hunt), the correctly fitting habit was socially enforced for women for every ride no matter the setting. Her dress could not be too long as it would irritate the horse, but neither could it be short enough to expose her boot, thus ruining her elegant image. As in Anne of Bohemia's era of sidesaddle riding, a woman's apparel was less about function and more about capturing a woman's grace. The length and weight of the habit necessitated male assistance in mounting, forcing women to relinquish what little independence the new sidesaddle had granted.

It was also important that a woman account for her shape in selecting her riding habit—it needed to fit well and flatter her figure. In *The American Horsewoman*, Karr recommends that a woman's riding jacket "be cut short over the hips, and is then especially becoming to a plump person, as it diminishes the apparent width of the back below the waist." Along with fit, color played an important role in the habit. Though Karr says color is merely "a matter of taste," she advocates that "black is always stylish, and is particularly becoming to a stout person. Dark blue, hunter's green, and dark brown are also becoming colors, especially for slender, youthful figures." The reader can see the resonance of this tradition in the hunt seat show ring today—these jacket colors are still the most prominent. Though the idea of making the rider appear slim is still popular today, the nineteenth century habit traded practicality for the sake of exaggerated femininity.

THE HORSE

In their texts, Mead, Karr and De Hurst all explore the ways women tried to adapt, learn and work with their horses while hindered by their required riding style, even providing detailed explanations on how to ask a horse perform various maneuvers. Both Mead and De Hurst, probably having only ever ridden astride, write from the viewpoints of horsemen looking in. Karr, in contrast, practices what she coins "horsewomanship" in the nineteenth century; however, both parties agree that a horse appropriate for a lady is quite different than a male rider's lively steed.

The characteristics that make a horse suitable for a woman are discussed at length in each of these texts. The ideal woman's mount needed to be dull and calm enough for a woman to handle given her compromising, one-sided position. For this reason, the horses intended for female riders were prepared and extensively trained for the duty of carrying a woman. In *Horsemanship for Women*, Mead includes an illustration to show how to acclimate a horse to fabric flapping against its left side. However, there is more to a woman's equine partnership than just the proper training and desensitizing that was required prior to her mounting her horse for the first time. Specifically, Karr and De Hurst describe in depth the acceptable equine statures depending on the woman's body type. Karr claims:

> A large, majestic looking woman would present a very absurd spectacle when mounted upon a slightly built, slender horse; his narrow back in contrast with that of his rider would cause hers to appear even larger and wider than usual, and thus give her a heavy and ridiculous appearance, while the little horse would look overburdened and miserable.

De Hurst echoes Karr in his book, *How Women Should Ride*, when he states that "a woman should buy a horse on which she will look well. Much will depend upon her mount being of an appropriate size and build. A woman of medium size will look her best on a horse of about

15.2."[1] Though the idea that a horse should never be overburdened was a common belief of the time (and still is today), there wasn't as much stress on a man's weight in proportion to his horse's build. This point is illustrated, for example, in paintings of fox hunting, which depict men aboard horses they would be considered too tall or large for today.

Approaching horses with kindness instead of force is another topic frequently stressed in each of these books, especially in Craige's dialogue, *A Conversation Between a Lady and Her Horse*, where the horse explains the miserable past of his species' abusive relationship with mankind, and the importance of receiving kindness from his riders. The horse articulates to his rider (and the reader) that even though his species is known for strength and stamina, they "must be used moderately, as we are only flesh, blood, bone and muscle, like yourself." The horse even warns his rider by explaining to her that "many persons have saved their lives by being on good terms with me, while on the contrary, many have lost them."

SEXISM AND THE SEXUALIZATION OF HORSEWOMEN

The equestrian sport is growing in popularity with competitions frequently televised and live-streamed, and Nickelodeon's new series, *Ride*. Despite this, people still separate the relationship between horses and women and that of horses and men. Miriam Adelman and Jorge Knijnik explain in their book, *Gender and Equestrian Sport*, that writers often make "explicit reference to the historic partnership of 'men and horses' or those that evoke women's presence." The primary difference is that the relationship between women and horses has been sexualized through centuries of literature and culture, and even subtly in the works anthologized in this book. For instance, many people today believe that women and girls ride horses partially because it gives them sexual gratification. This fallacy exists due to over-sexualized characters like the Wife of Bath, whose sexuality is visibly linked to the act of riding astride.

---

1 Horses were originally measured in the width of a man's hand from the top of the wither down to the ground. Over time the hand became standardized and now measures exactly four inches.

Even in the fundamental practices deemed important for horse-women to uphold, the not-so-archaic belief that women are objects still resonates: both sexually and as property that is traded from father to husband. The restrictive riding position that made women dependent on their male companions and the importance of the perfectly fitting habit emphasizes the idea that a woman is a body to be seen and not heard, an ornament of the horseman, not respected for her own intuitive horse sense. In comparing the dates in the timeline provided and the works in this anthology it is clear that the woman's role in the equestrian world regressed more than it advanced in the nineteenth century.

Even Mead, who urges women to take an active role in training young horses, writes about a horsewoman as an "enterprising damsel [who] manages to overcome all opposition, and, skirted, hatted, gloved, sets off in fine spirits," affirming the belief that even in defeating the resistance to her presence in the horse industry, a woman must be decorously clad on her horseback excursions. Riding Master Colonel Hitchcock encouraged women to embrace riding sidesaddle because it "is the most decorative, dignified, and graceful method, and pleases the male eye, which prefers the ultra-feminine woman to the type which emulates the male in attire or atmosphere." Hitchcock suggests that the enjoyment women received from feeling connected to a horse while galloping through open fields was merely to catch the eye of a prospective husband and to satisfy the eyes of her male companions.

Riding for women in nineteenth-century America was fraught with patriarchal impositions on her behavior, dress, and seat. During the turn of the century, there was what Luigi Gianoli, in *Horses and Horsemanship Through the Ages*, calls an "upsurge of feminism," where women abandoned the habit and started to wear breeches. In 1902, Mrs. Landenburg, the first woman to wear a split skirt while riding astride, led a movement in which she fought to abolish the sidesaddle in America. As a result, many women chose to ride astride, but not without backlash from male audiences. Gianoli captures the popular opinion of the time when he writes that riding astride in breeches took away "some of her poetry and grace" in the saddle. There are scarcely any acknowledgements of a woman's ability to be a proficient rider in these texts; instead, the female rider is left to overcome her restrictions of behavior and dress to be an effective rider within the bounds of nineteenth-century propriety.

Women like Nan Jeanne Aspinwall Gable Lambell, famous for her acts as a sharpshooter and roper in Buffalo Bill's Wild West Show with her husband, strived to change how the equestrian world viewed women. In 1911, mounted on her horse Lady Ellen, she became the first woman to ride alone from the Pacific Ocean across America to the Atlantic, all while riding astride and shoeing her own horse. Two years later, famous feminist Inez Milholland, aboard Gray Dawn, led a march dressed as Joan of Arc in an effort to promote women's suffrage, noted shouting, "you men ought to be ashamed of yourselves!"

Though the equestrian world likes to pride itself on being one of the few coeducational sports in which men and women compete at the same level, women spent much of the nineteenth century struggling to break out of their gender-imposed box, in order for the horse industry to reach its current state of relative equality. When the United States Equestrian Team began in 1949, it consisted of two men and two women. Even though they made up half of the team, women were not permitted to show jump in the Olympic Games until 1956. Women had to fight for their chance to ride some sharper horses, wear pants, get their right leg on the other side of their mounts, and be seen as horsewomen who could ride just as well as their male counterparts.

ELLIE WOZNICA, APRIL 2017
ALFRED, NY

CHRONOLOGY OF HORSEWOMANSHIP

2000BCE   Early evidence of horse domestication, used in ancient transportation and warfare to pull chariots.

500BCE   Persian carving depicts women riding and fighting in cavalry alongside men.

62CE   Death of Boadicea, British queen said to partaken in chariot races, breeding, and exporting horses to Rome, thought to be the first woman to maintain a racing stud.

1000s   Lady Godiva rides around town bareback and naked to convince her husband, Earl Leofric, to lift the taxes on horses.

1382   Anne of Bohemia introduces sidesaddle riding to England and creates the first model of the sidesaddle: a chair that sat the woman sideways on the horse. Women had no control, had to be led by a man.

1478   Geoffrey Chaucer publishes *The Canterbury Tales* where the Wife of Bath is described riding with "a paire of spores sharpe."

1500s   Margaret of the Netherlands only admits women into her court if they can get on their horses without male assistance. It is assumed that those who did not need assistance were riding astride, not sidesaddle.

           Catherine de Medici creates a more practical sidesaddle with the iconic leg hook.

1600   Riding astride generally believed to be unladylike and improper.

1700s   Catherine the Great, Empress of Russia, demanded all women of her court ride as she did: astride.

1830s	M. Pellier, Sr. invents the traditional sidesaddle, still in use today.
1851	Thomas Craige publishes *A Conversation Between a Lady and Her Horse*.
1884	Elizabeth Karr publishes *The American Horsewoman*.
1887	Theodore Hoe Mead publishes *Horsemanship for Women*.
1892	Founder of Olympic Games, Baron Pierre de Coubertin, writes: "Olympics with women would be incorrect, unpractical, uninteresting, and not aesthetic."
	C. De Hurst publishes *How Women Should Ride*.
1920	American woman are granted the right to vote.
1949	United States Equestrian Team (USET Inc.) is created. The team consisted of two men and two women, but the women were excluded from competing in the Olympic Games.
1956	Pat Smythe is the first woman to represent her country for the Olympic Games in equestrian event of show jumping.
1968	Kathy Kusner is the first woman to receive a jockey's license.

BIBLIOGRAPHY

Adelman, Miriam, and Jorge Knijnik, editors. *Gender and Equestrian Sport: Riding Around the World.* Springer, 2013.

Bloodgood, Lida Fleitmann. *The Saddle of Queens: The Story of the Side-Saddle.* J. A. Allen and Company, 1959.

Carr, K. E. "Riding Horses." *Quatr.us*, April 2016, www.quatr.us/environment/horses2.htm

Dashper, Katherine. *Human-Animal Relationships in Equestrian Sport and Leisure.* Routledge, 2017.

Gianoli, Luigi. *Horses and Horsemanship Through the Ages.* Crown Publishers, 1969.

Golden, Flora. *Women in Sports: Horseback Riding.* Harvey House, 1978.

Martin, Ann. *The Equestrian Woman.* Paddington Press, 1979.

O'Reilly, CuChullaine. "Sidesaddles and Suffragettes: The Fight to Ride and Vote." *The Long Riders Guild Academic Foundation,* 2014, www.lrgaf.org/articles/sidesaddles_and_suffragettes.htm

A
Conversation
Between a Lady
and her Horse

A

CONVERSATION

BETWEEN

A LADY AND HER HORSE.

———

BY THOMAS CRAIGE,

OF THE PHILADELPHIA RIDING SCHOOL.

———

PHILADELPHIA
PUBLISHED BY THOMAS CRAIGE,
And for sale at the N. W. corner of Fifth and Arch Streets.
1851.

A CONVERSATION BETWEEN A LADY AND HER HORSE

LADY   I should be much pleased to ride you this afternoon.

HORSE   If you will endeavor to make me as comfortable as possible, I will grant your request.

LADY   Are you not always comfortable?

HORSE   How can I be, when I am so much abused?

LADY   You appear to look as well as other horses.

HORSE   We are not always to be judged by our looks; but if you desire, you may ride me, if you will first see that the saddle will fit my back; that it is not girthed too tight; and when you are seated upon it, that you are equally balanced, that your whole weight may not be thrown upon my left side, hurt my shoulder, and keep me under a continual strain to support you in the saddle; also, that the bridle be not too hard for my mouth.

LADY   I think you are almost too particular: for I cannot see how it would be possible for a delicate creature like me, weighing only one hundred and forty-seven pounds, to hurt your back, if I were to ride you all day. I shall only ride you a short distance.

HORSE   What do you call a short distance?

1

LADY   Around the Wissahiccon to Germantown, and back by way of the Falls, where you shall have as much oats as they choose to give you, more water than you can drink, and a fine rest.

HORSE   These words sound delightful, but you forget the thermometer is 95 deg. and oh! those high hills, and loaded with a heavy saddle, that covers more than one half my body, your dress too, flowing back over my hip, and nearly your whole weight thrown upon my left side. You must remember that while you are riding I am on foot.

LADY   Do not complain, after what I have promised you.

HORSE   I shudder at such promises; when I get to the Falls, after my warm and weary journey, and you are getting supper, they do not choose to give me the oats you promised, for the very reason that you did not order it; and as for more water than I can drink, that does not cost any thing: weary and trembling, I thrust my head suddenly into the bucket, to cool my parched tongue, the groom, in a rage, strikes me on the head, and jerks me with the stiff bit in my mouth, until it bleeds, and then pokes me away back, under a dirty old shed, without a breath of air, with the saddle so tight that I can scarcely breathe, while you are refreshed with dainties from a sumptuous table.

LADY   My horse if you please! It is getting late, although mother knows I am out—mounted again! Come my good fellow, you can canter home finely, after so long a rest. You appear to be taking advantage, because I have treated you kindly; now, if you don' t stir yourself I shall be compelled to stir you. A bird that can sing and won't sing, must be made to sing.

HORSE   A bird that will sing, may sing all the time; if I were to canter until my tail dropped off, I have no doubt you would be sorry that I had not another to lose.

LADY   The object of your creation was expressly for our use.

HORSE   I have no doubt but that we were created expressly for your service, to labor for you, to carry you when and where you are not able to carry yourselves, and to do all that is in reason required of us for your ease and comfort; but at the same time, we are to be treated as creatures, sent by a wise and merciful Creator, placed under the care of intelligent beings, who will be accountable if they do not treat us kindly, feel for us when we suffer, and try to alleviate our pain. As we cannot relieve ourselves, it is to you we look for protection and sympathy; to observe and administer to our wants, and not think we are made of steel.

LADY   You astonish me! I thought you were such large, powerful creatures, that you could endure heat, cold or fatigue, and not be injured by it.

HORSE   We are large, strong and active, can endure a great amount of fatigue, but we must be used moderately, as we are only flesh, blood, bone and muscle, like yourself. If we are exposed to a chilly atmosphere when warm, our muscles become contracted, then we are not fit for use, and must endure great suffering and often become entirely useless.

LADY   I should like to know how to treat you when I ride you again; before, I never considered any thing but the pleasure I should enjoy from the ride, without the least intention of injuring you.

HORSE   As you are desirous of knowing, I will inform you.

LADY   I should like you to be particular, as you appear to understand your own feelings best, and can tell me what I cannot observe.

HORSE   In the first place, the bit should be suited to my mouth, the saddle to my back, and the crupper not too tight.

LADY   Suppose these were all wrong, what would be the consequence?

HORSE   If the saddle did not fit my back, I should suffer all the time
         you rode me; I could not perform one pleasant gait. If the
         crupper were too tight around my tail, it would hurt me,
         so that I would be obliged to kick up to get relief. If the
         bit were too hard and stiff for my mouth, and you should
         check me, I would rear up and perhaps fall over backward.
         When I do rear, it is often the effect of an unskillful hand,
         and then, whilst I am rearing, you would most likely check
         me again, that would complete the scene. Should you
         check me with the bridle and strike me at the same time
         behind the saddle, I would be apt to serve you as I did the
         young German trooper, in Third street, one morning.

LADY   Well, how did you serve him?

HORSE   When he mounted me, I soon felt that he could not ride
         and I was very sorry for him, as he was dressed so nicely,
         with his white pants, his spurs on his boots, and looking so
         proud.

LADY   I am anxious to know how you served him.

HORSE   I do not like to tell you, for I am afraid you will laugh.

LADY   You have excited my curiosity, do tell me, and I will en-
         deavor not to laugh.

HORSE   I could not help laughing myself, and if it made a horse
         laugh, who would not? I have told you about his dress and
         spurs; he was now ready; I was brought up and he mounted
         me. I felt somewhat alarmed, as he threw his right foot over
         the saddle and his sword came rattling down by my side.
         When he was seated in the saddle, off we started; I began to
         prance and felt so proud, for we had many spectators look-
         ing at us. I felt conscious all the time, if any thing occurred,
         he would fall off; but he had all confidence that he could
         ride me. To show me off to advantage, he gave me a sud-
         den check with the curb-rein and then struck me with both
         spurs, because I made a halt when he checked me and threw

up my head. Without knowing what I did, I reared as he checked me the second time, and as he spurred me, I threw up both heels, but oh, the poor Dutchman! I thought he would never come down; I stood aghast. When he did come down it was nose foremost, right on the hard stones; as he jumped up his eyes flashed fire; as for his nose it was flat on his face, while the blood flowed freely over his white pants, as he stood with both hands stretched out, his nose giving vent to his feelings. The poor soldier had the sympathies of many, while others considered it the fate of war. I stood perfectly quiet, until I was ordered to be taken back to the stable, as a vicious horse, not fit to be ridden on parade.

LADY   I should not like you to serve me as you did the trooper.

HORSE   When I am treated right, I will endeavor to do right.

LADY   Will you allow any one who may be ignorant of the art to ride you?

HORSE   I always try to accommodate myself first and then the rider; if those who are ignorant of the art will only be kind to me, and not begin as soon as they are mounted to whip me, jerk the reins and irritate me, so that I do not know what to do, I will endeavor to carry them safely.

LADY   From what you have told me, I shall almost be afraid to ride you.

HORSE   Those who learn to ride from their own experience and practice, without instruction, labor under many difficulties and are frequently injured through want of a knowledge of the art, as so much depends upon the management of the reins, to secure their safety and comfort.

LADY   I see many ride who have never had any instruction.

HORSE   They do not ride, but only imagine they do; for when they get upon my back they sit all doubled up in a heap, hanging upon one side of the saddle, or leaning nearly over my head, pulling and hauling the reins, first one side and then the other—sometimes jerking me, and not satisfied with that, but striking and scolding me at the same time, for being a stubborn disagreeable horse, that will not do any thing right.

LADY   When I hear all your complaints I feel sorry for you.

HORSE   You have heard but few of the difficulties I meet with.

LADY   How do you feel when ridden by a skillful hand?

HORSE   I feel just like a bird on the wing. I trip away with a light foot, and a light heart, and by every movement, convince my rider that I am well pleased. I find the reins are perfectly straight, that she is equally balanced in the saddle, so that I can carry her with ease to myself and comfort to my rider. At intervals, I feel her gentle hand patting me on the neck, smoothing down my mane, and her kind voice encouraging me. I have such confidence in her that let what may happen, I will not be frightened as long as I hear the voice of one who treats me with kindness.

LADY   Will kindness do so much with the animal creation?

HORSE   Kindness is the grand secret by which all the animal creation can be best governed. It creates in me an attachment for my rider, so that I always feel safe, especially when I hear the voice of one whom I know is my friend.

LADY   How strange it appears to hear you speak of so much kindness to a beast.

HORSE   We are a very sensitive race; all our senses are in requisition, for it is only through them we act. They are said by man to take the place of reason; but I can assure you that we have to act with reason, and our riders and drivers with instinct only; for I have been whipped of a dark night (when my rider could not see his hand before him,) to make me cross a bridge that was broken down, until I was compelled to make a desperate leap to clear it, taking my rider over safely. After doing so, he dismounted to see what was the cause, and found that I had saved his life by the leap, so that after he mounted me he caressed and patted me until we reached home, treating me with much kindness. Now, when he found that I would not go over the bridge, had he dismounted like a man of sense and examined into the cause, how much less trouble it would have been for him, and how much less I should have suffered.

LADY   How is it possible that you should know the bridge was broken down, when it was so dark your rider could not see it?

HORSE   Our senses are much more acute than yours, because we are more exposed to danger, and cultivate them for our own and the rider's safety. When I came to the bridge I could smell the effluvia arising from the marsh below, although I could not see that the bridge was broken, but felt certain after a close examination, that if forced I could leap it, or I should still have resisted the attempt to force me over.

LADY   I did not know that horses had so much instinct.

HORSE   You remember how Balaam abused the poor ass because he would not pass the angel with a drawn sword in his hand. If he had passed, it would have cost Balaam his life; but when his eyes were opened and he saw the angel standing before him, what a rebuke it must have been for his disobedience, getting a passion and abusing the poor beast.

LADY   Why is it that you so often shy at large stones on the road side, at a shadow thrown across it, at a dark spot, or where water has been thrown into the street?

HORSE   It is for safety that I do it. If I were to stumble over some large stone, or into a ditch, or sink into some place on the street that had just been filled up, without trying to avoid it, I would be severely whipped if the rider escaped with her life, and called a clumsy, blind, stupid animal, not worth owning. On the contrary, if I am watchful and avoid all danger, you say I shy at the least thing I see, and whip me for that. Now, pray, tell me what I shall do to do right?

LADY   Is there any sign by which I may know when you are alarmed? If so, how shall I manage you?

HORSE   If I approach an object that is likely to alarm me I prick up my ears and tail, and move on in rather a prancing mood, with my ears thrown forward and feel as though I should like to wheel to the right or left; then by patting me on the neck, and keeping my head directed to the object, I will, by perseverance on the part of the rider, pass on safely. On the contrary, if you whip, spur, or fight with me, the next object I see I will wheel around before I let you know much about it, fearing that you will whip me up to it again and frighten me more than I would otherwise be. But to be frightened by an object before me, and the whip or spur behind, driving me furiously up to it, would terrify old Sam himself.

LADY   Suppose you were to rear, kick, or run, how should I know your intention, and how should I manage you?

HORSE   If I rear, the reins must be moved forward immediately, until I come down again upon my feet; for if you draw the reins tight instead of moving them forward (which you most likely would,) then it is extremely dangerous, as I might be thrown over backward. If I design to kick, I throw my ears nearly flat on my head, with my head inclined downwards before I can conveniently do so. If you jerk my head up quickly, and then keep it up, I will cease at once; then, by your keeping a tight rein, I will not do it again. If I attempt to run, you must check me suddenly, and continue checking me until I stop, for if you let me get started, it is the more difficult to stop me. If you find it difficult to stop me with one hand, divide the reins, taking two in each hand, then check me first on one side, and then on the other, in quick succession, until I do stop. Never attempt to leave the saddle, if I get playful or run, as there is more safety in the saddle a hundred times than in trying to leap from it once; for if you remain in the saddle, I will stop some where, but if you attempt to leave it you will most assuredly be injured.

LADY   Riding on horseback requires mine instruction, attention, and acquaintance with the art than I had supposed.

HORSE   There is some danger in riding on horseback unless those who ride will be moderate, as there is much less danger in moderate exercise than in fast riding. I remember a lady who was anxious to ride for her health. She was very delicate and nervous, but could not be induced for some time to come near me, but after being assured that I would not hurt her she consented to mount me, trembling in every nerve. When seated upon my back she said she was dying, until assured that she was worth a thousand dead people. I moved off very gently, in order to assure her that I would not injure her, but had scarcely gone ten yards before she looked around, asking in a faint tone, if she could not go a little faster.

LADY   I suppose you meet with many adventures, and some of them very amusing?

HORSE   I meet with many, some of them very amusing and some very distressing. One afternoon a lady ordered for herself a first rate horse; as I was considered a good, safe, and well-trained one, I was sent to the door at the time appointed. I had not been there long before I saw the fair rider rushing out toward me, whip in hand. I felt somewhat alarmed, and started back a little as she approached for fear she would strike me. The groom patting me on the neck, brought me up to the curb-stone. The fair rider was thrown upon my back some how. She immediately drew up the reins all in a bundle, and as she did so gave me a number of cuts with the whip around my side, at the same time drawing the reins all to the left side. I commenced running around to the left, as she drew me, until I struck my foot against the curb-stone, and down I came, rider and all, flat in the gutter. As soon as I could get the use of the reins, I sprang to my feet again, finding myself straight on the street. I felt the whip again around my side, and away we went up the street like a locomotive just broken loose from the train. All the afternoon I was pulled and whipped, until I could scarcely stand; and when I returned in the evening I was sent home with a message from my rider that I was good for nothing, and fell down in the gutter before she could get me started from the door.

LADY   I think it looks unlady-like to ride fast through the city, and ladies should have some information on the subject.

HORSE   I am of your opinion, and would say to any rider, when I am brought to your door for an afternoon ride, approach me gently, pat me on the neck before you mount me, and glance over my equipments to see if they are all right; if so, adjust your reins, draw them sufficiently tight to prevent my starting while you mount, at the same time have them straight on both sides that I may not turn while you are mounting; after you are seated adjust your reins again. The curb rein should not be too tight at first, for fear of my mouth being tender. After being seated in the centre of the saddle, and your dress arranged, draw your reins a little tighter and speak to me, and with a slight motion of the reins forward, I will start off moderately without being touched with the whip; for if you will only signify what you wish me to do I am always ready and willing to obey. After starting, walk me some distance, then if you find all is right you can move me a little faster; but do not think of cantering me until you get off the pavement, as it is dangerous to us both, for I may slip unless I am on

the centre of the street. On the summer road there is not
the same danger; near the curb, the pavement inclines that
way, and I am very apt to slip if I go out of a walk, except
on the centre of the street. Always walk me when passing
vehicles in the city, if you are compelled to ride near the
side walk. When you reach the summer road, and find it
smooth and pleasant, you may canter me a quarter or half
a mile, if the weather be not too warm. After cantering,
let me walk; after walking me, then let me rack or trot a
little for a change before you canter me again. Let me walk
up and down all the hills; when ascending let the reins be
rather loose, when descending rather tight, but not so tight
that I cannot move. If you ride me faster than a walk down
hill, it is extremely dangerous even for a good rider. If you
ride me faster than a walk up hill, it not only injures, but
fatigues me, so that I cannot perform with any degree of
comfort after it. When I reach the summit of a hill, continue to let me walk a little until I recover from the fatigue
of ascending, before you canter me. You should watch me,
and if I begin to perspire too much, then walk me until I
cool off a little. Use your judgment in riding me; imagine
yourself walking at a rapid rate on a warm day, then you
can feel for me. When you stop at a public house, do not
let the groom run at me the first thing with a bucket of cold
pump water, for the sake of making a trifle, and founder
me, which would render me entirely useless or cause my
death. If you stop to get supper, have me put in a comfortable place, have the girths of the saddle loosened a little,
that I may breathe freely until starting, and then they can
be tightened again. If you order me to be fed, see that it is
done, or get some one to see to it for you. Let the first and
last part of your ride always be in a walk, as the contrary injures both you and me; it injures you, because you cannot
understand me or manage the reins. If you start me off fast
I cannot perform so pleasantly during the whole afternoon,
as I have not time to get any correct or natural step, and if
I do not get it in the beginning, it is not likely that I will

on returning home. If you ride me fast toward the close of the ride I shall suffer, for when I return to the stable, I will cool off too suddenly, then I take cold, my muscles become contracted, and I feel so stiff the next morning that I can scarcely walk. Now, if you wish to feel the benefit of the ride, come home moderately, so that you may dismount from your horse cool, that neither you nor I will take cold. You will enjoy the ride and wish to ride again, as it benefits you if you get the exercise as it is designed.

LADY   I remember now that I have always felt much better after I have taken a moderate ride; but then it is so fashionable and so exciting to ride fast, and so pleasant at the same time.

HORSE   Then I suppose you will be in the fashion if you even suffer for it afterward, or run the risk of breaking your neck. Those who are in the habit of riding fast are those who get out only once in a month or two, and when they do get out they feel as though all the world were let loose before them. The gentlemen who ride with them can scarcely get within a quarter of a mile of them, and you would often think they were not in company at all. Nothing looks more ridiculous than to see ladies going at such a speed. It looks as though some of their relations were dying, and they were going for a physician, or as though the city were on fire and they were trying to escape.

LADY   I must agree with you in some of your remarks, for I have seen a lady on the road myself start off from her company, so that when I saw her coming I was certain the horse had run away with her, until I saw her turn him back and run him to the company again.

HORSE   I have been served in the same way often, but take my word for it when you see a lady ride in that style she does not understand the art, gets out but seldom, and intends while she is out to make the most of it. Again, those who race and tear me about the most, feed me the least when they are out, for they have no time to feed me. It is all ride and go ahead with them, as though I were a locomotive, and the steam always at the highest pressure.

LADY   The more I ride the more pains I take to ride well. I shall endeavor for the future to ride moderately, to look graceful, and handle the reins well, to try and get all the information on the subject that I possibly can, so that I may not be intimidated if I happen to get on a horse that is difficult to manage, as I find every new or strange horse has new and strange ways to me. The more I learn about horses and riding, the more necessity I find for trying to ride those which are most difficult, for if I ride the same one all the time I will find out his ways, which would be very pleasant, no doubt, but my great desire and ambition is to be able to ride any horse well.

HORSE   Now you are getting on in the right way. If every lady would feel, think and act as you express yourself, how much pleasure we poor horses would have? We would be ridden well, but moderately, as the best riders always ride moderately, and take good care of us. They feel for us if we get weary and encourage us. They do not ride us like the Yankee did his horse. He said he could ride him so far in one day that he could not get back in three. There are too many of us poor horses ridden in that way. I have known them to go so far in one afternoon that they never got back.

LADY   From your conversation, some would almost be induced to believe that you are more than mortal.

HORSE   Have you never read in the Revelation of St. John what he saw in Heaven, in the vi. chap. and 2d verse. "And I saw, and behold, a white horse: and he that sat on him had a bow; and a crown was given unto him; and he went forth conquering, and to conquer. And when he had opened the second seal, I heard the second beast say, come and see. And there went out another horse that was red: and power was given to him that sat thereon to take peace from the earth, and that they should kill one another with the sword. And I beheld, and lo, a black horse; and he that sat on him had a pair of balances in his hand. And I looked, and behold a pale horse; and his name that sat on him was Death, and power was given unto him to kill with the sword, etc. a portion of those on the earth." The first horse was white, the rider had a bow, a crown was given him, and he went out as a conqueror. No doubt this is the reason why generals in armies, going out to battle, ride white or light colored horses. The next was red, an emblem of strife and contention; the next black, an emblem of justice, the rider holding the balances in his hand; the last the pale horse, and his rider that monster death! This beautiful vision of St. John's, you will remember when you ride the various colored horses, that he saw in that Celestial city, the streets of which are paved with gold.

LADY   Do you remember what Solomon, the wise man, said?

HORSE   I remember well that in Ecclesiastes, iii. chap. 20th and 21st verses, he says: "All go unto one place; all are of the dust, and all turn to dust again. Who knoweth the spirit of man that goeth upward, and the spirit of the beast that goeth downward?" Again, that good and patient man, Job, he was a good horseman, and understood the art well, or he could not have given such a beautiful description of the horse in his xxxix. chapter. "Hast thou given the horse strength? hast thou clothed his neck with thunder? canst thou make him afraid as a grasshopper? the glory of his nostrils is terrible. He paweth in the valley, and rejoiceth in his strength: he goeth out to meet the armed men: he mocketh at fear, and is not affrighted; neither turneth he back from the sword. The quiver rattleth against him, the glittering spear and the shield. He swalloweth the ground with fierceness and rage: neither believeth he that it is the sound of the trumpet. He saith among the trumpets,

Ha, ha! and he smelleth the battle afar off, the thunder of the captains, and the shouting." Who could surpass this description of our race? I think not one. Job was patient: he always treated our race with kindness. I wish there were more persons like him.

LADY   You speak of Job as being such a good man. I think we have just as good people now as Job was.

HORSE   It may be possible. I know they do much for the benefit of mankind. I know they form many societies for benevolent purposes; but they forget the poor horse, that labors incessantly for them. We assist in cultivating the soil; we haul the produce to market, draw materials to build your mansions, timber to build your ships; we assist in making your railroads and canals, we haul your merchandise, we go to your coaches, and take you out to enjoy the summer breeze; we carry you on our backs for your health and pleasure; we carry the hunter, and the child of the forest, in pursuit of the buffalo and other game; we travel through deserts, and carry heavy burdens; we assist in your wars, carry your generals and men to victory and to death. We go to your abominable omnibuses, until we are often stripped of nearly all the flesh on our bones, and sometimes a great deal of the skin too. To these destroyers of our race, we go and suffer every thing, until death pursues us so closely that he often overtakes us in the public street in performance of our duty, thus relieving us of our suffering. You have inspectors of flour, whiskey, and many other things, but no inspector at your Exchange to see that we poor horses are able to do what is required of us by our owners and often cruel drivers. Oh! what humanity in your city of Brotherly Love to overload those machines of destruction, and expect shadows to draw them. If we could only speak, what tales of sorrow and cruelty we would tell; but we are patient, we stand at your doors for hours in the heat, cold, or storm, without a murmur; and yet we are so cruelly treated by

many who ride and drive us, while at the same time they
are confident they cannot do without us.

LADY   I suppose in a state of nature you have little trouble, and
but few wants, as nature is simple in all her ways.

HORSE   Nature provides best for our wants, or, in other words, we are
created to suit the country and climate in which we are found.

LADY   Are you always happy in your native state?

HORSE   We are perfectly happy, as our Creator never formed any
thing to be miserable.

> When o'er the hills I oft did roam,
> Free as the air without a home,
> With unshod feet, but full of grace;
> The wilderness my resting place.
>
> From mountain top so oft I've seen
> The vale decked out in beauteous green;
> My roving spirit knew no bound,
> As earth was bliss in every sound.
>
> The rivulet from which I drank,
> Or ocean wide I never shrank.
> The tempest flood with cloudy spray
> Received my form, why should I stay?
>
> The angry waves I viewed with scorn;
> They swell, they toss my sprightly form.
> I toil amid them as they roar,
> In triumph gain the rocky shore.
>
> When roving through my native air,
> No dread of savage beasts I fear.
> But savage men in wild array
> Disturb my peace, or make me stray.
>
> Their hideous yells, fantastic look,
> Compare to none in nature's book.
> They rave, they whoop, the lasso hurl,
> Like fiends just from the lower world.

Mistaken dream of earthly bliss
That tore me from such happiness.
From highest joys I'm severed now;
Submissive to my fate I bow.

They took me from my wild woods' home—
Those scenes of pleasure I bemoan;
And sold me to the white man, where
There's naught but toil, there's naught but care.

I now am in the Riding School,
Where some get high and some keep cool;
While some get frightened, and implore,
I never saw the like before.

Some whip me much when I do right;
Some scold, some laugh, some hold me tight.
A time amid such scenes I'm told
Will make the youngest horse grow old.

Some say I trot—they pull and strike—
While others say 'tis what I like.
One thing I know, some have compassion,
Although they ride me every fashion.

When first I entered in this place,
Methought it was an Indian race;
Like forests bound in living green,
Along the rocky cliffs I've seen.

They moved around in joyous mirth;
Some think the pleasure best on earth;
Some look so happy, and of course,
Some look like death on the pale horse.

They ride, and soon with pleasure view
The pale cheek take the rosy hue;
The budding flower it sought for room,
And burst spontaneous into bloom.

The Indian girls, the way they ride,
Is hand and foot on either side.
When mounted now, I am so tried
To find both feet on the same side.

You see what trials we pass through,
To please each one I try to do.
I hope from hence that I may tell
Each one of you has used me well.

Then if you wish to be my friend,
Some kindness now to me extend;
For if you don't, all I can say
Is I'll kick up and run away.

Now in these days when lightnings stream,
You all expect to go by steam;
The pressure high without distrust,
And then you'll see my boiler burst.

In cities large your churches rise
In towering height to reach the skies.
You have such intellectual feasts,
But not one word for us poor beasts.

They get behind me on my back,
It's nothing now but whip and crack.
Oh, preacher! from your pulpit tell
To saint and sinner use me well.

LADY   How is it possible that you can understand us when we speak to you, as there are so many different words used by different persons to convey the same meaning?

HORSE   Man, as we understand, was created a little lower than the angels. We were created inferior to man, with an understanding precisely suited to that of man, that he might communicate his thoughts and desires to us by words, so that we should fully comprehend them; thus you see how wise and how kind was our Creator in his dispensations. When we are domesticated, we look up to man as our superior, because he has power over us. We were created to assist him in all his labors upon the earth, and can be made entirely subject to his will. He has power to halter and lead us, to saddle, bridle and ride us; to tie us to a tree or stake, and there let us starve to death if he wishes. We obey without resistance, and thus the great responsibility resting upon him. I listen when you speak to me, and if you make any particular motion or sign with the hand, speaking to me at the same time, I will remember both the words and motion of the hand, and when you repeat it again, speaking the same words, I will do just what you taught me to do before; for instance, if you are riding me, and wish me to trot, put your right hand on my neck, as near my head as you can, loosen the reins a little, and say, come sir, trot, I will do so as soon as my head gets nearly level with my body, as I can trot much easier when my head is not too high. Again, if you draw up the reins rather tight, and give me a slight check with them, and speak to me, then I will canter. If I do not canter with the first motion of the hand, it should be repeated; at the same time, touch me with the heel of the foot, or a slight touch with the whip on the shoulder, in front of the saddle, and I will be almost certain to canter; if not, repeat it again. So it is with every thing you wish me to do. I observe all your actions toward me. If you are cruel and unkind to me, when you are riding or driving me, I will try to run away if possible, as I am always afraid of the whip. If, on the contrary, you are kind to me, and any accident should occur, or anything should break while you are riding or driving, and I can only hear your voice, bidding me to stop, I will do so immediately, as I know you wish me to stop, and I am not afraid you will whip me when I am obedient. I delight to obey those who treat me with kindness; for I am certain that when I stop you will come up to me, pat me on the neck, caress me, and say, you are a fine fellow! How is it possible that I can forget these things, when it is my business to be watchful and observe every thing that is going on around me, especially that in which I am most concerned. If you treat me kindly, I will follow you almost any where; if you do not, I will try and keep as far from you as possible, as I never stay near an enemy if I can avoid it.

LADY   If so much depends on your friendship, I shall by all means endeavor to gain it.

HORSE   Many persons have saved their lives by being on good terms with me, while on the contrary, many have lost them. I knew a horse that had a drunken master, but what was singular for such a person, he always treated him with the greatest kindness. I have known him to fall out of his wagon on the road under the wheel, but the horse could not be induced to stir one step while he was lying in that position; and those who have found him on the road under his wagon intoxicated, have taken him up, and placed something under the wheel in his place, and tried to get his horse to start, but could not until the obstacle was removed entirely from under the wheel, the horse fearing it was his master.

LADY   You have told me many things that I should do. I would like you to tell me what I should not do.

HORSE   If I should tell you all you should not do, it would take me so long that you would grow weary of listening. I will, therefore, only mention a few. Never pass by my heels when you approach or when you leave me. Never strike me when I stumble, but examine my feet and shoes that you may ascertain the cause. Never run suddenly toward me to mount me, flourishing your whip, as it frightens me.

Never ride me up or down hill out of a walk.

Never ride me fast on a warm day because others do.

Do not imagine when you are riding me that I am perpetual motion.

Do not ride me out to where there are a number of your friends boarding, and invite each of them to ride me up and down the lane all the afternoon to tire me and hurt my back.

Do not, when you return from an afternoon's ride, let your sister, cousin, or friend mount me and ride me two or three hours more.

Do not, when you take me out for an afternoon, keep me out all night, but remember that I have to go out at five in the morning, rest or no rest, while you are sleeping.

Do not change my saddle when you have me from home, as another might injure my back.

Do not sit on my back like a politician, all on one side.

Do not let me drink when I am warm, as it will founder and perhaps kill me.

Do not put me in a current of air to cool when I am warm, but walk me.

Do not have your habit so long and so fashionable that I shall put my hind feet through it, and pull you off, and perhaps kick you while you are falling.

Do not strike me about the head with your whip, as I have but two eyes, need them both, and can scarcely see enough with them.

Do not forget when you are out to tea that I like oats better than tea.

Do not forget to speak for me, as I cannot speak for myself.

Do not strike me without first speaking to me, as it is very impolite.

Do not forget to ride moderately, as it is more genteel.

Do not feel sorry after you have ridden me too far, or too fast, but always feel sorry before you do it.

Do not tickle me about the head, neck or ears with your whip, as I shall become restive and throw you if I can.

Do not stay out so late in the evening when you are in good company that you must ride me half to death in order to get home in good time.

Do not stop your ears with ribbons and rosettes when you ride, as horses with vehicles often run away behind you, and you cannot hear them coming. You may see those before you, but those behind most endanger your life.

Do not fret me, nor let me fret when you find I am very ambitious, as it will injure me.

LADY   Is there any means by which you can understand each other?

HORSE   All animals have a language; we, by ours, understand each other. You are willing to believe that I can understand you when you speak to me. Would it not be strange then if we could not understand each other? The great Creator is well acquainted with each of our race—with each and all of the immense herds that traverse the wilderness and prairies of the far west, where the foot of man has never trodden—just as well as he is with your beautiful coach or saddle horses in the crowded city. While in his providence He provides for the one, man, as his agent, provides for the other; and it is just as much his will that you should be kind to his creature horse as it is that you should be kind to his creature man.

LADY   What is it that alarms you most when passing through the populous city?

HORSE   I feel alarmed at the sudden rattling noise of a heavy cart or wagon over the pavement coming behind me, at the wheel-barrow before me, at the porter with his push-cart, loaded with beds or boxes, so that I cannot see his person. If I could always see him pushing it, I would not he so much fright-ened. The cart loaded with lumber passing near or over my head, the omnibus with the top loaded with passengers, the mortar bed and lime box, the noise of engines running, the military parade, or a buffalo robe, the sight and smell of all wild animals, or their skins, terrify me exceedingly. The bray of the jack I cannot endure. It terrifies me.

LADY   As you have mentioned some of the things that alarm you passing through the city, I would like to know what alarms you most in the country?

HORSE   The locomotive and train of cars alarm me very much until
         I become accustomed to them. The sudden clattering of
         horses' feet, coming behind me with or without vehicles.
         A rough stone lying on the road side; a horse, colt, cow,
         of calf lying in the field near the fence, or a calf springing
         suddenly from his leafy bed on the inside of the fence along
         the woods; the farmer in the field near the road sharpening
         his scythe; and a variety of objects that I cannot remember,
         but your memory will be refreshed by them as they appear.

LADY   As I mount you on a bright morning in May, and leave
         the large city with its crowded streets of gayety and fash-
         ion, we pass on toward the country under a cloudless sky.
         As I feel you prancing under me, we wander along the val-
         ley or mountain side, where nature is clothed in its richest
         verdure, where the stillness of its beauty is broken only
         by the warblings of the sweet songster as he flutters from
         tree to tree, and the fresh breeze of heaven is wafting the
         fragrance of the wild flowers along its mossy banks, my
         nerves are strengthened with the delightful exercise as my
         prancing steed amuses himself with the bit, enjoying the
         rustling of the leaves under his feet, or leaps gently over
         the sparkling brook that crosses our foot-path in search of
         its native waters below. I am enchanted with the glory of
         the scene by which we are surrounded, and I cannot pass
         without adoring the great Creator of this earthly paradise.
         As I leave these enchanted regions, and turn my horse in
         the direction of the great city with its massive buildings,
         towering spires, and enterprising citizens, where we find
         the merchant in his counting-room, the mechanic in his
         shop, and a great variety of persons, who are naturally
         engaged in in-door occupations, and who seldom breathe
         the fresh air, with the great mass of pleasure-loving citi-
         zens, who attend at all the fashionable places of amuse-
         ment, the circus, theatre, ball-room, etc., I cannot but
         think how much more rational it would be if those who
         wish to enjoy health and long life would take out-door

exercise. They would soon feel their physical constitutions renewed with health and vigor.

HORSE I wish you would let many of your fashionable ladies and gentlemen pursue their own course and attend to their own amusements, for if you divert their attention from them to riding out in the open air, we will have more employment and the undertakers will have less. But with all their wisdom, many of them never think of riding us while they enjoy their health, but leave it as a last resort and until death stares them in the face; then they expect us to perform. miracles, to heal the sick, restore sight to the blind, and almost raise the dead.

LADY I have great faith in riding for the benefit of my health, for I am certain that all the quack medicines in the world cannot do half as much toward restoring the weak or delicate constitution as riding you in the Riding School or in the open air would do.

HORSE Yes, poor me! I have to do wonders. You take your quackery until you make a patent medicine depot of your stomach, and then expect us poor horses to cure you!

LADY I think you are too hard on the quack doctors, for they labor much to cure their patients.

HORSE You talk about my being hard on the quack doctors. You say they do much to cure their patients, but I think not. Let them take their patients on their backs, as I do, on a warm afternoon, and jolt them over hill and dale for fifteen or eighteen miles into the country, where all the world can see how I cure them, and they would not be quite so fat as they are, but would soon quit the business, or get as thin as I often do.

LADY As you have said so much about kindness to your race, I should like to know if it is necessary at any time to use the whip?

HORSE   It is sometimes essential. After you have used all other means, then try the whip. Use it with judgment, not in excitement or passion, but in mercy, to aid you in accomplishing what might be otherwise impossible. If you are compelled to use it, be resolute and bring me to obedience, or I will trifle with you all the time. After I become submissive pat me on the neck, caress me and show me that all you desire is obedience; that you feel kindly disposed toward me, that you are still my friend. Remember also that I know the moment you feel alarmed or become timid.

LADY   How is it possible that you can tell when I am timid?

HORSE   I understand your feelings perfectly by the way in which you handle the reins; by your position in the saddle; your manner, voice and actions all convince me that you are timid and that you have no confidence in yourself. If you are a timid rider you can assume an air of boldness and determination that will tend to deceive me; then I will be more obedient, and when you find that it has the desired effect, it will make you a bold and fearless rider.

LADY   If we should meet the locomotive and train of cars and you become alarmed, how then am I to manage you?

HORSE   You should always stop and listen before you get near the railroad, that you may ascertain if the train be in sight, "if so," let me stand still and prepare me to meet them. Always keep my head toward the cars or train, for if you suffer me to turn my head from them, I will become more restive and endeavor to run. Your only safety then is in keeping my head toward them, and my attention attracted in that direction. Do not get excited and become so much alarmed that you will hold me so tight that I will run back and turn around. If you find I run back it is because you hold me too tight; then move the reins forward but keep my head straight, patting me on the neck and caressing me all the time; speak loud to me that I may hear your voice above the noise of the train. When I hear your voice, it gives me confidence. After the train has passed do not start me off immediately; let me recover a little from the excitement, and then I will proceed quietly. If you start me the moment the cars have passed, and I cross the track, they will seem to be behind me, which is often really the case; then I will begin to prance, and become restive or try to run with you. When you cross the track always let my head down by moving the reins forward, that I may find my way without getting my feet fast in the rails, which sometimes throws me down. When you are passing over a very stony road loosen the reins that I may select the best path among the stones, as I can do so better than you can guide me.

LADY   I am very glad that you have told me so much about the locomotive and train of cars, as it has always been a source of trouble to me, especially when I have had a horse that I did not understand, but we must all live and learn.

HORSE   I hope you may not have to learn as we often do. I was just thinking what a time I and a companion had one morning before breakfast. A European gentleman, who had not been long in this country, came to my master one evening and engaged a couple of horses for two of his ladyfriends to ride the next morning. He said the ladies understood the art well, and as for himself he could ride BESSER AS MOST ANY MAN. Myself and companion were sent early next morning. The ladies made their appearance, and the gentleman assisted them to mount; while he was mounting I happened to cast my eye in that direction, as I am always on the look-out, and to my astonishment saw that he had in his hand a large wagon or coach whip. Just as we were starting, he got behind us, when the first thing I felt was a cut across my back with the long whip, my companion sharing the same fate. I sprang forward in an instant, and came near throwing my fair rider over my head. He rode behind us all the morning, and whipped us out to the

Wissahiccon and back to our great annoyance, but much to the amusement of the ladies and spectators. I have often started up in a fright when I have been sleeping in the stable, dreaming that he was after me with his long whip.

LADY   How is it that there are so many dangerous horses?

HORSE   It is the fault of those who break, train and use us that we become dangerous.

LADY   How can it be the fault of those who break, train and use you?

HORSE   If they would first study our nature, temper and disposition, and then treat us accordingly, we would all be gentle and safe.

LADY   Am I to understand that you would all be gentle and safe alike?

HORSE   Far from it, but we would all be good and safe alike according to our temper and disposition, as I have said before.

LADY   How shall I know the difference?

HORSE   One will stand easy and quiet at your door, another that is high tempered will be continually excited and fretful at the most trifling cause. They are of a nervous temperament, and require care and watchfulness on the part of those who use them. Horses are like children. How much better and how much more pleasant it is to instruct and watch over them all the time to prevent them doing wrong, than to have to break them after they have done wrong, and then be compelled to watch them without having the least confidence in them. You generally expect too much of us. You appear to think that we should start, stop, stand, back, turn, walk, rack, canter, trot, and do many other things without having been taught. First teach us what to do, but teach us correctly, caress and pat us, then we are convinced that you are pleased, and we will not forget it, but will do just as you wish. My memory is good. I remember things for years. If you should stop with me on a strange road at a certain house and then pass that way in one or two years after on a dark night, I will stop again at the very same house or gate. If I get frightened or run at any particular place on the road, when I pass that way again I will remember the spot, and will feel alarmed until I pass it, but will not be alarmed on any other road more than usual, except where I was frightened. You should at that place be kind to me, and with a little patience I will not mind it after having passed that way several times and find that there is no real cause for alarm. I will hear your voice in tones of kindness and will not fear.

LADY   Is there any particular kind of dress that you would prefer I should wear for your comfort as well as my own?

HORSE   I often feel irritated when I have a rider who wears her dress so long that it almost drags the ground, as it is continually flowing back over my hip until it covers my left side. It also heats and fatigues me. It drags around my left hind leg so that I cannot move with ease or comfort. If you were to be thrown from my back, as ladies sometimes are, you could not recover your feet without standing on your dress. It would be impossible for you to walk or run. You would certainly fall in the attempt, drawing up your dress from under your feet to enable you to get out of the way would not occur to you at the time, as you would feel excited. The long flowing dress you may imagine looks graceful, but let me assure you that it endangers your life. And then the half peck of beautiful curls flying over your face and eyes so that you cannot see; I am pulled about because you are uncomfortable. Your cap too with the streamers flying in the breeze, enough to frighten a poor timid horse out of his senses; also the thick buckskin gloves, with which you often ride, will prevent your handling the reins with that ease and quickness often requisite. Your riding dress should be made of something that will not change its color if it should happen to get a sprinkle of rain. Common Alpaca changes more perhaps than any other article. Your dress should not be more than nine or ten inches longer than your height. I do not mean that much longer than your walking dress, but that much longer than your full height from the floor. Then you will be able to run or walk more quickly without much inconvenience. If your dress be too tight, you cannot ride with comfort and it injures your health. You can sew small quantities of shot in small pieces of muslin, and tack them around the inside of the skirt at equal distances on the front breadth. Your hat or cap should be made as light as possible, that it may not give you a pain in your head in warm weather. There should not be any loose ribbons or strings flying about your cap or dress to irritate and frighten me. Your hair should be fastened up securely so that it will not trouble you, nor interfere with your comfort while riding. Your gloves must be such that you can use your reins with ease, for as regards your safety much depends upon it.

LADY   Is it more difficult to manage you at one season of the year than at another, or are they all the same to you?

HORSE   As for the change in the seasons it would not make any material difference with me if I were properly managed or regularly used by a skillful rider, with whom I am acquainted and who understands me; but as I am ridden by different persons, and each of them differing in the management of the reins, it will be more difficult to ride me during the changes of the seasons than at any other time. In cold weather I am very lively. At the breaking up of the winter, and at the opening of spring, I will be more difficult to manage, as I will not be likely to get that regular out-door use which is so important to keep me quiet. If you ride me out in the opening of the spring, or late in the fall, when the air is cool and blowing fresh from the west, north-west, or north, I will prance and be playful, as it is bracing and calculated to arouse all my energy.

LADY   How do you like your present mode of life—the duties you are now obliged to perform compared with your former life and duties?

HORSE   Oh, happy days! when I wandered through the green meadows, by the sparkling brook and drank of its crystal waters, or plunged into the billows of some majestic river and spouted the spray from my nostrils. I have passed through many trying and some pleasant scenes in the wild west. In the chase, in the Indian wars, where the savage riders fought hand to hand, while the war-whoop rent the air, together with the falling of riders and the yells of savages, made the scene most exciting. I have passed through a frontier life, labored in western towns, and at last have arrived in the great Atlantic city, have become a good saddle horse, and now it appears that I am destined for a while to carry the more refined lady and gentleman for health and pleasure; but sometimes I find myself mistaken, and get a Jakey or a b'hoy upon my back in the garb of a gentleman, then all Philadelphia must get out of the way, especially when we get on Broad street.

LADY   How should I manage if I were compelled to cross a large stream or river? Would there be any danger, or how would I know whether you could swim?

HORSE   We can all swim, and can endure the fatigue of swimming according to our strength. When you ride me into the stream, if it be wide or the current strong, it will be better for you to go a short distance up above where you wish to cross, that I may not have to swim against the tide, and I will reach the shore where you desire with less fatigue. When I enter the water hold the reins rather tight, as sometimes there are holes near the shore into which I may stumble and throw you off. When you reach the deep water where I cannot walk any farther, I will appear to go down suddenly, then loosen the reins at once, or I cannot swim. They must be entirely loose that I may have the free use of them without the least restraint. You must guide me with loose reins, for the moment you attempt to tighten them I will struggle and drown. I have often had the rider to fall off my back when swimming me for amusement, when he would catch hold of my tail; then I could swim with more ease than when he was on my back, and I would not hurt or kick him. A gentleman who owned a horse, a friend of mine, in the summer of 1850, had occasion to drive him a few miles up the Schuylkill one very warm day, after getting him perfectly cool and giving him a rest, he procured a son of the Emerald Isle to ride him into the Schuylkill to wash and refresh him. He mounted him and rode into the water, but as soon as the horse began to swim Paddy got frightened, threw down the reins, caught him around the neck with both arms, and held on until he choked him, when the horse and Paddy disappeared entirely several times. The owner was standing on the bank calling to Paddy to let go of his neck as he was drowning him, but it was of no use, Paddy had a good hold and had heard that a bird in the hand was worth two in the bush. The horse plunged and struggled in the most violent manner, until he reached the shore with his rider still choking him, and exclaiming, there, sir! I have saved your horse from drowning, for he cannot swim, and if I had not kept my arms around his neck, sir, and pulled him up, he would have been a dead horse, so you may thank me for saving his life. The owner of my friend was so much amused at Paddy's ingenuity and ignorance that he could not say a single word in reply.

LADY   On which side of you should a gentleman ride for my safety and your comfort?

HORSE   There has been much controversy on the subject, but you will remember that it has not been between horsemen, as they do not often trouble themselves about such things. They generally try to know for themselves and act accordingly. They do not trouble the public with newspaper arguments.

LADY   I suppose there is a right and a wrong side to almost every question, and as so much has been said concerning this, I feel anxious to know the right if there be any?

HORSE   I remember when the first halter was put upon my head that my master approached me gently on the left or near side; he caressed me, and when he had placed the halter upon my head, repeated it. He led me away, walking by my left side. I remember too, that when he came to saddle, bridle and mount me that it was from the left side. I was harnessed and unharnessed on that side; when fed or watered in the stable, it was always the same. I was groomed on both sides; but as I have been handled generally on the near side, I am always more quiet when you approach me on that side. When a gentleman is riding in company, I feel more comfortable if he is on my left side, because I am accustomed to being haltered, led, bridled, saddled and mounted from that side. The most important question is the safety of my fair rider, as every one will admit. If the gentleman rides on my left side, as he should do, his left hand will be engaged with the reins, he then has his right hand disengaged, that he may assist the lady if she requires it. If I become restive, and he rides near me, speaks to me, or lays his hand on my neck and caresses me, I will in most cases listen to his voice if it be in kindness, and be passive; but if I still feel irritable, he can take me by the bridle with his right hand, and speak to me until I become quiet. Touch, speak to me, and handle me on the left side, and it will have the effect. If my rider's dress becomes disordered, the gentleman can arrange it with his right hand; if she is in danger, he can better aid and support her in the saddle with his right hand, or stop me if he wishes. She is comparatively safe with the gentleman on her left side, being secure from the interruption and danger of vehicles. as they pass on the right, and will not then expose myself and rider to danger. My rider's dress and feet being next to the gentleman, will not incommode him if he can ride; as to those cannot, every thing is in the way. If the gentleman should be on the right side, and I become restive, his left hand is engaged with the reins, so that to assist my rider he must first change them into his right hand, with which he cannot use his reins as well. If he takes hold of my bridle on my right side with his left hand when I become restive, it will make me more so, as I am not in the habit of being led or held on that side. If my rider should lose her balance in the saddle, he, with his left band, would most likely pull her off in the attempt to assist her, as for her dress he cannot arrange it without riding around to my left side. The safety of my rider is all important, and a gentleman riding on the left side has all the advantage of safety and comfort.

LADY   How is it that so few ladies learn to ride well?

HORSE   The true secret of learning to ride well is to ride slowly.

LADY   I remember when I commenced riding that I could never get a horse that would go fast enough, until riding out one day with a gentleman, I challenged him to race with me. We started, my horse ran with me between one and two miles to a public house, and there stopped, when I fainted, remaining on the saddle until I was lifted from it. After that I felt very timid, and have since been satisfied with moderate riding.

HORSE   I have often carried ladies who would not ride moderately until they had met with some accident. I recollect having been ridden by a careless rider quite fast. I fell and threw her over my head, after which she rode slowly. Another lady riding out one day with a party, was running me through a lane, at the end of which was a gate; on one side the lane turned off, but the lady not being a skillful rider, did not even attempt to turn me as she approached the end of it, when I suddenly stopped before the gate and threw her on it, where she remained until relieved by one of the party.

LADY After hearing these anecdotes of your companion, I feel anxious to know whether they are true, or only given for the sake of instruction?

HORSE I have not told you a single word that is not true, and the incidents are but few compared with the thousands which have occurred in my experience. I could fill a volume with incidents concerning Paddy, which might interest and amuse you, some of them having been witnessed by your friends.

LADY Did you ever know a horse that could not be ridden?

HORSE I had a companion called Paddy that was very difficult to ride. He had been trained so that by a word, look or sign, he would throw any person who would mount him. Paddy was a chestnut-sorrel, about fourteen hands high, which is rather under the usual size, short mane and tail. A hand is four inches. The place to measure a horse is on the highest part of the withers, that is just in front of the saddle. A gentleman came riding in one afternoon on a horse which a friend of his could not ride, as he had thrown him off on the road. My master asked him if the horse was not quiet, he replied in the affirmative, at the same time saying, "if he was not, he could rite him; could rite te tevil if he could find him!" My master told him that he had him in the stable, and that if he and his friends would come in they could ride him. So in they came. The gentleman shouted, "pring him out and I will rite him!" Paddy was brought out; the rider mounted him, while his friends anxiously awaited the result. Paddy made one bound, and sent his rider about fifteen feet over his head; and if you had seen him you would have said at once that he was the Flying Dutchman. He came down right on the crown of his head, knocking his hat into a cocked hat; he stood about perpendicular, his eyes, nose and mouth filled with tan. As soon as he could get his feet to the ground, and his eyes, nose and mouth free from tan, and recover himself a little, he mounted him again without a word, except from his friends, who shouted to him to go it again. As soon as Paddy was ready he made one spring, threw up his heels, and away went the rider exactly into his former position, about twenty feet over Paddy's head, crushing his hat in a most ridiculous manner. He sprang to his feet, and roared out in broken English, "He is worse as te tevil," while his friends cheered him and insisted on his trying to do it better, but his courage failed. His hatter sold a new hat on the strength of the performance; and he said "He did not wish to rite te tevil again."

A gentleman from South America related the following incident to my master. Riding through the wilderness of Venezuela one dark night, he lost his way, when his horse refused to proceed. He whipped and spurred, but the horse remained immovable, finally he dismounted, took the reins over the horse's head, and groped about in the deep darkness to satisfy himself (if possible) as to the cause of this unexpected delay, when he suddenly slipped, lost his footing, but still having his hold on the reins, he was enabled to replace himself by the side of the horse, where he concluded to wait the approach of day. When the first faint light appeared, imagine, if you can, his feelings on seeing before him a precipice several hundred feet in depth, over which he had slipped the night before, and where he certainly must have perished had it not been for the sagacity of his faithful horse.

Upon one occasion, a gentleman who considered himself a first rate rider, was about mounting a horse in the Riding

School. He intended to mount without using the stirrups. Of course he was fully equipped, whip and spur. Jim stood perfectly quiet. As the gentleman threw his right foot over the saddle, he unintentionally struck the spur into the side of the horse, which caused him to plunge and kick, while he was endeavoring to rise into the saddle. The tighter he held, the more Jim plunged and kicked, at last he became desperate, and with one violent effort threw his rider five or six feet above the saddle. He came down on his face, hands and side, and then sprang to his feet in a perfect rage. He said to my master, "I gifes you fifty tollars if you lets me shoot him." Now Jim did nothing but what he was compelled to do in self-defence. It cost the rider something to be cupped, but Jim did not appear any the worse for his part of the performance.

LADY   I have often felt that I should like to know something about purchasing a horse for my own use, but I feel myself incapable of judging of the qualities that are calculated to suit a lady.

HORSE   It is very difficult for a lady to find in a horse just what will please her.

LADY   As there is such a variety of horses, and every lady or gentleman who owns one will say I have the finest horse that can possibly be found, now when there are so many fine horses, it cannot be difficult for me to get one.

HORSE   You will find a great number of fine looking horses, but very few of them are suitable for ladies to ride.

LADY   It appears so strange to hear you say that so few are fit for our use.

HORSE   A wealthy lady who was looking for a fine, safe horse for herself, said she had often heard it remarked that money would purchase anything, but that she had traveled through a portion of New York and Pennsylvania, had offered high prices, and had purchased several horses at two hundred and fifty and three hundred dollars each, but could not get one suitable for herself to ride. She finally came to the conclusion that either there were not any good ladies' horses or that money would not purchase them.

LADY   I think the lady of whom you speak must have been very difficult to please, or there must have been more scarcity of ladies' horses than I had imagined.

HORSE   You may well be at a loss to know what qualities a horse should possess in order to please her, for I am certain that there is not one in ten kept for that purpose which has the requisite qualities. Horses are somewhat like persons. They have many imperfections, and if they had not some redeeming qualities to counterbalance them, I should feel very sorry. They all have their perfections as well as imperfections, so that when we find one that has more of the former than the latter, we should endeavor to be satisfied, provided there be no serious objections. I have known persons who have owned good horses, which suited them admirably, to sell them and get fine, spirited young horses that did not suit them, because they were not safe or well-broken, and therefore not fit to be trusted. I have told you that a hand is four inches. A lady's horse may be fifteen or fifteen and a half hands high, which is a very good size. Ponies are not safe, do not become a lady so well, and are not generally so well able to carry them. They are not safe, because they are tormented by all around them, and thus acquire many bad habits. There are other reasons why they are not safe. The rider is too near the ground, so that her dress will almost sweep it, and vehicles in passing will be more likely to come in contact with her. When a lady is seated upon a good sized horse, she is comparatively free from danger. She can handle him with much more ease, looks more graceful, and feels more like riding.

LADY   I wish to hear a description of a horse suitable for a hackney.

HORSE   You have heard what size he should be. His body should be full and round, but not clumsy, his head small, his muzzle sharp, his ears slender and pointed, or with a handsome curve towards the tip, narrow through the top of his head between the ears, so that they may come near together, rather broad between the eyes, which should be round, full and prominent. Neck long, smooth and arched, chest not too broad, but deep through the shoulder, limbs clean with flat bone and strong muscle, tail long and flowing, good, strong black hoofs, but not too small. He should not be too young, say from seven to fifteen, if he has been well used. When you get such a horse he will be likely to be gay, carry himself well, and be sure footed. As to color, there are good and bad horses of all colors, though a dark color is preferable. You must see that his step is light, free and graceful, as much depends upon his movements as regards his being a good saddle horse. A good walking horse is most likely to become a fine saddle horse.

LADY   I should suppose from the description you have given me of a good saddle horse, that it would be difficult to find one.

HORSE   It is rather difficult I must admit. You may find some fine horses that will differ from that which I have described, and when you handle them it will be well for you to do so moderately and with judgment.

LADY   I am getting tired of such a long description of a horse. I would rather be riding one, or hearing something about how to ride them, as it interests me more and adds greatly to my enjoyment. I am doubtful of your ability to persuade us that you are correct in your opinions, as it takes time to change the order of things.

HORSE   I was just thinking how your grandmother used to ride! How well she rode, and how she enjoyed it; and the reason why she enjoyed it so much, was that her constant daily exercise kept her in health and vigor; her nerves were strong; she did not understand the term Neuralgia. The disease was not known in her day. It is one peculiar to the present generation. Exercise is a remedy. It is its most deadly foe. It pursues it, puts it to flight, conquers and destroys it!

LADY   It is impossible for us to get the daily exercise that appears requisite for our health, as the extent of the city prevents our getting out into the country air. We are therefore confined within the limits of the city for exercise, for if we should ride into the country often, it would be very expensive.

HORSE   Where there is a will there is a way. I am fully aware of the difficulties under which you labor, but you forget how much time and money you spend in city amusements. In crowded houses heated to excess, where the air is calculated to injure your lungs and debilitate your whole system. If the same amount were expended in useful gymnastic exercises, or in the Riding School, or upon our backs in the open air, what a difference would soon be perceived in the female portion of your large cities. But while fashion rules you will be its votaries, at the expense of health and even of life. You should look back at the olden times, when the country was in its infancy, and see your grandmothers and great-grandmothers—when exercise on horseback was a part of their daily business—when they took the produce of their farms to market on horseback—and the country girls would mount the unruly horse and contend with him until he became submissive, having strength and courage equal to the task. They could walk, ride, spin, knit, and perform many duties in the house and on the farm with a happy smile upon their rosy faces. But, oh! refinement and fashion, what have ye done? Turned the world upside down, and persuaded ladies that it is disgraceful to labor, knowing, as they do, that their forefathers gloried in it, and by it have reared this beautiful Union, which I hope will be perpetuated to the end of time. But as I was saying, refinement, or a false opinion of it, has degenerated the population of your cities, and persuaded multitudes of their inhabitants that they were created to live without exercise or labor. Let me tell you, although I am a horse, if I stand in the stable a day or two without exercise, I feel badly; if for many days, I am sure to get sick, and cannot eat or work with comfort. Let me assure you, fair lady, that without a certain amount of exercise daily you cannot enjoy health. You recollect when Adam was expelled from the garden of Eden how the ground was cursed for his sins. He was told that in the sweat of his brow he should eat his bread all the days of his life until he returned to the ground. Now all this was wisely appointed for your benefit, proving at once that you must labor; and if you will not labor you must take that exercise which will be equivalent.

LADY   I have often heard of vicious horses being tamed in a short time, and brought under the influence and control of man, so that they would be perfectly docile and tractable under the care of such persons only as seemed to possess the power.

HORSE   I suppose you have heard of Sullivan, the great English horse-tamer. From all accounts of this singular man, he certainly did perform what might when not understood be called miracles. He would take the most vicious horse, and in an hour, or a few hours, make him as submissive as a child. He died without imparting the secret. We have horse-tamers in the United States, who can take the most vicious horse and tame him so that you would be surprised at the change. You will naturally ask by what power can man influence our race to such an extent? The extent of the power of kindness is but little known. By it the most noble results have been attained. Its effects on the animal creation are most marvelous, securing their affection as long as it is exerted. It brings to submission the fierce lion, the huge elephant, and the noble horse; through it, the birds of the air can be made to hover around you, and the fish in the water may be fed from your hand. If you remember, at the creation all these were made subject to the power of man, and would doubtless have remained so had it not been for his cruelty, which has tended to drive them from him, so that instead of loving they really fear him.

LADY   I cannot see why the animal creation should fear him more now than at the first, as man is the same and so are animals.

HORSE   Man has changed greatly since the creation. He has degenerated, and still continues to do so. In the beginning man lived to be hundreds of years old, now they seldom live to be one hundred years. Then they lived a natural life, now an artificial one. Then they lived in the open air in tents, and breathed the fresh air of heaven, now they live in cities and in towns, and seldom breathe the pure fresh air. Then their exercise or labor was in the open air—they were entirely exempt from the cares of city life.

LADY   As you seem to be somewhat acquainted with the afflictions of the human family, I should like to know whether you really think that ladies can be much benefited by riding you, whose lungs are weak or diseased?

HORSE   I have had much experience in these things. I have for years carried different ladies, who have been afflicted in a variety of ways, and I am convinced that those who have weak lungs will, in forty-nine cases out of fifty, recover if they will ride and persevere for a length of time. I have carried ladies frequently who have been pronounced incurable, and in a few weeks their cough has left them, the rose has returned to their cheek, beauty to their countenances, and buoyant spirits have taken the place of languor and listlessness. Indeed I have reason to know that their strength was increased, when I consider the manner in which they have plied the whip around my shoulder and side, often too, when I was doing my very best for them. I am almost afraid to tell you how much benefit may be derived from riding me, as it may only serve to increase my duties. However, I suppose you understand for yourself that this kind of exercise brings into requisition nerves and muscles, which would not otherwise be called into action, thus strengthening the system and leaving permanently good results.

LADY   Do you think a lady's position in the saddle a safe one; I mean is it quite as secure as that of a gentleman—their knowledge of the art being equal?

HORSE   When a lady is seated in the saddle she is about as safe as a gentleman, and it is just as difficult to get her out of the saddle as it would be to displace a gentleman. When she begins to learn she gets accustomed to the position, and habit, you know, is second nature. The position of the gentleman is decidedly more easy, as he sits facing the horse, and is not obliged to exert himself to bring forward the left shoulder, in order to bring him into the proper position. A lady finds a difficulty in balancing herself if she expects to ride with ease to the horse, whereas the gentleman finds none. I have seen many gentlemen thrown from their horses; that is, many more than ladies. I suppose that, ladies think that gentleman have more control over the horse than they have. If strength, activity, and freedom from the incumbrance of dress could confer any advantage, the gentlemen have it. But the tone of a lady's voice has more power to quiet us than that of a gentleman's, yet it is sometimes absolutely necessary for a lady to be determined. She must endeavor to act as the case may require. A well-bred horse is more sensitive and more susceptible to kindness than a common-bred one can be, and there is not as much danger to be anticipated from a well-bred horse, as he is free and bold, while the other is not so much to be relied upon.

LADY   How do the Indian women ride?—in the same manner that we do?

HORSE   They generally ride astride. It would look quite as singular to them to see a lady riding sideways as their style of riding would look to you. A gentleman who happened to be among the Indians, together with a number of his friends, was invited to one of their festivals. After their principal amusements were over, in which he and his friends had taken an active part, the Indians cleared a space in the woods among the large trees where they were all to take their turns in riding a short distance through the woods. Some of the Indians were concealed behind the large trees, and when the riders passed they rushed out on their hands and knees to frighten the horses. The whites were thrown off in every direction amid the whoops and shouts of the Indians, while their own party, being better horsemen, retained their seats.

LADY   I have been thinking whether your herds on the prairies and in the wilderness were ever attacked by beasts of prey?

HORSE   We are sometimes attacked by wild beasts, which attempt to take the young from the herds.

LADY   Have you any means of defence, or are they ever successful?

HORSE   They are seldom or never successful, as nature has provided us with means of defence, which are a certain protection.

LADY   I should suppose, as you are so fleet in your movements, that you would seek safety in flight.

HORSE   We would not run that risk, as it would be dangerous in the extreme. When we are attacked, the dams and their foals crowd together, forming a circle, while the horses, which have more courage, form a circle around them, with their heads to the centre and their heels out, then we can defy all the beasts of the forest, and it is certain death to attempt to penetrate our midst. Now when a number of ladies and gentlemen are out riding, and we become alarmed just form a circle with our heads to the centre, and all the steam engines in the world cannot frighten us.

LADY   How is it that you are so timid, and appear frightened when I approach you?

HORSE   I will tell you. When I was out one afternoon, not long since, the company stopped at the Falls. We were tied, some of us, to posts, and some under the shed. When we were about starting, the gentleman who rode me, came running in great haste, and flourishing his whip, caught hold of the reins, and in the act of untying me, gave me a sudden jerk, so that I have always been afraid since to have any one approach me unless in a very quiet manner, first patting me on the neck, which gives me confidence.

LADY   Some ladies and gentlemen complain that they can never hire a fine horse.

HORSE   Those who treat us kindly, and ride us moderately, and bring us home in good condition, can always get the finest of our race.

LADY   As you have given me many ideas of things I did not understand, I should like to know if anything more could be said which might profit or interest me, as I feel a deep interest in the welfare of your race, and I hope that the information which you have given me may be useful to ladies and profitable to your race?

HORSE   I do not understand much about music, but I do assure you, although I am a horse, I am very fond of it. To learn to ride me easily and beautifully is far more difficult for you than to excel in music. Now, many persons think they understand how to ride, and how to treat me after having been upon my back but a few times, whilst there are those who, having made it their study during their whole lives, still consider themselves learners. It is almost impossible to convince the former of their entire ignorance of the art;

but the day is coming, and not far distant, when it will be better understood, and we shall be rightly appreciated. Why, we are the favorites, and often the companions of kings and queens, and great ones of the earth! who pride themselves in us, and treat us with kindness. But in these United States, we are universal favorites as well as servants of the people, where every lady may be a queen if she will. We are with you in nearly all your pleasure excursions, and are often the subject of conversation at your parties as well as in the social circle, at the table and by the fire-side; in the stillness of the night, when your eyes are closed upon surrounding objects, your thoughts are wandering amid the beauties of nature, and you ofttimes imagine yourselves seated upon our backs, riding along some retired spot through the deep woods, or following the course of the sparkling river, enjoying the delightful breeze as it ripples the silvery surface. If all these enjoyments be desirable, is it not worth your time and attention to become acquaint-ed with us in order to know our habits—that method of treatment which will secure our comfort, and that style of riding and driving which will secure your safety? When la-dies possessing refinement and talent, and goodness, reflect that it has cost years of persevering labor to fit me for their use, I feel persuaded that they cannot be so cruel as to ride me so far or so fast that I will be injured by it, or per-haps made to drag out a miserable existence. The subject of horsemanship is boundless; it might be written upon for ages; it is inexhaustible, like the sands upon the shore, or like a sea without a shore: in it perfection dwells not. To see a lady mounted on a handsome steed—to see her ride him gracefully, and fearlessly manage the wild, restless, sprightly creature with rolling eyes and flowing mane, and nostrils expanding with fierceness and rage; to see his every movement controlled by her delicate hand—is certainly the perfection of beauty!

THE
AMERICAN
HORSEWOMAN

THE

AMERICAN HORSEWOMAN

BY

MRS. ELIZABETH KARR

"Gold that buys health can never be ill spent,
Nor hours laid out in harmless merriment."
J. WEBSTER

BOSTON
HOUGHTON, MIFFLIN AND COMPANY
New York: 11 East Seventeenth Street
The Riverside Press, Cambridge
1884

EDITOR'S REPLICATION OF ORIGINAL TITLE PAGE

THE AMERICAN HORSEWOMAN

PREFACE

IN PRESENTING THIS volume to the women of America, the author would remark that, at least as far as she is aware, it is the first one, exclusively devoted to the instruction of lady riders, that has ever been written by one of their own countrywomen. In its preparation, no pretension is made to the style of a practiced author, the writer freely acknowledging it to be her first venture in the (to her) hitherto unexplored regions of authorship; she has simply undertaken,—being guided and aided by her own experience in horseback riding,—to write, in plain and comprehensive language, and in as concise a manner as is compatible with a clear understanding of her subject, all that she deems it essential for a horsewoman to know. This she has endeavored to do without any affectation or effort to acquire reputation as an author, and wholly for the purpose of benefiting those of her own sex who wish to learn not only to ride, but to ride well. She has also been induced to prepare the work by the urgent solicitations of many lady friends, who, desirous of having thorough information on horseback riding, were unable to find in any single work those instructions which they needed.

Many valuable works relating to the subject could be had, but none especially for ladies. True, in many of these works prepared for equestrians a few pages of remarks or advice to horsewomen could be found, but so scant and limited were they that but little useful and practical information could be gleaned from them. The writers of these works never even dreamed of treating many very important points highly essential to the horsewoman; and, indeed, it could hardly be expected that they would, as it is almost impossible for any horseman to know, much less to comprehend, these points. The position of a man in the saddle is natural and easy, while that of a woman is artificial, one-sided, and less readily acquired; that which he can accomplish with facility is for her impossible or extremely difficult, as her position lessens her command over the horse, and obliges her to depend almost entirely upon her skill and address for the means of controlling him.

If a gentleman will place himself upon the side-saddle and for a short time ride the several gaits of his horse, he will have many points presented which he had not anticipated, and which may puzzle him; that which appeared simple and easy when in his natural position will become difficult of performance when he assumes the rôle of a horsewoman. A trial of this kind will demonstrate to him that the rules applicable to the one will not invariably be adapted to the other. The reader need not be surprised, therefore, if in the perusal of this volume she discovers in certain instances instructions laid down which differ from those met with in the popular works upon this subject by male authors.

Another inducement to prepare this volume existed in the fact that the ladies throughout the country, and especially in our large cities and towns, are apparently awakening to an appreciation of the importance of out-door amusement and exercise in securing and prolonging health, strength, beauty, and symmetry of form, and that horseback riding is rapidly becoming the favorite form of such exercise. Instructions relating to riding have become, therefore, imperative, in order to supply a need long felt by those horsewomen who, when in the saddle, are desirous of acquitting themselves with credit, but who have heretofore been unable to gain that information which would enable them to ride with ease and grace, and to manage their steeds with dexterity and confidence. The author—who has had several years' experience in horseback riding with the old-fashioned, two-pommeled saddle, and, in later years, with the English saddle, besides having had the benefit of the best continental teaching—believes she will be accused of neither vanity nor egotism when she states that within the pages of this work instructions will be found amply sufficient to enable any lady who attends to them to ride with artistic correctness.

Great care has been taken to enter upon and elucidate all those minute but important details which are so essential, but which, because they are so simple, are usually passed over without notice or explanation. Especial attention has also been given to the errors of inexperienced and uneducated riders, as well as to the mistakes into which beginners are apt to fall from incorrect modes of teaching, or from no instruction at all; these errors have been carefully pointed out, and the methods for correcting them explained. A constant effort has been made to have these practical hints and valuable explanations as lucid as possible, that they may readily be comprehended and put into practical use by the reader.

From the fact that considerable gossip, including some truth, as to illiteracy, rudeness, offensive familiarity, and scandal of various kinds has in past years been associated with some of the riding-schools established in our cities, many ladies entertain a decided antipathy to all riding-schools; to these ladies, as well as to those who are living in places where no riding-schools exist, the author feels confident that this work will prove of great practical utility. Yet she must remark that, in her opinion, it is neither just nor right to ostracize indiscriminately all such schools, simply because some of them have proven blameworthy; whenever a riding-school of good standing is established and is conducted by a well-known, competent, and gentlemanly teacher, with one or more skilled lady assistants, she would advise the ladies of the neighborhood to avail themselves of such opportunity to become sooner thorough and efficient horsewomen by pursuing the instructions given in this work under such qualified teachers.

ELIZABETH KARR.

NORTH BEND, OHIO.

A BRIEF SYNOPSIS OF CONTENTS

waist.—The basque or jacket.—Length of riding habit.—White material not to be worn on horseback.—Riding shirt.—Riding drawers.—Riding boots.—Riding corset.—Riding coiffure or head-dress.—Riding hat.—Minutiæ to be attended to in the riding costume.—How to hold the riding skirt while standing.—Riding whip.

THE SADDLE AND BRIDLE

Saddle of ancient times, and the manner of riding.—Planchette.—Catherine de Medici deviser of the two-pommeled saddle.—M. Pellier, Sr., inventor of the third pommel.—English saddle.—Advantages of the third pommel.—Saddle should, invariably, be made and fitted to the horse.—Seat of saddle.—Kinds of saddles for different ladies.—Proper application of the third pommel.—Saddle recommended and used by the author.—Points to be attended to in procuring a saddle.—Girths.—New mode of tightening girths.—Stirrups and stirrup-leathers.—Safety stirrups.—How to attach the stirrup-leather.—The bridle and reins.—Martingales.—Snaffle-bits.—Curb-bits.—Curb-chain.—Tricks of horses with bits, and their remedy.—Adjustment of the bit and head-stall.—Care of the bit.—How to correctly place the saddle on the horse.—Remarks concerning girthing the horse.—Great advantages derived from knowing how to saddle and bridle one's horse.

MOUNTING AND DISMOUNTING

Timidity in presence of a horse should be overcome.—First attempts at mounting.—Mounting from a horse-block.—Mounting from the ground.—Mounting with assistance from a gentleman; how this is effected.—What the gentleman must do.—A restive horse while mounting; how to be managed.—Attractiveness of correct mounting.—To dismount with assistance from a gentleman; what the gentleman must do.—Attentions to the skirt both while mounting and dismounting.—Dismounting without aid; upon the ground; upon a very low horse-block.—Concluding remarks.

lengthen the curb-reins.—To tighten a rein that has become loose.—To change the double bridle from the left to the right hand; to return it to the left hand.—Management of reins when making quick turns.—European manner of holding the double bridle-reins, a pair in each hand.—The equestrienne should practice and perfect herself in these various manoeuvrings with the reins.—The proper rein-hold creates a correspondence between the rider's hand and the horse's mouth, and gives support to the animal.—Give and take movements.—The dead-pull.—In collecting the horse the curb must be used.—The secret of good riding.—The management of the reins with restive horses.—Liberty of the reins sometimes necessary.—Movements of horse and rider should correspond.—Horse united or collected.—Horse disunited.—To animate the horse.—To soothe the horse.—What to do in certain improper movements of the horse.—Concluding remarks.

The movements of the horse in walking.—A good walk is a certain basis for perfection in other gaits.—A lady's horse should be especially trained to walk well.—Every change in the walk, as turning, backing, and stopping, should be well learned, before attempting to ride in a faster gait.—The walk is a gait more especially desirable for some ladies.—The advance, the turn, the stop, the reining back, in the walk.—Remarks on the reining back.

The movements of the horse in trotting.—The trot a safe gait for a lady.—The jog trot.—The racing trot.—The true trot.—The French trot.—The English trot; is desirable for ladies to learn.— Objections to the French trot.—How to manage the horse and ride the English trot.—Which is the leading foot of the horse in the trot.—To stop a horse in the English trot.—

Trotting in a circle.—Circling to the right, to the left.—The amble.—The pace.—The rack.

horse to leap.—A lady should never attempt the leap, except with a horse well trained in it.—Horses do not all leap alike.—The flying leap.—Important points to know relative to the flying leap.

ILLUSTRATIONS

INTRODUCTION

"How melts my beating heart as I behold
Each lovely nymph, our island's boast and pride,
Push on the generous steed, that sweeps along
O'er rough, o'er smooth, nor heeds the steepy hill,
Nor falters in the extended vale below!"

The Chase.

AMONG LADIES OF wealth and culture in England, the equestrienne art forms a portion of their education as much as the knowledge of their own language, of French, or of music, and great care is taken that their acquirements in this art shall be as thorough as those in any other branch of their tuition. The mother bestows much of her own personal supervision on her daughter's instruction, closely watching for every little fault, and promptly correcting it when any becomes manifest. As a result universally acknowledged, a young English lady, when riding a well-trained and spirited horse, is a sight at once elegant and attractive. She exhibits a degree of confidence, a firmness of seat, and an ease and grace that can be acquired only by the most careful and correct instruction. The fair rider guides her steed, without abruptness, from walk to canter, from canter to trot, every movement in perfect harmony; horse and rider being, as it were, of one thought.

"Each look, each motion, awakes a new-born grace."

Unfortunately, at the present day, from want of careful study of the subject, the majority of American lady riders, notwithstanding the elegance of their forms and their natural grace, by no means equal their English sisters in the art of riding. In most instances, a faulty position in the saddle, an unsteadiness of seat, and a lack of sympathy between horse and rider, occasion in the mind of the spectator a sense of uneasiness lest the horse, in making playful movements, or, perhaps, becoming slightly fractious, may unseat his rider,—a feeling which quite destroys the charm and fascination she might otherwise exercise. If my countrywomen would but make a master stroke, and add correct horseback riding to the long list of accomplishments which they now possess, they would become irresistible, and while delighting others, would likewise promote their own physical well-being. There is no cosmetic nor physician's skill which can preserve the bloom and freshness of youth as riding can, and my fair readers, if they wish to prolong those charms for which they are world renowned, charms whose only fault is their too fleeting existence, must take exercise, and be more in the fresh air and sunshine.

How much better to keep old age at bay by these innocent means, than to resort to measures which give to the eye of the world a counterfeit youth that will not deceive for a moment. Even an elderly lady may without offense or harsh criticism recall some of the past joys of younger years by an occasional ride for health or recreation, and, while gracefully accepting her half century, or more, of life, she can still retain some of the freshness and spirit of bygone years.

Not only is health preserved and life prolonged by exercise on horseback, but, in addition, sickness is banished, or meliorated, and melancholy, that dark demon which occasionally haunts even the most joyous life, is overcome and driven back to the dark shades from whence it came. Should the reader have the good fortune to possess an intelligent horse, she can, when assailed by sorrows real or fancied, turn to this true, willing friend, whose affectionate neigh of greeting as she approaches, and whose pretty little graceful arts, will tend to dispel her gloom, and, once in the saddle, speeding along through the freshening air, fancied griefs are soon forgotten, while strength and nerve are gained to face those troubles of a more serious nature, whose existence cannot be ignored.

To the mistress who thoroughly understands the art of managing him, the horse gives his entire affection and obedience, becomes her most willing slave, submits to all her whims, and is proud and happy under her rule.

In disposition the horse is much like a child. Both are governed by kindness combined with firmness; both meet indifference with indifference, but return tenfold in love and obedience any care or affection that is bestowed upon them. The horse also resembles the child in the keenness with which he detects hypocrisy; no pretense of love or interest will impose on either.

To the lady rider who has neither real fondness for her horse nor knowledge of governing him, there is left but one resource by means of which the animal can be controlled, and this is the passion of fear. With a determined will, she may, by whipping, force him to obey, but this means is not always reliable, especially with a high-spirited animal, nor is it a method which any true woman would care to employ. If, in addition to indifference to the horse, there be added nervousness and timidity, which she finds herself unable to overcome by practice and association, the lady might as well relinquish all attempt to become a rider.

Should any of my readers think that these views of the relations between horse and rider are too sentimental, that all which is needed in a horse is easy movement, obedience to the reins, and readiness to go forward when urged, and that love and respect are quite unnecessary, she will find, should she ever meet with any really alarming object on the road, that a little of this despised affection and confidence is very desirable, for, in the moment of danger, the voice which has never spoken in caressing accents, nor sought to win confidence will be unheeded; fear will prevail over careful training, and the rider will be very fortunate if she escapes without an accident. The writer is sustained in the idea that the affection of the horse is essential to the safety of the rider, not only by her own experience, but also by that of some of the most eminent teachers of riding, and trainers of horses.

Maud S. is an example of what a firm yet kind rule will effect in bringing forth the capabilities of a horse. She has never had a harsh word spoken to her, and has never been punished with the whip, but has, on the contrary, been trained with the most patient and loving care; and the result has been a speed so marvelous as to have positively astonished the world, for although naturally high tempered, she will strain every nerve to please her kind, loving master, when urged forward by his voice alone.

Some ladies acquire a dislike for horseback riding, either because they experience discomfort or uneasiness when in the saddle, or because the movements of their horses cause them considerable fatigue.

There may be various reasons for this: the saddle may be too large, or too small, or improperly made; or the rider's position in the saddle may be incorrect, and as a consequence, the animal cannot be brought to his best paces. Discomfort may occasionally be caused by an improperly made riding-habit. The rider whose waist is confined by tight lacing cannot adapt herself to the motions of her horse, and the graceful pliancy so essential to good riding will, therefore, be lost. The lady who wears tight corsets can never become a thorough rider, nor will the exercise of riding give her either pleasure or health. She may manage to look well when riding at a gait no faster than a walk, but, beyond this, her motions will appear rigid and uncomfortable. A quick pace will induce rapid circulation, and the blood, checked at the waist, will, like a stream which has met with an obstacle in its course, turn into other channels, rushing either to the heart, causing faintness, or to the head, producing headache and vertigo. There have even been instances of a serious nature, where expectoration of blood has been occasioned by horseback riding, when the rider was tightly laced.

The naturally slender, symmetrical figure, when in the saddle, is the perfection of beauty, but she whom nature has endowed with more ample proportions will never attain this perfection by pinching her waist in. Let the full figure be left to nature, its owner sitting well in the saddle, on a horse adapted to her style, and she will make a very imposing appearance, and prove a formidable rival to her more slender companion.

There is a mistaken idea prevalent among certain persons, that horseback riding induces obesity. It is true that, to a certain extent, riding favors healthy muscular development, but the same may be said of all kinds of exercise, and this effect, far from being objectionable, is highly desirable, as it contributes to symmetry of form, as well as to health and strength, conditions that in a large proportion of our American women are unfortunately lacking. Those who ride on horseback will find that while gaining in strength and proper physical tissue, they will, at the same time, as a rule, be gradually losing all excess of flesh; it is impossible for an active rider to become fat or flabby; but the indolent woman who is prejudiced against exercise of any kind will soon find the much dreaded calamity, corpulency, overtaking her, and beauty of form more or less rapidly disappearing beneath a mountain of flesh.

There are many persons who entertain the mistaken idea that instinct is a sufficient guide in learning to ride; that it is quite unnecessary to take any lessons or to make a study of the art of correct riding; and that youth, a good figure, and practice are all that is required to make a finished rider. This is a most erroneous opinion, which has been productive of much harm to lady riders. The above qualifications are undoubtedly great assistants, but without correct instruction they will never produce an accomplished and graceful rider.

The instinctive horsewoman usually rides boldly and with perfect satisfaction to herself, but to the eye of the connoisseur she presents many glaring defects. Very bold, but, at the same time, very bad riding is often seen among those who consider themselves very fine horsewomen. In order to gain the reputation of a finished rider, it is not essential that one should perform all the antics of a circus rider, nor that she should ride a Mazeppian horse. The finished rider may be known by the correctness of her attitude in the saddle, by her complete control of her horse, and by the tranquillity of her motions when in city or park; in such places she makes no attempt to ride at a very rapid trot, or flying gallop-gaits which should be reserved for country roads, where more speed is allowable.

There is still another false idea prevalent among a certain class of people, which is that a love for horses, and for horseback riding necessarily makes one coarse, and detracts from the refinement of a woman's nature. It must be acknowledged that the coarseness of a vulgar spirit can be nowhere more conspicuously displayed than in the saddle, and yet in no place is the delicacy and decorum of woman more observable. A person on horseback is placed in a position where every motion is subject to critical observation and comment. The quiet, simple costume, the easy movements, the absence of ostentatious display, will always proclaim the refined, well-bred rider. Rudeness in the saddle is as much out of place as in the parlor or salon, and greatly more annoying to spectators, besides being disrespectful and dangerous to other riders. Abrupt movements, awkward and rapid paces, frequently cause neighboring horses to become restless, and even to run away. Because a lady loves her horse, and enjoys riding him, it is by no means necessary that she should become a Lady Gay Spanker, indulge in stable talk, make familiars of grooms and stable boys, or follow the hounds in the hunting field.

There are in this work no especial instructions given for the hunting field, as the author does not consider it a suitable place for a lady rider. She believes that no lady should risk life and limb in leaping high and dangerous obstacles, but that all such daring feats should be left to the other sex or to circus actresses. Nor would any woman who really cared for her horse wish to run the risk of reducing him to the deplorable condition of many horses that follow the hounds. In England, where hunting is the favorite pastime among gentlemen, the number of maimed and crippled horses that one meets is disheartening. Every lady, however, who desires to become a finished rider, should learn to leap, as this will not only aid her in securing a good seat in the saddle, but may also prove of value in times of danger.

Before concluding I would again urge upon my readers the importance of out-of-door exercise, which can hardly be taken in a more agreeable form than that of horseback riding,—a great panacea, giving rest and refreshment to the overworked brain of the student, counteracting many of the pernicious effects of the luxurious lives of the wealthy, and acting upon the workers of the world as a tonic, and as a stimulus to greater exertion.

THE AMERICAN HORSEWOMAN

CHAPTER I
THE HORSE

"Look, when a painter would surpass the life,
In limning out a well-proportioned steed,
His art with Nature's workmanship at strife,
As if the dead the living should exceed;
So did this horse excel a common one,
In shape, in courage, color, pace, and bone."

• • • • • • • • • • • • • • • • • • •

—"what a horse should have he did not lack,
Save a proud rider on so proud a back."

Venus and Adonis.

I T IS SUPPOSED that the original home of the horse was central Asia, and that all the wild horses that range over the steppes of Tartary, the pampas of South America, and the prairies of North America, are descendants of this Asiatic stock.[1] There is, in the history of the world, no accurate statement of the time when the horse was first subjugated by man, but so far back as his career can be traced in the dim and shadowy past, he seems to have been man's servant and companion. We

---

1 A very interesting work, by C. A. Piétrement, has recently been issued in France, entitled *Les chevaux dans les temps prehistorique et historique.* The author shows that wild horses were hunted and eaten by man in the rough stone age. He also determines in what European and Asiatic regions the eight extant horse families were domesticated, and traces their various wanderings over the earth, deducing many interesting facts from the history of their migrations.

find him, on the mysterious ruins of ancient Egypt, represented with his badge of servitude, the bridle; he figures in myth and fable as the companion of man and gods; he is a prominent figure in the pictured battle scenes of the ancient world; and has always been a favorite theme with poet, historian, and philosopher in all ages.

The first written record, known to us, of the subjection of the horse to man is found in the Bible, where in Genesis (xlvii. 17) it is stated that Joseph gave the Egyptians bread in exchange for their horses, and in 1. 9, we read that when Joseph went to bury his father Jacob, there went with him the servants of the house of Pharaoh, the elders of the land of Egypt, together with "chariots and horsemen" in numbers. Jeremiah compares the speed of the horse with the swiftness of the eagle; and Job's description of the war charger has never been surpassed.

Ancient Rome paid homage to the horse by a yearly festival, when every one abstained from labor, and the day was made one of feasting and frolic. The horse, decked with garlands, and with gay and costly trappings, was led in triumph through the streets, followed by a multitude who loudly proclaimed in verse and song his many good services to man.

This adulation of the horse sometimes went beyond the bounds of reason, as in the case of Caligula, who carried his love for his horse, Incitatus, to an insane degree. He had a marble palace erected for a stable, furnished it with mangers of ivory and gold, and had sentinels guard it at night that the repose of his favorite might not be disturbed. Another elegant palace was fitted up in the most splendid and costly style, and here the animal's visitors were entertained. Caligula required all who called upon himself to visit Incitatus also, and to treat the animal with the same respect and reverence as that observed towards a royal host. This horse was frequently introduced at Caligula's banquets, where he was presented with gilded oats, and with wine from a golden cup. Historians state that Caligula would even have made his steed consul of Rome, had not the tyrant been opportunely assassinated, and the world freed from an insane fiend.

In the legends of the Middle Ages the knight-errant and his gallant steed were inseparable, and together performed doughty deeds of valor and chivalry. In our present more prosaic age, the horse has been trained to such a degree of perfection in speed and motion as was never dreamed of by the ancients or by the knights of the crusades; and there has been given to the world an animal that is a marvel of courage, swiftness, and endurance, while, at the same time, so docile, that the delicate hand of woman can completely control him.

The Arabian is the patrician among horses; he is the most intelligent, the most beautifully formed, and, when kindly treated, the gentlest of his race. He is especially noted for his keenness of perception, his retentive memory, his powers of endurance, and, when harshly or cruelly treated, for his fierce resentment and ferociousness, which nothing but death can conquer. In his Arabian home he is guarded as a treasure, is made one of the family and treated with the most loving care. This close companionship creates an affection and confidence between the horse and his master which is almost unbounded; while the kindness with which the animal is treated seems to brighten his intelligence as well as to render him gentle.

When these horses were first introduced into Europe they seemed, after a short stay in civilization, to have completely changed their nature, and, instead of gentleness and docility, exhibited an almost tiger-like ferocity. This change was at first attributed to difference of climate and high feeding, but, after several grooms had been injured or killed by their charges, it began to be suspected that there was something wrong in the treatment. The experiment of introducing native grooms was therefore tried, and the results proved most satisfactory, the animals once more becoming gentle and docile.[2] Since

2   "The Bedouin (and every other race of Orientals that I am acquainted with seems to possess somewhat the same quality) exhibits a patience towards his horse as remarkable as is the impatience and roughness of the Englishman.... In his (the Oriental's) mental organization some screw is tight which in the English mind is loose; he is sane on a point where the Englishman is slightly cracked, and he rides on serene and contented where the latter would go into a paroxysm of swearing and spurring. I have seen an Arab horse, broken loose at a moment when our camp was thronged with horses brought for sale, turn the whole concern topsy-turvy, and reduce it to one tumult of pawing and snorting and belligerent screeching; and I never yet saw the captor when he finally got hold of the halter show the least trace of anger, or do otherwise than lead the animal back to his picket with perfect calmness. Contrast this with the 'job' in the mouth and the kick in the ribs and the curse that the English groom would bestow under similar circumstances, and you have, in a great measure, the secret of the good temper of the Arab horse in Arab hands."— *Blackwood's Magazine*, 1859.

then the nature of the Arabian has become better understood, and, both in this country and in Europe, he shows, at the present day, a decided improvement upon the original native of the desert. He is larger and swifter, yet still retains all the spirit as well as docility of his ancestors. In America his descendants are called "thorough-breds," and Americans may well be proud of this race of horses, which is rapidly becoming world renowned.

Before purchasing a saddle-horse, several points should be considered. First, **the style of the rider's figure**; for a horse which would be suitable for a large, stout person would not be at all desirable for one having a small, slender figure. A large, majestic looking woman would present a very absurd spectacle when mounted upon a slightly built, slender horse; his narrow back in contrast with that of his rider would cause hers to appear even larger and wider than usual, and thus give her a heavy and ridiculous appearance, while the little horse would look overburdened and miserable, and his step, being too short for his rider, would cause her to experience an unpleasant sensation of embarrassment and restraint. On the other hand, a short, light, slender rider, seated upon a tall broad-backed animal, would appear equally out of place; the step of the horse being, in her case, too long, would make her seat unsteady and insecure, so that instead of a sense of enjoyment, exhilaration, and benefit from the ride, she would experience only fatigue and dissatisfaction.

If the rider be tall and rather plump, the horse should be fifteen hands and three inches in height, and have a somewhat broad back. A lady below the medium height, and of slender proportions, will look equally well when riding a pony fourteen hands high, or a horse fifteen hands. An animal fifteen hands, or fifteen hands and two inches in height, will generally be found suitable for all ladies who are not excessively large and tall, or very short and slender. In all cases, however, the back of the horse should be long enough to appear well under the side-saddle, for a horse with a short back never presents a fine aspect when carrying a woman. In such cases, the side-saddle extends from his withers nearly, if not quite, to his hips, and as the riding skirt covers his left side, little is seen of the horse except his head and tail. Horses with very short backs are usually good weight-carriers, but their gaits are apt to be rough and uneasy.

Another point to be considered in the selection of a horse is, what gait or gaits are best suited to the rider, and here again the lady should take her figure into consideration. The walk, trot, canter, and gallop are the only gaits recognized by English horsewomen, but in America the walk, rack, pace, and canter are the favorite gaits. If the lady's figure be slender and elegant, any of the above named gaits will suit her, but should she be large or stout, a brisk walk or easy canter should be selected. The rapid gallop and all fast gaits should be left to light and active riders.

The fast or running walk is a very desirable gait for any one, but is specially so for middle-aged or stout people, who cannot endure much jolting; it is also excellent for delicate women, for poor riders, or for those who have long journeys to make which they wish to accomplish speedily and without undue fatigue to themselves or their horses. A good sound horse who has been trained to this walk can readily travel thirty or forty miles a day, or even more. This gait is adapted equally well to the street, the park, and the country road; but it must be acknowledged that horses possessing it rarely have any other that is desirable, and, indeed, any other would be apt to impair the ease and harmony of the animal's movements in this walk.

The French or cavalry trot should never be ridden on the road by a woman, as the movements of the horse in this gait are so very rough that the most accomplished rider cannot keep a firm, steady seat. The body is jolted in a peculiar and very unpleasant manner, occasioning a sense of fatigue that is readily appreciated, though difficult to describe.

The country jog-trot is another very fatiguing gait, although farmers, who ride it a good deal, state that "after one gets used to it, it is not at all tiresome." But a lady's seat in the saddle is so different from that of a gentleman's that she can never ride this gait without excessive fatigue.

A rough racker or pacer will prove almost as wearisome as the jog-trotter. Indeed, if she wishes to gain any pleasure or benefit from riding, a lady should never mount a horse that is at all stiff or uneven in his movements, no matter what may be his gait.

The easiest of all gaits to ride, although the most difficult to learn, is the English trot. This is especially adapted to short persons, who can ride it to perfection. A tall woman will be apt to lean too far forward when rising in it, and her specialties, therefore, should be the canter and the gallop, in which she can appear to the greatest advantage. The rack, and the pace of a horse that has easy movements are not at all difficult to learn to ride, and are, consequently, the favorite gaits of poor riders.

In selecting a horse his **temperament** must also be considered. A high-spirited, nervous animal, full of vitality, highly satisfactory as he might prove to some, would be only a source of misery to others of less courageous dispositions. First lessons in riding should be taken upon a horse of cold temperament and kindly disposition who will resent neither mistakes nor awkwardness. Having learned to ride and to manage a horse properly, no steed can then be too mettlesome for the healthy and active lady pupil, provided he has no vices and possesses the good manners that should always belong to every lady's horse.

It is a great mistake to believe, as many do, that a weak, slightly built horse is yet capable of carrying a woman. On the contrary, a lady's horse should be the soundest and best that can be procured, and should be able to carry with perfect ease a weight much greater than hers. A slight, weak animal, if ridden much by a woman, will be certain to "get out of condition," will become unsound in the limbs of one side, usually the left, and will soon wear out.

Before buying a horse, the lady who is to ride him should be weighed, and should then have some one who is considerably heavier than herself ride the animal, that she may be sure that her own weight will not be too great for him. If he carries the heavier weight with ease, he can, of course, carry her.

In selecting a horse great care should be taken to ascertain whether there is the least trace of **unsoundness in his feet and legs**, and especially that variety of unsoundness which occasions stumbling. The best of horses, when going over rough places or when very tired may stumble, and so will indolent horses that are too lazy when traveling to lift their feet up fully; but when this fault is due to disease, or becomes a habit with a lazy animal, he should never be used under the side-saddle.

If the reader will glance at Figs. 1 and 2, she will observe the difference between the head of the low-bred horse and that of the best bred of the race. Fig. 1 represents the head of an Arabian horse; the brain is wide between the eyes, the brow high and prominent, and the expression of the face high-bred and intelligent. Fig. 2 shows the head of a low-bred horse, whose stupid aspect and small brain are very manifest.

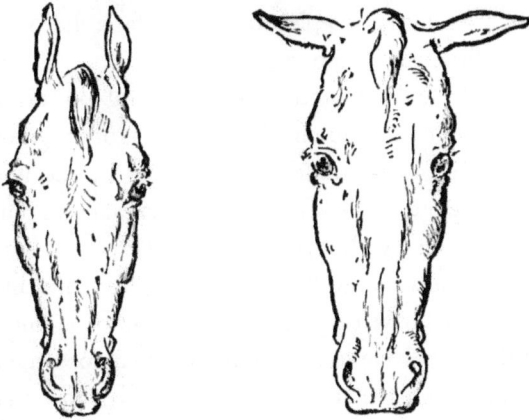

FIG. 1—HEAD OF THE ARABIAN STEED   FIG. 2—HEAD OF THE LOW-BRED HORSE

The one horse will be quick to comprehend what is required of him, and will appreciate any efforts made to brighten his intelligence, while the other will be slow to understand, almost indifferent to the kindness of his master, and apt, when too much indulged, to return treachery for good treatment. The whip, when applied to the latter as a means of punishment, will probably cow him, but, if used for the same purpose on the former, will rouse in him all the hot temper derived from his ancestors, and in the contest which ensues between his master and himself, he will conquer, or terminate the strife his own death, or that of his master.

Another noticeable feature in the Arab horse, and one usually considered significant of an active and wide-awake temperament, is the width and expansiveness of the nostrils. These, upon the least excitement, will quiver and expand, and in a rapid gallop will stand out freely, giving a singularly spirited look to the animal's face.

The shape and size of the ears are also indications of high or low birth. In the high-bred horse they are generally small, thin, and delicate on their outer margins, with the tips inclined somewhat towards one another. By means of these organs the animal expresses his different emotions of anger, fear, dislike, or gayety. They may be termed his language, and their various movements can readily be understood when one takes a little trouble to study their indications. The ears of a low-bred horse are large, thick, and covered with coarse hair; they sometimes lop or droop horizontally, protruding from the sides of the head and giving a very sheepish look to the face; they rarely move, and express very little emotion of any kind.

The eye of the desert steed is very beautiful, possessing all the brilliancy and gentleness so much admired in that of the gazelle. Its expression in repose is one of mildness and amiability, but, under the influence of excitement, it dilates widely and sparkles. A horse which has small eyes set close together, no matter what excellences he may possess in other respects, is sure to have some taint of inferior blood. Some of the coarser breeds have the large eye of the Arabian, but it will usually be found that they have some thorough-bred among their ancestors.

Width between the sides or branches of the lower jaw is another distinctive feature of the horse of pure descent. (Fig. 3.) A wide furrow or channel between the points mentioned is necessary for speed, in order to allow room for free respiration when the animal is in rapid motion.

FIG. 3—WIDTH OF THE LOWER JAW IN THE THOROUGH-BRED

The coarser breeds have very small, narrow channels (Fig. 4), and very rapid motion soon distresses them.

The mouth of the well-bred horse is large, allowing ample room for the bit, and giving him a determined and energetic, but at the same time pleasant, amiable expression. The mouth of the low-bred horse is small and covered with coarse hair, and gives the animal a sulky, dejected appearance.

FIG. 4—WIDTH OF THE LOWER JAW IN THE LOW-BRED HORSE

The light, elegant head of the Arabian is well set on his neck; a slight convexity at the upper part of the throat gives freedom to the functions of this organ, as well as elasticity to the movements of the head and neck; and the *encolure*, or crest of the neck, is arched with a graceful curve. But it is especially in the shape of the shoulders that his horse excels all others, and this is the secret of those easy movements which make him so desirable for the saddle. These shoulders are deep, and placed obliquely at an angle of about 45°; they act like the springs of a well-made carriage, diminishing the shock or jar of his movements. They are always accompanied by a deep chest, high withers, and fore-legs set well forward, qualities which make the horse much safer for riding. (Fig. 5.)

FIG. 5—OBLIQUE SHOULDER

The animal with straight shoulders, no matter how well shaped in other respects, can never make a good saddle-horse, and should be at once rejected. These shoulders are usually accompanied by low withers, and fore-legs placed too far under the body, which arrangement causes the rider an unpleasant jar every time a fore-foot touches the ground. Moreover, the gait of the horse is constrained and not always safe, and if he be used much under the saddle his fore-feet will soon become unsound. This straight, upright shoulder is characteristic of the coarser breeds of horses, and is frequently associated with a short, thick neck. Such horses are not only unfit for the saddle, but, when any speed is desired, are unsuitable even for a pleasure carriage. (Fig. 6.)

FIG. 6—STRAIGHT OR UPRIGHT SHOULDER

The haunch of the low-bred horse is generally large, but not so well formed as that of the thorough-bred. This portion of the Arabian courser is wide, indicating strength, and force to propel himself forward, while his tail, standing out gayly when he is in motion, projects in a line with his back-bone. His forearm is large, long, and muscular,[3] his knees broad

---

3   "There is, however, a medium in this, and the advantage of length in the arm will depend on the use to which the horse is applied. The lady's horse, the cavalry horse, every horse in which prancing action is esteemed a beauty, and in which utility is, to a certain degree, sacrificed to appearance, must not be too long in the arm. If he is long there, he will be proportionally short in the leg; and although this is an undoubted excellence, whether speed or continuance is regarded, the short leg will not give the grand and imposing action which fashion may require. In addition to this, a horse with short legs may not have quite so easy

and firm, his hocks of considerable size, while his cannon-bone, situated between the knee and the fetlock, is short, although presenting a broad appearance when viewed laterally.

On each front leg, at the back of the knee, there is a bony projection, giving attachments to the flexor muscles, and affording protection to certain tendons. The Orientals set a great value upon the presence of this bone, believing that it favors muscular action, and the larger this prominence is the more highly do they prize the animal that possesses it. The pasterns of the high-bred horse are of medium length, and very elastic, while the foot is circular and of moderate size.

In the preceding description, the author has endeavored to make plain to the reader the most important points to be observed in both the high-bred and the low-bred horse, and has given the most pronounced characteristics of each.

Between these extremes, however, there are many varieties of horses, possessing more or less of the Arabian characteristics mingled with those of other races. Some of the best American horses are numbered among these mixed races, and, by many, are considered an improvement upon the Arabian, as they are excellent for light carriages and buggies. The more they resemble the Oriental steed, the better they are for the saddle.

The lady who, in this country, cannot find a horse to suit her, will, indeed, be difficult to please. It will be best for her to tell some gentleman what sort of horse she wishes, and let him select for her; but, at the same time, it can do no harm, and may prove a great advantage to her to know all the requisite points of a good saddle-horse. It will not take long to learn them, and the knowledge gained will prevent her from being imposed upon by the ignorant or unscrupulous. Gentlemen, even those who consider themselves good judges of horse-flesh, are sometimes guilty of very serious blunders in selecting a horse for a lady's use; and should the lady be obliged to negotiate directly with a horse-dealer, she must bear in mind constantly the fact that, although there are reliable and honorable dealers to be found, there are many who would not scruple to cheat even a woman. A careful perusal of the

---

an action as another whose length is in the shank rather than in the arms."—*W. Youatt.*

present work, together with the advice of an *upright* and *trustworthy* veterinary surgeon, or a skilled riding-master, will aid her in protecting herself from the impositions of unprincipled horse-jockeys and self-styled "veterinary doctors."

In any case, whatever be the other characteristics of the animal selected, be sure that he has the oblique shoulder, as well as depth of shoulder, and hind-legs well bent. Without these characteristics he will be unfit for a lady's use, as his movements will be rough and unsafe, and the saddle will be apt to turn.

If it be desired to purchase a horse for a moderate price, certain points which might be insisted on in a high-priced animal will have to be dispensed with; for instance, his color may not be satisfactory; he may not have a pretty head, or a well-set tail, etc., but these deficiencies may be overlooked if he be sound, have good action, and no vices. He may be handsome, well-actioned, and thoroughly trained, but have a slight defect in his wind, noticeable only when he is urged into a rapid trot, or a gallop. If wanted for street and park service only, and if the purchaser does not care for fast riding, a horse of this sort will suit her very well. Sometimes a horse of good breed, as well as of good form, has never had the advantages of a thorough training, or he may be worn out by excessive work. Should he be comparatively young, rest and proper training may still make a good horse of him, but great care should be taken to assure one's self that no permanent disease or injury exists. The Orientals have a proverb, that it is well to bear in mind when buying an animal of the kind just described:— "Ruin, son of ruin, is he who buys to cure."

Always examine with great care a horse's mouth. A hard-mouthed animal is a very unpleasant one for a lady to ride, and is apt to degenerate into a runaway. Scars at the angles of the mouth are good indications of a "bolter," or runaway, or at least of cruel treatment, and harsh usage is by no means a good instructor.

While a very short-backed horse does not appear to great advantage under a side-saddle, he may, nevertheless, have many good qualities that will compensate for this defect, and it may be overlooked provided the price asked for him be reasonable; but horses of this kind frequently command a high price when their action is exceptionally good. Corns on the feet generally depreciate the value of a horse, although they may sometimes be cured by removing the shoes, and giving him a free run of six or eight months in a pasture of soft ground; if he be then properly shod, and used on country roads only, he may become permanently serviceable. There is, however, considerable risk in buying a horse that has corns, and the purchaser should remember the Oriental proverb just referred to, and not forget the veterinary surgeon.

Before paying for a horse, the lady should insist upon having him on trial for at least a month, that she may have an opportunity of discovering his vices or defects, if any such exist. She must be careful not to condemn him too hastily, and should, when trying him, make due allowance for his change of quarters and also for the novelty of carrying a new rider, as some horses are very nervous until they become well acquainted with their riders. Should the horse's movements prove rough, should he be found hard-mouthed, or should any indications of unsoundness or viciousness be detected, he should be immediately returned to his owner. It must be remembered, however, that very few horses are perfect, and that minor defects may, in most instances, be overlooked if the essentials are secured. Before rejecting the horse, the lady should also be very sure that the faults to which she objects are not due to her own mismanagement of him. But if she decides that she is not at fault, no amount of persuasion should induce her to purchase. In justice to the owner of the horse, he ought to be reasonably paid for the time and services of his rejected animal; but if it be decided to keep the horse, then only the purchase-money originally agreed upon should be paid.

The surest and best way of securing a good saddle-horse is to purchase, from one of the celebrated breeding farms, a well-shaped four-year-old colt of good breed, and have him taught the gaits and style of movement required. Great care should be taken in the selection of his teacher, for if the colt's temper be spoiled by injudicious treatment, he will be completely ruined for a lady's use. A riding-school teacher will generally understand all the requirements necessary for a lady's saddle-horse, and may be safely intrusted with the animal's education. If no riding-school master of established reputation as a trainer can be had, it may be possible to secure the services of some one near the lady's home, as she can then superintend the colt's education herself and be sure that he is treated neither rashly nor cruelly.

The ideas concerning the education of the horse have completely changed within the last twenty-five years. The whip as a means of punishment is entirely dispensed with in the best training schools of the present day, and, instead of rough and brutal measures, kindness, firmness, and patience are now the only means employed to train and govern him. The theory of this modern system of training may be found in the following explanation of a celebrated English trainer, who subdued his horses by exhibiting towards them a wonderful degree of patience:—"If I enter into a contest with the horse, he will fling and prance, and there will be no knowing which will be master; whereas if I remain quiet and determined, I have the best of it."

The following is an example of the patience with which this man carried out his theory:—

Being once mounted on a very obstinate colt that refused to move in the direction desired, he declined all suggestions of severe measures, and after one or two gentle but fruitless attempts to make the animal move, he desisted, and having called for his pipe, sat there quietly for a couple of hours enjoying a good smoke, and chatting gayly with passing friends. Then after another quiet but unsuccessful attempt to induce the colt to move, he sent for some dinner which he ate while still on the animal's back. As night approached and the air became cool, he sent for his overcoat and more tobacco, and proceeded to make a night of it. About this time the colt became uneasy, but not until midnight did he show any disposition to move in the required direction. Now was the time for the master to assert himself. "Whoa!" he cried, "you have stayed here so long to please yourself, now you will stay a little longer to please me." He then kept the colt standing in the same place an hour longer, and when he finally allowed him to move, it was in a direction opposite to that which the colt seemed disposed to take. He walked the animal slowly for five miles, then allowed him to trot back to his stable, and finally—as if he had been a disobedient child—sent him supperless to bed, giving him the rest of the night in which to meditate upon the effects of his obstinacy.

To some this may seem a great deal of useless trouble to take with a colt that might have been compelled to move more promptly by means of whip or spur; but that day's experience completely subdued the colt's stubborn spirit, and all idea of rebellion to human authority was banished from his mind forever. Had a contrary course been pursued, it would probably have made the creature headstrong, balky, and unreliable; he would have yielded to the whip and spur at one time only to battle the more fiercely against them at the first favorable opportunity, and his master would never have known at what minute he might have to enter into a contest with him. That a horse trained by violent means can never be trusted is a fact which is every day becoming better recognized and appreciated.

"A great many accidents might be avoided," says a well-known authority upon the education of the horse, "could the populace be instructed to think a horse was endowed with senses, was gifted with feelings, and was able in some degree to appreciate motives."... "The strongest man cannot physically contend against the weakest horse. Man's power reposes in better attributes than any which reside in thews and muscles. Reason alone should dictate and control his conduct. Thus guided, mortals have subdued the elements. For power, when mental, is without limit: by savage violence nothing is attained and man is often humbled."

The lady who has the good fortune to live in the country where she can have so many opportunities for studying the disposition and character of her animals, and can, if she chooses, watch and superintend the education of her horse from the time he is a colt, has undoubtedly a better chance of securing a fine saddle-horse than she who lives in the city and is obliged to depend almost entirely upon others for the training of her horse. Indeed, very little formal training will be necessary for a horse that has been brought up under the eye of a kind and judicious mistress, for he will soon learn to understand and obey the wishes of one whom he loves and trusts, and if she be an accomplished rider she can do the greater part of the training herself.

The best and most trustworthy horse the author ever had was one that was trained almost from his birth. Fay's advent was a welcome event to the children of the family, by whom he was immediately claimed and used as a play-fellow. By the older members of the family he was always regarded as part of the household,—an honored servant, to be well cared for,—and he was petted and fondled by all, from paterfamilias down to Bridget in the kitchen. He was taught, among other tricks, to bow politely when anything nice was given him, and many were the journeys he made around to the kitchen window, where he would make his obeisance in such an irresistible manner that Bridget would be completely captivated; and the dainty bits were passed through the window in such quantities and were swallowed with such avidity that the lady of the house had to interfere and restrict the donations to two cakes daily.

Fay had been taught to shake hands with his admirers, and this trick was called his "word of honor;" he had his likes and dislikes, and would positively refuse to honor some people with a handshake. If these slighted individuals insisted upon riding him, he made them so uncomfortable by the roughness of his gaits that they never cared to repeat the experiment. But the favored ones, whom he had received into his good graces and to whom he had given his "word of honor," he would carry safely anywhere, at his lightest and easiest gait. Fay never went back on his word, which is more than can be said of some human beings.

The great difficulty in training a horse for a lady's use is to get him well placed on his haunches. In Fay's case this was accomplished by teaching him to place his fore-feet upon a stout inverted tub, about two feet high. When he offered his "hand" for a shake, some one pushed forward the tub, upon which his "foot" dropped and was allowed to remain a short time, when the other foot was treated in the same manner. After half a dozen lessons of this sort, he learned to put up his feet without assistance; first one, and then the other, and, finally, both at once. These performances were always rewarded by a piece of apple or cake, together with expressions of pleasure from the by-standers. Fay had a weakness for flattery, and no actor called before the curtain ever expressed more pleasure at an *encore* than did Fay when applauded for his efforts to please. That the tub trick would prove equally effectual with other horses in teaching them to place themselves well on their haunches cannot be positively stated. It might prove more troublesome to teach most horses this trick than to have them placed upon their haunches in the usual way by means of a strong curb, or by lessons with the lunge line. It proved entirely successful in Fay's case, and a horse lighter in hand or easier in gait was never ridden by a woman.

Fay's training began when he was only a few weeks old: a light halter and a loose calico surcingle were placed on him for a short time

each day, during which time he was carefully watched lest he should
do himself some injury. When he was about eight months old, a small
bit, made of a smooth stick of licorice, was put into his mouth, and to
this bit light leather reins were fastened by pieces of elastic rubber: this
rubber relieved his mouth from a constant dead pull, and tended to
preserve its delicate sensibility. Thus harnessed he was led around the
lawn, followed by a crowd of youthful admirers and playmates, who
formed a sort of triumphal procession, with which the colt was as well
pleased as the spectators. Every attempt on his part to indulge in horse-
play, such as biting, kicking, etc., was always quickly checked, and no
one was allowed to tease or strike him.

Nothing heavier than a dumb jockey was put on his back until
he was four years old, when his education began in sober earnest.
After a few lessons with the lunge line, given by a regular trainer, a
saddle was put on his back, and for the first time in his life he carried
a human being.

When learning his different riding gaits on the road, he was always
accompanied by a well-trained saddle-horse, aided by whose example
as well as by the efforts of his rider he was soon trained in three different styles of movement, namely, a good walk, trot, and hand gallop.
Fear seemed unknown to this horse, for he had always been allowed as
a colt to follow his dam on the road, and had thus become so accustomed to all such alarming objects as steam engines, hay carts, etc.,
that they had ceased to occasion him the least uneasiness. This high
spirited and courageous animal had perfect confidence in the world
and looked upon all mankind as friendly. His constant companionship
with human beings had sharpened his perceptive faculties, and made
him quick to understand whatever was required of him. The kindness
shown him was never allowed to degenerate into weakness or over-in-
dulgence, and whenever anything was required of him it was insisted upon until complete obedience was obtained. In this way he was
taught to understand that man was his master and superior.

Although it is not absolutely essential that a lady's horse should
learn the tricks of bowing, hand-shaking, etc., yet the lady who will
take the pains to teach her horse some of them will find that she not
only gets a great deal of pleasure from the lessons, but that they enable
her to gain more complete control over him, for the horse, like some

other animals, gives affection and entire obedience to the person who makes an effort to increase his intelligence.

Lessons with the lunge line should always be short, as they are very fatiguing to a young colt, and when given too often or for too great a length of time they make him giddy from rush of blood to the head; not a few instances, indeed, have occurred where a persistence in such lessons has occasioned complete blindness.

A lady's horse should be taught to disregard the flapping of the riding-skirt, and it is also well for him to become accustomed to having articles of various kinds, such as pieces of cloth, paper, etc., fluttering about him, as he will not then be likely to take fright should any part of the rider's costume become disarranged and blow about him.

He should also be so trained that he will not mind having the saddle moved from side to side on his back. The best of riders may have her saddle turn, and if the horse be thus trained he will neither kick nor run away should such an accident occur.

It is also very important that the horse should be taught to stop, and stand as firm as a rock at the word of command given in a low, firm tone. This habit is not only important in mounting and dismounting,—feats which it is difficult, if not impossible, for the lady to perform unless the horse be perfectly still,— but the rider will also find this prompt obedience of great assistance in checking her horse when he becomes frightened and tries to break away; for he will stop instinctively when he hears the familiar order given in the voice to which he is accustomed.

A lady should not fail to visit her horse's stable from time to time, in order to assure herself that he is well treated and properly cared for by the groom. Viciousness and restlessness on the road can often be traced to annoyances and ill-treatment in the stable. Grooms and stable boys sometimes like to see the horse kick out and attempt to bite, and will while away their idle hours in harassing him, tickling his ears with straws, or touching him up with the whip in order to make him prance and strike out. The result of these annoyances will be that, if the lady during her ride accidentally touches her horse with the whip, he will begin prancing and kicking; or, if it is summer time, the gnats and flies swarming about his ears will make him unmanageable. In the latter case, ear-tips will only make the matter worse, especially if they have dangling tassels. When such signs of nervousness are noticeable, especially in a horse that has been hitherto gentle, they may usually be attributed to the treatment of the groom or his assistants.

Most grooms delight in currying their charges with combs having teeth like small spikes and in laying on the polishing brush with a hand as heavy as the blows of misfortune. Some animals, it is true, like this kind of rubbing, but there are many, who have thin, delicate skins, to whom such treatment is almost unmitigated torture. Should the lady hear any contest going on between the horse and groom during the former's morning toilette, she should order a blunt curry-comb to be used; or even dispense with a comb altogether, and let the brush only be applied with a light hand. Grooms sometimes take pleasure in throwing cold water over their horses. In very warm weather, and when the animal is not overheated, this treatment may prove refreshing to him, but, as a general rule it is objectionable, as it is apt to occasion a sudden chill which may result in serious consequences.

The stable man may grumble at the lady's interference and supervision, but she must not allow this to prevent her from attending carefully to the welfare of the animal whose faithful services contribute so largely to her pleasure. When she buys a horse she introduces a new member into her household, who should be as well looked after and cared for as any other faithful servant or friend. Indeed, the horse is the more entitled to consideration in that he is entirely helpless, and his lot for good or evil lies wholly in her power. If the mistress is careless or neglects her duty, the servants in whose charge the horse is placed will be very apt to follow her example, and the poor animal will suffer accordingly.

Perhaps the lady, however, may object to entering the stable, and agree with the groom in thinking it "no place for a woman." Or she may fear that in carrying out the ideas suggested above she will expose herself to the ridicule of thoughtless acquaintances who can never do anything until it has received the sanction of fashion.

For the benefit of this fastidious individual and her timid friends we will quote the example of the Empress of Austria, who, although occupying an exalted position at a court where etiquette is carried to the extremes of formality, yet does not hesitate to visit the stable of her favorite steeds and personally to supervise their welfare; and woe to the perverse groom who in the least particular disobeys her commands.

Many other examples might be given of high-born ladies, such as Queen Victoria, the Princess of Wales, the Princess of Prussia, and others, who do not seem to consider it at all unfeminine or coarse for a woman to give some personal care and supervision to her horses. But to enter into more details would prove tiresome, and the example given is enough to silence the scruples of the followers of fashion.

Like all herbivorous creatures that love to roam in herds, the horse is naturally of a restless temperament. Activity is the delight of his existence, and when left to nature and a free life he is seldom quiet. Man takes this creature of buoyant nature from the freedom of its natural life, and confines the active body in a prison house where its movements are even more circumscribed than are those of the wild beasts in the menagerie; they can at least turn around and walk from side to side in their cages, but the horse in his narrow stall is able only to move his head from side to side, to paw a little with his fore-feet, and to move backwards and forwards a short distance, varying with the length of his halter; when he lies down to sleep he is compelled to keep in one position, and runs the risk of meeting with some serious accident. In some stables where the grooms delight in general stagnation, the horses under their charge are not allowed to indulge in even the smallest liberty. The slightest movement is punished by the lash of these silence-loving tyrants, in whose opinion the horse has enough occupation and excitement in gazing at the blank boards directly in front of his head. If these boards should happen to be whitewashed, as is often the case in the country, constant gazing at them will be almost sure to give rise to shying, or even to occasion blindness. If the reader will, for several minutes, gaze steadily at a white wall, she will be able to get some idea of the poor horse's sensations.

Is it then to be wondered at, that an animal of an excitable nature like the horse should, when released from the oppressive quiescence of his prison-house, act as if bereft of reason, and perform strange antics and caperings in his insane delight at once more breathing the fresh air, and seeing the outside world. But, while the horse is thus expressing his pleasure and recovering the use of limbs by vigorous kicks, or is expending his superfluous energy by bounding out of the road at every strange object he encounters, the saddle will be neither a safe nor pleasant place for the lady rider. To avoid such danger, and to compensate, in some degree, the liberty-loving animal for depriving him of his natural life and placing him in bondage, he should be given, instead of the usual narrow stall, a box stall, measuring about sixteen or eighteen feet square. In this box the horse should be left entirely free, without even a halter, as this appendage has sometimes been the cause of fearful accidents, by becoming entangled with the horse's feet.

The groom may grumble again at this innovation, because a box stall means more work for him, but if he really cares for the horses under his charge he will soon become reconciled to the small amount of extra work required by the use of a box stall. Every one who knows anything about a horse in the stable is well aware of the injury done to this animal's feet and limbs by compelling him to stand always confined to one spot in a narrow stall. A box will prevent the occurrence of these injuries, besides giving the horse a little freedom and enabling him to get more rest and benefit from his sleep.

Some horses are fond of looking through a window or over a half door. The glimpse they thus get of the outside life seems to amuse and interest them, and it can do no harm to gratify this desire. Others, however, seem to be worried and excited by such outlooks; they become restless and even make attempts to leap over the half door or through the window. In such cases there should, of course, be no out-of-door scenery visible from the box.

The groom should exercise the horse daily, in a gentle and regular manner; an hour or two of walking, varied occasionally by a short trot, will generally be found sufficient. Being self-taught in the art of riding, grooms nearly always have a very heavy bridle hand, and, if allowed to use the curb bit, will soon destroy that sensitiveness of the horse's mouth which adds so much to the pleasure of riding him. The man who exercises the horse should not be permitted to wear spurs; a lady's horse should be guided wholly by the whip and reins,—as will be explained hereafter, and in no case whatever should the spur be used. If the lady wishes to keep her horse in good health and temper she must insist upon his being exercised regularly, and must assure herself that the groom executes her orders faithfully; for some men, while professing to obey, have been known to stop at the nearest public house, and, after spending an hour or two in drinking beer and gossiping with acquaintances, to ride back complacently to the stable, leaving the horse to suffer from want of exercise. Other grooms have gone to the opposite extreme, and have ridden so hard and fast that the horse on his return was completely tired out, so that when there was occasion to use him the same day it was an effort for him to maintain his usual light gait. Grooms who are always doctoring a horse, giving him nostrums that do no good but often much harm, are also to be avoided. In short, the owner of a horse must be prepared for tricks of all kinds on the part of these stable servants; although, in justice to them, it must be said that there are many who endeavor to perform all their duties faithfully, and can be relied on to treat with kindness any animals committed to their care.

Should the lady rider be obliged to get her horse from a livery stable, she should not rely entirely upon what his owner says of his gaits or gentleness, but should have him tried carefully by some friend or servant, before herself attempting to mount him. She should also be very careful to see, or have her escort see, that the saddle is properly placed upon the back of the horse and firmly girthed, so that there may be no danger of its turning.

CHAPTER II
THE RIDING HABIT

"Her dress, her shape, her matchless grace,
Were all observed, as well as heavenly face."

DRYDEN

A RIDING HABIT should be distinguished by its perfect simplicity. All attempts at display, such as feathers, ribbons, glaring gilt buttons, and sparkling jet, should be carefully avoided, and the dress should be noticeable only for the fineness of its material and the elegance of its fit.

One of the first requirements in a riding dress is that it should fit smoothly and easily. The sleeves should be rather loose, especially near the arm-holes, so that the arms may move freely; but should fit closely enough at the wrist to allow long gauntlet gloves to pass readily over them. It is essential that ample room should be allowed across the chest, as the shoulders are thrown somewhat back in riding, and the chest is, consequently, expanded. The neck of the dress should fit very easily, especially at the back part. Care must be taken not to make the waist too long, for, owing to a lady's position in the saddle, the movements of her horse will soon make a long waist wrinkle and look inelegant. To secure ease, together with a perfect fit without crease or fold, will be somewhat difficult, but not impossible. Some tailors, particularly in New York, Philadelphia, London, and Paris, make a specialty of ladies' riding costumes, and can generally be relied on to supply comfortable and elegant habits.

The favorite and most appropriate style of **riding jacket** is the "postilion basque;" this should be cut short over the hips, and is then especially becoming to a plump person, as it diminishes the apparent width of the back below the waist. The front should have two small darts, and should extend about three inches below the waist; it should then slope gradually up to the hips,—where it must be shortest,—and then downward so as to form a short, square coat-flap at the back, below the waist. This flap must be made without gathers or plaits, and lined with silk, between which and the cloth some stiffening material should be inserted. The middle seam of the coat-flap should be left open as far as the waist, where about one inch of it must be lapped over from left to right; the short side-form on each side must be lapped a little toward the central unclosed seam. The arm-holes should be cut rather high on the shoulders, so that the back may look less broad. If the lady lacks plumpness and roundness, her jacket must be made double-breasted, or else have padding placed across the bust, for a hollow chest mars all the beauty of the figure in the saddle, and causes the rider to look round-shouldered. The edge of the basque should be trimmed with cord-braid, and the front fastened with crocheted bullet buttons; similar buttons should be used to fasten the sleeves closely at the wrist, and two more should be placed on the back of the basque just at its waist line.

Great care must be taken to have the jacket well lined and its seams strongly sewed. The coat-flaps on the back of the basque, below the waist-line, should be held down by heavy metallic buttons, sewed underneath each flap at its lower part, and covered with the same material as that of the dress. Without these weights this part of the dress will be apt to be blown out of position by every passing breeze, and will bob up and down with every motion of the rider's body, presenting a most ridiculous appearance.

For winter riding an extra jacket may be worn over the riding basque. It should be made of some heavy, warm material, and fit half tightly. If trimmed with good fur, this jacket makes a very handsome addition to the riding habit.

Poets have expatiated upon the grace and beauty of the long, flowing riding skirt, with its ample folds, but experience has taught that this long skirt, though, perhaps, very poetical, is practically not only inconvenient but positively dangerous. In the canter or gallop the horse is very apt to entangle his hind-foot in it and be thrown, when the rider may consider herself fortunate if she escapes with no worse accident than a torn skirt. Another objection to this poetical skirt is, that it gathers up the mud and dust of the road, and soon presents a most untidy appearance; while if the day be fresh and breezy its ample folds will stream out like a victorious banner; if made of some light material the breeze will swell it out like an inflated balloon; and if of heavy cloth its length will envelop the rider's feet, and make her look as if tied in a bag.

To avoid all these dangers and inconveniences the **riding skirt** should be cut rather short and narrow, and be made of some heavy material. Two yards and a quarter will be quite wide enough for the bottom of the skirt, while the length need be only about twelve inches more than the rider's ordinary dress. The skirt should be so gored as to form no gathers or plaits at the waist. Tailor-made skirts are so neatly gored as to remain perfectly smooth when the rider is seated in the saddle. As the pommels take up a good deal of room, the front part of the skirt, which passes over them, should be made a little longer than the back, so that, when the rider is seated in the saddle, her dress may hang evenly. If made the same length all around it will, when the lady is mounted, be entirely too short in front, and, besides presenting an uneven, trail-like appearance, will be apt to work back, or to blow up and expose the right foot of the wearer.

The bottom of the skirt should have a hem about three inches wide, but should never be faced with leather, as this will give a stiff, bungling effect, and if the rider should be thrown, and catch the hem of her skirt on either pommel or stirrup, the strength of the leather lining would prevent the cloth from tearing and thus releasing her. Shot, pieces of lead, or other hard substances are also objectionable, because by striking against the horse's side they often cause him to become

restless or even to run away. To keep the skirt down in its proper position a loop of stout elastic, or tape, should be fastened underneath, near the bottom, and through this loop the foot should be passed before being put into the stirrup. The point where the loop should be fastened must be determined by the position of the lady's foot when she is correctly seated in the saddle. Some riders use a second elastic for the right foot, to prevent the skirt from slipping back, but this is not absolutely necessary.

The basque and skirt should be made separate, although it is a very good plan to have strong hooks and eyes to fasten them together at the sides and back, as this will prevent the skirt from turning, or slipping down below the waist, should the binding be a little too loose. The placket-hole should be on the left side and should be buttoned over, to prevent it from gaping open; it must be only just large enough to allow the skirt to slip readily over the shoulders.

The best material for a riding habit is broadcloth, or any strong, soft fabric that will adapt itself readily to the figure. The color is, of course, a matter of taste. Black is always stylish, and is particularly becoming to a stout person. Dark blue, hunter's green, and dark brown are also becoming colors, especially for slender, youthful figures. In the country, a linen jacket may be worn in warm weather, and will be found a very agreeable substitute for the cloth basque, but the skirt should never be made of so thin a material, as it will be too light to hang well and too slippery to sit upon.

To secure ease and freedom in the saddle, a garment closely resembling a pair of **pantaloons** will have to be worn under the riding skirt, and be fastened down securely by means of strong leather or rubber straps, which pass under the foot and are buttoned to the bottom of the pantaloons. These pantaloons should be made of some soft cloth the color of the dress, or else of chamois skin, faced up to the knee with cloth like that of the skirt. Most people prefer the chamois skin for winter use, as it is very warm and so soft that it prevents much of the chafing usually occasioned by the rubbing of the right leg on the pommel.

No under **petticoats** are necessary where the pantaloons are used, but if the rider wear one, it should be of some dark color that will not attract attention if the riding skirt be blown back. Black silk will be an excellent material for such a skirt in summer, something warmer being used in winter. This skirt should have no folds or gathers in it, but if the rider be very thin a little padding around the hips and over the back will give her the desired effect of plumpness.

An important article of every-day wear will have to be discarded and a **riding-habit shirt** used in its place. This shirt must be made short, that the rider may not have to sit upon its folds and wrinkles, which she would find very uncomfortable. The collar should be high and standing, *à la militaire*, and made of the finest, whitest linen; it should be sewed to the shirt for greater security, and should just be seen above the high collar band of the basque.

The **drawers** must also be made very much like those of a gentleman, and the lower parts be tucked under the hose. The garters should be rather loose, or elastic.

Buttoned boots, or those with elastic sides, should not be worn when riding. For summer use, the shoe laced at the side, and having a low, broad heel, is liked by many. The ladies' Wellington boot, reaching nearly to the knee, is also a favorite with some, and, when made without any seam in front, prevents the stirrup-iron from chafing the instep. To be comfortable, it should have a broad sole and be made a little longer than the foot. This boot, however, gives the wearer rather an Amazonian appearance, and has also the great disadvantage of being very difficult to get off, the lady usually being obliged to appropriate the gentleman's bootjack for the purpose. The **best boot** for riding purposes, found to be the most comfortable, and one easy to get on and off, is made of some light leather, or kid, for summer use, and of heavier leather for winter; it extends half way to the knee, laces up in front, has broad, low heels and wide soles, and is made a little longer than the wearer's foot, so that it may be perfectly easy, as a tight boot in riding is even more distressing than in walking.

The **corset** is indispensable to the elegant fit required in a riding habit, but should never be laced tight. It should be short on the sides and in the front and back. If long in front it will be almost impossible for the rider to pass her knee over the second pommel when she attempts to mount her horse, and will cause her, when riding, to incline her body too far back; when long at the sides it will be even more inconvenient, for, if at all tight, it will make the rider, when in the saddle, feel as if her hips were compressed in a vise; when too long behind, it will interfere with that curving or hollowing in of the back that is so necessary to an erect position; it will also tend to throw the body too far forward. If the rider have any tendency to stoutness all these discomforts will be exaggerated. The C. P. or the Parisian *la Sirene* is undoubtedly the best corset for riding purposes, for it is short, light, and flexible, and not prejudicial to the ease and elegance of good riding, as is the case with the stiff, long-bodied corset.

The **hair** should be so arranged that it cannot possibly come down during the ride. To effect this, it must be made into one long braid, which must be coiled upon the back of the head, and fastened firmly, but not too tightly, by means of a few long hairpins. The coil may be put on the top of the head, but this arrangement will be found very inconvenient, especially where the hair is thick, for it will make the hat sit very awkwardly on the head. The hair should never be worn in ringlets, as these will be blown about by the wind, or by the movements of the rider, and will soon become so tangled as to look like anything but the "smooth flowing ringlets" of the poet. Nor should the hair be allowed to stream down the back in long peasant-braids, a style mistakenly adopted by some young misses, but which gives the rider a wild and untidy appearance. When the horse is in motion these braids will stream out on the breeze, and an observer at a short distance will be puzzled to know what it is that seems to be in such an extraordinary state of agitation. It is also a mistake to draw the hair back tightly from the forehead, as this gives a constrained look to the features; it should, on the contrary, be arranged in rather a loose, unstudied manner, which will tend to soften the expression of the face. It is the extreme of bad taste to bang or frizz the hair across the forehead, or to wear the hat somewhat on the back of the head. These things are sometimes done by very young girls, but give to the prettiest and most modest face an air of boldness and vulgarity.

The **riding hat** at present fashionable, and most suitable for city or park, is made of black silk plush with a Stanley curved brim, and bell-crown, and is trimmed with a narrow band around the crown, directly above the brim. Another favorite is a jockey-cap, made of the same cloth as that of the habit. Either of these may be obtained at the hat stores. For riding in the country, where one does not care to be so dressy, the English Derby, or some other fashionable style of young gentleman's felt hat, may be used; with a short plume or bird's wing fastened at the side, a hat of this description has a very charming and coquettish air. There is another style of silk hat manufactured expressly for ladies, which may also be obtained at any hatter's; it has a lower crown than a gentleman's silk hat, and looks very pretty with a short black net-veil fastened around the crown, as this relieves the stiff look it otherwise presents. This style of hat is very appropriate for a middle-aged person. Care must be taken to have the hat neither too loose nor too tight; if too tight, it will be apt to occasion a headache, and if too loose will be easily displaced.

Long veils, long plumes, hats with very broad brims, or very high crowns, as well as those which are worn perched on the top of the head, should be especially avoided. The hat must always be made secure on the head by means of stout elastic sewn on strongly, and so adjusted that it can pass below the braid or coil of hair at the back of the head. An ordinary back-comb firmly fastened on the top of the head will prevent the hat from gradually slipping backwards.

These apparently trifling details must be attended to, or some prankish breeze will suddenly carry off the rider's hat, and she will be subjected to the mortification of having it handed back to her, with an ill-concealed smile, by some obliging pedestrian. Many little particulars which seem insignificant when in the dressing-room will become causes of much discomfort and suffering when in the saddle. The pleasure of many a ride has been marred by a displaced pin, a lost button, too tight a garter, a glove that cramped the hand, or a ring that occasioned swelling and pain in the finger. These details, unimportant as they may seem, must be carefully attended to before starting for a ride. Pins should be used sparingly. If a watch is worn, it should be well secured in its pocket, and the chain carefully fastened to a button of the jacket.

The **riding gauntlets** should be made of thick, soft, undressed kid, or chamois skin, be long wristed, and somewhat loose across the hands, so that the reins may be firmly grasped. With the exception of the watch, the chain of which should be as unostentatious as possible, it will not be in good taste to wear jewelry. A cravat or small bow of ribbon will be in much better taste than a breast-pin for fastening the collar, and may be of any color that suits the fancy or complexion of the wearer. The costume may be much brightened by a small *boutonnière* of natural flowers; these placed at the throat or waist in an apparently careless manner give an air of daintiness and refinement to the whole costume.

There is one accomplishment often neglected, or overlooked, even by the most skillful lady riders, and that is, expertness in **holding the riding skirt** easily and gracefully when not in the saddle. In this attainment the Parisian horsewoman far excels all others; her manner of gathering up the folds of her riding skirt, while waiting for her horse, forms a picture of such unaffected elegance, that it would be well for other riders to study and imitate it. She does not grab her skirt with one hand, twist it round to one side, allow it to trail upon the ground, nor does she collect the folds in one unwieldy bunch and throw it brusquely over her arm. Instead of any of these ungraceful acts, she quietly extends her arms down to their full length at her sides, inclines her body slightly forward, and gathers up the front of her skirt, raising her hands just far enough to allow the long part in front and at the sides to escape the ground; then by bringing her hands slightly forward, one being held a little higher than the other, the back part of the skirt is raised. While accomplishing these movements her whip will be held carelessly in her right hand, at a very short distance below the handle, the point being directed downwards, and somewhat obliquely backwards. The whole of this graceful manoeuvring will be effected readily and artlessly, in an apparently unstudied manner. In reality, however, all the Parisian's ease and grace are the results of careful training, but so perfect is the instruction that art is made to appear like nature.

In selecting a **riding whip** care should be taken to secure one that is straight and stiff; if it be curved, it may accidentally touch the horse and make him restless; if flexible it will be of no use in managing him. The handle of the whip may be very plain, or the lady may indulge her taste for the ornamental by having it very elaborate and rich, but she should be careful never to sacrifice strength to appearances. Any projecting points that might catch on the dress and tear it must be dispensed with. That the whip may not be lost if the hand should unwittingly lose its hold upon it, a loop of silk cord should be fastened firmly to the handle, and the hand passed through this loop. When riding, the whip should always be held in the right hand with a grasp sufficient to retain it, but not as if in a vise; the point should be directed downward, or toward the hind-leg of the horse, care being taken not to touch him with it except when necessary.

CHAPTER III
THE SADDLE AND BRIDLE

"Form by mild bits his mouth, nor harshly wound,
Till summer rolls her fourth-revolving round.
Then wheel in graceful orbs his paced career,
Let step by step in cadence strike the ear,
The flexile limbs in curves alternate prance,
And seem to labor as they slow advance:
Then give, uncheck'd, to fly with loosen'd rein,
Challenge the winds, and wing th' unprinted plain."

VIRGIL, *Sotheby's Translation.*

IN YE ANCIENT times, the damsel who wished to enjoy horseback riding did not, like her successor of to-day, trust to her own ability to ride and manage her horse, but, seated upon a pad or cushion, called a "pillion," which was fastened behind a man's saddle, rode without a stirrup and without troubling herself with the reins, preserving her balance by holding to the belt of a trusty page, or masculine admirer, whose duty it was to attend to the management of the horse. We learn that as late as A.D.1700, George III. made his entry into London with his wife, Charlotte, thus seated behind him. Gradually, however, as women became more confident, they rode alone upon a sort of side-saddle, on which by means of the reins and by bracing her feet against a board, called a "planchette," which was fastened to the front of the saddle, the rider managed to keep her seat. Such was the English horsewoman of the seventeenth century, in the time of Charles II.,— "the height of fashion and the cream of style."

To the much quoted "vanity of the fair sex" do we owe the invention of the side-saddle of our grandmothers. About the middle of the sixteenth century Catherine de Medici, wife of Henry II. of France, having a very symmetrical figure which she wished to display to advantage, invented the second pommel of the saddle, and thus, while gratifying her own vanity, was unconsciously the means of greatly benefiting her sex by enabling them to ride with more ease and freedom. To this saddle there was added, about 1830, a third pommel, the invention of which is due to the late M. Pellier, Sr., an eminent riding teacher in Paris, France. This three-pommeled saddle is now called the **English saddle**, and is the one generally used by the best lady riders of the present day.

This so-called "English saddle" was promptly appreciated, and wherever introduced soon supplanted the old-fashioned one with only two pommels. (Fig. 7.)

A lady who has once ridden one of these three-pommeled saddles will never care to use any other kind. It renders horseback riding almost perfectly safe, for, if the rider has learned to use it properly, it will be nearly impossible for a horse to throw her. It gives her

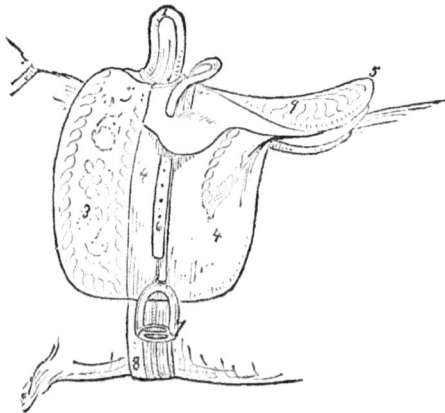

FIG. 7–ENGLISH SADDLE

1, second pommel; 2, third pommel; 3, shield; 4, saddle-flap;
5, cantle; 6, stirrup-leather; 7, stirrup; 8, girths; 9, platform.

a much firmer seat even than that of a gentleman in his saddle, and at the same time, if rightly used, does not interfere with that easy grace so essential to good riding. In many of our large cities where this saddle is employed twenty lady riders may now be seen in the park or on the road where formerly there was one; and this is wholly due to the sense of security it gives, especially to a timid rider, a feeling never attainable in the two-pommeled saddle, where the seat is maintained chiefly by the balance, or by using the reins as a means of support.

By sitting erect, taking a firm hold upon the second pommel with the right knee, and pressing the left knee up against the third pommel, a perfectly secure seat is obtained, from which the rider cannot be shaken, provided the saddle is well girthed and the horse does not fall, while her hands are left free to manage the reins, a very important point where the horse is spirited or restless. To insure the greatest safety and comfort for both horse and rider, it is very important that the saddle should be accurately constructed. If possible, it should be made especially for the horse that is to carry it, so that it may suit his particular shape. If it does not fit him well, it will be likely to turn, or may gall his back severely, and make him for a long time unfit for service. It may even, in time, give rise to fistulous withers, will certainly make the horse restless and uneasy on the road, and the pain he suffers will interfere with the ease and harmony of his gaits. Many a horse has been rendered unfit for a lady's use solely because the saddle did not fit well.

The under surface of the arch of the saddle-tree, in front, should never come in contact with the animal's withers, nor should the points of the saddle-tree be so tightly fitted as to interfere with the movements of his shoulders. On the other hand, they should not be so far apart as to allow the central furrowed line of the under surface of the saddle (the chamber) to rest upon the animal's back. The saddle should be so fitted and padded that this central chamber will lie directly over the spinal column of the horse without touching it, while the padded surfaces, just below the chamber, should rest closely on the sides of the back, and be supported at as many points as is possible without making the animal uncomfortable.

When a horse has very high withers, a breast-plate, similar to that employed in military service, may be used, to prevent the saddle from slipping backwards. This contrivance consists of a piece of leather passing round the neck like a collar, to the lowest part of which is fastened a strap that passes between the fore-legs of the horse and is attached to the saddle girth. Two other straps, one on each side, connect the upper part of the collar piece with the upper part of the saddle. The under strap should never be very loose, for should the saddle slip back and this strap not be tight enough to hold down the collar piece, the latter will be pulled up by the upper straps so as to press against the wind-pipe of the horse and choke him. Should the horse have low withers and a round, barrel-like body, false pannels or padded pieces may be used; but an animal of this shape is not suitable for a lady, for it will be almost impossible to keep the saddle from turning, no matter how carefully it may be girthed.

A sufficiently spacious seat or platform to the saddle is much more comfortable for both horse and rider than a narrow one. It gives the rider a firmer seat, and does not bring so much strain upon the girths. This platform should also be made as nearly level as possible, and be covered with quilted buckskin. Leather, now so often used for this purpose, becomes after a time so slippery that it is difficult to retain one's seat, and the pommels when covered with it are apt to chafe the limbs severely.

To secure a thoroughly comfortable saddle it is necessary that not only the horse, but also the rider, should be measured for it; for a saddle suitable for a slender person could hardly be used with any comfort by a stout one, and it is almost as bad to have a saddle too large as too small. Care must be taken to have sufficient length from the front of the second pommel to the cantle. In the ready-made saddles this dis-tance is usually too short, and the rider is obliged to sit upon the back edge of the seat, thereby injuring both herself and her horse. It is much better to err in the other direction and have the seat too long rather than too short. The third pommel should be so placed that it will just span the knee when the stirrup-leather is of the right length. It should be rather short, slightly curved, and blunt. If it be too long and have too much of a curve, it will, in the English trot, interfere with the free action of the rider's left leg, and if the horse should fall, it would be al-most impossible for her to disengage her leg and free herself in time to escape injury. The third pommel must be so placed as not to interfere with the position of the right leg when this is placed around the second pommel with the right heel drawn backwards. To get the proper pro-portions for her saddle, the lady must, when seated, take her measure from the under side of the knee joint to the lower extremity of her back, and also—to secure the proper width for the seat—from thigh to thigh. If these two measurements are given to the saddle-maker he will, if he understands his business, be able to construct the saddle properly.

The saddle recommended by the author, one which she has used for several years, and still continues to use, is represented in Fig. 7. The third pommel of this saddle is of medium size, and instead of being close to the second one is placed a short distance below it, thus enabling the rider to use a longer stirrup than she otherwise could; for if the two pommels be very close together, the rider will be obliged to use a very short stirrup in order to make this third pommel of any use. The disadvantage of a short stirrup is that, in a long ride, it is apt to occasion cramp in the left leg. It also interferes with an easy and steady position in the saddle. But with a stirrup of the right length, and the arrangement of the pommels such as we have described, a steadiness is given to the left leg that can never be obtained with the old-fashioned two-pommeled saddle.

The third pommel must be screwed securely into the saddle-tree, and once fixed in its proper place, should not again be moved, as if frequently turned it will soon get loose, and the rider will not be able to rely upon its assistance to retain her balance. It should be screwed into place inversely, that is, instead of being turned to the right it must be turned to the left, so that the pressure of the knee may make it firmer and more secure, instead of loosening it, as would be the case if it were screwed to the right. This pommel should be well padded, so that the knee may not be bruised by it.

The second pommel should also be well padded, and should always be curved slightly so as to suit the form of the right leg. It must not be so high as to render it difficult, in mounting and dismounting, to pass the right knee over it. The off-pommel, since the English saddle has come into vogue, has almost disappeared, being reduced to a mere vestige of its former size. This is a great improvement to the rider's appearance, as she now no longer has that confined, cribbed-up look which the high pommeled saddle of twenty years ago gave her.

The distance between the off-pommel and the second one should be adapted to the size of the rider's leg, being wide enough to allow the leg to rest easily between the two; but no wider than this, as too much space will be apt to lead her to sit sideways upon the saddle.

A saddle should be well padded, but not so much so as to lift the rider too high above the horse's back. The shield in front should not press upon the neck of the horse, but should barely touch it. The saddle flaps must be well strapped down, for if they stand out stiffly, the correct position of the stirrup leg will be interfered with. A side-saddle should never be too light in weight, for this will make the back of the horse sore, especially if he be ridden by a heavy woman.

The tacks or nails in the under part of the saddle should be firmly driven in, as they may otherwise become loose and either injure the horse, or make him nervous and uneasy. To avoid trouble of this kind, some people advocate the use of false pannels, which are fastened to the saddle-tree by rods or loops, and can be removed and replaced at will. It is said that by using them, the same saddle can be made to fit different horses. The author has no personal knowledge of this invention, but it has been strongly recommended to her by several excellent horsemen. A felt or flannel saddle cloth, of the same color as the rider's habit, should always be placed under the saddle, as it helps to protect the horse's back, as well as to prevent the saddle from getting soiled.

Every finished side-saddle has three girths. Two of these are made of felt cloth, or strong webbing, and are designed to fasten it firmly upon the horse's back. The third one, made of leather, is intended to

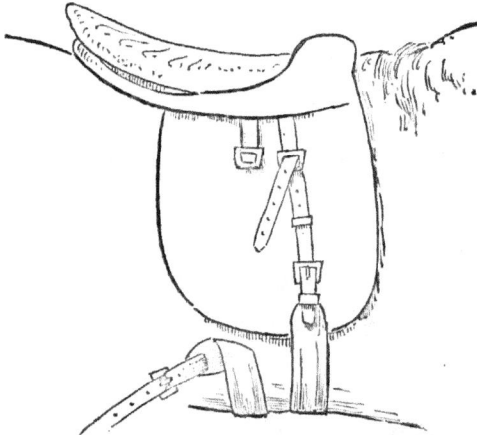

FIG. 8—STOKES' MODE OF GIRTHING THE SADDLE

keep the flaps down. There should always be, on each side, three straps fastened to the saddle-tree under the leather flaps; upon two of these the girths are to be buckled, while the third is an extra one, to be used as a substitute in case of any accident to either of the others. Between the outside leather flaps and the horse's body there should be an under flap of flannel or cloth, which should be well padded on the side next

the horse, because, when tightly girthed, the girth-buckles press directly upon the outside of this flap, and if its padding be thin, or worn, the
animal will suffer great pain. This is a cause of restlessness which is
seldom noticed, and many a horse has been thought to be bad tempered when he was only wild with pain from the pressure of the
girth-buckles against his side.

The credit of introducing a new method of tightening girths belongs, so far as we know, to Mr. Stokes, formerly a riding-teacher in
Cincinnati. This method enables one to girth the horse tightly, without using so much muscular effort as is usually required, so that by its
means, a lady can, if she wish, saddle her own horse. (Fig. 8.)

The following is a description of Mr. Stokes' manner of girthing:
At the end of each of the leather girth straps, which hang down between the flaps on the off-side of the saddle, is fastened a strong iron
buckle without any tongue, but with a thin steel roller or revolving
cylinder on its lower edge. On the near side of the saddle the girths
are strapped in the usual manner, but, on the *outer* end of each cloth
girth there is, in addition to an ordinary buckle, with a roller on the
upper side of it, a long strap, which is fastened to the under side of the
girth, the buckle being on the upper side. This strap, when the saddle is
girthed, is passed up through the tongueless buckle, moving easily over
the steel roller, and is then brought down to the buckle with tongue on
the end of the girth, and there fastened in the usual manner.

The slipper stirrup, when first introduced, was a great favorite, for
in addition to furnishing an excellent support, it was believed that it

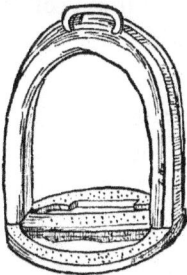

FIG. 9–VICTORIA STIRRUPS

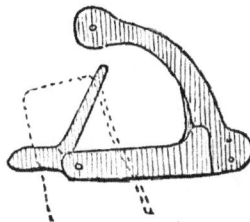

FIG. 10–SPRING-BAR FOR
STIRRUP-LEATHER

would release the foot instantly should the rider be thrown. This latter
merit, however, it was found that it did not possess, as many severe

accidents occurred where this stirrup was used, especially with the two-pommeled saddle. Instead of releasing the rider in these cases, as it was supposed it would, the stirrup tilted up and held her foot so firmly grasped that she was dragged some distance before she could be released. This stirrup, therefore, gradually fell into disfavor, and is now no longer used by the best riders.

There are, at the present time, three kinds of stirrups which are favorites among finished riders. The first is called the "Victoria" be-

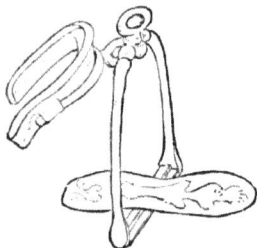

FIG. 11–LENNAN'S
SAFETY STIRRUP

cause it is the one used by the Queen of England. (Fig. 9.) In this stirrup the platform on which the foot rests is broad and comfortable, and is slightly roughened to prevent the foot from slipping. A spring-bar attachment (Fig. 10) is placed at the top of the stirrup-leather under the saddle-flap, and at the end of this bar there is a spring, so that, if the rider be thrown, the stirrup-leather becomes instantly detached from the saddle.

The second variety of stirrup, known as "Lennan's safety stirrup," has all the merit of the preceding one. If kept well oiled and free from mud, it will release the foot at once, when an accident occurs. It may, if desired, be accompanied by the spring-bar attachment, and thus rendered doubly secure. (Fig. 11.) Some people, however, dislike the spring-bar attachment, and prefer to rely entirely upon the spring of the stirrup to release the foot.

The third stirrup, called "Latchford's safety stirrup," consists of a stirrup within a stirrup, and is so arranged that, when a rider is thrown, the inner stirrup springs open and releases the foot. (Fig. 12.) Either of these stirrups can be procured in London, England, or from the best saddle-makers in this country.

A **stirrup-iron** should never be made of cast metal, but invariably of the best wrought steel: it should be adapted to the size of the rider's foot, and should, if possible, have an instep pad at the top, while the bottom platform, upon which the foot rests, should be broad, and roughened on its upper surface.

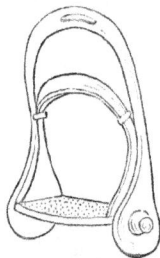

FIG. 12–LATCHFORD'S
SAFETY STIRRUP

The **stirrup-leather** should be of the very best material, and should have neither fissures nor cracks in any part of it. It is very important to examine this leather frequently, and see that it is neither wearing thin, nor breaking at its upper part at the bar, nor at the lower part where it is fastened to the stirrup.

A novel arrangement of the stirrup-leather, by means of the so-called "balance-strap," has of late years been used by some riders. The stirrup is, in this case, fastened to the balance-strap, which consists of a single strap passing up through the ring-bar, and then brought down to within two or three inches of the lower edge of the saddle-flap; here it is passed through a slit in the flap, then carried under the horse to the other side and buckled to another strap, which is fastened, for this purpose, just below the off-pommel. By this arrangement the saddle-flaps on both sides are held down, and the rider, without dismounting, can change the length of her stirrup by merely tightening or loosening this strap. Although highly recommended by some riders, this balance strap has one objectionable feature, which is that, as the measurement of the horse's girth is not constant during a long ride, it will be necessary to tighten the strap frequently in order to keep the stirrup of the proper length. The old way of fastening is much better, for too much complication in the saddle and bridle is apt to annoy and confuse the rider, especially if a novice. The **golden rule** in riding on horseback is to have everything accurate, simple, safe, and made of the very best material that can be procured.

The **bridle** should be neatly and plainly made, with no large rosettes at the sides, nor highly colored bands across the forehead. The reins and the head-piece should never be made of rounded straps, but always of flat ones, and should be of the best and strongest leather, especially the reins. These should be carefully examined from time to time, in order to be sure that there are no imperfections in them. Any roughness or hardness is an indication of defectiveness, and may be detected by dexterously passing the fingers to and fro over the flat surfaces, which should be smooth, soft, and flexible. There can hardly be too much care taken about this matter, for the snapping of a rein always alarms a horse; and, feeling himself free from all control, he will be almost certain to run away, while the rider, if she has no other reins, will be powerless to protect herself, or to check him in his purpose.

Martingales are rarely used by riders, as they are troublesome, and can very well be dispensed with, unless the horse has the disagreeable trick of raising his head suddenly, from time to time, when a martingale will become necessary in order to correct this fault. The French martingale is the best. This consists of a single strap, fastened either to the under part of a nose-band at its centre under the jaw, or by branches to each side of the snaffle-bit at the corners of the horse's mouth and then carried between the fore-legs and fastened to the girth. When the horse raises his head too high this strap pulls upon the nose-band, compresses his nostrils, interferes with his breathing, and causes him to lower his head promptly. The horse should not be too much confined by the martingale, for the object is simply to prevent him from lifting his head too high, and all other ordinary movements should be left free.

Among the many **bits** which have been used, that known as the "Pelham" has been highly praised, although, at the present time, it is almost, if not entirely, out of use. It might, however, from the severity

of its curb prove of service in controlling a hard-mouthed horse, although such a one should never be ridden by a lady. The Chifney bit is another very severe one, and is very useful in managing a horse that pulls hard. But if the animal have a tender mouth, this bit should be used with great caution, and

FIG. 13—CHIFNEY BIT

not at all by an inexperienced rider. (Fig. 13.)

The bit known as the "snaffle," when made plain and not twisted, is the mildest of all bits, and some horses will move readily only when this is used, the curb instantly rousing their temper. Others, again, do best with a combination of the curb and the snaffle, and although the former may seldom require to be used, its mere presence in the mouth of the horse will prove a sufficient check to prevent him from running away. Most horses, however, especially those ridden by ladies, require a light use of the curb to bring them to their best gait.

The bit used and recommended by many, but not by the author, is a curb so arranged as to form a combination bit in one piece. It consists of a curb (Fig. 14), to each side of which, at the angles of the horse's mouth, a ring is attached, and to each of these rings is fastened a rein. This gives a second pair of reins and converts the curb into a kind of snaffle. In this way it answers the purpose of both curb and snaffle without crowding the horse's mouth with two separate bits.

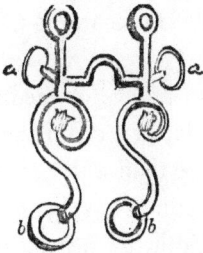

FIG. 14—THE COMBINATION BIT
a, a, rings fastened on each side to small bar, at right angles to and directed backward of the cheek; b, b, rings for the curb reins.

If two bits should be used—the curb and bridoon—instead of the above combination bit, the bridoon should be placed in the horse's mouth in such a way as not to interfere with the action of the curb; it must, therefore, be neither too thick nor too long, and so fitted into the angles of the mouth as to neither wrinkle nor draw back the lips.

The bit should always be made of the best steel, be well rounded, and perfectly smooth. Above all it should be accurately fitted to the horse's mouth: if it be too narrow it will compress his lips against the bars of his mouth, and the pain thereby occasioned will render him very restive. The mouth-piece should be just long enough to have the cheeks of the bit fit closely to the outer surface of the lips without compressing them, and must not be so long as to become displaced obliquely when a rein is pulled.

According to Major Dwyer, who is a high authority on the subject of bits,—and whose little work should be carefully studied by all bit-makers,—it seems to be the general rule to have the lower bar or cheek of the curb-bit twice as long as the upper one; but, as there is no standard measure for the upper one the other is frequently made too long. Major Dwyer states that the mouth-piece, for any horse of ordinary size, should be one and three fourths inches for the upper bar, and three and a half inches for the lower one. This makes five and one fourth inches for the en-

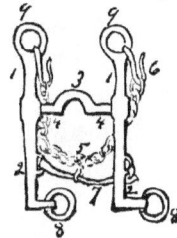

FIG. 15—DWYER'S CURB-BIT
1, 1, upper bars or cheeks; 2, 2, lower bars; 3, the port; 4, 4, the canons; 5, curb-chain; 6, curb-hook; 7, lip strap and ring; 8, 8, rein rings; 9, 9, head stall rings.

tire length of the two bars, from the point at which the curb-hook acts above to that where the lower ring acts below. (Fig. 15.) For ordinary ponies the upper bar may be one and a half inches, and the lower one three, making a total length of four and a half inches.

Every lady rider should know that the longer the lower bar, the thinner the mouth-piece, and the higher the "port," the more severe and painful will be the action of the bit upon the horse's mouth. For a horse of ordinary size, the width of the port should be one and one third inches; for a pony, one inch. The height will vary according to the degree of severity required.

The curb-chain, for a horse that has a chin-groove of medium size, should be about four fifths of an inch wide, as a chain that is rather broad and flat is less painful for the horse than a thin, sharp one. If the chin-groove be very narrow, a curb-chain of less width will have to be used, and should be covered with cloth; or, instead of a chain, a narrow strap of leather may be used, which should be kept soft and pliable. The proper length for the curb-chain, not including the curb hooks, is about one fourth more than the width of the animal's mouth. The hooks should be exactly alike, and about an inch and a quarter long.

Some horses are very expert in the trick of catching the cheek of the bit between their teeth. To remedy this vice a lip-strap may be used; but it will be found much better to have each cheek or bar bent into the form of the letter S, remembering, however, that the measurement of the length, referred to above, must in the case of curved bars be made in a straight line. Sometimes the upper bar of the curb-bit will, on account of the peculiar form of the horse's head, press against and gall his cheeks. When this is noticed, most people change the bit, and get one with a longer mouth piece; but where the mouth-piece is of the same length as the width of the mouth, the proper remedy for this difficulty will be to have the upper bar bent out enough to free the cheeks from its pressure.

The curb-bit once made and properly adjusted to the head-stall, the next step will be to **fit it accurately** to the horse's mouth. Every rider should thoroughly understand not only how to do this, but also how to place the saddle correctly upon the horse. Upon these points nearly all grooms require instruction, and very few gentlemen, even, know how to arrange a side-saddle so as to have it comfortable for both horse and rider. Moreover, should the lady be riding alone, as frequently happens in the country, and meet with any accident to saddle or bridle, or need to have either adjusted, she would, without knowledge on these subjects, be completely helpless, whereas with it she could promptly remedy the difficulty.

In order to adjust the bit permanently to the head-stall, so that afterwards the horse can always be properly bridled, one must proceed as follows: having first fitted the head-stall to the horse's head by means of the upper buckles, the bit must then be adjusted, by means

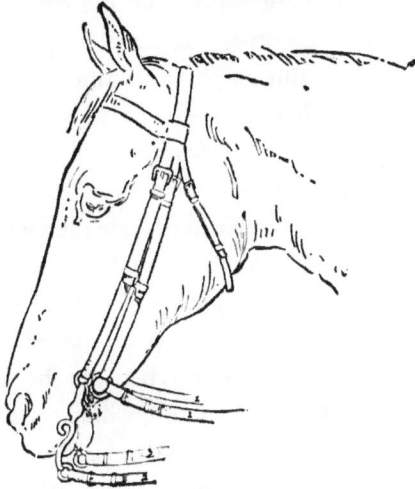

FIG. 16–THE BIT ADJUSTED

of the lower ones, in such a manner that the canons of the mouth-piece will rest on the bars of the horse's mouth, exactly opposite the chin-groove. (Fig. 16.) Should the tusks of the horse be irregularly placed, the mouth-piece must be adjusted a little higher than the projecting tusks, so as to just avoid touching them. The curb-chain may now be hooked into the ring of the upper bar on the off-side, leaving one link loose, after which the other hook must be fastened to the ring of the bar on the near-side, leaving two links loose. Care should be taken to have the curb-chain rest with its flat surface against the chin-groove in such a way that it will have no tendency to rise up when the reins are pulled upon. The curb-chain should never be tight; there must always be room enough between it and the chin to insert the first and second fingers of the right hand flatwise; and, while the fingers are thus placed, if the reins are drawn up, it will be easy to ascertain whether the chain pinches. If, when the reins are tightened, the bit stands stiff and immovable, it will show that the chain is too short and needs to be lengthened a link or two. If the horse gently yields his head to the tightening of the reins, without suddenly drawing back, or thrusting out his nose as the tension is increased, it will prove that the bit is correctly placed. But if the lower bars of the bit can be drawn back quite a distance before the horse will yield to the pull of the reins, then the chain is too long, and should be shortened. "Lightness, accuracy, easy motion, a total absence of stiffness, constraint, or painful action, are the characteristics of good bitting; and if these be attained, ready obedience to the rider's hand will be the result."—*F. Dwyer.*

When the bit has once been correctly adjusted to the head-stall and to the horse's mouth, there will be little difficulty in bridling him upon any subsequent occasion. Thus: standing at the left of the horse's head, the head-stall, held by its upper part in the right hand, should be lifted up in front of the horse's head, while the left hand, holding the bit by its mouth-piece, should put this between the animal's lips, press it against his teeth, and into his mouth, which he will generally open a little in order to admit it. As soon as this has been accomplished, the upper part of the head-stall must be promptly raised so as to bring its upper strap or band across the forehead, while at the same time the horse's ears are passed between the forehead band and the strap which forms the upper part of the head-stall.

During these manoeuvres, the curb-chain must be passed under the chin, so as to rest against the chin-groove, and care be taken to keep the fingers of the left hand out of the horse's mouth while the mouth-piece is being put in. The bit and head-stall having been properly arranged, the whole should be secured by buckling the throat-strap loosely on the left side. If this strap be buckled tightly, the horse will be unable to bend his neck properly. The mouth-piece of the bit should be washed, dried, and then rubbed with fresh olive or cotton-seed oil, each time after use, to preserve it from rust.

Neither a rusted bit nor a very cold one should ever be put into a horse's mouth. In frosty winter weather the bit should always be warmed. Many a valuable horse has had his mouth seriously injured by having an icy cold mouth-piece put into it, to say nothing of the pain and suffering it must invariably occasion.

In order to produce a neat and pleasing appearance, there should be no unsightly ends or straps left dangling from the loops of the head-stall. They should be so snugly fitted into their places that they cannot work out of their loops.

The forehead band should never be too tight for the horse's comfort, and the small rosettes that lie over his temples should be well oiled underneath and kept soft.

A side-saddle may be made accurately according to all recognized rules, and yet lose nearly all its good effects by being improperly put on; the rider will be made uncomfortable, the horse's back will be injured, and the saddle will eventually have its padding so compressed in the wrong direction that it will be impossible to put it on in the right way.

Every lady rider should know as well how to have her saddle properly adjusted as how to sit her horse or manage the reins. On a well-formed horse, with rather high withers and sloping shoulders, the centre of the saddle should be placed over the middle of the back, and be so arranged that the front part of the saddle-tree shall be a very short distance back of the horse's shoulder-blade, for if allowed to rest upon the shoulder-blade it will interfere very much with the action of the shoulder muscles. It is a common fault of grooms to place the saddle a little sideways, and too far forward on the withers. The well-taught rider can, however, easily decide whether the saddle is in the right position: standing on the off-side of the horse, she must pass her right hand under the arch of the saddle-tree, which should be directly over the withers, and see whether it sits perfectly even, bearing no more to one side than to the other; then stepping behind the horse, but at a safe distance from his heels, she can see whether the long central furrow of the under surface of the saddle-seat from front to rear (chamber) is in a direct line with the animal's backbone, and forms an open space over it. If these conditions are fulfilled, the saddle is properly adjusted. If the horse have rather straight shoulders, together with a plump, round body, the saddle will require to be placed rather farther forward, but with the chamber still in a line with the backbone. On some horses of this shape, the saddle, to be held securely, will need to be set so far forward that the girths will have to pass close to the fore-legs. A horse of this description is not suitable for the side-saddle, but as ladies in the country and in the far West are sometimes obliged to ride such, it is very important for their safety to know how these ill formed animals should be saddled, because should the saddle be put too far back on such horses, it will be sure to turn.

It not infrequently happens that after the saddle has been placed in the correct position, it becomes slightly displaced while being fastened. To avoid this, it should always be girthed on the off-side, and great care be taken, when fastening the girths, especially the first one, that the saddle be not jerked over to the left; and that in pulling upon the short strap on the off-side, to which the girth is to be buckled, the saddle be not forced to the right.

When girthing the saddle, the lady may place her left hand on the middle of the seat and hold it steady while she arranges the first girth, and with her right hand draws it as tightly as she can, without using violent exertion, or making any sudden jerk; she will then be able, with both hands, to tighten the girth as much as is necessary, doing this with an even, regular pull, so that the saddle will not be moved out of place. Before fastening the other girths, she should step behind the horse and assure herself that the chamber is in a line with the horse's backbone, as before described. If it is not, she must loosen the girth, and, after straightening the saddle, proceed as before. The girth to be first fastened is the one nearest the horse's fore-legs; the second girth is the one back of the first, and should be placed evenly over the first one and fastened equally tight; the third is the leather girth which is intended to keep down the saddle flaps; this must be placed evenly over the other two, but it is not essential to have it drawn so tight as they, but just enough so to hold the flaps. Most horses have a trick, when they are being girthed, of expanding their sides and abdomen, for the purpose of securing a loose girthing; and girths that seem almost too tight when they are first buckled are often found to be too loose after the rider has mounted. Too tight a girth is injurious to the horse, but too loose a one may cause the saddle to turn. A round, plump horse with low withers will need tighter girthing than a better shaped one. The lady rider should study the shape of her horse, and use her own judgment as to how tight the girths should be drawn, making due allowance for the trick alluded to above. If there is any second person present while the saddle is being arranged, matters may be facilitated if this person will hold the saddle firmly by the off-pommel while the girthing is being done.

The author has been thus particular in describing the bit and saddle with their proper arrangement, as well as the girthing of the horse, because so few lady riders bestow any attention upon these very important matters; and yet, if one desires to ride safely and well, a knowledge of them is positively necessary. Grooms cannot always be depended upon, and, indeed, seldom know much about the side-saddle; there is an adage which is applicable to many of them: "Too much must not be expected from the head of him who labors only with his hands." In the instructions given by gentlemen writers, useful as they may be in many respects, there is usually a good deal of practical information omitted which a lady rider ought to know, but the necessity of which it is perhaps impossible for a gentleman fully to appreciate or understand; this knowledge the lady will have to gain either from her own experience or from one of her own sex who has studied the subject carefully.

In preparing for horseback riding, nothing should be omitted that can give greater security to the rider, or protect her more completely from accident of any sort. Every article should be of the very best material, so that a breakage or casualty of any kind may be only a remote possibility. The knowledge that everything is right, and firmly and properly placed, creates a confidence which adds greatly to the pleasure of the ride.

CHAPTER IV
MOUNTING AND DISMOUNTING

"'Stand, Bayard, stand!'—the steed obeyed,
With arching neck and bending head,
And glancing eye and quivering ear,
As if he loved *her voice* to hear."

Lady of the Lake.

A NOVICE IN riding always experiences in a greater or less degree a sense of trepidation and embarrassment when, for the first time, a horse duly caparisoned for a lady rider is put before her, and she is expected to seat herself in the saddle. If she be a timid person, the apparent difficulty of this feat occasions a dismay which the good-natured champing of the bit and impatient head shakings of the horse do not tend to diminish. If, however, she be accustomed to horses as pets, and understand their ways, she will be much less apprehensive about mounting than the lady who has only observed them at a distance and is entirely ignorant of their nature. The author has known ladies, after their horses had been brought to the door, to send them back to the stable because courage failed them when it became necessary to trust themselves on the back of an animal of which they knew nothing. To overcome this timidity the lady must become better acquainted with her horse, and, to do so, should visit him occasionally in his stable, feed him with choice morsels, and lead him about the yard from time to time. By these means a mutual friendship and confidence will be created, and the lady will gradually gain enough courage to place herself in the saddle.

The first attempt at mounting should be made from a **high horse-block** with some one to hold the head of the horse and keep him still. Turning her right side somewhat toward the horse's left, and slightly raising the skirt of her riding habit, the lady should spring from her left foot towards the saddle, at the same time raising her right leg so that it will pass directly over the second and third pommels. This accomplished, the left foot may be placed in the stirrup.

Another method of mounting from a rather high horse-block, when the pommels are high, is for the lady to face the horse's left side, and, seizing the off-pommel with the right hand and the second one with the left, to spring towards the saddle from her left foot, and seat herself sidewise. She can then turn her body so as to face the horse's head, place her right leg over the second pommel,—adjusting her skirt at the same time,—and slip her left foot into the stirrup and her left knee under the third pommel.

Should the **horse-block be low** and the lady short, she will be obliged to mount somewhat after a man's fashion, thus: Placing her left foot in the stirrup, and grasping the second pommel with her left hand, she should spring from her right foot, and, as she rises, grasp the off-pommel with her right hand; by means of this spring, aided by the pommels and stirrup, she can seat herself sideways in the saddle, turning her body for this purpose just before gaining the seat. In the absence of a horse-block, from which to mount, the assistance of a chair or stool should never be resorted to unless there is some one to hold it firm and steady.

When the rider is obliged to **mount** without assistance and **from the ground**, if the balance-strap, before referred to, be used with her stirrup, she can let this strap down far enough to enable her to put her foot in the stirrup easily, and to use it as a sort of stepping-stone by means of which, and a spring from her right foot, she can reach the saddle sideways. In doing this she must grasp the second pommel firmly with her left hand, in which she also should hold her whip and the reins; on rising she must aid herself by grasping with the right hand the off-pommel as soon as she can reach it. When she is seated, the stirrup can be adjusted from the off-side by means of the balance-strap.

If, however, she uses the old-fashioned stirrup-leather, and there is no assistance of any kind at hand, neither horse-block, chair, nor stool, not even a fence or steep bank from which to mount,— a situation in which a rider might possibly be placed,—then reaching the saddle becomes a very puzzling affair, unless the lady be so active that she can

spring from the ground to her saddle. To try the plan of lengthening
the stirrup-leather will be dangerous, because, in order to readjust it
after mounting, she will have to sit on the back part of the saddle, bend
over the horse's left side, and pull up the stirrup-leather in order to
shorten and buckle it; while in this position, if the horse should start,
she would probably be thrown instantly. Her safest course would be to
lead the horse until a place is found where she can mount. If she should
have to use a fence for this purpose let her be sure that the posts are
firmly fixed in the ground, and that the boards are neither loose nor
easily broken.

When mounting, the whip and reins should be held in the left
hand, the former with the point down, so that it may not hit the horse,
and the latter grasped just tightly enough to feel the horse's mouth
without pulling on it. In order to arrange the folds of the riding skirt
after mounting, the reins and whip must be transferred to the right
hand; then, resting this hand upon the off pommel, the rider should
raise herself free from the saddle by straightening her left knee and
standing on the stirrup, also aiding herself by means of the right hand
on the pommel. While thus standing she can quickly arrange the skirt
with her left hand.

None of the methods of mounting just described—with the exception of the first one—are at all graceful, and they should never be used
except in case of absolute necessity. The most graceful way for a lady to
reach the saddle, and the one that is taught in the best riding schools,
is by the **assistance of a gentleman**. The rider's education will not be
complete until she has learned this method of mounting, which, when
accomplished easily and gracefully, is delightful to witness. It should
be learned after the preliminary lessons at the horse-block have been
taken. In using this simple manner of reaching the saddle, the rider
will have three distinct points of support, namely, the shoulder of the
gentleman who assists her, the united palms of his hands, and her own
hold upon the pommel.

The stirrup having been placed across the shield of the saddle in
front of the pommels, the lady, holding the reins and the whip with its
point down in her right hand,—which must rest upon the second
pommel,—should stand with her right side toward the horse's left,
about four or five inches from it, her left shoulder being slightly turned

back. Then, taking a firm hold upon the second pommel with her right hand, she should with the left lift her riding skirt enough to enable her to place her left foot fairly and squarely into the gentleman's palms, which should be clasped firmly together. This done, she should drop the skirt, place her left hand upon his right shoulder, bend her knee, or give the word "ready," as a signal, and at once spring from her right foot up and a little towards the horse. The gentleman, at the same

FIG. 17—LADY READY TO MOUNT HER HORSE

moment, must raise his hands, and move them toward the horse. The lady must, when rising, press or bear lightly upon his shoulder, and also keep a firm hold upon the second pommel, which she must not relinquish until she is seated. If correctly performed, this manoeuvre will place the rider in the saddle sideways. The gentleman should then remove the stirrup from the front of the saddle, while the lady transfers the reins to her left hand, passes her right knee over the second pommel and her left under the third. She will then be ready to have her foot placed in the stirrup. (Fig. 17.)

It will, however, be found very difficult to mount in this manner, gracefully, unless the gentleman who assists thoroughly understands his duties; should he be awkward about helping her, the lady will find it much better to depend upon the horse-block. If, for instance, he should raise his hands too high, or with too much energy, when she makes her spring, he may push her too far over, or even—if she should loosen her grasp of the second pommel,—cause her to fall from the off-side of the horse. This is a dangerous accident, and almost certain to occasion severe injuries. On the other hand, if he does not use energy enough, or neglects to carry his hands toward the body of the horse as the lady rises, she may not reach the saddle at all, and will he apt to fall to the ground on the left side of the horse, especially if she relinquishes her hold on the second pommel. The gentleman must also be careful not to let his foot rest on the lady's skirt, as this will pull her back, and perhaps tear the dress, as she makes her spring.

In assisting a lady to mount, the **gentleman** should first arrange the snaffle-reins evenly and of the proper length, and place them in her right hand, leaving the curb-reins to lie loosely on the neck of the horse. Then, after putting the stirrup out of the way, as described above, he should take a position facing her, with his left shoulder toward the left shoulder of the horse. Clasping his hands together with the palms turned up, he should stoop sufficiently to enable her to put her left foot upon them, and, in raising them as she springs, he must gradually assume the erect posture. When the lady is seated, he should return the stirrup to its proper position and place her foot in it, after first, with his left hand, adjusting her skirt so that it will fall evenly; he should then place the curb-reins in her left hand, with the others. No gentleman is a finished equestrian, nor a desirable companion for a lady on horseback, who does not know how to assist her dexterously and gracefully to mount and dismount.

A lady who is not very nimble in her movements, or who is very heavy, should be extremely careful in mounting not to accept assistance from a gentleman who is not strong enough to support her weight easily and firmly. It will be much better for her to use a horse-block or something of the kind. But if she does accept the aid of a gentleman, the following changes in the methods described above have been recommended: instead of facing her, he should stand close to her side, with his face turned in the same direction as hers: she should then place her left foot in his united hands, and in order to do so must pass her left leg between his right arm and his body. He will thus be enabled to support and lift her with greater ease, and, as she rises, her left leg will

readily escape from under his right arm, and she will be able to seat
herself sideways in the saddle, as by the former method. During this
manoeuvre she must sustain herself by the second pommel, as in the
preceding instance.

If a horse is restless and uneasy when being mounted, he should be
held by a third person, who must stand in front of his head and take a
firm hold of the curb-bit on each side, but without touching the reins,
which should always be held and managed by the rider only. It is *always*
a better plan, when mounting, to have the horse held, although a well-
trained horse will stand quietly without such control.

Mounting is a part of the rider's education which should be carefully studied and practiced, for when properly and gracefully accomplished it is the very poetry of motion, and will enable her to display
more pliancy and lightness than she can even in the ball-room. There
is another branch of the rider's education which also requires careful
study, as it is rarely accomplished satisfactorily, and is apt to occasion
as much embarrassment and dismay to a beginner as mounting. This
is **dismounting**. To alight from a horse easily and well, without disar-
ranging the dress, and without being awkwardly precipitated into the
arms of the gentleman who assists, is by no means an easy task, and
very few lady riders accomplish it with skill and address.

When assisting his companion from the saddle, the gentleman
should stand about a foot from her with his face toward the horse,
while she, after taking her foot from the stirrup and disengaging
her right leg from the pommel, must turn her body so as to face
him. After putting the stirrup over the shield of the saddle, as in
mounting, he should then extend his hands so as to support her
by the elbows, while she rests a hand upon each of his shoulders.
Then, by giving a gentle spring, she will glide lightly to the ground,
he meanwhile supporting her with his hands, and, as she descends,
bending his body, and moving his right side slightly backward. She
can also assist him to lessen the shock as she touches the ground by
bending her knees a little, as if courtesying.

Another way of assisting the lady, especially if she be rather stout
and not very active, is for the gentleman to clasp her waist with both
hands, instead of holding her by the elbows. He should, in this case,
stand as far from her as he can while still supporting her, and, as she

descends, should make a step backward with his right foot, and turn a little away from the horse, which should be held by a third person, in the manner described before, in mounting.

Another, and more graceful way of dismounting is the following: The gentleman, standing about a foot from his companion and directly facing her, takes in his left hand her bridle,—as near as he can to the horse's mouth, that he may hold him as firmly and

FIG. 18—LADY READY TO DISMOUNT

securely as possible,—the lady now drops the reins on the horse's neck, disengages her foot from the stirrup, and her leg from the second pommel, and then seats herself sideways in the saddle, so as to face her assistant, who now places the stirrup on the front of the saddle with his right hand; he then offers his right shoulder to the lady for her support. She, after gathering up in her left hand a few folds of her riding skirt, in order to have her feet free when she alights, places upon his shoulder the hand which holds the skirt, and with the other, in which she holds her whip point downward, grasps the second pommel and springs lightly from the saddle, the gentleman bending over a little as she descends. On reaching the ground, she should, as before described, bend her knees slightly to lessen the shock of the descent. (Fig. 18.)

In all these modes of dismounting, the lady, before attempting to alight, should be sure that her skirt is quite free from the pommels, especially from the second one, and that it is so adjusted that it will not be trodden upon when she reaches the ground, but will fall evenly about her, without being in any way disarranged.

It happens not infrequently that a lady is obliged to dismount without **any one to assist her**, and in this case she should ride up to a horse-block so as to bring the left side of her horse close to it, let the curb reins fall upon his neck, retaining, however, the whip and snaffle-reins in her left hand, and then, removing her foot from the stirrup and her right leg from the pommel, she should seat herself a little sideways upon the saddle. Now, with a slight turn of her shoulders to the right, she should place her left hand—still holding the whip and reins—upon the second pommel, and her right hand upon the off one, and thus alight sideways with her face toward the horse's head. In effecting this manoeuvre, she must be careful to retain her hold upon the snaffle-reins and also upon the second pommel until she is safe upon the horse-block; she must also remember the caution given before, in regard to having her skirts free from the pommels.

To **dismount upon the ground**, or upon a very low horse-block, **without** assistance, is a difficult feat to execute gracefully, but some young ladies in the country, who are active and light, accomplish it so easily and quickly that they do not appear awkward. The manner in which this is to be done is nearly the same as that just explained, the only difference being, that the gliding down must be effected quickly and lightly, and the rider, as she passes down, must release her hold upon the off-pommel, but retain that upon the second, also taking care to have the reins quite loose. This mode of alighting is, however, entirely out of place except in the country, where assistance cannot always be had readily, or in cases where the lady is obliged to dismount very quickly.

If the lady rider, after carefully studying these different methods of mounting and dismounting with assistance, will select the one she thinks suits her best, and then practice it a few times with her gentleman escort, she will soon find herself able to perform with ease these apparently difficult feats, and will have no need of resorting to a horse-block, nor to some secluded spot, where she can mount or dismount unobserved. A lady once told the author that the pleasure of her daily ride was at one time almost spoiled by the knowledge that she must mount and dismount in front of a hotel, the piazza of which was always crowded with observers, for, not having been properly taught to execute these manoeuvres, she was rather awkward at them. She, however, placed herself under correct tuition, and soon overcame the difficulty. She can now execute these movements with such grace and elegance as to fascinate gentlemen, and excite the envy of rival belles who are still obliged to seek the aid of a horse-block.

CHAPTER V
THE SEAT ON HORSEBACK

"Bounded the fiery steed in air,
The rider sat erect and fair,
Then like a bolt from steel cross-bow
Forth launched, along the plain they go."

Lady of the Lake.

A CORRECT SEAT is very seldom attained by the self-taught lady rider, for her attitude on the horse is so artificial that she cannot, like the gentleman rider, whose seat is more easy and natural, fall directly into the proper position. Competent instruction alone can enable her to gain the safe and easy posture which will give the least possible fatigue to herself and to her horse. It is true that a natural rider, or she who professes to ride instinctively, may to-day accidentally assume the proper position in the saddle, but, as she has no rule by which to guide herself, and is entirely unacquainted with the "whys and wherefores" of a correct seat, she will to-morrow assume the incorrect position, so natural to a self-taught rider, and the pleasant ride of to-day will be followed by a rough and unpleasant one to-morrow. On the one occasion, the poor horse will receive much praise for his easy motion, and on the next be highly censured for the roughness of his gait, for the lady will not suspect that the real difficulty lies in her own ignorance of a correct attitude, and in her bad management of the poor beast.

Upon the position of the upper part of the body depends not only grace and pliancy, and that harmony between horse and rider which is so highly desirable and, indeed, necessary, but also the ability to manage the reins properly; for, if the rider be not well balanced, her hands will be unsteady, and seldom in the right position for controlling the animal.

But the proper position of the body above the saddle depends upon the correct arrangement of the lower limbs; if they are not in the right position, the rider will lean too far forward, or too far back, or too much to one side or the other. She will also lose all firmness of seat, and, consequently, all safety in riding. This faulty position of the lower limbs has been, and still is, the occasion of much incorrect riding, but is a point which is seldom regarded by the gentleman teacher. He, indeed, cannot possibly know how the legs are arranged, when they are covered by the riding skirt, and probably seldom gives the subject any thought; yet he wonders, after carefully watching and correcting the position of the body, why his pupil does not retain the erect position as directed. A lady teacher of experience is, therefore, much to be preferred to a gentleman, unless the lady pupil is willing to wear, while taking her lessons, trousers similar to those worn during calisthenic exercises.

It sometimes happens that a lady, even after being carefully instructed how to sit in the saddle, and when she seems to understand what is necessary, will yet present a very erect but stiff appearance, as if she were made of cast-iron, or some other unyielding material. This may be due to nervousness, fear, tight-lacing, or affectation. Practice in riding, loose corsets, and less affectation, will soon remedy this stiffness.

Another faulty position is one which may be termed "the dead weight seat," which is only possible when riding on an English saddle. It consists in sitting or bearing chiefly upon the left side of the saddle, the right leg firmly grasping the second pommel, and the left leg squeezed tightly between the stirrup and the third pommel, as if held in a vise. In this position the rider will be fastened to her horse as closely as if she were a package of merchandise strapped upon the back of a pack-horse. She will appear indolent and inanimate, besides riding heavily, and thus distressing and discouraging her horse; for a well-trained horse will always prefer to keep in unison with the movements of his rider, but will find it impossible to do so, when she adopts this constrained, unyielding seat. The rider will also be made miserable, for the constant effort to keep steady by a continuous pressure of the left knee against the third pommel will not only prove wearisome, but will be apt to bruise her knee, as well as strain the muscles of the upper part of the leg, and the next day she will feel very stiff and lame. In addition to which it will be impossible for her to rise in the English trot, or to move her body to the right in the gallop or canter when the horse leads with his left leg. Moreover, should the lady who thus hangs upon the pommel be rather heavy, her horse's back will be sure to receive more or less injury, no matter how well the saddle may be made and padded.

Although the second pommel should be firmly grasped by the right knee, and the left knee be strongly pressed up against the third one, when the horse is unruly or trying to unseat his rider, these supports should not be habitually employed, but kept for critical situations, and even then the body must be kept erect, yet flexible. A rider who depends entirely upon the pommels to enable her to keep her seat is a bad rider, who will soon acquire all kinds of awkward and ridiculous positions, and expose herself to much severe criticism.

The opposite of the "dead-weight seat" is what may be termed the "wabbling seat." This is seen where the old-fashioned saddle is used; the rider, instead of sitting firm and erect, bounds up and down like a rubber ball tossed by an unseen hand. This can be remedied by the substitution of the English saddle, whose third pommel, when used judiciously and aided by a proper balance of the body, will give the required firmness of seat, which should be neither too rigid nor too yielding.

The correct seat, universally adopted by finished riders, is the following: The lady should seat herself exactly on the centre of the saddle, with her body erect, and her backbone in a direct line with that of the horse, at a right angle with it. A spectator can readily tell whether the rider is in the centre of the saddle by observing whether the space between the buttons on the hind flaps of her riding-jacket corresponds with the backbone of the horse, and also with the chamber of the saddle. (Fig. 19.) Or the lady can herself decide the question by placing her fingers between these two buttons, and then carrying the former in a straight line directly down to the chamber of the saddle; if these coincide, and if she has placed herself far enough back on the saddle to be able to grasp the second pommel comfortably with her right knee, while the left one is just spanned by the third pommel, then she is in a position to ride with ease to herself and horse, for she now sits upon that part of the animal which is the centre of motion in his forward movement, and in this position can keep in unison with the cadence of

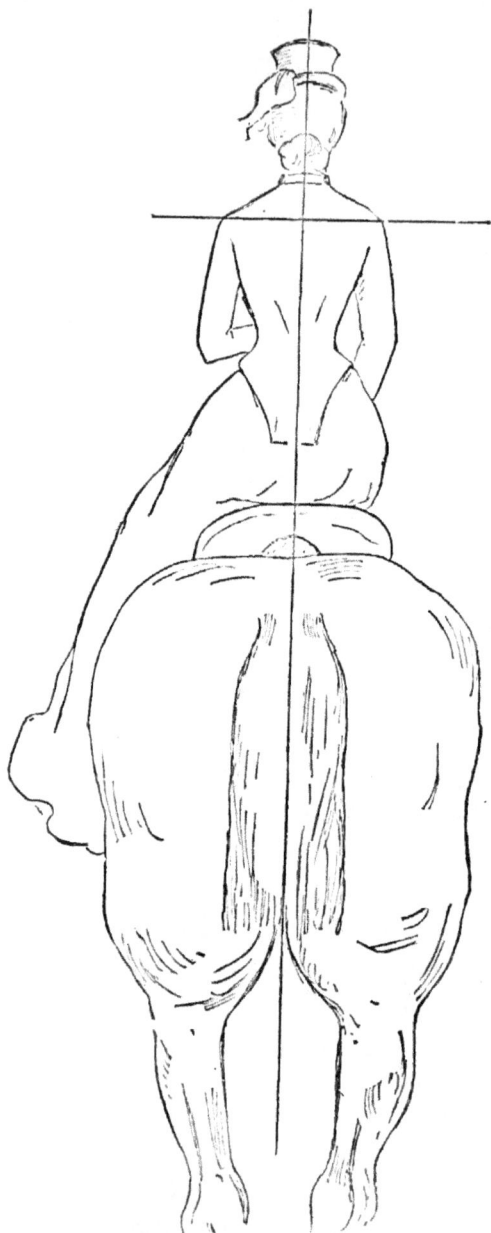

FIG. 19—CORRECT SEAT FOR A LADY
(*BACK VIEW*)

his various gaits. Again, her weight being exactly upon the centre of motion, she can with difficulty be unseated or shaken off by the most violent efforts of the horse, for, whether he springs suddenly forward, or sideways, or whirls around, the rider is in a position at once to anticipate his movement, to keep a firm seat, and quickly to gain her balance.

When the horse advances straight forward, the rider—sitting with head erect and her body so placed that its entire front is directed toward the horse's head, or, in other words, that *a straight line drawn from one hip to the other would form a right angle with one drawn along the centre of the horse's head and neck*—must throw her shoulders somewhat back, so as to expand her chest, taking care, however, to keep the shoulders in line, and not to elevate one more than the other. There should also be, at the back of the waist, a slight inward bend which will throw the front of the waist a little forward. The arms, from the shoulders to the elbows, must hang perpendicularly, and the elbows be held loosely but steadily and in an easy manner, near the rider's sides, and not be allowed to flap up and down with every movement. The hands must be held low and about three or four inches from the body. The bearing of the head, the backward throw of the shoulders, and the curve at the waist, are exactly like those assumed by a finished waltzer, and if the reader is herself a dancer, or will notice the carriage of a good dancer gliding around the ball-room, she can readily understand the attitude required for a correct seat in the saddle.

The right knee should grasp the second pommel firmly, but not hang upon it in order to help the rider keep her seat and balance. The right leg, from the hip to the knee, must be kept as steady as possible, because from a woman's position in the saddle, the movements of her horse tend to throw her toward his left side, and she must guard against this by bearing slightly toward his right. From the knee to the foot, the right leg must be in contact with the fore-flap of the saddle, the heel being inclined backward a little.

The left knee should be placed just below the third pommel, so that this will span it lightly, close enough to assist in preserving a firm seat, yet not so close as to interfere with the action of the leg in the English trot. From the knee to the foot this left leg must be held in a straight line perpendicular to the ground, and the knee be lightly pressed against the side-flap of the saddle. The ball of the foot must be placed evenly in the stirrup, the heel being a little lower than the toes, which should be pointed toward the shoulder of the horse. (Fig. 20.)

If the rider will seat herself in the saddle in the manner just de-

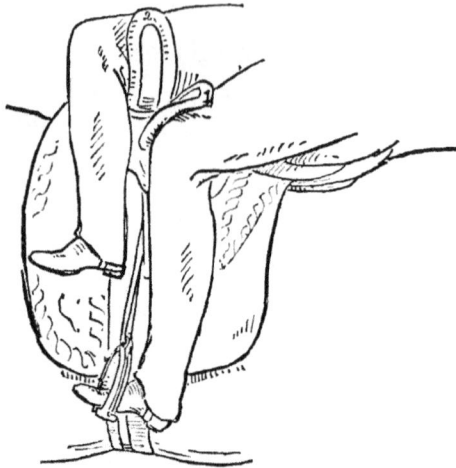

FIG. **20**—CORRECT SEAT FOR A LADY (*SIDE VIEW*)

scribed, she will find that she has a very firm seat, from which she cannot easily be displaced; but in order to appear graceful she must be flexible, and adapt herself readily to the motions of her horse. The shoulders, for example, although thrown back, must not be rigid, and the body, while erect, must be supple; the head be upright and free, and, in the leap, or when circling in the gallop, the body must be pliant, yielding and bending with the movements of the horse, but always resuming afterward the easy erect position. But it must be borne in mind that the above directions in regard to carriage apply to the times when the horse is moving, and need not be observed in full rigor at other times. When, for instance, the horse is standing, the rider may assume a more easy posture, collecting herself and steed simultaneously when she wishes him to move.

The novice in riding should never be allowed to touch rein or whip until she has acquired a good seat, and a correct balance. During her first lessons, some one should ride by her side and lead her horse, while she, folding her hands in front of her waist, should give all her attention to gaining a correct seat; or, she may practice circling to the right by means of the lunge line, which will prove excellent training, and will teach her to bear toward the off or right side, for it has already been stated that the motion in the side-saddle has a tendency to impel the rider toward the left, and this tendency must always be guarded against by bearing the body a little to the right. Circling to the right, when riding in the track of the riding-school, is also a useful exercise for this purpose, but as riding-schools are not always to be had conveniently, the lunge line will be found very useful, many riders, indeed, considering it even better than riding in the ring, as it keeps the horse well up to his gait.

During a few of the first lessons, that the rider may not fall from the saddle, the stirrup-leather may be somewhat shortened, but as soon as an idea of the proper balance has been acquired and the reins and whip are placed in her hands, the stirrup must be lengthened, as this secures a firmer and more easy seat. This leather will be of the correct length when, by a little pressure on it with her foot, and a simultaneous straightening of her knee, the rider can spring upward about four or five inches from the saddle; but it must never be so long as to render the third pommel nearly, if not quite, useless.

It is better to have the first lessons in riding rather short, so that the pupil may become gradually accustomed to the exercise. As soon as she begins to feel at all fatigued, she should at once dismount, and not try to ride again until the tired feeling is wholly gone. These intervals of fatigue will gradually become less and less frequent, until at last the rider will find herself so strong and vigorous that riding will no longer require any fatiguing effort. In the case of an active, healthy woman, accustomed to exercise of various kinds, these short preliminary lessons may not be necessary; her muscles will be already so well developed that she will not be easily fatigued by exercise of any kind. But for a lady who has always been physically inactive, these short lessons at first are absolutely necessary. The general system of such a person has become enfeebled, her muscles are weak and flabby, and any sudden or long continued exercise would tend to produce very injurious results, so that riding, unless begun very gradually, would probably do her more harm than good.

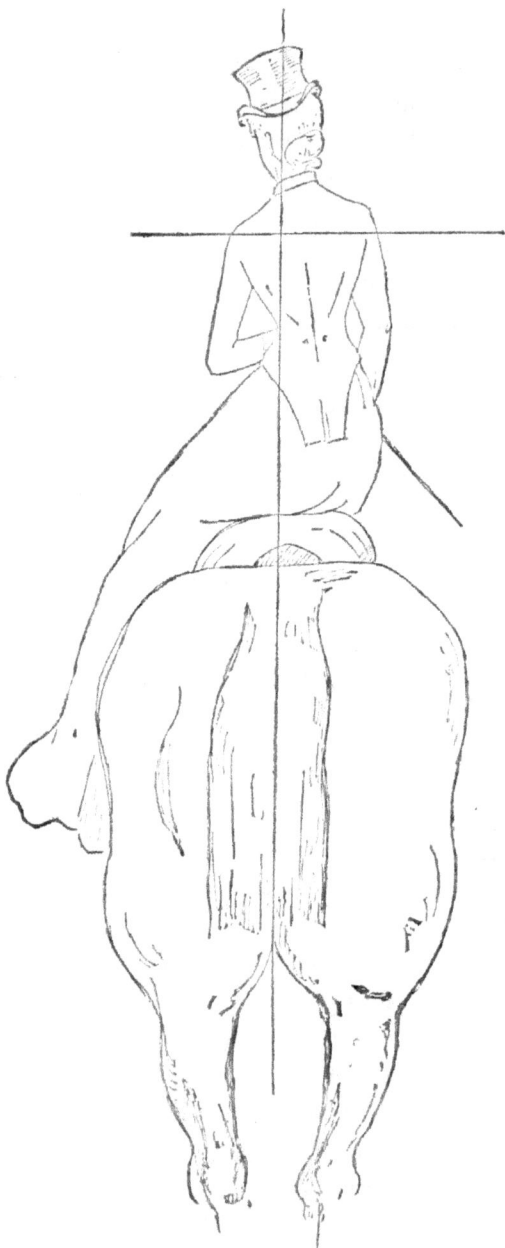

FIG 21—CROOKED POSITION IN THE SADDLE
(*MISS X.*)

But after reading all the directions just given about riding, the reader may ask what need there is of so much study and circumspection to enable a woman to mount a horse and ride him, when hundreds of ladies ride every day, and enjoy doing so, without knowing anything about the make of the saddle, or the position they ought to take when seated in it.

Although it seems almost a pity to disturb the serenity and self-complacency of ignorance, we shall be obliged, in justice to those who really wish to understand the principles of good horsewomanship, to point out some of the mistakes of those who think that riding is an accomplishment which can be acquired without instruction and study.

It is not too sweeping an assertion to state that, of one hundred ladies who attempt a display of what they consider their *excellent* horsewomanship in our streets and parks, ninety-five are very imperfect riders; and the five who do ride well have only learned to do so by means of careful study and competent instruction. They have fully appreciated the fact that nature never ushered them into the world finished riders, any more than accomplished grammarians or Latin scholars, and that although one may possess a natural aptitude for an accomplishment, application, study, and practice are positively necessary to enable her to attain any degree of perfection in it. Yet the idea unfortunately prevails very largely in this country that women require very little instruction to become good riders, and the results of this belief are apparent in the ninety-five faulty riders already referred to.

Let us now watch some of the fair Americans whom the first balmy day of spring has tempted out for a horseback ride, and notice the faulty positions in which they have contrived to seat themselves in their saddles. With regard to their beauty, elegance of form, and style of dress, nothing more could be desired; but, alas! the same cannot be said of their manner of riding.

Take Miss X. and Mrs. Y., for examples. These ladies have the reputation of being fine and fearless horsewomen, and certainly do ride with that dash and confidence which long practice in the saddle is sure to give, but we regret to say that we can bestow no further praise upon them. Miss X. has taken a position that is almost universal with American horsewomen, and is exactly the one which a rider nearly always assumes when seated sideways on a horse without a saddle. Instead of sitting squarely, with the entire front of her body facing in the direction toward which the horse is going, she sits crosswise. It will be seen by looking at Fig. 21, that the central vertical line of her back, instead of being directly in the centre of the saddle, is placed toward the right corner of it, and that her shoulders are out of line, the left one being thrown back, and the right one advanced forward. This position makes it impossible for her to keep in unison with her horse when he is moving straight forward at an easy pace. When he changes his gait to a canter the rider will, for a short distance, appear to be more in harmony with him, because he is now turning himself slightly to the left and leading with his right fore-leg, a position which is more in unison with that of his rider. But, after a short time, the horse gets tired of this canter, turns to the right, and leads with his left fore-leg. This change entirely destroys the apparent harmony which had before existed between the two.

The lady, knowing nothing about the position of a horse when galloping or cantering, is ignorant of the fact that he always turns a little to the right or left according to the leg with which he leads, and that she ought to place her body in a corresponding position. She has but one position in the saddle,—the crooked one already described,—and this she maintains immovably through all the changes of her horse's gaits.

Let us now turn to Mrs. Y., who is even a more faulty rider than her companion. She has likewise taken a crosswise position in the saddle; but having given a peculiar twist to her body so that, by turning her right shoulder backward, she can look to the right, she seems to imagine that by these means she has placed herself squarely upon the saddle. (Fig. 22.) As she is riding a racking horse and seated on a two-pommeled saddle, she holds the reins firmly in her left hand and by a steady pull on them she balances herself and keeps her horse up to his gait. But this steady pull will soon ruin the tenderness and sensitiveness of any horse's mouth, and this is the reason why racking horses generally have very hard mouths, many of them requiring to be well held up or supported in their rack by the reins. As this pulling upon the reins also gives considerable support to the rider, many ladies prefer a racking horse. Now notice Mrs. Y., who is attempting to turn her hard-mouthed racker. Instead of doing this by an almost

FIG. 22–CROOKED POSITION IN THE SADDLE

(MRS. Y.)

imperceptible movement of the hand, her left hand and arm can be distinctly seen to move, and to fairly pull the animal around. Her right hand—probably acting in sympathy with the left, so tightly clasped over the reins—holds the whip as if it were in a vise intended to crush it. In odd contrast with the rigidly held hands is the body with its utter lack of firmness.

It can be seen at a glance why the lady will only ride an easy racker, for it is well known that on a good racker or pacer the body of a rider in a faulty position is not jolted so much as in other gaits. For this reason also the rack and pace are the favorite gaits of most American horsewomen.

Nearly every lady who rides has an ambition to be considered a finished horsewoman, but this she can never be until she is able to ride properly the trot and gallop, can keep herself in unison with

FIG. **23**–INCORRECT POSITION OF LEGS AND FEET (*SIDE VIEW*)

her horse, whether he leads with the left or right fore-leg, and has hands that will "give and take" with the horse's movements and bring him up to his best gait. From this point of view, Miss X. and Mrs. Y., then, are by no means the "splendid riders" that their friends suppose them, but having all the confidence of ignorance they ride fast and boldly and with a certain *abandon* that is pleasing; but by those who understand what good riding is, they must always be regarded as very faulty riders.

Another common fault, against which we have already warned the reader, is that of riding with too short a stirrup-leather, thus pressing the left knee up against the third pommel, carrying the left heel backward and slightly upward, and dropping the toes of the left foot more or less down toward the ground, while those of the right are raised and pointed toward the horse's head. (Fig. 23.) Although the lower limbs are concealed by the skirt, it can easily be told whether they are in the position just described, from the effect produced upon the upper part of the body, which then leans too far forward and too much to the right (Fig. 24); while the rider, in her efforts to balance herself, inclines her shoulders to the left. This is a very awkward as well as a very dangerous attitude, because, by thrusting her leg backwards, the action of spurring is imitated, and, if the horse is very high-spirited, this may cause him to become restive, or even to run away. Should the leg, moreover, as is very apt to be the case, be firmly and steadily pressed against the animal's side, he may suddenly pirouette or turn around to the right, especially if he has been accustomed to carrying gentlemen as well as ladies. This short stirrup-leather and improper use of the third pommel should be carefully avoided.

The use of too long a stirrup-leather is apt to be the mistake of those who ride upon the old fashioned saddle, but is a fault which has become much less common since the English saddle has been more generally used. The objection to too long a stirrup-leather is that, when the foot is pressed upon it, the leg at the same time is straightened, and extends down so far as to cause the rider to sit too much to the left of the saddle. As the pressure and weight are thus thrown wholly upon the left side, the saddle is very likely to turn, and if this faulty position be persisted in, it will be certain to injure the horse's back and may give rise to fistulous withers.

Besides looking very awkward and inelegant, when stooping forward in the saddle and rounding the back without the slightest curve inwardly, the rider will also run great risk, if her horse stumbles or makes any sudden movement, of being unseated, or at least thrown violently against the front of the saddle, as it is almost impossible for her, under such circumstances, to adapt herself to the change in his motion quickly enough to preserve her equilibrium. In all violent movements of the horse, except rearing, the body must be inclined backward, so as

FIG. 24—INCORRECT POSITION WHEN LEGS AND FEET ARE WRONGLY PLACED
(*BACK VIEW*)

to keep the balance. When he is moving briskly in his ordinary gaits, the body must be kept erect; and when he is turning a corner rapidly, it should be inclined backward somewhat, and toward the inner bend of the horse's body; or, in other words, toward the centre of the circle, of which the turn forms a segment.

Here come two ladies who have evidently received very limited instructions in the art of riding. Notice how the head of one is thrust forward, while the other, though holding her head erect allows it to be jerked about with every motion of her horse. It shakes slowly when the animal is walking, but as he quickens his pace to a canter, it rocks with his motion, and, during his fast pace, the poor head moves so rapidly as to make one fear that the neck may become dislocated, while the arms dance about simultaneously with the movements of the head in a way that reminds one of the toy dancing-jacks, pulled by an unseen hand for the amusement of children. The head should, in riding, be kept firm and erect, without stiffness, the chin being drawn in slightly, and not protruding high in the air, because the latter gives one a supercilious look. The head and shoulders should adapt themselves, in their direction, to the movements of the head and fore-legs of the horse, and the arms should be held as steady as possible.

But here come several ladies who have taken lessons at the riding-school and may, therefore, reasonably be expected to be finished riders; but such, alas! is not the case. They have been trying "to walk before they could creep," or, in other words, their lessons in riding have been conducted too hastily. They have begun to try a canter or a rapid gallop before they knew how to sit correctly upon their horses, or even to manage them properly in a walk. This desire to make too rapid progress is more frequently the fault of the pupil than of the riding teacher. Most teachers have an ambition to make finished riders of their pupils, and take much pride in doing so, especially as such a result adds greatly to the prestige of their school. This ambition is often defeated, however, by the impatience of the pupils, who are not satisfied to learn slowly and well, but overrule the teacher's objections and undertake to gallop before they have acquired even the first principles of horsewomanship. Moreover, many of these ladies never take any road lessons, so highly important to all who would become thoroughly accomplished in this art; nor do they remain long enough under instruction in the school, but seem to think that a few short lessons are enough to make them finished riders. They often refuse to learn the English trot, although this is a very important accomplishment for the beginner, as it enables her to gain a correct idea of the balance. Or, if they do attempt to learn it, they insist upon circling only to the right, as this is easier than going the other way.

Again, many pupils will insist upon riding the same favorite horse, instead of leaving the selection to the judgment of the teacher, who is well aware that it is much better for the lady's progress that she should ride a variety of horses with different gaits. He is often driven to his wit's end when two or three ladies who patronize his school, and whom it is an honor to have as pupils, express a desire to ride the same horse on the same occasion. Should he favor one more than the others, the latter will become highly offended, and the poor man in his perplexity is often obliged to resort to some subterfuge to pacify them.

It is not difficult, then, to understand why some ladies, although they have taken lessons at a riding-school, are, nevertheless, not finished riders, their faults being due, not to the instruction but to their own lack of judgment or inattention. It is true that occasionally the teacher, although he may be an excellent instructor for gentlemen, is not so good a one for ladies, or he may become careless, believing that if he gives them well-trained horses to ride very little else is required of him. Or, again, he may think, as many foreigners do, that very few American ladies know how a woman should ride, and are satisfied with being half taught.

It cannot be too strongly impressed upon riding teachers that in every riding-school where ladies are to be taught there should be at least one lady assistant. A gentleman can give all the necessary instructions about the management of the horse and the handling of the reins better than most ladies; but, in giving the idea of a correct seat and the proper disposal of the limbs, the presence of a lady assistant becomes necessary; in these matters she can instruct her own sex much better than a man can.

CHAPTER VI
TO HOLD THE REINS, AND MANAGE THE HORSE

"What a wild thought of triumph, that this girlish hand
Such a steed in the might of his strength may command!
What a glorious creature! Ah! glance at him now,
As I check him awhile on this green hillock's brow;
How he tosses his mane, with a shrill, joyous neigh,
And paws the firm earth in his proud, stately play!"

GRACE GREENWOOD.

THE POSITION OF the rider in the saddle has a decided influence upon the horse's mouth, rendering his movements regular or irregular, according to the correctness and firmness of the seat; for, if the rider be unsteady or vacillating in the saddle, this will exert an influence upon the hand, rendering it correspondingly unstable, and will thereby cause the horse's movements to be variable. And should she endeavor to remedy this unsteadiness of hand and seat by supporting herself upon the reins, the horse will defend himself against such rigid traction by making counter-traction upon the reins, thrusting his head forward, throwing himself heavily upon his fore-legs, thus forcing the hands of the rider, and compelling her to support the weight of his neck and shoulders. On the contrary, if she be firm in her seat, and not in the least dependent upon the reins, her hand will be light, and the animal will yield a ready obedience and advance in his best pace. The preceding remarks explain why a horse will go lightly with one rider and heavily with another.

A lady should have a thorough knowledge of the management of her horse, and of the means by which she may command him in every degree of speed, and under all circumstances; without this knowledge she can never become a safe and accomplished horsewoman. A gentleman may guide and control his horse, and obtain obedience from a restive one, by a firm, strong hand, and by his courage and determined will; but as a rule, a lady cannot depend upon these methods; she will have to rely entirely upon the thorough training of her horse, a properly arranged bit, her firm, yet delicate touch, and her skill in handling the reins. The well-trained hand of a woman is always energetic enough to obtain the mastery of her horse, without having to resort to feats of strength and acrobatic movements; and a *lady* should never seek to gain prestige by riding restless or vicious horses, in order that she may display her skill in conquering them; though every rider should be thoroughly taught how to control her steed in cases of emergency.

When one sees how little skill most lady riders exhibit in managing the reins, it seems almost miraculous that so few accidents occur to them, and is indeed a positive proof of the excellent temper of their horses. From some mysterious cause, most horses will bear more awkwardness and absurdity in the handling of the reins by a woman than by a man, and will good-naturedly submit to the indifferent riding of the gentle being in the side-saddle, while the same character of riding and treatment from a man would arouse every feeling of defense and rebellion. The probable cause of this difference of action on the part of the horse is, that a lady rider, with all her ignorance of seat and rein, will talk kindly to and pet her steed, and will rarely lose her temper, no matter in what eccentricities he may indulge, and her gentleness causes the animal to remain gentle.

On the contrary, when a man throws his weight upon the reins, jerking and pulling upon them, his horse, seeking to defend himself against such rough measures, arouses the temper of his rider, and this anger is soon communicated to the animal, which then becomes obstinate and rebellious; moreover, a man will often whip and spur for some trivial offense in instances where a woman would simply speak to her horse, or take no notice. Hence, the ignorant horsewoman often rides in safety under circumstances in which the ignorant horseman, who has resorted to violent measures, meets with an accident.

Although a horse may submit to an awkward rider and carry her with safety, still she will have no power to make him move in his best and most regular manner, and there will exist no intelligence or harmony between the two. Yet this same horse, when mounted by a lady who understands the **management of the reins**, will be all animation and happiness. There will soon be established a tacit understanding between the two, and the graceful curvetings and prancings of the steed will manifest his pride and joy in carrying and obeying a gentle woman, who manages the reins with spirit and resolution, and yet does not, with the cruelty of ignorance or indifference, convert them into instruments of torture.

The **reins** should not be employed until a firm, steady position upon the saddle has been acquired, and then, for first lessons, the snaffle only should be used, **a rein in each hand**. It will be better to have the reins marked at equal distances from the bit, either by sewing colored thread across each, or otherwise; this will be useful because, with the novice, the reins will imperceptibly slip through her hands, or one rein will become longer than the other, and the markings will enable her to notice these displacements, and promptly to remedy them. By holding the snaffle-reins separately, in first lessons, the pupil will be aided in assuming a square position upon the saddle, and will likewise be prevented from throwing back her right shoulder, out of line with the left, a common fault with beginners, especially when the reins are held only in the left hand. This rein-hold is very simple; the right rein of the snaffle must be held in the right hand, and the left rein in the left.

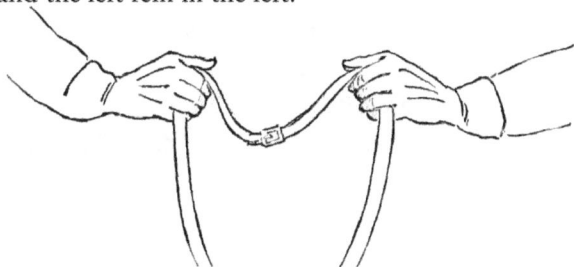

FIG. 25—SNAFFLE-REINS; ONE IN EACH HAND

The hands being closed, but not too tightly, must be held with their backs toward the horse's head, and each rein, as it ascends from the bit, must be passed between the third and fourth fingers of its appropriate hand, carried across the inner surface of the third, second, and first fingers, and then be drawn over the outside (or side next to the thumb) of the first finger, against which it must be held by firm

pressure of the thumb. The thumbs must be held opposite each other
and uppermost, the finger-nails toward the body, and the back of the
wrists must be rounded a little outwardly, so as to make a slight bend
of the closed hand toward the body. The little fingers must be held
down and nearly in a horizontal line with the tips of the elbows; and
the hands be kept as low as possible, without resting upon the knees,
and be about four inches distant from the body, and from four to six
inches apart. (Fig. 25.)

This arrangement of hands and reins may be termed the "original position" when a snaffle-rein is held in each hand, of which all
the others are variations. In this position,—the reins being held just
short enough to feel the horse's mouth,—if the hands be now slightly
relaxed by turning the nails and thumbs toward the body, the latter
being, at the same time, inclined a little forward, the horse will be
enabled to advance freely, and, as soon as he **moves onward**, the
original position of the hands must be gently resumed. It is proper
to remark here, that when using the snaffle-reins only, the curb-bit
should always be in the horse's mouth, its reins being tied and allowed to rest upon his neck, although the pupil must not be allowed
to meddle with it. The presence of the curb in the horse's mouth,
although not used, has a restraining influence, especially with an animal accustomed to it.

To turn the horse to the right, the right rein must be shortened so
as to be felt at the right side of his mouth; to effect this, the little finger
of the right hand must, by a turn of the wrist, be moved in toward the
body and sufficiently toward the left, with the nails up and the knuckles down, while, in order to aid the horse, the rider will simultaneously
turn her face and shoulders slightly to the right. The animal having
made the turn, the hand must gently return to the original position,
and the body again face to the front.

To turn the horse to the left, the left rein must be shortened, by
a turn of the left wrist, carrying the little finger of the left hand toward the body and to the right, nails upward, etc., while the pupil will
slightly turn her face and shoulders to the left. The turn having been
effected, the original position must be resumed, the pupil, in all these
cases, taking great care that the markings on her reins are even and in
the correct position.

To stop the horse, both reins must be shortened evenly; this must be accomplished by a turn of both wrists that will bring the little fingers toward the body with the finger-nails uppermost, the body of the pupil being, at the same time, slightly inclined backward. Now, by bending the wrists to a still greater degree, and bringing the hands in closer to the body, which must be inclined a little forward, and nearly in contact with each other, thus throwing more strength upon the reins, the horse will be compelled **to back**. To make him **move on again**, the hands and body must resume the original position, and the hands must be relaxed, etc., as stated above.

When the pupil becomes more advanced, and can command her horse, in all his gaits, with the reins separate, one in each hand, she will then be prepared for lessons in handling **both reins with the left hand only**, still employing the snaffle, as her touch may not be delicate enough for the curb.

For this purpose, the reins being held for the time being in the right hand, the left, having its back toward the horse's head, will seize them as follows: its little finger must be passed directly between the

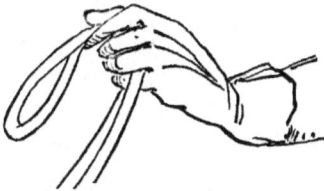

FIG. 26—SNAFFLE-REINS; BOTH
IN THE LEFT HAND

two reins, the left rein being on the outer side of this finger and the right one on its right side, between it and the third finger. This done, the reins must be drawn up nearly even to the marks upon them,[4] so as just to feel the animal's mouth, noticing that these marks are nearly on a line with each other, while that portion of the reins lying within the hand must be carried across its palm to the index finger, to a point between its first and second joints, against which point, being placed evenly with one overlying the other, they are to be firmly held

---

4   It is stated in this paragraph that the *marks on the reins* should be "nearly even," or "nearly on a line with each other," because, in its passage under the little finger, across the hand, and on the outside of the right rein, the left one will be shortened so that its marking will be about half an inch nearer the bit than that of the right one; consequently, in order to make the pressure upon the horse's mouth even, the right rein will have to be shortened to the extent named.

by pressure of the thumb; the right hand may now quit its hold upon
the reins. (Fig. 26.)

The reins having been properly placed in the left hand according
to the directions just given, this hand, being closed, but not too tightly,
must be held at a distance of about three inches from the front part of
the waist, with the wrist slightly rounded, the nails toward the body,
the back of the hand toward the horse's head, and the little finger down
and a little nearer the body than the others. The under surface of the
bridle arm and hand, from the tip of the elbow to the first joint of
the little finger, should be held nearly in a horizontal line. The elbow
must be held somewhat close to the side but not in contact with it,
and should be kept steady. Care must be taken, when the reins are
held in the left hand, that the right shoulder be not thrown back, nor
the left one elevated, faulty positions common to beginners when not
otherwise instructed. The right arm should be allowed to hang easily and steadily at the side, the whip being lightly held in it, with its
point downward. When the snaffle-reins are held in the left hand as
described, we may term this the "original position," of which all the
others are variations.

In order that the horse may **move onward**, the left hand, holding
the reins as just described, should be relaxed by turning the thumb
downward and toward the body until the back of the hand is up and
the finger-nails down; at the same time, the pupil should slightly incline her body forward, being careful not to round the shoulders,—
aiding the movement by the voice, or, if necessary, by a gentle tap of
the whip. The horse having started onward, the original position must
be gently resumed.

In order to **turn the horse to the right**, the left wrist must be
turned so as to bring the nails down and the knuckles up,—the
thumb being toward the body,—at the same time carrying the little finger slightly to the left, and drawing the reins a little upward.
This movement will effect the necessary shortening of the right rein,
without allowing any looseness of the left one. The turn having been
accomplished, the hand must resume the original position. It must
not be forgotten, that while making this turn the face and shoulders
must be turned somewhat to the right, or in the direction in which
the horse is moving.

To turn to the left, the bridle-hand being in the original position, its wrist must be turned so as to carry the finger-nails up, and the knuckles down, simultaneously moving the little finger toward the right and pressing it against the left rein, both reins being drawn slightly upward. This manoeuvre shortens the left rein, without relaxing the right. In this turn the movements of the horse should be aided by the rider's face and shoulders being turned a little to the left. The turn having been made, the original position must be resumed.

The horse **may be stopped** by simply turning the wrist so as to carry the finger-nails up, the knuckles down, and the little finger toward the body, which must be slightly inclined backward. Now, by bracing the muscles of the hand, bending the wrist and carrying the hand farther in toward the waist, at the same time advancing the body, the animal will be made **to back**; though, in backing a horse, it will be better to employ both hands. After having stopped, or backed the horse, to make him **move onward**, a course should be pursued, with both reins in the bridle-hand, similar to that described for the same purpose when a rein is held in each hand.

To change the snaffle-reins from the left to the right hand, as is sometimes necessary in order to adjust the skirt, to relieve the left hand, etc., the following course must be pursued, whether the horse be in rapid or slow motion: While the left hand must retain its position and gentle pressure of the reins upon the horse's mouth, the right must be carried to and over the left hand, its forefinger be passed between the two reins, so that the left rein will be on the left side of this finger, and the right on its right side, between the first and second fingers; both reins must now be carried to the right, across the palm, to the little finger; the hand must then be firmly closed, and the thumb be pressed against the left rein, holding it in contact with the index finger,—the left hand now gives up the reins. In this change, while the right hand is being carried over to the left, this latter must be held stationary, as any movement of it to meet the right hand may cause the animal to turn or swerve from his course, and will at the same time interfere with his gait.

To return the reins to the left hand, the following course must be pursued: While the right hand must remain steady and sustain the gait of the horse, the left must be carried to and over it, insert its little finger between the two reins, so that the left one will be on the left or outer side of this finger, and the right one on its right side, between it and the third finger; then the reins must be drawn through the left hand, and be arranged and held in this hand in the same manner as explained when describing the original position of both snaffle-reins in the bridle-hand.

These various changes must be made quickly and expertly, without altering the degree of pressure or pull upon the horse's mouth. The novice will find it greatly to her advantage to learn the management of the reins before mounting the horse, and can do so by fastening the bit-end of the reins to some stationary object, and then practicing the different changes, until she can perform all these manoeuvres without looking at her hands or the reins.

When both the reins are held in the left hand, the rider has not so much command over her horse as when they are held one in each hand. For this reason, unless her steed be exceptionally well trained and obedient, it will be better, when in a crowded thoroughfare, where quick turns have to be made, to hold a rein in each hand, and this will become absolutely necessary if the animal be hard mouthed or unruly.

When the horse is in motion and the reins are held in the left hand, their **separation** may be quickly effected by carrying the right hand to and over the left, the latter retaining its steadiness all the time, and then passing the first three fingers of the right hand between the two reins, so that they may readily close upon the right rein; the thumb will then keep this rein firm by pressing it against the first joint of the index finger. The position of the hands and reins will then, after a movement of the left little finger to place the rein between it and the third, be the same as described for the original position where a snaffle-rein is held in each hand.

Should the reins become too long when held separately, they can readily **be shortened** by returning the right rein to the bridle-hand, placing it directly over the left rein between the third and little finger, and then, by means of the right hand, drawing the loose rein or reins through the bridle-hand to the proper length, after which the right rein may again be taken in the right hand, as already described.

When the reins are held in one hand, they can be **shortened or lengthened** by simply seizing them at their free, disengaged ends with the right hand, and while this holds them and sustains the horse, the left hand must be slipped along the reins, up or down, as may be required, but without changing their arrangement.

Another way of holding the reins in the bridle-hand is to pass the right rein to the right of, and underneath, the index finger, and then carry it across the palm, so as to escape beyond the little finger; while the left rein must be passed to the left of the little finger (or between it and the third finger), and then be carried across the palm to escape beyond the index finger. The author cannot recommend this manner of holding the reins to ladies who desire to become accomplished and graceful riders, because the movements of the hands and arms, when turning, or managing the horse, are much more conspicuous; and there is not that delicate correspondence with the animal's mouth that can be obtained by the other methods described.

After the pupil has become expert in riding with the snaffle, she will be ready for the **double bridle**, or **the curb-bit and bridoon**. The double bridle must be **held in the left hand** in the following manner: The *bridoon* or *snaffle-reins* are first to be taken up, evenly, by the right hand and then the second finger of the left hand be passed between these reins (the left rein being between the second and third fingers, and the right rein between the first and second), the back of the hand being directed somewhat upward, with the knuckles toward the horse's head; the reins should then be pulled up by the right hand just enough to feel the horse's mouth, and carried across the palm to the index finger, where they should be held in position by firm pressure with the thumb.

The *curb-reins* are now to be taken evenly by the right hand, and then the little finger of the left hand be passed between the two reins, the left rein being upon the left or outer side of the little finger, and the

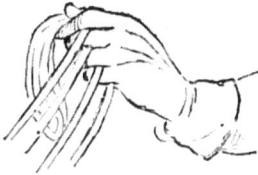

right rein between the little and third fingers; both curb-reins should next be drawn upward by the right hand until they are nearly the length of the snaffle, and carried across the palm, one rein overlying the other, to the index finger, between its first and second joints, and between the snaffle-reins and the thumb, at which point all the reins must be firmly held by pressure of the

FIG. 27—DOUBLE BRIDLE;
ALL REINS IN THE
BRIDLE-HAND

thumb against them; the right hand will now remove its hold. (Fig. 27.) The above manoeuvring of the reins will give the "original position" for the double bridle in the left hand. All these reins should be of nearly equal length, the snaffle being slightly the shortest, so that, while riding with the latter, the curb may be ready for instant use; this may be brought into play by simply turning the wrist so as to carry the little finger up and toward the waist. And the full power of the curb may be brought into action by turning the wrist so as to carry the knuckles down and the nails up, at the same time drawing the little finger toward the waist.

To shorten or lengthen both the curb and snaffle reins evenly without abandoning the horse to himself for a moment, or without ceasing to keep up his action, the following method may be pursued: The loose, disengaged ends of all the reins that extend beyond the index finger of the left hand must be taken between the thumb and forefinger of the right hand, care being taken during this manoeuvre to keep up the support to the horse with this hand; the grasp of the left hand upon the reins must now be sufficiently relaxed to allow this hand to slide along the reins downward to shorten them, or upward to lengthen them; this must be effected without deranging their adjustment; when the proper range has been obtained, remove the right hand.

To shorten the curb and lengthen the snaffle-reins: The loose, disengaged ends of all the reins must be held in the same manner as stated in the preceding paragraph, between the thumb and index finger of the right hand, not omitting to keep up a support to the horse; the grasp of the left hand must now be slightly relaxed, and this hand be slid up along all the reins, which movement will lengthen them in the left hand. The grasp of the right hand upon the snaffle-reins must now be relaxed, and the left hand be slid down along the curb-reins, carrying the snaffle-reins with it, until the proper range or distance has been attained, when the right hand may be removed. While these changes are being made, the right hand must sustain the horse by the curb-reins until the left has obtained a firm hold upon all.

To shorten the snaffle and lengthen the curb reins, a course similar to the one just preceding must be pursued, except that in this case the right hand must retain the snaffle-reins, and support the horse by them, while the left hand, in sliding down, will carry those of the curb.

In all these changes of the various reins, it must be remembered that after each change has been effected the reins must be held in place by firm pressure of the thumb, as already described.

When **either of the reins** held in the left hand **becomes loose**, it may be tightened, by carrying the right hand to and over the left one, seizing the loose rein by its disengaged end that hangs loosely from the left index finger, and drawing it up as far as is necessary. While this is being done, the left hand must not be removed from its position, and should continue to keep up a steady pressure upon the horse's mouth.

In requiring the horse **to stop, to back, to turn,** or **to advance,** the management of the double bridle-reins will be exactly the same as stated in the directions given when holding the snaffle-reins in the left hand.

When both **the curb and the snaffle reins** are held in the bridle-hand, they may be **changed to the right hand**, when this is desired, as follows: The right hand must be carried to the left; the second finger of the right hand must be placed between the snaffle-reins (already separated by the second finger of the left hand); and the little finger of the right hand between the curb-reins (already separated by the little finger of the left hand); this done, the thumb and fingers of the right hand must be closed upon the reins, which must, at the same time, be released by the left hand.

To restore these reins to the left hand, the pupil must proceed as follows: Carrying the left hand to the right, the second finger of the left hand must be placed between the snaffle-reins, and the little finger of this hand between the curb-reins; this having been done, the thumb and fingers must be closed upon all the reins, while the right hand releases its hold. These several changes can be made whether the horse be moving slowly or rapidly, care being taken to effect them so quietly that the horse will not be abandoned to himself from want of support, nor interrupted in the rhythm of his gait.

If when riding with the double bridle in the bridle-hand, very quick turns have to be made, or when the horse will not yield readily to the movements of the bridle-hand, it will become necessary to **separate the reins** by taking that of the right snaffle in the right hand; this can be quickly effected by carrying the right hand to and over the left, and seizing the right snaffle-rein with the first three fingers of the right hand; this rein will pass between the third and little fingers and across the palm, so that the loose, disengaged end will escape from between the thumb and forefinger.

In America, most lady riders prefer to guide the horse with the bridle-hand only; in doing this, although they may appear more careless and graceful, they certainly lose much command over the animal. The method at present employed by the best European horsewomen, who *seldom ride with the reins in the left hand alone*, is as follows: The little finger of the right hand is to be passed between the right curb and snaffle reins in such a way that the curb-rein will be on the outer side of this finger, and the snaffle between it and the third finger; both reins must then be carried across the palm, and be firmly held by the thumb against the forefinger. The little finger of the left hand is also to be passed between the left snaffle and curb reins, in a similar manner to that just described, and the reins must be held firm by the thumb and forefinger of this hand. (Fig. 28.) This arrangement may be termed the "original position" for a curb and snaffle rein in each hand.

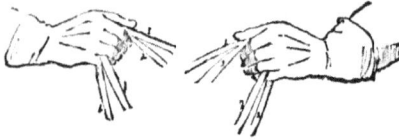

FIG. 28—DOUBLE BRIDLE; A SNAFFLE AND A CURB REIN IN EACH HAND

When the reins are thus separated, the action upon the horse's mouth will be much more powerful than when they are all placed in the bridle-hand. They should be held nearly even, the snaffle being somewhat shorter than the curb, so that the hold or pressure upon the animal's mouth may be made by the former; but should it be required on any occasion to employ the curb, this can be brought into instant use by a slight turn of the wrists, that will carry the little fingers up and toward the rider's waist. To *stop*, to *back*, to *turn*, or to *advance*, the reins must be managed in the same way as when one snaffle-rein alone is held in each hand. In all these various ways of holding the double bridle, the snaffle-reins should, as they pass upward from the bit, always be placed above those of the curb; indeed, it would be rather awkward to hold them otherwise.

As already stated, when the object for which any change of hands and reins has been made is effected, the hands should always resume the original position, as explained for the snaffle-reins when one is held in each hand,—thus, hands four inches from the body, four inches apart, etc. The arms and elbows must be kept as steady as possible, all movements of the reins being made with the wrists and fingers, unless the horse be hard mouthed or badly trained, when the arms will have to be employed and more force will be required. But a horse of this kind should never be ridden by a woman; and the directions herein given will be found amply sufficient to control a well-trained, properly-bitted animal.

The preceding directions relative to holding and managing the reins may appear very tedious and exceedingly complicated. But if the pupil, commencing with the snaffle-reins, one in each hand, will carefully study and practice each method in succession, she will soon find that all these apparently difficult manoeuvres are very simple when put into practice, and can be readily learned in half a dozen lessons. When she has once fully mastered them, she will be astonished to find how little management, when it is of the right kind and based upon correct principles, will be required to make her steed move in an easy and pleasant manner.

After the rein-hold has been acquired, and the pupil properly seated in the saddle, she will, if the reins are held steady, observe with each step of the horse as he advances in the canter or gallop, a slight tug or pull upon the reins. This pull will also be simultaneously felt by the horse's mouth, between which and the rider's hand or hands there will be what may be termed a **correspondence**. This correspondence gives a *support* to the horse, provided the rider, while maintaining an equal degree of tension upon the reins, will "**give and take**," or, in other words, will allow the movements of the bridle-hand to concur with those of this tug or pull. A *dead pull* may be made by bracing the muscles of the hand, tightly closing the fingers upon the reins, and holding the hand immovable; but this should never be done, except to convey some imperative command to the horse, or when he attempts to gain the ascendency. This kind of pull will interfere with the natural movements of the horse's head, making him move in a confined, irregular manner, and will oblige him to *force the rider's hand* or *hands*; that is, in order to relieve himself from this restraint, he will give a sudden downward jerk of his head, which may take the reins from her hands, unless she be upon her guard; or else he will move heavily upon his fore-legs, and make his rider support the weight of his head and neck.

Should the curb be used instead of the snaffle, the result may be still worse; because when the curb-reins are pulled upon, the port or arched part of the bit will come in contact with the roof of the animal's mouth, and will press upon it to a degree corresponding to the power used upon the reins, while the curb-chain will be forced against the lower jaw, and if this continual pressure or dead pull be kept up the animal will experience considerable pain. To relieve himself, he will suddenly throw his head either up or down and may even rear. In the latter case, if his rider does not instantly relax her hand, he will be apt to fall backward, which is one of the most serious accidents that can happen when riding. If this rigid pull upon the curb be continued, the horse will be certain, ultimately, to become hard mouthed, if not vicious. This is a reason why so many riders, though having the double bridle-reins, use only the snaffle, and allow the curb-reins to hang quite loosely, being afraid to employ them, as experience has taught them that this rigid hold upon the reins will be instantly resented by the horse. Hence the curb-reins appear to be attached to the head-gear of their horses more as an article of ornament than of utility.

In order that a lady's horse may move lightly and well upon his haunches, the curb will have to be employed occasionally to *collect* and *restrain* him; and when it is managed properly, he will advance in better style than when the snaffle alone is used. The snaffle will answer a better purpose when employed to guide the horse in turning completely around, or in movements to the right or to the left; while the curb will answer during a straightforward motion to keep the animal well up to his action and to bring out his best gait, as well as to collect and restrain him.

An easy "give and take" feeling can be effected by slightly loosening or opening the fingers of the bridle-hand or hands as the horse springs forward; as the hand feels the pull upon the reins, it must yield to this sensation, and will thus allow the animal liberty in his spring or advance movements. Then, as the action of the horse lessens or recedes, the reins will be felt to slacken, when the fingers should be closed, which will tighten the reins, support the animal, and keep him under control. This "give and take" movement should occur alternately and simultaneously with the cadence of each step of the steed, and should be effected without any backward or forward movements of the arm or arms, which must be held steady,—except in a rapid gallop, in which case both the hand and arm will, to a certain extent, have to move to and fro. In the "give and take" movement the reins should not be allowed to slip in the slightest degree, nor to be jerked from the rider's hand by any sudden motion of the horse's head; on the contrary, they should always be held firm between the thumb and the first and second joints of the index finger, the *other fingers alone* performing the alternate action of loosening and tightening the reins.

The reader will be better enabled to understand this explanation if she will take a piece of elastic, pass it around her right hand, which will correspond to the horse's mouth, and then hold the two ends in her left hand, exactly in the manner explained for holding the double bridle-reins in one hand. Now, by making tension on the elastic (or reins) with the left hand, so that the right (or supposed horse's mouth) can just feel this pressure, a *correspondence* will be formed between these two hands (or bridle-hand and supposed horse's mouth) through which the slightest movement of the left hand, or of its second, third, or fourth fingers, will be immediately felt by the right hand; then, while holding the elastic (or reins) firmly, by pressure, between the thumb and index finger, by alternately opening and closing the fingers of the left hand, she will observe that when her fingers are closed there will be quite a tension upon the elastic and consequently upon the right hand, and when they are slightly opened this will become flaccid. The relaxation and contraction of the hand constitutes the "give and take" movement, which causes the horse to move easily, pleasantly, and with perfect freedom, while at the same time he is kept in entire obedience to his rider. Indeed, this movement is *the grand secret of good riding and correct management of the horse, and there can be no good riding without it.*

With this movement there should always be a certain support or pull upon the horse's mouth,— firmer or lighter according to the sensitiveness of his mouth, as some animals are harder mouthed than others, and consequently require a firmer support;—this tension or pressure should be rather light in the walk and canter, firmer in the trot, and very light in the hand gallop. In the rapid gallop, the horse requires considerable support.

In all cases of *restiveness*, except in rearing, raising the bridle-hands will give more command over the horse, as it will cause him to keep up his head, and thus while lessening the power of the animal will at the same time add to that of the rider. On the contrary, should the horse lower his head, and the bridle-hands be held low, the power of the animal will be augmented and he can bid defiance to his rider, unless she can raise his head. She will have to do this in a gentle but firm manner, soliciting, as it were, the desired elevation of his head by raising her hands and quickly relaxing and contracting the fingers, but being careful to keep the reins in place between the thumb and index finger of each hand; she will thus gradually oblige him to raise his neck with his chin drawn in, so that control over his mouth may be regained.

Should he resist this method, the reins must be momentarily slackened, and then a decided jerk or pull be given them in an upward direction; this will cause a sharp twinge in his mouth, and make him raise his head. In these manoeuvres the curb-bit should be used, and as the animal raises his head the rider should gently relax the reins, and also be on her guard lest he rear. In some instances a decided "sawing" of his mouth with the snaffle—that is, sharply pulling upon one rein and then upon the other, and in rather quick succession—will cause him to raise his head and neck.

When a horse is obedient, all changes in the degree of pressure upon his mouth should be made gradually, because, if a sudden transition be made from a firm hand to a relaxed one, he will be abruptly deprived of the support upon which he has been depending and may be thrown forward on his shoulders. Again, to pass precipitately from a slack rein to a tight one will give a violent shock to his mouth, cause him to displace his head, and destroy the harmony of his movements. As a means of punishment, some riders jerk suddenly, repeatedly, and violently upon the reins; this "jagging on the reins" is a great mistake, and will be likely to result in more harm to the rider than to the horse, as the latter may suddenly rear, or else have a bad temper aroused that will be difficult to overcome.

When riding on the road there will be times when the horse will require more liberty of the reins, as, for instance, when his head or neck becomes uncomfortable from being kept too long in one position, when he has an attack of cough, when he wants to dislodge a troublesome fly, etc. In giving this liberty when occasion requires, the reins must not be allowed to slip through the hands, but the arms should be gradually advanced, without, however, inclining the body forward.

The movements of the body must correspond with those of the horse and of the rider's hands; thus, when the animal is moving regularly and straight forward, the hands, or bridle-hand, being held firm and steady immediately in front of the waist, the body must then be seated squarely, with its front part to the front, so that the rider can look directly between the ears of her steed. When the animal turns completely around to the right or to the left, the shoulders and head of the rider must also turn a little toward the direction taken by the horse, while the hand must be slightly carried in an opposite direction. When turning a corner, the entire body from the hips upward must incline toward the centre of the circle of which the turn forms an arc, or, in other words, the body must incline toward the direction taken by the horse, and the degree of this inclination must be proportioned to the bend of the horse's body, and to the rapidity of his pace while turning.

When the horse advances, and the hands are relaxed, the body must momentarily lean slightly forward without rounding the shoulders; this will aid the horse in commencing his forward movement. In stopping him, the rider's body must be inclined slightly backward as the hands rein him in. All these movements should be made gradually, and never abruptly.

When a horse stumbles, or plunges from viciousness or high spirits, the rider's body must be inclined backward, as this will enable her to maintain her balance more effectually as well as to throw more weight upon the reins. On the contrary, when he rears the bridle-hand must be instantly advanced or relaxed, the body at the same time being inclined well forward, which will throw the rider's weight upon the animal's shoulders and fore-legs, and cause him to lower his fore-feet to the ground.

A horse is said to be **united** or **collected** when he moves easily in a regular, stylish manner, well on his haunches, with head and neck in proper position, his rider exercising perfect control over him by gentle pressure upon his mouth, and keeping up the regular movements of the animal by a quiet and dexterous "give and take" action of her hands.

He is **disunited** when he moves in an irregular manner, or heavily upon his fore-legs, occasioning the rider to support the weight of his neck and shoulders; also, when the reins are too slack and exercise no pressure upon his mouth, in which case, having no aid or support from his rider's hand, he will move carelessly, or exactly as he pleases.

In **collecting a horse**, the aid of the whip and the left leg will frequently be required, as the rider's hand alone may not be sufficient. In such a case, the left leg must be lightly pressed against his left side and the whip at the same time be pressed against his right side; these in conjunction with the action of the bridle-hand,[5] as heretofore explained, will collect him and bring him up to his bridle with his haunches well under him,—the proper position for starting. As soon as he moves there should be only a light pressure on his mouth. In order to perform the above feat effectively, the whip must not be too limber and must always be held with its lash downward. This simultaneous pressure of the whip and left leg has the same effect in collecting the horse as that of the horseman's right and left legs. Should the horse flag in his movements or move heavily upon his fore-legs, a repetition of this pressure of the leg and whip, in conjunction with the proper movements of the bridle-hand, will bring him well on his haunches and lighten his action.

The horse is always animated by mild taps of the whip, light pressure of the hand upon the curb, a clacking of the tongue, or an urging tone of his mistress's voice. He is soothed and rendered confident by mild and encouraging tones of voice, by the rider's sitting easily, by a gentle hold upon the reins, and by caressing pats upon his neck and shoulders.

In the directions given in this chapter, necessarily involving more or less repetition, the author has endeavored to be as clear, comprehensible, and simple as possible. And the rider will find it of much greater advantage to have these instructions printed, than to be required to learn them orally, as she can read and re-read them at pleasure and have them thoroughly committed to memory before mounting her horse. And, although it has required many pages to present these instructions

---

5   The bridle-hand being in the *original position* for the double bridle, the curb should be brought into action by a turn of the wrist, which will carry the little finger in toward the waist; and this, in conjunction with the leg and whip, will collect the horse.

to the reader, she will find that their application will prove very simple, and will also be agreeably surprised to observe the great control she will have over the feelings and movements of her steed through their agency. Horses are generally very sagacious, and appear to recognize promptly any timidity, awkwardness, or ignorance on the part of their riders, and, according to their temper or disposition, will take advantage of such recognition, either by advancing carelessly or by manifesting trickiness or viciousness. The best trained horse always requires to be kept under command, but by kind treatment and correct management. The horse, when ridden by a finished horsewoman, knows that although allowed to move with a light rein he is under the control of a masterly hand that will aid him in his efforts to please, but will instantly bring him into submission if he does not yield entire obedience.

CHAPTER VII
THE WALK

"And do you not love at evening's hour,
By the light of the sinking sun,
To wend your way o'er the widening moor,
Where the silvery mists their mystery pour,
While the stars come one by one?
Over the heath by the mountain's side,
Pensive and sweet is the evening's ride."

E. PAXTON HOOD.

IN WALKING, THE horse moves nearly simultaneously the two legs that are diagonally opposite to each other, first one pair, and then the other. Thus, the right fore and the left hind leg make one step nearly at the same time, and when these have touched the ground, the left fore and the right hind leg are raised and advanced in a similar manner, and so on in succession. In this manner as one pair of legs moves onward the other pair sustains the weight of the animal; and of the two legs that act together the fore one is raised from as well as placed upon the ground slightly previous to the hind one. This is the reason why a horse which walks well and in a regular manner will nearly or quite cover the foot-marks of his fore-feet with those of his hind ones. If the hind-foot should fall short of covering the track of the fore one, the animal will not be a good walker; if, on the contrary, it should pass somewhat beyond the mark of the fore-foot, it will indicate him to be a fast walker, although he may overreach.

In both the walk and the trot, when the horse is moving regularly, a quick ear can detect four distinct beats or tappings of the feet; when these beats mark equal time and sound exactly alike for each footstep, it may be inferred that the horse is a good walker as well as a good trotter, and that all his legs are sound. But if one beat be lighter than the

others, it may be assumed that there is some disease in the foot or leg
that produces this beat. Horse-dealers will often endeavor to disguise
this defect by adopting means to disable the animal temporarily in his
healthy leg, as the treads will then be made more nearly alike, though
the slight shade of difference thus effected can be readily detected by a
quick, experienced ear. These hoof-beats are best heard when made on
a hard road.

A horse that is a good walker will move with a quick step, his hind-
legs well under him, his foot taps marking regular time, and his feet
measuring exact distances, while he will lift his feet just high enough
to escape obstructions on the road, thrusting each foot well forward,
and placing it lightly, though firmly and squarely, upon the ground. He
will advance in a straight line, vacillating neither to the right nor left,
and should be able to accomplish at least from four to four and a half
miles per hour.

The walk of a lady's horse is almost always neglected, and as a good
walk is a sure foundation for perfection in all other gaits, a lady should
positively insist that her steed be thoroughly trained in this particular;
especially if she be large and majestic looking, because the walk will
then become her specialty. A stout woman does not ride to the best
advantage at a rapid gait, but upon a horse that has the walk in perfection she presents an imposing, queen-like appearance. If her steed,
however, be allowed to saunter along in a careless, listless manner, all
the charm will be destroyed, and the *tout ensemble* will present by no
means a pleasing picture.

The beginner in riding should learn to sit and manage her horse in
a walk, and should never attempt to ride a faster gait until she can collect her steed, make him advance, turn him to the right and to the left,
and rein him back; this last movement is a very important one, with
which few teachers strive to make their pupils thoroughly acquainted.
Reining back will not only bring the horse under better command,
but, with a lady's horse, a short reining back from time to time will
improve his style of motion in his various gaits; besides which, the rider
may on some occasion be placed in a situation in which, for her own
safety, she will be compelled to move her horse backward.

To begin the walk: The pupil, having placed herself in the saddle,
must not allow her horse to move until she is quite prepared, her skirt

adjusted, and the whip and reins properly arranged in her hands. Then, drawing gently upon the curb and snaffle reins, a little more upon the former than upon the latter, and at the same time gently pressing against the animal's side with her left leg, and against his right side with the whip, as heretofore explained, she will thus *collect her horse*, and start him upon the walk. As soon as he has begun to move forward, the pressure of the leg and whip must cease, and the hand or hands must be held steady on the snaffle, the curb no longer being required, unless the animal flags in his movements. The hold upon the snaffle must be only tense enough to enable the rider to feel the beat of the horse's action as he places each foot upon the ground, and to give him a slight support and keep up an even action. Should this support be too heavy, his step will be shortened, and he will be unable to move freely; should it be insufficient, he will carry his head low, will not raise his feet high enough to escape stumbling, will knock his toes against every inequality of the ground, and both he and his rider will present an indolent and listless aspect. Her attitude should be easy and erect, but she should yield herself slightly to the movements of the horse although without showing any lack of steadiness. (Fig. 29.)

Should the horse be too much animated by the reins and whip at the commencement of the walk, he may enter upon a jog trot, or an amble, in which case he must be checked by gradually reining him in until he has settled into a walk. Should he, on the contrary, not be sufficiently animated, he will not exert himself and will move in an irregular and indolent manner; in this case, he must be made to raise his head by a slight pull upon the curb-reins, as already explained, and be again collected and animated by the aid of the leg and whip.

A short, abrupt **turn in the walk** should never be made, if it can possibly be avoided; it is only in case of emergency that it should be attempted, and even then it is more or less dangerous, because, as the horse moves his legs diagonally in the walk, he may, when abruptly turned, place one leg in the way of the other, be thrown off his balance, and fall. When turning a horse completely around, it should always be done in a deliberate manner. This rule should never be forgotten, especially by a novice.

During her first lessons in the walk, the pupil, in attempting to turn her horse to the right, to the left, or completely around, must move him very slowly, pressing her whip and left leg against his sides, and keeping him well-balanced by proper support upon *both* snaffle-reins. In making a **turn to the right**, with a snaffle-rein in each hand, the left hand must not abandon the horse, but retain a steady pressure upon his mouth, while the tension upon the right rein must be increased by moving the right hand and its little finger up and toward the body, at the same time holding this hand a little lower than the left one. The tension upon the right rein should be nearly double that made upon the left, and should be kept up until the turn has been completed. In the turn to the right, the left leg should make a little stronger pressure than that made by the whip, to prevent the animal from throwing his croup too far to the left; and in making the turn to the left, the whip should press more strongly than the leg, in order to prevent the croup from being carried too far to the right.

In attempting **to turn** completely around **to the left**, the same manoeuvring, though in an opposite direction, will be required; the above directions for the two hands being simply reversed.

Should the horse fail to turn in a regular manner, or refuse to obey the reins readily, he must be collected, and brought up to the bridle in the manner already described. This will cause him to raise his head and place himself in a position to move in the required manner, and when this is done the rider must slacken the tension upon the curb, and turn him with the snaffle-rein.

In making these turns, care must be taken to have ample space, and it must not be forgotten, that while increasing the tension upon the rein required to direct the turn, the other should not be slackened or abandoned, but should continue to give support to the horse, though in a less degree; and also that this tension upon the reins is much more important when making a partial or complete turn, than when the animal is moving forward in a straight line. For, if the reins be slackened, and the horse left to himself, he will turn in an awkward manner, may get one leg in the way of the other, and perhaps stumble or fall, especially if the ground be slippery, or rough and uneven.

It is a habit with many lady riders, as well as with multitudes of horsemen, to make the turn by carrying the bridle-hand in the direction of the turn, thus pressing the outward rein, or the one opposite to the direction of the turn, against the horse's neck,—the inward

FIG. 29—THE WALK

rein being completely slackened. This is a very dangerous fault and one that instantly betrays ignorance of correct horsemanship, because the animal is thus left without any support at a time when it is most needed. If a rider has any regard for her own safety, she will remember this very important rule, namely, *to support the horse on both reins when making a turn.*

When all the reins are held in the bridle-hand and a turn is to be made to the left, the fault is sometimes committed of carrying the right hand over to assist the left by pulling upon the left rein; this is frequently done by ladies who have not been properly instructed, and gives them an awkward appearance. When riding with the double bridle in the bridle-hand, if the movements of the horse be controlled by this hand and wrist, as explained in the preceding chapter, the turn to the right or to the left can be effected without abandoning the horse by relaxing one of the reins, and also without the assistance of the other hand. These manoeuvres, accomplished easily and gracefully, indicate the well-instructed and correct bridle-hand, the well-trained horse, and the accomplished horsewoman, who will appear to manage her steed more by mental influence than by any perceptible movements of her hands.

To **stop in the walk**, in a correct and regular manner, is a sure criterion of a good horsewoman, one that has her steed under complete control, for this stop renders him more obedient, and tends to collect him and to bring his haunches into a pliant condition. To accomplish this stop properly, the rider must brace her arms firmly against her sides,—being careful not to let her elbows protrude backward,—throw her shoulders back, hold both reins evenly and firmly, and tighten the tension upon them by turning the hand and little fingers up and carrying them toward the waist, at the same time not omitting to press gently against the horse's sides with the leg and whip. All this should be accomplished by one simultaneous movement, and the degree of tension made on the reins should be in proportion to the sensitiveness of the horse's mouth.

If the left leg and whip be not employed in making the stop, the horse when brought to a stand may throw his weight upon his shoulders and fore-legs,—which he should never be allowed to do, as it will destroy the pleasing effect of the stop, and cause him to become disunited. The animal should be so nicely balanced upon his haunches when he stops, that, with a little more liberty of rein, he can readily move forward in a united and collected manner. The reins must not be abruptly jerked, but be drawn upon, as stated before, in a gradual and equal manner. After the stop is completed, the reins may be so far relaxed as to enable the horse to again advance, should it be required. The stop should always be made when the animal is advancing straight forward, and never, if it can possibly be avoided, when making a turn or going around a corner.

If, when attempting to stop the horse, he should *toss up his head*, the bridle-hand must be kept low and firm, and the right hand be pressed against his neck until his head is lowered, when the rein-hold may be relaxed. In such a case, the rider must be on her guard, as a horse which stops in this manner may rear, when she must immediately yield the reins.

The stop, especially in rapid gaits and when effected suddenly, is very trying to the horse; it should therefore be made only when necessary, and never to display the rider's superior command and excellent horsewomanship; many horses, particularly those having weak loins, have been caused much suffering and have had their dispositions completely ruined by a too frequent and injudicious practice of the stop.

In reining back or **backing in the walk**, the horse bends his haunches and places one of his hind legs under his body, upon which to rest and balance himself; this enables him to collect force to impel his croup backward. To favor this movement, the horse must be collected, brought to stand square and even on his fore-legs, and then be reined backward by a firm, steady, and equal pull upon both the right and left snaffle-reins.[6] The hands should be held low and directly in front of the body, with the knuckles down, and the little fingers turned up and carried toward the body. During this whole movement care must be taken not to elevate the hands. The body of the rider must bend somewhat forward, with the waist drawn in, but without any rounding of the shoulders, while the leg and the whip must make gentle pressure against the horse's sides, so as to "bring him up to the

---

6   If the horse be tender in the mouth the snaffle-reins had better be used in backing; if not, the curb.

bridle," and prevent his deviating from the line in which it is desired to back him. The backing must never be made by one continuous pull; but as soon as the movement is commenced, the hands and body of the rider must yield so that the horse may regain his balance, after which he may again be urged backward. These actions should occur alternately, so that with every step backward the rider will yield her hands, and immediately draw them back again, continuing these movements until the horse has backed as far as desired. If, instead of this course, a steady pull be made, the horse may lose his balance and fall, or may be compelled to rear.

When reining the horse back the body must never be inclined backward, as is necessary when stopping the horse; on the contrary, it must always be inclined somewhat forward, as this will enable the hands to manage the reins more effectively, will give the horse more freedom to recede, and, should he rear, will place the rider in the proper balance. Should the rider unfortunately incline her body backward, and the horse rear, she would probably be unseated, and should she pull upon the reins in order to sustain herself and keep her seat, the animal would be drawn backward, and probably fall upon her.

In backing, the pull upon the reins must never be made suddenly, but always gradually, the hand rather soliciting than compelling. When the reins are suddenly pulled upon, the horse is very apt to get his hind-legs too far forward under him, in which case it is impossible for him to move backward.

In reining the horse directly backward, should his croup move out of line to the right, the pressure of the whip must be increased, or gentle taps be given with it upon his right side back of the saddle-flap, the hand at the same time increasing the tension upon the right rein. The taps of the whip must be very light, lest the animal turn too much to the left.

Should the croup swerve to the left, the rider must press her left leg against her horse's side, or give light taps with her left heel upon his side, turning the point of the toe out, moving the leg a little back, and slightly separating the knee from the side of the saddle, in order to give these taps; at the same time she must increase the tension upon the left rein until the horse is brought into line.

When it is desired to rein back, but with an inclination to the right, a slight extra bearing or pull must be made upon the left rein, without relaxing the steady tension upon the right one. A pressure with the whip upon the right side of the horse must at the same time be kept up, in order that he may not carry his croup too far to the right.

In reining back with an inclination to the left, the pull upon the right rein must be slightly increased, still keeping a steady feeling upon the left one; then, by a constant pressure with the left leg upon the horse's side, he will be prevented from carrying his croup too far to the left. Reining back teaches the horse to move lightly, and improves the style of his different gaits, but its effect is very severe upon him, hence its practice should not be too frequent, and always of short duration.

CHAPTER VIII
THE TROT, THE AMBLE, THE PACE, THE RACK

"We ride and ride. High on the hills
The fir-trees stretch into the sky;
The birches, which the deep calm stills,
Quiver again as we speed by."

OWEN INNSLY.

I N THE TROT, the horse moves his legs in the same diagonal manner as in the walk, the only difference being that in the trot they are moved more rapidly. When trotting regularly and evenly, the right fore-foot and the left hind-foot strike the ground nearly simultaneously, and then the left fore-foot and the right hind-foot do the same; and so on alternately, two legs being diagonally upon the ground at about the same moment, while two legs are raised in the air.

The strokes of the hoofs upon the ground are called "beats," and are loud and quick, harmonizing with the animal's rapidity of motion and length of step. The trot is the safest gait for a rider if the horse be free from any defect in his limbs, as he will be less apt to stumble; it is also less tiresome for the animal, because while two legs are diagonally off the ground, the other two support the weight of his body, and thus one pair alternately and quickly relieves the other.

There are three varieties of trot, namely, the jog trot, the flying or racing trot, and the true or even trot. In the *jog trot* each foot is placed nearly in the same track it occupied before it was raised, though somewhat in advance of it, and it remains upon the ground a longer time than when raised in the air, thus rendering the gait almost as slow as the walk. If the horse be young and spirited, he will prefer this gait to that of the walk, and, if permitted, will naturally adopt it. This should be guarded against, and under no circumstances should he be allowed to break into a jog trot; because, however accomplished the rider may be, she will find it a very unpleasant and excessively fatiguing gait, and one which will make her look very awkward. This variety of trot, however, occasions less injury to the horse's feet and legs than any other gait, and, on this account, it is preferred by most farmers.

In the *racing* or *flying trot*, the horse is allowed to step out without the least constraint, the legs being extended as far as possible, and moving straight forward, while the animal spiritedly enters into the occasion and gives out his full power. In this trot all the legs are moved very rapidly, and the hind ones with more force than the fore-legs, in order that the horse's body may, with each bound, be propelled as far forward as possible. Between the two successive bounds all four legs are momentarily off the ground. Very springy fetlocks tend to diminish speed in the flying trot, and hence, not having such elastic fetlocks, a good trotting racer is rough in his action and an undesirable saddle-horse.

In the *true* or *even trot*, the action of the horse is regular, all his limbs moving in an even manner, his feet measuring exact distances, his hoof-beats being in equal time of *one, two, three, four*, and his feet, when moving rapidly, touching the ground only for an instant. There are two ways in which this trot may be ridden: one is to sit closely to the saddle, moving as little as possible, and making no effort to avoid the roughness of the gait. This is the method practiced by the cavalry of this country, as well as by the armies in Europe, and is called the "cavalry" or "French trot."

The other method is to relieve the joltings by rising in the saddle in time with the horse's step. This is called the "English trot," and is the favorite gait of the European and the American civilian horsemen. It is only during the last few years that this trot has been gradually coming into favor with American horsewomen, although the ladies of England, and of nearly all continental Europe, have for a long time ridden this gait as well as the canter and hand gallop, having found that by alternating the latter gaits with the trot they could ride greater distances upon hard roads, and with much less fatigue to themselves and their steeds. The English trot does not wear out the horse so quickly as the gallop and canter; indeed, it has been generally found that the horse's trot improves as he grows older, many horses having become better trotters at their tenth or twelfth year than at an earlier age. The trot in which the hoof-beats are in time of only *one, two,* is very difficult to ride.

In America, many persons condemn the English trot for lady riders, which is hardly to be wondered at when one observes the various awkward and grotesque attitudes that are assumed, even by many gentlemen, when attempting to rise in the saddle. As for the ladies who have undertaken this innovation, their appearance on horseback, from want of proper training or from lack of attention to given rules, has, with but few exceptions, been simply ridiculous. Even with correct teaching and proper application, some ladies, although they acquire the English trot, and do not make caricatures of themselves while employing it, yet do not appear to such advantage as when in the canter or hand gallop. This is also the case with European ladies, who differ very much in their power to make this gait appear graceful. A small, slightly built person, having a short measurement from the hip to the knee, can, when correctly taught, ride this trot with much ease and grace. A tall woman will have to lean too far forward with each rising movement of her steed, as her length of limb will not permit a short rise; she will therefore appear to much less advantage in this gait; while a stout built person will look rather heavy in the rise from the saddle.

However, whether a lady is likely to present an elegant appearance or not when riding the English trot, she must, if she desires to become an accomplished horsewoman, learn to ride this particular gait, as it will enable her to gain a correct seat, to keep a better and more perfect balance, and to become more thorough in the other gaits. From a hygienic point of view, it will prove beneficial, and will preserve both rider and horse from excessive fatigue when traveling long distances. Under certain circumstances, it will also enable a lady to ride a man's horse, which will be very apt to have this trot in perfection, and but little knowledge of, or training in, any other gaits. In the country a regular and sure trotting horse may often be readily obtained, while it will be much more difficult to procure one with a light, easy canter or gallop. This trot, when well cadenced and in perfect time, is very captivating, as the rider escapes all jolting, and feels more as if she were flying through the air than riding upon a horse.

There is, however, one objection to the English trot to which attention should be directed; namely, if the lady ride on a two-pommeled saddle, and the horse happens to shy, or to turn around suddenly, while she is in the act of rising, she is very likely to be unseated or thrown from her horse. With the three-pommeled saddle, however, this accident will be much less liable to occur, but the lady should always be on her guard when riding this trot, especially if her steed be nervous; and to avoid an accident of the kind just named, she should keep her left knee directly under the third pommel, but without pressing up against it enough to interfere with the rising motion, or just so close, that in pressing upon the stirrup and straightening her knee she can rise about four inches from the saddle; the distance between the upper surface of the knee and the under surface of the pommel will then be about one and a half, or two inches. If, in the rise, she does not find herself embarrassed by the third pommel, she may know that the stirrup leather is of the correct length for this trot. The more rapid and regular the trot, the easier and shorter will be the rise, and the less noticeable the movements of the rider, because, when trotting fast, the rise will be effected with but very little effort on her part, and will be almost entirely due to the rapid action of the horse. To rise when trotting slowly, will be neither easy nor pleasant for the rider, and in this gait she will not appear to much advantage.

In the **French** or **cavalry trot**, the body should be inclined a little backward, being kept as firm as possible but without stiffness, while at the same time the rider should sit as closely to the saddle as she can, with the left knee directly under the third pommel, not using force to press up against it, but simply holding it there to sustain the limb and to assist in keeping it as firm and steady as possible during the roughness of this gait—while the reins should be held a little firmer than for the walk. This trot should never be ridden by ladies after their first lessons in riding, unless the horse moves so easily in it that his rider is not jolted in the least. To trot so softly that no shock will be experienced by the rider as the horse's feet touch the ground will require a thorough-bred of rare formation.

Before the invention of the three-pommeled saddle the French trot was always employed in the best riding-schools, a beginner being required to practice it for a long time, in order to acquire the proper firmness in the saddle; but since the invention of the third pommel the cavalry trot has been almost entirely dispensed with, as this pommel at once gives a firmness of seat that could be obtained on an old-fashioned two-pommeled saddle only after taking many fatiguing lessons in the French trot. It was this fatigue that caused so many persons to condemn horseback riding for ladies, and it also proved a cause of discouragement to the pupils in the riding-school, frequently giving rise to a decided dislike for horseback exercise. But since the employment of the third pommel, it is only necessary for the pupil to take two or three lessons in the French trot, just enough to enable her to understand the movement, after which she may proceed to rise in the English style. However, a knowledge of the cavalry trot will be found useful, as a horse, when reined in from a gallop or canter, will often trot a short distance before stopping; and if the rider understands this trot, she will be able to sit close to the saddle, and not appear awkward by jolting helplessly about.

Of all the styles of riding, there is none so difficult to describe or to learn as the **English trot**. We will make an effort, however, to render it comprehensible to the reader. Considerable study and practice will be required to learn it perfectly, but when once learned it will indicate the thoroughly accomplished horsewoman. (Fig. 30.)

To commence the English trot, the rider must collect her horse, as for the walk, and then, as he advances, keep a firm, even tension upon the *snaffle-reins*, because, in this trot, the animal will rely wholly upon his rider to support him and hold him to the pace, without the "give and take" movements of the hands required in the other gaits. It is not meant by this that a dead pull is to be made, but that the support must be firm and steady, with a proper correspondence between the bridle-hand and the horse's mouth. The elbows must be held steady and lightly near the rider's sides, but not close against them. As the horse extends his trot, an unpleasant roughness or jolting will be experienced, which will give an upward impetus to the rider's body; the moment she is conscious of this impetus, she must allow herself to be raised from her horse in regular time with his step or hoof-beats. In this trot, the horse will always have a leading foot, either the right or left, and the foot he leads with is the one to which the rider must rise,—rising when the leading foot is lifted, and touching the saddle when this foot touches the ground. Most riders do this instinctively, as it were, rising and falling with the leading foot.

FIG. 30—THE TROT

In *this rise* the action of the horse alone will give the impetus; no effort must be made by the lady, *except* to press slightly, or rather to sustain herself gently upon the stirrup, and keep her knee and instep yielding and flexible with the rise. Care must be taken not to allow the leg to swing forward and backward. The rise should be made as straight upward as possible, the upper part of the body inclining forward no more than is necessary to effect the rise with ease. The back must be kept well curved, and the shoulders square to the front of the horse, without lifting them up, or rounding them in rising.

The **leading foot of the horse** is that fore-foot or leg with which he commences his advance in the gait; it will always be carried somewhat beyond its fellow, while, at the same time, that side of the animal's body which corresponds with the leading foot will be a little more advanced toward this foot, though almost imperceptibly so. Every rider should be taught to know with which foot her horse leads.

When a horse trots evenly and quickly, and with rather a short step, the rise in the saddle will be barely perceptible; but when he trots slowly and with a long step, the rise will have to be higher, in order that the rider may keep time with the slowness and length of his step. In this gait a tall woman will be very apt to prefer a long step to a short one.

In making the rise, the rider must never assist herself by pulling upon the reins, which should be held firm and low to give support *to the horse alone*, not allowing them to slip in the least from between the thumb and forefinger that should hold them steady.

The descent of the body to the saddle must be effected as gently as possible. The right knee should be pressed against the second pommel, and the left foot lean lightly upon the stirrup, the left foot and instep being kept yielding and flexible with the descent, and the body and right leg bearing[7] a little to the right. The descent should be made just in time to catch the next impetus of the horse's movement, so that the saddle will be hardly touched before the rider's body will again be thrown upward to make the rise.

---

7   By "bearing to the right" is not meant an inclination of the body to this side, but a resistance sufficient to keep the body from inclining toward the left. As hereafter stated, trotting in a circle to the *right* will be found an excellent exercise to teach one this bearing.

It presents a very comical and inelegant appearance for a rider, whether man or woman, when attempting the rising trot, to elevate and protrude the shoulders, curve the back out so as to round it, lean forward toward the horse's ears, with elbows sticking out from the rider's sides and flopping like the wings of a restless bird, while the body is bobbing up and down like a dancing jack, out of all time with the movements of the animal. One reason why some persons are so awkward in the rise is that they sit too far back upon the saddle. This obliges them to sustain themselves upon the stirrup obliquely, thus causing them to lean too far forward in order to accomplish the rise more easily. Another cause of awkwardness in the rising trot is an improperly constructed saddle. The seat or platform should be as nearly level as a properly made saddle will permit. When the front part or arch is much higher than the seat, it will be difficult to use the second pommel as a point of support for the right knee, which support is highly essential during the descent, in this trot. It is a common thing to see riders exaggerate the rise by pressing hard upon the stirrup and supporting themselves by the reins, thus rising higher than necessary, and coming down with a heavy thump upon the saddle; to which equestrian gymnastics they give the name of "English trot."

When rising and descending in the English trot, the left leg, from knee to instep, must be held perpendicular and steady; the foot, from toe to heel, must rest horizontally in the stirrup, and in a line with the horse's side. The foot should not be allowed to turn out, nor the leg to swing backward and forward: if the foot be pointed out, this will tend to carry the body and leg too much toward the left, on the rise; and, if the leg be allowed to swing, it will cause the rider to lose the rhythm of the trot. Again, the stirrup must not be too strongly pressed upon, as this will throw all the rider's weight upon the left side, and may cause the saddle to turn. On making the rise, great care must be taken not to advance the left shoulder, nor to turn the body to the left; many riders do these things with the idea that they will enable them to rise with more ease. But this is an error, for such movements will not only occasion fatigue, but will also render the rein-hold unsteady, and the action of the foot and knee uncertain. The body and shoulders must always be square to the front when the horse is trotting straight forward, the body remaining as erect as the action of the horse will allow.

To stop a well-trained horse **in this gait**, it will simply be necessary for the rider to cease rising, sit down to the saddle, and gradually loosen the reins. Many horses, however, are trained to make the stop in the usual way, by having the reins tightened. The advance and the turns are to be conducted in the same manner as that described for the walk.

In the English trot, the horse must be kept well up to his gait; should he appear to move heavily or disunitedly the reins must be gradually shortened, and the animal be collected. Should he step short, in a constrained manner, the reins must be gradually lengthened, to give him more freedom. If he break into a gallop when it is desired that he should trot, he must be gradually reined in to a walk, and then be started again upon a trot, and this course must be repeated until he obeys, stopping him every time he attempts to gallop, and then starting the trot anew. If he trot too rapidly, he must be checked, by bracing the bridle-hand and increasing the pull upon the reins. If the trot be too slow, the hand must relax the reins a little, and the horse be animated by the voice, and by gentle taps with the whip. To regulate the trot, to keep it smooth and harmonious, to rein in the horse gently without rendering him unsteady, and then gradually to yield the hand so that he may move forward again in a regular manner, are very difficult points for beginners to accomplish while still keeping up the proper support upon the bit, and will require study and considerable practice.

A horse should never be urged into a more rapid trot than he can execute in an even, regular manner; if compelled to exceed this, he will break into a rough gallop, or into such an irregular trot as will render it impossible for the rider to time the rise.

An accomplished horsewoman, when trotting her horse, will make no observable effort, and there will be perfect harmony between her steed and herself. When the English trot is ridden in this manner, the person who can condemn it must, indeed, be extremely fastidious. However, it must be acknowledged that it will require the lithe, charming figure of a young lady to exhibit its best points, and to execute it in its most pleasing and graceful style. The very tall, the inactive, or the stout lady may ride this gait with ease to herself and horse, and when properly taught will not render herself awkward or ridiculous, but she can never ride it with the willowy grace of the slender woman of medium size.

Trotting in a circle may be practiced in a riding-school, or upon a level, open space or ground, having a circular track about seventy-five or eighty feet in diameter. It is very excellent practice, especially in teaching the rider to rise in unison with the horse's trot, whether he leads with the right or left leg. For first lessons, the pupil must commence by circling to the right, as this is the easiest to learn, and will teach her to bear toward the right side of the horse. It is very essential that in first lessons she should do this; because in the English trot she will have to guard carefully against inclining to the left in the rise and descent, a fault common to all beginners who are not better instructed.

In circling, the horse will always incline toward the centre of the circle, with which inclination the rider's body must correspond, by leaning in the same direction; if this precaution should be neglected and the horse be trotting rapidly, the rider will lose her balance, and fall off on the side opposite to that of the inclination. The distance she should lean to the right or to the left must be in proportion to the size of the circle that is being passed over, and also to the inward bearing of the horse's body. Should the circle be small and the gait rapid, the inclination of the rider's body will have to be considerable to enable her to maintain her seat and keep in unison with the horse. If the circle be large, say eighty feet in diameter, the inclination will be slight.

In order to *circle to the right*, when holding a curb and a snaffle rein in each hand, the pupil must collect her horse by the aid of curb, leg, and whip, as already explained, and start him forward on the snaffle, holding the right rein a little lower than the left, and drawing it enough to enable her to see plainly the corner of his right eye; the reins must be held steadily, no sudden jerks being given to them, as these will cause the horse to move irregularly and swerve about. Should his croup be turned too much to the right, the pressure of the whip will bring it to the left; if it be turned too much to the left, the pressure of the left leg will bring it to the right.

In *circling to the left*, the horse will incline his body to the left, toward the centre of the circle. It is not very easy to learn to circle to the left, but when once learned, it will be found no more difficult than circling to the right, provided the animal has been properly trained and made supple, so as to lead with either leg. Horses that have been trained to lead with the right leg only will, when required to change and lead with the left, move in a confined, inflexible, and irregular manner, so that it will be impossible to time the rise from the saddle. In riding in the circle to the left, the directions for circling to the right must be reversed, the rider leaning to the *left*, pulling the *left* rein a little tighter, etc. Great care must be taken, however, not to lean too much toward the left in making the rise. The degree of inclination should not in this case be so great as the corresponding inclination when circling to the right, for if it is the rider will throw her weight too much upon the stirrup side, and may cause the saddle to turn.

In practicing riding in a circle, it will be found very advantageous to vary the size of the circle, first riding in a large one, then gradually contracting it, and again enlarging it; or the rider, while practicing upon a large circle, may make a cross-cut toward the centre of this circle, so as to enter upon another one of smaller diameter, and, after riding for a short time in the smaller circle, she may again pass out to resume her ride upon the larger one. These changes from large to narrow circles form excellent practice for pupils, but should always, if possible, be performed under competent instruction.

The first lessons in trotting in a circle should always be of short duration, and the pupil required to ride slowly, the speed being gradually increased as she gains knowledge and confidence. The moment she experiences fatigue she should dismount, and rest, before resuming the lesson.

In **the amble** the horse's movements very strongly resemble those of the camel, two legs on one side moving together alternately with the two legs of the other side. Thus one side of the animal supports the weight of his body, while the other side moves forward, and so on in alternation. This is an artificial gait, and one to which the horse must usually be trained; though some horses whose ancestors have been forced to travel in this gait, have themselves been known to amble without any training. In the feudal ages it was the favorite pace for a lady's palfrey, but at the present day it is no longer countenanced by good taste.

The pace, however, which is so well liked by many ladies in this country, is a kind of amble, although the steps taken are longer. A good pacer can frequently travel faster than most horses can in the trot. When the steed moves easily and willingly, the pace is very pleasant for short rides, but for long journeys, unless the animal can change his gait to a hand gallop or a canter, it will become very unpleasant and tiresome. Many pacers are almost as rough in their movements as the ordinary trotter; and although they do not jolt the rider up and down upon the saddle, yet they jerk her body in such a manner as successively and alternately to throw one side forward and the other slightly back with each and every step, rendering a ride for any distance very fatiguing.

The rack, at one time so much liked, has become almost obsolete. This is a peculiar gait, not easily described, in which the horse appears to trot with one pair of legs and amble with the other, the gait being so mixed up between an amble and a defective trot as to render it almost a nondescript. When racking, the horse will appear constrained and uncomfortable, and will strongly bear upon the rider's hand; some animals so much so, as completely to weary the bridle hand and arm in a ride of only an hour or two. This constant bearing of the horse's head upon the reins soon renders him hard mouthed, and, consequently, not easily and promptly managed. The rack soon wears out a horse, besides spoiling him for other gaits, and so injures his feet and legs that a racker will rarely be suitable for the saddle after his eighth year. It is an acquired step, much disliked by the horse, which has always to be forced into it by being urged forward against the restraint of a curb-bit; and he will, whenever an opportunity presents, break into a rough trot or canter, so that the rider has to be constantly on the watch, and compel him to keep in the rack against his will. And although the motion does not jolt much, the aspect of the horse and rider is not as easy and graceful as in the canter and hand gallop, there being an appearance of unwillingness and restraint that is by no means pleasing. The directions for the French trot will answer for both the pace and the rack, except that in the latter the traction upon the reins must be greater.

CHAPTER IX
THE CANTER

"When troubled in spirit, when weary of life,
When I faint 'neath its burdens, and shrink from its strife,
When its fruits, turned to ashes, are mocking my taste,
And its fairest scene seems but a desolate waste,
Then come ye not near me, my sad heart to cheer
With friendship's soft accents or sympathy's tear.
No pity I ask, and no counsel I need,
But bring me, oh, bring me my gallant young steed,
With his high arched neck, and his nostril spread wide,
His eye full of fire, and his step full of pride!
As I spring to his back, as I seize the strong rein,
The strength to my spirit returneth again!
The bonds are all broken that fettered my mind,
And my cares borne away on the wings of the wind;
My pride lifts its head, for a season bowed down,
And the queen in my nature now puts on her crown!"

GRACE GREENWOOD.

IN THE GALLOP, the horse always has a leading foot or leg. In *leading with the right fore-foot*, he will raise the left one from the ground, and then the right will immediately follow, but will be advanced somewhat beyond the left one; and this is the reason why, in this case, the right side is called the "leading side." In the descent of the fore-feet, the left one will touch the ground first, making the first beat, and will be immediately followed by the leading or right fore-foot which will make the second beat. The hind-legs are moved in a similar way, the left hind-foot making the third beat, and the right one the fourth. These beats vary in accordance with the adjustment of the horse's weight, but when he gallops true and regular, as in the canter, the hoof-beats distinctly mark *one, two, three, four*. In the rapid gallop the hoof-beats sound in the time of *one-two*, or *one-two-three*.

In *leading with the left foot*, the left side of the horse will be advanced slightly and the left leg be carried somewhat beyond the right, the action being just the reverse of that above described when leading with the right leg. In this case the left side is termed the "leading side." The hoof-beats of horses in the trot and gallop have been admirably rendered by Bellini, in the opera of "Somnambula," just previous to the entrance of Rudolfo upon the stage. There are three kinds of gallop, namely, the *rapid* or *racing*, the *hand gallop*, and the *canter*.

The canter is a slow form of galloping, which the horse performs by throwing his weight chiefly upon his hind-legs, the fore ones being used more as supports than as propellers. Horses will be found to vary in their modes of cantering, so much so as to render it almost impossible to describe them accurately. Small horses and ponies have a way of cantering with a loose rein, and without throwing much weight upon their haunches, moving their feet rapidly, and giving pattering hoof-beats. Most ponies on the Western prairies canter in this manner, and it is said to be a very easy gait for a horseman though very unpleasant, from its joltings, for a lady.

Another canter is what might be termed the "canter of a livery-stable horse." This appears to be partly a run and partly a canter, a peculiarity which is due to the fact that one or more of the animal's feet are unsound, and he adopts this singular movement for the purpose of obtaining relief. The little street gamins in London recognize the sound of this canter at once, and will yell out, in time with the horse's hoof-beats, "three pence, two pence," in sarcastic derision of the lady's hired horse and the unhappy condition of his feet.

In the true canter, which alone is suitable for a lady, the carriage of the horse is grand and elegant. In this gait, the animal has his hind-legs well under his body, all his limbs move regularly, his neck has a graceful curve, and responds to the slightest touch of the rider's hand upon the reins. A horse that moves in this manner is one for display; his grand action will emphasize the grace of a finished rider, and the appearance of the *tout ensemble* will be the extreme of elegance and well-bred ease.

Horses intended for ladies' use are generally trained to lead in the canter with the right or off fore-foot. Most lady riders, whose lessons in riding have been limited, sit crosswise upon their saddles. This position, without their being aware of it, places them more in unison with the horse's movements, and thereby renders the canter with this lead the easiest gait for them. But if a horse be constantly required to canter with this lead he will soon become unsound in his left hind-leg, because in leading with the right fore-foot he throws the greater part of his weight upon his left hind-leg, and thus makes it perform double duty. For this reason the majority of ladies' horses, when the canter is their principal gait, will be found to suffer from strained muscles, tendons, and articulations.

A finished rider will from time to time relieve her horse by changing the lead to the left leg, or else she will change the canter to a trot. Should her horse decidedly refuse to lead with the foot required, whether right or left, it may be inferred that he is unsound in that leg or foot; in which case he should be favored, and permitted to make his own lead, while the canter should frequently be changed to a walk.

To **commence the canter**, the horse must be brought to a walk, or to a stand, then be placed on his haunches, and collected by means of the curb, left leg, and whip; and then the bridle-hand must be raised, while the second, third, and fourth fingers are moved to and fro, so as to give gentle pulls upon the curb-reins, thus soliciting the animal to raise his fore-feet. In performing these manoeuvres, the rider must be careful to direct the leg with which she desires her horse to lead. This may be done as follows: If she desires to have the **right leg lead**, the tension upon the left curb-rein must, *just before* the animal rises to take his first step, be increased enough to make him incline his head so far to the left that the rider can see his left nostril, while, simultaneously, her left leg must press against his side. By these means, the horse will be prompted to place himself obliquely, with his head rather to the left, and his croup to the right.

The rider, if seated exactly in the centre of her saddle, must take a position corresponding to that of the horse, by throwing her right hip and shoulder somewhat forward, her face looking toward the animal's head, while her body is held erect with the shoulders gracefully inclined backward, and the hollow of the back well curved inward. Any stiffness or rigidity of the body must be guarded against in these movements and positions. The rider must hold herself in a pliant manner, and yield to the motions of the horse. The left leg must be held steady, the knee being placed directly underneath the third pommel, and care must be taken not to press upon the stirrup, as this will tend to raise the body from the saddle, and convey its weight almost wholly to the left side.

The hands must be held somewhat elevated and steady, and, as the horse advances, the tension on the reins must be even, so that the fingers can feel every cadence of his step, and give and take with his movements. Unlike the trot, in which the horse must be supported by the snaffle, the canter will require the curb to sustain and keep up his action. After the animal has started in the canter with the right leg leading, should he incline too much to the left, the tension upon the right rein must be increased, so as to turn his head more to the right and bring him to the proper inclination for the lead of the right leg. This correction must be effected gradually and lightly, so as not to disturb the gait, or cause him to change his leading leg. This canter with the right leg leading is very easy to learn, and will not require much practice to master.

However, should the horse fail to obey these indications of the left rein and leg, and start off in a false and disunited manner, as explained under "the turn in the canter," another course should be pursued, namely: the tension upon the right or off curb-rein must be increased so as to bring the animal's nose to the right, as if he were going to turn to the right on a curve, while at the same time the left leg must be pressed against his side in order to have him carry his croup slightly to the right. Now he must be made to lift his fore-feet by increased tension on both curb reins, and then be urged forward. As he advances, the hands should be extended a little to give him more freedom in the spring forward, and he will then naturally lead with the right side advanced. When once started in this gait, the rider must equalize the tension upon the reins, having placed herself in the saddle, in the manner explained for the canter. To have him lead with the left leg, a similar but reversed course must be pursued, using pressure with the whip, instead of the leg, to make him place his croup to the left.

To canter with the **left leg leading** will be found more difficult to acquire, and will demand more study and practice. The horse, having been collected, must then be inclined obliquely to the right. To accomplish this, the rider must increase the tension of the right curb-rein,

FIG. 31—ENTERING UPON THE CANTER WITH THE RIGHT LEG LEADING

and press her whip against the animal's right side, which will urge his head to the right and his croup to the left. In order that the position of the rider's body may correspond with that of the horse, her left hip and shoulder must be slightly advanced, in precedence of her right hip and shoulder. It will be observed that the manoeuvring in this lead is similar to that in which the right leg leads, except that the *direction* of the positions, of the management of the reins, and of the horse's bearing during the canter is simply reversed; in either lead, however, the tension or bearing upon the reins, as the horse advances in the canter, must be equal.

It may be proper to state here that, as the amount of tension needed upon the reins when cantering varies considerably with different horses, some needing only the lightest touch, the rider will, consequently, have to ascertain for herself how much will be suitable for her horse. Some horses, after having fairly started in the canter, will bend their necks so as to carry their chin closer to the throat, while others again will extend the neck so as to carry the chin forward. In the first instance, the reins will have to be shortened in order to give the animal the proper support in the gait, as well as to keep up the correspondence between his mouth and the bridle hand; in the latter they will require to be lengthened, to give him more freedom in his movement. Should the reins be held too short, or the rider's hand be heavy and unyielding, the horse will be confined in his canter; should the reins be held too long, he will canter carelessly, and will either move heavily upon his fore-legs, or break into an irregular trot.

A rider may by attending to the following directions readily determine whether her horse be leading with the leg she desires, and also whether he be advancing in a true and united manner: If he be moving regularly and easily, with a light play upon the reins in harmony with the give and take movements of the hand, his head being slightly inclined in a direction opposite to that of the leading leg, and his action being smooth and pleasant to the rider, he will, as a rule, be cantering correctly. But if he be moving roughly and unevenly, giving the rider a sensation of jolting, if his head is inclined toward the same side as that of the leading leg, and he does not yield prompt obedience to the reins, then he is not cantering properly, and should be immediately stopped, again collected, and started anew. If necessary this course should be repeated until he advances regularly and unitedly.

Some horses, after having fairly entered upon the canter, will change the leading leg, and will even keep changing from one to the other, at short intervals. This is a bad habit, and one that will never be attempted by a well-trained animal, unless his rider does not understand how to support him correctly and to keep him leading with the required leg. A horse should never be allowed to change his leading leg except at the will of his rider; and should he do so, he should be chidden and stopped instantly, and then started anew.

If the rider when trotting rapidly wishes to change to a canter, she must first moderate the trot to a walk, because the horse will otherwise be apt to break from the trot into a rapid gallop. Should he insist upon trotting, when it is desired that he should canter, he must be stopped, collected with the curb-bit, as heretofore described in the directions for commencing the canter, and started anew. This course must be repeated every time he disobeys, and be continued until he is made to canter.

It may be remarked here that, in the canter, whenever the horse moves irregularly, advances heavily upon his fore-legs, thus endeavoring to force his rider's hand, or when he fails to yield ready obedience, he should always be stopped, collected, and started anew,—repeating this course, if necessary, several times in succession. Should the animal, however, persist in his disobedience, pull upon the reins, and get his head down, his rider must, as he moves on, gently yield the bridle-reins, and each time he pulls upon them she must gradually, but firmly, increase the tension upon them, by drawing them in toward her waist. This counter-traction must be continued until the horse yields to the bridle and canters properly. When he pulls upon the reins his rider in advancing her hands to yield the reins should be careful to keep her body erect, and not allow it to be pulled forward.

The turn in the canter. In turning to *the right*, if the horse is leading with the inward leg, or the one toward the centre of the circle of which the distance to be turned forms an arc, in the present instance the right fore-leg which is followed by the right hind-leg, he is said to be true and united, and will be able to make the turn safely. Should the turn be made toward *the left*, the horse leading with his inward or left fore-leg, followed by the left hind-leg, he will likewise be true and united.

On the contrary, the animal will be disunited when, in cantering to the right, he leads with the right fore-leg followed by the left hind-leg, or when he leads with the left fore-leg followed by the right hind-leg. In either case, from want of equilibrium in action and motion, a very slight obstruction may make him fall.

In turning toward the left, in a canter, the horse will be disunited if he leads with the left fore-leg followed by the right hind-leg, or if he leads with the right fore-leg followed by the left hind-leg, as in the preceding instance, he will be liable to fall. A horse is said to go false when, in turning to the right, in the canter, he leads with both left legs, or advances his left side beyond his right; also, when in cantering to the left he leads with both right legs or advances his right side beyond his left; in either of these false movements he will be very liable to fall.

When it is desired to **turn to the right**, in the canter, the horse must be kept well up to the bridle, so as to place his haunches forward and well under him, thus keeping him light on his fore-legs, and preventing his bearing too heavily upon his shoulders; and, while the inward rein is being tightened in order to make the turn, the outward one must continue to support the horse, being just loose enough to allow him to incline his head and neck toward the inner side of the turn. Pressure from the left leg of the rider will keep the animal from inclining his haunches too much to the left, during the turn. Should the steed be turned merely by means of the inward rein, without being kept well up to the bridle, and without either leg or whip being used upon his outer side, he will turn heavily upon his forehand, and will be obliged to change to the outward leg in order to support himself. This will cause him, after the turn has been accomplished, to advance in a disunited way in the canter.

When it is desired to **turn to the left**, the instructions in the preceding paragraph may be pursued, the directions, however, being reversed and pressure with the whip being employed instead of that with the leg.

Sudden, sharp turns, are always dangerous, however sure-footed the horse may be, and especial care should be taken not to turn quickly to the right when the left fore-leg leads, nor to the left when the right fore-leg leads, as in either case the animal will almost certainly be thrown off his balance. In turning a "sharp corner," especially when the rider cannot see what she is liable to encounter, it will be better for her to make the turn at a walk, and keep her own side of the road, the right.

The stop in the canter. In bringing the horse to a stand, in the canter, he should be well placed on his haunches by gradually increasing the pull upon the curb-reins just as his fore-feet are descending toward the ground; the hind-feet being then well under the horse will complete the stop. The rider must guard against leaning forward, as this will not only prevent the horse from executing the stop in proper form, but should he suddenly come to a stand, it will throw her still farther forward, and the reins will become relaxed. Now, while she is thus leaning forward, should the animal suddenly raise his head, the two heads will be very likely to come into unpleasant contact; or should the horse stumble, his liability to fall will be increased, because the rider will not be in a proper position to support him, and will increase the weight upon his shoulders, by being so far forward.

Many ladies not only lean forward while effecting the stop, but also draw the bridle-hand to the left, and carry the bridle-arm back so that the elbow projects behind and beyond the body, while at the same time they elevate the shoulder on this side. This is an extremely awkward manner of bringing a horse to a stand. The stop should be made in the same manner as that described in the walk, that is, by gradually drawing the bridle-hand toward the waist, etc.

Nearly all horses, unless exceptionally well trained, will trot a short distance before coming to a stand in the canter or gallop, and it is here that a knowledge of the French or cavalry trot will prove essential, because the rider will then comprehend the motion, and will sit closely to the saddle until the horse stops. In all cases, the horse should be brought to a stand in a regular, collected manner, so that with a little more liberty of rein he can promptly reënter upon the canter, should this be desired.

CHAPTER X
THE HAND GALLOP.—THE FLYING GALLOP

"Now we're off like the winds to the plains whence they came;
And the rapture of motion is thrilling my frame!
On, on speeds my courser, scarce printing the sod,
Scarce crushing a daisy to mark where he trod!
On, on like a deer, when the hound's early bay
Awakes the wild echoes, away, and away!
Still faster, still farther, he leaps at my cheer,
Till the rush of the startled air whirs in my ear!
Now 'long a clear rivulet lieth his track,—
See his glancing hoofs tossing the white pebbles back!
Now a glen dark as midnight—what matter?—we'll down
Though shadows are round us, and rocks o'er us frown;
The thick branches shake as we're hurrying through,
And deck us with spangles of silvery dew!"

GRACE GREENWOOD.

THE HAND GALLOP is an intermediate gait between the canter and the flying gallop. Its motion, though rather rapid, is smooth, easy, and very agreeable for both rider and steed. Nearly all horses, especially spirited ones, prefer this movement to any other; the bronchos on the plains of the far West will keep up this long, easy lope or hand gallop for miles, without changing their gait, or requiring their riders to draw rein, and without any apparent fatigue. This pace is likewise a favorite one with riding parties, as the motion is so smooth that conversation can be kept up without difficulty. If the animal's movements are light, supple, and elegant, the lady rider presents a very graceful appearance when riding this gait, as the reactions in it are very mild; it is the gait *par excellence*, for a country ride.

On a breezy summer morning, there is nothing more exhilarating than a ride at a hand gallop, on a willing, spirited horse; it brightens the

spirits, braces the nerves, refreshes the brain, and enables one to realize
that "life is worth living."

> "I tell thee, O stranger, that unto me
>   The plunge of a fiery steed
> Is a noble thought,—to the brave and free
> It is music, and breath, and majesty,—
>   'Tis the life of a noble deed;
> And the heart and the mind are in spirit allied
> In the charm of a morning's glorious ride."

Let all gloomy, dyspeptic invalids try the cheering effects of a hand
gallop, that they may catch a glimpse of the sunlight that is always
behind even the darkest cloud of despondency.

When the horse is advancing in a collected canter, if the rider will
animate him a little more by gentle taps with the whip, and then as he
springs forward give him more liberty of the curb-rein, he will enter
upon a **hand gallop**. In this gait he will lead either with the left or the
right foot, but the oblique position of his body will be very slight. The
management of the reins, the turns to the right or to the left, the stop,
and the position of the rider's body, must, in this gait be the same as
in the canter, except that the body need not be quite so erect, and the
touch upon the reins must be very light, barely appreciable.

If riding a spirited horse, the lady must be upon her guard, lest he
increase his speed and enter into a flying or racing gallop. Any horse
is liable to do this when he has not been properly exercised, especially
if he is with other horses, when a spirit of rivalry is aroused, and he
sometimes becomes almost unmanageable from excitement. Many livery-stable horses, although quiet enough in the city, will, when ridden
upon country roads, especially in the spring, require all the skill of
their riders to keep them under control. The change from the stone
and brick of the city or town to the odor of the fresh grass and the
sight of green fields has an exhilarating effect upon them, and makes
them almost delirious with gladness, so that they act like anything but
sensible, quiet, well-worked horses.

When her horse manifests any such disposition, the rider must
retain her presence of mind, and not permit any nervousness or excitement on her part to increase that of her horse. She must keep him
well under the control of the curb-bit, and not allow him to increase

his speed; when he endeavors to do so, she must sit erect, and every time his fore-feet touch the ground she must tighten the curb-reins, by drawing them gradually but firmly toward her waist. She will thus check the animal's desire to increase his speed, by compelling him to rest upon her hand at short intervals until he can be brought under command and again made obedient. Care must be taken not to make this strong pull upon the animal's mouth constant, as this will be more apt to increase than to lessen his speed, and will also prevent her from turning him readily should she encounter any object upon the road.

Should the horse, however, continue to disobey the commands of his rider, and persist in his efforts to increase his speed, she must then lean well back, and "saw his mouth" with the snaffle reins, that is, she must pull first one of these reins and then the other in rapid succession; this may cause him to swerve out of a straight course, but if he has a snaffle-bit separate from the curb this sawing will generally have the desired effect, and stop him.

If the horse should get his head down and manifest a disposition to change the full gallop into a runaway, the rider must, as she values her own safety, keep her body well inclined backward, for some horses, when excited, will, while their riders are endeavoring to check or control them, kick up as they gallop along, and the rider, unless she is prepared for such movements, will be in danger of being thrown. In such a case every effort must be made to raise the horse's head. To do this, the rider must slacken the curb-reins for a moment, and then suddenly give them a strong, decided jerk upward; this will cause a severe shock to the horse's mouth, and make him raise his head and stop suddenly, a movement that may throw her toward or upon the front of the saddle with considerable force, unless she guard herself against such an accident by leaning well back.

Should the horse, when galloping at full speed, turn a corner in spite of the efforts of his rider, she must keep a steady pull upon the outer curb-rein, and lean well back and in toward the centre of the curve which the horse is describing in his turn. All this must be done quickly, or she will lose her balance and fall off upon the outer side.

During all these violent efforts of the horse the rider must keep a firm, steady seat, pressing her left knee up strongly against the third pommel, and at the same time holding the second clasped firmly by the bend of her right knee. If she recollects to do all this, there will be little cause for alarm, as it will then be very difficult for her horse to unseat her. The combined balance and grip of limbs will give her a firmer seat than it is possible for a man to acquire in his saddle.

In **the flying or racing gallop** the horse manifests the utmost capabilities of his speed, his body at every push of his hind-legs being raised from the ground so quickly that he will appear as if almost flying through the air; hence the name "flying gallop." In this gait it is unimportant with which leg the horse leads, provided the advance of the hind-leg on the same side as that of the leading one be made correspondingly. It is advisable that every lady rider should learn to sit the flying gallop, as she will then be better able to maintain her seat, and to manage her horse should she ever have the misfortune to be run away with. (Fig. 32.)

Many ladies, when riding in the country, enjoy a short exhilarating flying gallop; and for their benefit a few instructions are here given that will enable them to indulge their *penchant* for rapid riding, without danger to themselves, or injury to their horses. Before the lady attempts rapid riding, however, she must be thoroughly trained in all the other gaits of the animal, must possess strong, healthy nerves, and must have sufficient muscular power in her arms to hold and manage her horse, and to stop him whenever occasion requires; she must also have fitted to his mouth a curb-bit which possesses sufficient power to control him and to bring him to a stand, when this is desired. Above all, her horse must be sure-footed, and free from any and every defect that might occasion stumbling.

Every point having been carefully attended to, and the lady being ready for the ride, she must sit firmly upon the centre of the saddle, grasping the second and third pommels, as described above. She must be careful not to press strongly upon the stirrup, as this will tend to raise her body from the saddle. From the hips down the body and limbs must be held as immovable as possible. The body, below the waist, must by its own weight, aided by the clasp of the right and left legs upon their respective pommels, secure a firm seat upon the saddle. From the waist up the body must be pliable, the shoulders being well back, and the back curved in, so that the rider may keep her balance, and control the horse's action. The reins must be held separately, in the

FIG. 32—THE FLYING GALLOP

manner described for holding the double bridle-reins in both hands. The animal must be ridden and supported by the snaffle-reins, the curb being held ready to check him instantly should he endeavor to obtain the mastery. The hands must be held low, and about six or eight inches apart, and the rider's body must lean back somewhat.

Leaning forward is a favorite trick of the horse-jockey when riding a race, as it is supposed to assist the horse, and also enable the rider to raise himself on the stirrups; but as lady riders are not horse-jockeys, and are not supposed to ride for a wager, but simply for the enjoyment of an exhilarating exercise, it will not be at all necessary for them to assume this stooping posture. Many of the best horsemen, when riding at full gallop in the hunting field, or on the road, prefer to incline the body somewhat backward, this having been found the safest as well as most graceful position for the rider.

As the horse moves rapidly forward, the rider, while keeping a firm hand upon the snaffle-reins so as to give full support to the horse, must be sure with every stride of the animal to "give and take," and this motion, instead of being limited to the hands and wrists, as in all other gaits, must in this one embrace the whole of the fore-arms, which, using the elbows as a hinge, should move as far as is necessary.

To **stop the horse** in a flying gallop, the curb-reins must be drawn upward and toward the waist gradually, for should they be pulled upon suddenly it would be apt to stop him so abruptly that he would either become overbalanced, or cross his legs, and fall.

In this gait, the rider should never attempt to turn her horse except upon a very large circle, because, even when in the proper position, unless she possesses great muscular power, she will be almost certain to be thrown off on the outward side by the forcible and vigorous impetus imparted.

CHAPTER XI
THE LEAP—THE STANDING LEAP—THE FLYING LEAP

"Soft thy skin as silken skein,
Soft as woman's hair thy mane,
 Tender are thine eyes and true;
All thy hoofs like ivory shine,
Polished bright; oh, life of mine,
 Leap, and rescue Kurroglou!"

Kyrat, then, the strong and fleet,
Drew together his four white feet,
 Paused a moment on the verge,
Measured with his eye the space,
And into the air's embrace
 Leaped as leaps the ocean serge.

    LONGFELLOW, *The Leap of Roushan Beg.*

A LADY RIDER who has the nerve and confidence to ride a hand gallop, or a flying gallop, will be ready to learn to leap. Indeed, instruction in this accomplishment should always be given, as it is of great assistance in many emergencies. The most gentle horse may become frightened, shy suddenly to one side, or plunge violently for some reason or other, and these abrupt movements strongly resemble those of leaping; if, therefore, the rider understands the leap, she will know better how to maintain her equilibrium. Or she may meet some obstruction on the road, as the trunk of a tree felled by a storm; when, instead of being compelled to return home without finishing her ride, she can leap over the obstacle. Again, should she at any time be in great haste to reach her destination she may, by leaping some low gap in a fence, or some small stream, be able to take one or more short cuts, and thus greatly lessen the distance she would have had to ride on the road.

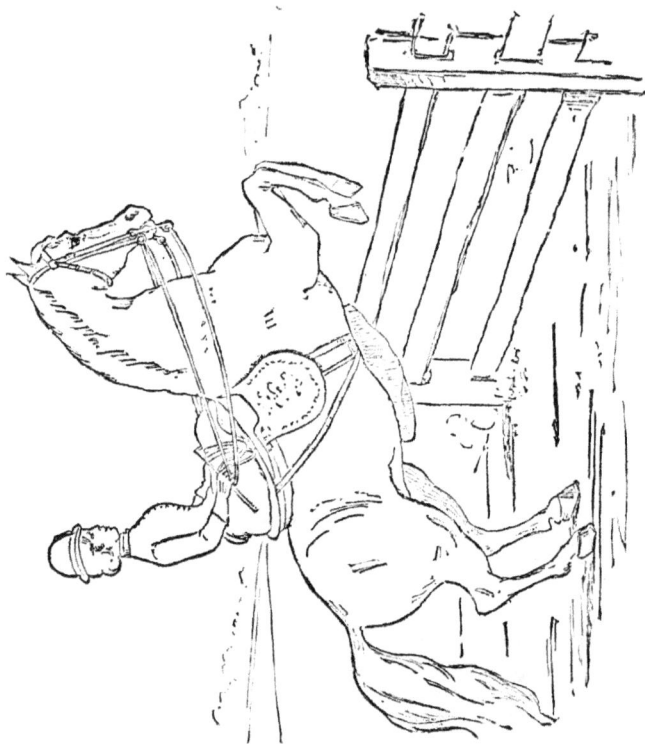

FIG. 33—THE STANDING LEAP—RISING

Leaping is by no means difficult to learn. With an English saddle, the third pommel will prevent the rider from being shaken off
by the violence of the motion, and will thus make leaping entirely
safe for a lady provided the horse be well-trained and sure-footed.
Before venturing upon a leap, three requisites are necessary: first, the
horse must be a good and fearless leaper; second, the rider must have
confidence in herself and steed, because any nervousness on her part
will be apt to cause the animal to leap awkwardly; and third, she must
always be sure of the condition of the ground on the opposite side of
the object over which the leap is to be made—it must neither slope
abruptly down, nor present any thorny bushes, nor be so soft and
soggy that the horse will be apt to sink into it. No risk must be taken
in the leap, except in cases of emergency, when, of course, the rider
may have neither time nor opportunity to select her ground, and be
obliged to leap her steed over the nearest available point. The author
once avoided what might have proved a serious accident to both herself and horse, by promptly leaping him over a hedge of thorn bushes,
upon the other side of which was a river: this was done in order to
avoid colliding in a narrow road with a frightened, runaway team,
which was quite beyond the control of its driver.

The **standing leap** will prove more difficult to learn than the flying
leap, but, nevertheless, it should be the first one practiced, and when
once acquired, the other will be mere play. A bar twelve feet long,
raised two feet from the ground, will be sufficient for practice in this
exercise; if a lady can manage a leap of this height with expertness and
grace, she will be fully able to bound over a still higher obstacle, should
she desire to do so, and her horse be equal to the occasion. Before attempting the leap, she must be sure that she is perfectly secure upon
the saddle, with her left knee directly under the third pommel so as to
press it firmly against the latter as the horse rises to the leap; her left
leg, from the knee to the stirrup, must hang perpendicularly[8] along the
side of the horse, the inner surface or side of the knee lightly pressing
against the saddle-flap; her foot must be well placed in the stirrup; her
seat directly in the centre of the saddle; her body erect and square to

---

8   If the leap be a very high one, the left foot may be thrust a little more
forward to enable the rider to lean back as far as is necessary.

the front; her shoulders well back; and the small of her back curved in.
The right leg must firmly grasp the second pommel as the horse rises,
and the right heel be held somewhat back, and close to the fore-flap
of the saddle. The hands must be held low, and about six inches apart,
with a snaffle-rein in each, and the curb-reins must be so placed that
the rider will not unconsciously draw upon them, but must not hang
so loosely as to become caught accidentally upon any projecting article
with which they may come in contact. If all these points be carefully
attended to, just previous to walking the horse up to the bar, the rider
will be in correct position and ready for the leap, which she will accomplish very quickly, with perfect security, and with a much firmer seat
than that obtained by the most finished horseman.

The principal movement for which the rider should be prepared
in leaping is that of being thrown forward on the saddle, both when
the horse makes the spring and when his fore-feet touch the ground.
In order to avoid this accident, the rider, keeping a firm seat and
grasp upon the pommels, must incline her shoulders somewhat backward, both when the horse springs from the ground and also during
the descent, the amount of inclination varying with the height of
the leap. The erect position should be resumed when the hind-legs
have again touched the ground. In a very high leap, the rider's body
should be bent so far back during the descent as to look almost as if
in contact with the back of the horse.

When the points named above have been attended to, the horse
must be collected, with his hind-legs well under him, and then be
briskly walked up to the bar or obstacle to be leaped and placed directly before it, but not so close that he cannot clear it without striking his
knees against it as he rises,—sufficient room must always be allowed
him for his spring. Now, after receiving a light touch or pull upon the
reins to tell him that his rider is ready, he will raise himself upon his
hind-legs for the leap. As he rises, the rider's body, if properly seated,
as heretofore explained, will naturally assume a sufficient inclination
forward without any effort on her part. While in this position she must
not carry her shoulders forward, but must keep them well back, with
the waist well curved in as when sitting erect. It should never be forgotten that in the rise during the leap, just previous to the spring, no
efforts whatever must be made by the rider to support the horse, or to

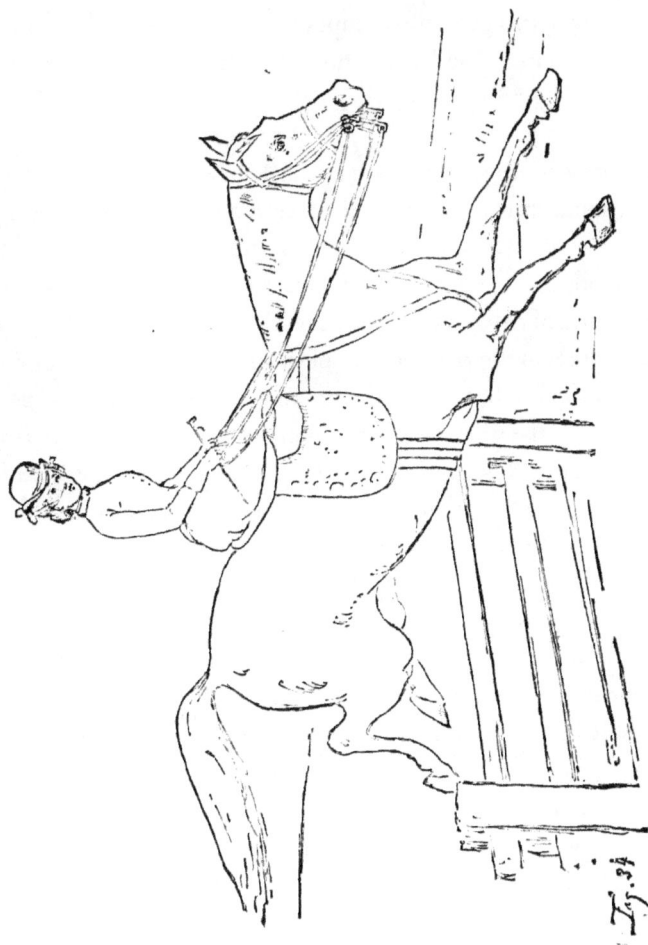

FIG. 34—THE STANDING LEAP—DESCENDING

lift him, but instead, she should simply hold the reins so lightly that his mouth can just be felt, which is called "giving a free rein." If the reins be allowed to hang too loosely they may catch upon some object not noticed by the rider, and not only be wrenched from her hands, but also give the horse's mouth a severe jerk, or perhaps throw him upon the ground. Too loose a rein would, moreover, be apt to make it impossible for her to give timely support to the animal as his fore-feet touched the ground. The leap, it must be borne in mind, is effected very quickly. (Fig. 33.)

As the horse springs from his hind-legs to make the leap, the rider must advance her arms, with her hands held as low as possible so as to give him a sufficiently free rein to enable him to extend himself; this position of the arms will also prevent the reins from being forcibly wrested from her hands by the horse's movements. At the moment of the spring and the advance of the arms, the rider's body must be inclined backward, the erect position of the waist and shoulders being, however, maintained. As the animal's fore-feet touch the ground, the hands must be gently drawn in toward the waist in order to support him, as such support will be expected by the horse, and must be continued even after his hind-legs rest upon the ground, so that the animal will not become disunited, but will move onward in a collected manner. (Fig. 34.)

Many riding-teachers instruct their pupils to incline the body well forward as the horse rises, while others require their pupils to lean well back. The advocates of the former method say that this forward inclination conforms to the position of the horse at the time, and so places the weight of the body as to assist the horse in his spring. They who adopt the other method maintain that if the body be inclined forward in the rise, it will be almost, if not quite, impossible for the rider, from the rapidity with which the horse extends himself, to make the backward inclination in time to enable her to regain her balance quickly. A happy medium will prove the best. If the rider be seated correctly at the time the horse rises, her body *will naturally incline a little forward*, and there will be but little weight upon the horse's hind-quarters, while, as he springs and extends himself in his leap, she can promptly adapt herself to his movements and incline her body backward.

By leaning back as the horse rises on his hind-legs, the weight of his rider will be thrown upon his hind-quarters, and she will present an awkward appearance; while at the same time she will be very apt to shorten the reins, and thus confine the horse so much that his leap will become clumsy and dangerous.

On commencing the leap the rider, as heretofore stated, must never attempt to raise the horse by the reins; a light, gentle touch or pull given to them with the fingers, as when starting upon a hand gallop, is all that will be necessary. The horse must be left free to take the leap in his own way, using his own instinct or judgment in order that he may clear his fore feet from the bar or object over which he has to pass. During the rise, the rider must carefully guard against raising her hands, and also against jerking or holding back the reins, as either of these movements will discourage the horse, and, should he be tender mouthed, he will refuse to leap at all, his own instinct warning him that it is dangerous to attempt it under such conditions.

A rather hard mouthed, courageous animal, that has had experience with awkward riders, will, as he extends himself in the leap, force his rider's hands by a sudden jerk of his head, so as either to pull the reins out of her hands, or, should she manage to retain her hold upon them, to pull her forward upon the saddle.

Many ladies, in their fear of becoming displaced during the leap, will unconsciously press their left leg and foot strongly against the side of the horse, thus causing him to swerve or to refuse to leap. Gentlemen teachers are apt to be unaware of this pressure, as the leg is hidden underneath the riding skirt, and not unfrequently they have been puzzled to comprehend why a well-trained, docile horse should leap very well with some of their lady pupils, and awkwardly, or not at all, with others.

A common error, in attempting to leap, is to sit too far back upon the saddle, a position that not only prevents the rider from supporting herself properly by the pommels, but is also likely to occasion her a severe jar as the horse's feet touch the ground. When in the correct position, the body is placed as far forward upon the saddle as the pommels will permit, the waist and shoulders only being inclined backward, as already described.

Pressing heavily upon the stirrup is another fault. This not only destroys the usefulness of the third pommel, but, as has already been remarked, such pressure will tend to lift the body from the saddle. The foot should merely be kept light and steady in the stirrup.

It will be better for a beginner to leap with a snaffle-rein in each hand. After having thoroughly learned how to make the leap properly, she may then prefer to hold all the reins in the left hand. In this case, she must be very careful not to throw up the unoccupied right hand and arm as the horse passes over the obstacle; for, besides being a very ungraceful movement, it may lead the horse to suppose that he is about to be struck with the whip, and so cause him to make the leap precipitately, and upon reaching the ground to gallop wildly off.

The rider must hold her head firm, not only for the sake of appearances, but also to escape biting her tongue and receiving a violent jerk of the neck, when the horse's feet touch the ground.

If a horse, just before leaping, be too much confined or collected by an unnecessary degree of tension upon the reins, especially if he be not thoroughly trained, he will rise from all four legs almost simultaneously, and also alight upon them all together. In horse-jockey's *parlance* this is termed a "buck-leap." It is an awkward manner of leaping, and gives a severe shock to the animal beside fearfully jolting his rider. Again, a horse not well trained in the leap, or somewhat indolent, may, if not animated and properly collected just before rising, fail to leap over the obstacle, or in passing over it may strike it with his hind-feet, for he will attempt the leap in a loose, straggling manner. An animal that is well trained, and accustomed to leaping, will take care of himself, and will require very little assistance from his rider; a light hand upon the reins just before he rises, a free rein as he extends himself, and support when he touches the ground being all that is necessary.

Should the lady be expert in riding, and desire to teach her steed to leap, she can readily do so by pursuing the following course: Let a bar about twelve feet in length, and two feet from the ground, be so arranged that the horse cannot pass around it. If possible, he should be allowed to see a well-trained horse leap over this bar a number of times; then taking advantage of a time when her horse is hungry, his mistress should give him a few oats and, passing over the bar, she should rattle the oats and call to him, when he will bound over to obtain them. This course should be followed at each meal, and she should reward him by feeding, caressing, and praising him every time he leaps the bar,— the object being to accustom him to leap it without being whipped or treated harshly. By thus being allowed to take the leap of his own accord and without assistance, he will gain confidence, and will not be apt to refuse when his rider is placed upon his back. In the course of this training, the appearance of the bar should be changed in various ways, as, for example, by placing different bright colored articles upon it, such as pieces of carpet, rugs, shawls, etc. If he be accustomed to leap only over an object that invariably presents the same appearance, he may refuse to leap one of a different aspect.

Having thus trained the horse until he has become quite familiar with the movements of the leap, and does not refuse to pass over the bar, whatever appearance it may present, he will then be ready for his rider. For the first few trials the lady should take care to have the bar consist of some material that can readily be broken, in order to prevent any accident should the horse, in passing over with her weight upon his back, strike it with either his fore or hind feet. Once mounted, she should teach him to clear the bar in a deliberate manner, not allowing him to rush at it and jump from all four feet at once. She will have to collect him, cause him to place his hind-legs under him so that, as he rises, his weight will be thrown upon his haunches, and, as he leaps over, she must be exceedingly careful not to restrain him in the least, as any thoughtless act or awkwardness on her part may give him a great distaste for an exercise which, otherwise, he would have no reluctance in performing.

With regard to teaching a young horse to leap, the author is much gratified to know that her views are sustained by several eminent equestrians, and among them Mr. E. Mayhew of England, who states that a horse should never be allowed to leap until he has attained at least his fifth year, and who in his excellent work, entitled "The Illustrated Horse Management," etc., remarks: "To place a rider upon an animal's back and then to expect a bar to be cleared is very like loading a young lady with a sack of flour, as preparatory to a dancing lesson being received. This folly is, however, universally practiced; so is that of teaching the paces, when the quadruped's attention is probably engrossed by the burden which the spine has to sustain.

"Leaping is best taught by turning the horse into a small paddock having a low hedge or hurdle fence across its centre. A rider should, in sight of the animal, take an old horse over several times. The groom who brings the corn at the meal hour then goes to that side where the animal is not and calls, shaking up the provender all the time his voice sounds. The boundary will soon be cleared. When half the quantity is eaten, the man should proceed to the opposite compartment and call again. If this is done every time the young horse is fed, the fence may be gradually heightened; after six months of such tuition, a light rider may be safely placed upon the back.

"Instruction, thus imparted, neither strains the structures nor tries the temper. The habit is acquired without those risks which necessarily attend a novel performance, while a burden oppresses the strength, and whip or spur distracts the attention. The body is not disabled by the imposition of a heavy load before its powers are taxed to the uttermost. The quadruped has all its capabilities unfettered, and, in such a state, leaping speedily becomes as easy of performance as any other motion."

Horses leap in different ways; the best leapers being those which just glide over the object without touching it,—they appear to measure the height required for the leap, and, whether the object be high or low, they skim close to it. Such animals can be trusted, and may be allowed to leap without urging or hurrying them, for they require very little assistance from their riders, and do better when left to themselves. Other horses exaggerate the leap and rise higher than is required; they make a very fine appearance when leaping, but are apt to light too close to the opposite side of the bar or obstacle, because they expend all their energies on height instead of width. The worst leapers are those which, instead of clearing the bar at a single bound, make two bounds, as it were, in passing over it: the fore-part of the horse having passed over, the body will seem to be resting for an appreciable time upon the fore-legs.

The **flying leap** can be taken, without stopping, from any gait that is more rapid than a walk, though commonly taken from the gallop. It is a very easy leap, being little more than an extended gallop. The rider takes the same firm, central position upon the saddle as has been described for the standing leap. In the flying leap the body must be inclined well back from the start, care being taken not to make any forward inclination whatever. When the horse has fairly landed, after the leap, the body must again become erect. The degree of the backward inclination must be in accordance with the height and width of the leap. During the whole period of the leap the hands must be kept low and the reins be freely given to the animal, which must be supported as he lands on the opposite side. As the horse runs toward the object to be leaped over, the rider must, when about twelve or fifteen yards from it, gradually relax the reins, by advancing her bridle hand or hands; and, if her horse be a willing and good leaper, he may be allowed to select his own pace, and use his own judgment as to the proper distance from which to make the spring.

If the horse be unused to leaping, or be unwilling, the rider must be upon her guard lest he attempt to defend himself and avoid the leap, either by suddenly swerving to one side or by stopping before the object to be leaped and then backing, or rearing. These actions are generally the result of the horse's want of confidence in his own powers, and severity will only make matters worse. In a dilemma of this kind, the rider will have to convert the flying into the standing leap, as follows:—

She must turn her horse and walk him a short distance away from the object, then, turning him again toward it, she must encourage him to advance slowly that he may take a good look at it; at the same time she must have a light and ready hand on the reins, just firm enough to keep his head steady and maintain control over his neck, so as to prevent him from swerving to the right or to the left. She should then kindly and firmly encourage him to make the bound; and by patience and perseverance in this course he will generally be induced to do so. After he has obeyed, she must not make him repeat the movement several times in succession, as if she were triumphing over him, because he might regard such a process as a sort of challenge, and renew the contest; instead of such measures, he should be allowed to pass on quietly, no further attention being given to the matter. By this change from the flying to the standing leap the horse can be better prevented from shying, and on the next occasion will be apt to make the flying leap over the object without swerving.

The whip or spur should never be employed to make an obstinate or timid horse leap, as he will ever after associate such objects as those over which he has been thus urged or forced to leap with fear of punishment, and his rider will never be sure of him when approaching one of them, for he will either shy, or else bound over it in such a flurried manner as will prove dangerous both to himself and his rider.

An indolent horse, that requires to be roused by whip or spur, is not a suitable one for a lady to ride at a leap. Some horses will refuse to leap when traveling alone, but will do so spiritedly and excellently when in company with others of their kind.

CHAPTER XII
DEFENSES OF THE HORSE.—CRITICAL SITUATIONS

"High pampered steeds, ere tamed, the lash disdain,
And proudly foam, impatient of the rein."
VIRGIL, *Sotheby's Translation*.

"The startling steed was seized with sudden fright."
DRYDEN.

A LADY'S HORSE is generally selected for his gentleness, soundness, good training, and freedom from vice, and the rider's management of him is usually so kind and considerate that he is seldom roused to rebellion; hence, she is rarely called upon to enter into a contention with him. The docility of a lady's steed is almost proverbial, and when purchasing a horse the highest recommendation as to his gentleness and safeness is the assurance that he has "been used to carry a woman." Horse-dealers are well acquainted with this fact, and attach a high value to it, as a sure criterion of the animal's kindly nature. No lady rider, however expert she may be, will, if she be wise and have a regard for her own safety, ride or endeavor to conquer a really vicious horse; yet there may be times when even the hitherto most docile animal will suddenly display that which in Yorkshire dialect is called "mistech;" that is, there may be unexpectedly developed a restive trait, for which there seems to be no reason. Even a really good-natured horse may, owing to high feed and little work, shy, plunge, and kick, in his exuberance of spirits, and should his rider not know how to control these sudden and unexpected manifestations, he may gain the ascendency, and she be thrown from the saddle. That which, on the part of the horse, is intended for good-humored play, may thus, from want of control, degenerate into positive viciousness. A skillful rider will manage and endure the prancings, pawings, and impatience of her

211

steed,— which are frequently only his method of expressing satisfaction and happiness in carrying his kind mistress,—and will continue riding and controlling him until he becomes calm and quiet, and ceases to display his impulsive sensitiveness. Again, a lady may have occasion to ride a strange horse, of whose disposition she knows very little. It is, therefore, very important that every horsewoman should be prepared to meet and to overcome any eccentric demonstrations on the part of the animal she may be riding.

Some horses are constitutionally nervous and timid, always fearful and upon the lookout, constantly scrutinizing every object around them, and keeping their riders incessantly on the watch. These horses, though disagreeable to ride, are seldom dangerous, as they will readily obey the reins and yield to the hand that has many times proved its reliability and correctness.

SHYING.— The position in which a horse places his ears is a sure indication of his immediate intentions. When he raises his head and points his ears strongly forward, it is because he sees some object at the side of the road, or approaching, which renders him uneasy or even fearful. In such a case, his rider must be prepared for a sudden leap to one side, a whirl around, or a quick darting from the road. She must not allow herself to become nervous and jerk or suddenly tighten the reins, for then the animal will think that she is likewise afraid, and that he is justified in his own fright. On the contrary, she must maintain her presence of mind, quietly and calmly take a snaffle-rein in each hand, draw them just tight enough to feel the horse's mouth, keep his head high and straight forward, and, as he approaches the object that has alarmed him, gently turn his head away from it, so that in passing he can see as little of it as possible; at the same time she should press her leg or whip against the horse on the side toward which he is likely to shy,—also speaking to him in a firm and assuring tone of voice, that he may be led to understand there is nothing to fear.

In following these directions the rider must be mindful of her balance, because, notwithstanding all her efforts, the horse may leap out of the road; she should sit erect, keep a firm hold on both pommels with the legs, check him as soon as possible, and then bring him again upon the road. Should he swerve and attempt to rush past the object, his rider must not try to pull his head toward it, but, holding the reins with steady hands, must keep him headed straight forward, and, after he has passed, gradually rein him in.

Should he make a half turn from the object, he must be turned completely around, so as to face it, and then be urged forward by the aid of the left leg and whip, while he is at the same time spoken to in a quiet, encouraging tone. If the horse have confidence in his rider, and his fright be not a pretense, he will thus be induced to go by, and on future occasions will pass by the same object with indifference. Severity, such as scolding and whipping, will only render him more fearful, and since he will always regard the object of his fright as being the cause of his punishment, he will, consequently, the next time of meeting with it become still more unmanageable. But, having passed it at first without experiencing any pain, he will gain confidence in the judgment of his rider, imagine he has made a mistake in being alarmed, and be satisfied that, after all, there was no occasion for dread.

A horse should never be caressed, patted, or coaxed, either just before or just after he has passed any object he dislikes, because he may misinterpret these acts, and imagine that he has done just right in shying, and will, therefore, be very apt to repeat the act in order again to receive the praise of his rider. It will always be better, in such cases, to ride on as usual, and act as if the matter were of no consequence. On the other hand, a horse should never be whipped after he has passed an object that terrifies him. Some riders are afraid to whip the horse while he is in the act of shying, but will lay on the lash after he has passed the cause of his dread; this will not only be "a tardy vengeance that crowns a cowardly act," but will cause the animal to conclude that he has done wrong in passing by, and on the next occasion for alarm he will either delay as long as possible in dread of the remembered whipping, or else will plunge quickly by the object, and, perhaps, add to the vice of shying that of running away. The course pursued by some persons of making a horse pass and repass a number of times in succession an object which has caused him to shy is an erroneous one, as it gives him a chance for again resisting, and makes the rider appear vainglorious and pretentious.

Whether a horse shies from real fright, or from mere pretense or affectation, the severe use of whip or spur to force him by the object he is shying at will always do more harm than good. Mildness and forbearance, combined with firmness, will invariably do much more to tranquillize him and to render him obedient than severity and harsh measures. Horsemen who, from actual experience, are well able to advise say, "Let the horse alone, neither letting him perceive that we are aware we are advancing toward anything that he dislikes, nor doing more with him when in the act of shying than is necessary for due restraint and a steady hand upon the reins."

When a horse shies from pretense of fright, it is either from exuberance of spirits, because he has not been sufficiently exercised, or else because he has detected timidity in his rider, and shies from pure love of mischief and the desire to amuse himself by augmenting her fears. Although not intending any real harm, he may manage, to his own astonishment, to unseat her, and, by thus discovering what he can do, may become a vicious rogue, and make every strange object an excuse for a dangerous shy. The only remedy for this affectation and mischievousness will be a courageous and determined rider on his back, who will give him more work than he likes; he will then, of his own accord, soon tire of his tricks.

When a horse that has had plenty of work and a good rider to manage him nevertheless continues to shy, it will generally be found that his vision is defective. If he is a young horse, with very prominent eyes, the probability is that he is near-sighted; if an old horse, that his vision—having undergone a change similar to that of a human being who is advanced in years—is imperfect for near objects, which appear confused and blurred; in other words, that he is troubled with long sightedness, or presbyopia. In these cases the horse becomes fearful and suspicious, and his quick imagination transforms that which he cannot distinctly see into something terrifying. Ocular science has not advanced so far as to have determined a remedy for these visual difficulties except by the use of glasses; and to place spectacles upon a horse to improve his sight would be inconvenient as well as decidedly unique. Animals thus afflicted are unsuited for either saddle or harness, as they are more dangerous than if they are totally blind, and the only safe course to pursue when one is compelled to use them will be the very undesirable one of completely blindfolding them. Many a horse has been severely punished and condemned for viciousness, when his fault arose from defective vision.

Sometimes a horse becomes discontented and uneasy from being always ridden over the same road; this dull routine is irksome to him, especially if he be spirited, and he ventures upon some act of disobedience in order to create variety and excitement. He may commence by sideling toward other horses or objects on his left, or by suddenly turning around to the right. In the first case, the rider must instantly take a snaffle-rein in each hand, and instead of attempting to turn him from the object, she must rein his head directly toward it, and then back him from it. By these means, his body will form a concavity on the side toward the object, thus preventing injury to the rider or horse, and she will be able to retreat in safety.

In the second instance, the horse instinctively knows that he is opposing his strongest side to the weakest one of his rider, and it is useless to contend with him by pulling upon the left snaffle-rein, as he will be watching for this very movement and be prepared to resist it. He should be foiled by having the right rein tightened so as to turn him completely around and place him in the same position he was in before he began to turn. He will perceive to his astonishment that he has gained nothing by his abrupt movement; and as soon as he has reached the position stated, he should be urged forward by the aid of both leg and whip.

This method is usually successful unless the steed be very obstinate; he may then refuse to advance at all, and may make another turn to the right, in which case his rider should repeat the course just named, and oblige him to turn completely around three or four times in succession, and then while his head is in the right direction, a stroke of the whip behind the girths should instantly be given in order to compel him to go forward before he has time to defend himself and make another turn. Should he again refuse, and succeed in making still another turn, the tactics of his rider must be changed; taking care not to use her whip, she must turn him around as before, and then rein him backward in the direction she desires him to go; she must keep doing this until he concludes to move onward. Should this course have to be continued for some time, it will be advisable occasionally to head him in the desired direction, in order to ascertain whether he will go forward; if he will not, he must again be turned and backed. A horse can readily be induced to move backward, when he has determined not to go forward.

During this contest with the horse, the rider must be careful to retain her balance, to keep her left knee directly under the third pommel, and to incline her body quickly to the right as her animal turns. She should likewise be watchful of surrounding objects, in order to protect herself and her horse from any dangerous position in which he may be disposed to place himself. In case she is not a very expert horsewoman, or has little confidence in her ability to manage the horse, it will be better to have him led a short distance, and then, if possible, she should change the road to one he has not been accustomed to travel; this will divert him, and cause him to forget his contumacy.

BALKING.— When a horse stops on the road and refuses to move in any direction, it may be owing to disease (immobility), or to obstinacy. In either case, it will be better for the rider to make no effort to induce him to move, but she should quietly and patiently remain in the saddle until he evinces a disposition to advance, when he should be made to stand a little longer. If his defense be due to obstinacy, this course will be a punishment; but should it be due to disease, the detention will be no disadvantage nor punishment to him, but rather an advantage, as it will enable him to gain composure. It is rarely, however, that a horse proves balky, unless as the result of some disease of the brain or of the heart, rheumatic pain, etc.

BACKING.— Should a horse commence backing, when on the road, he must have his head quickly turned toward the direction in which he is backing. Thus, if he be backing toward a dangerous declivity, he will be able to see that what he is doing threatens danger to himself, and will be checked. Then he must be backed some little distance away from the danger, and in the direction toward which he is desired to go. If, however, the horse continues to back toward the dangerous place, notwithstanding the rider's efforts to turn him, the safest course will be to dismount instantly. Backing is sometimes, if not very frequently, due to confused vision, rush of blood to the head, pain in the head, etc.

GAYETY.— When a horse moves one ear back and forth, or keeps agitating first one and then the other, at the same time moving his head and neck up and down, and, perhaps, also champing upon his bit, he is feeling gay, and his rider must be on her guard, as he may unexpectedly jump. While keeping a steady hand upon the reins, she must urge him to move forward at a regular and somewhat rapid gait, for this will be what he wants in order to work off his superfluous spirits.

KICKING.— A horse, when defending himself against anything whatever, will always lay his ears flat upon the back of his head; this is his attitude and signal for a battle, and he is then ready to kick, bite, plunge, or rear. When the ears are only momentarily placed back, it may be from playfulness, but when maintained in this position, he is angry and vicious, and may make a desperate effort to throw his rider. In the company of other horses he will attempt to bite or kick at them. As soon as he is observed to gaze fixedly upon any animals in his vicinity, while at the same time he puts his ears back, and turns his croup toward his companions, he is then about to kick, and his rider must frustrate his intention, as soon as she feels his croup move, by quickly raising his head and turning it in the direction in which the kick was to be made. Should he attempt to bite, he must be driven to a proper distance from the object of his anger, and his attention be diverted by keeping him moving on.

A horse will kick when feeling gay, when he is annoyed, when he suffers pain from any cause, when feeling playful or malevolent toward other animals, and, sometimes, when he wishes to dislodge his rider. Whenever her horse manifests an inclination to kick, the rider must endeavor to keep his head up, because he will then be unable to accomplish much in the way of raising his hind-legs; but once allowed to get his head down, he will have everything his own way, and will be able to kick as high as he pleases.

Every time the horse attempts to lower his head, he must be punished by a pull upon the curb-bit strong enough to make him keep his head up. His mouth must also be sawed upon with the curb, should he succeed in getting his head down. The rider must remember to lean well back, and have her left knee well braced against the third pommel, as in this position it will be almost impossible for him to unseat her by his kicking. If the kick be made during a stand-still, a sharp, vigorous stroke of the whip upon the animal's shoulder will be apt to check him; but if the kick be made while he is on the gallop, a stroke of the whip will be apt to make him run away. Should kicking be an old vice of the horse, he must be ridden with a severe curb-bit, that he may be prevented from getting his head down.

PLUNGING, BUCKING.— Plunging is a succession of bounds, in which the four legs of the horse are almost simultaneously raised from the ground, the animal advancing with each bound. It is frequently an effort made by the horse to rid himself of something that pains him, as the sting of an insect, the pinching of the saddle or the girth, etc. All that can be done in any case of plunging will be to endeavor to keep up the animal's head, brace one's self firmly in the saddle, and sit the plunges out; they will rarely amount to more than three or four. When a horse that is not vicious commences to plunge, it may be due to fear or pain; he should, therefore, be spoken to kindly, and be soothed. As soon as he is brought under control, the rider should endeavor to ascertain the cause of his movements, and, if possible, remove it.

Bucking is a desperate effort to throw the rider; the horse will gather his legs under him in as close a group as possible, curve his back upward like an angry Tabby when she espies Towser, lower his head, endeavor to burst the saddle-girths by forcibly expanding his abdomen, and then without making any advance or retreat bound up and down upon all four legs, which are held as rigid as iron rods. Sometimes he will produce a see-saw movement by repeatedly and rapidly throwing himself from his hind to his fore legs. These motions will be kept up as long as he can hold his breath, which generally becomes exhausted after five or six bounds; he will then renew his breath and may repeat the bounds.

When a horse "bucks," the rider must keep her seat the best way she can. Her body should be held as straight as possible, although the natural tendency will be to lean forward and to round the shoulders; she should also take a firm knee-grasp upon both the second and third pommels, keep a steady hold upon the reins, and be especially on her guard against allowing her body to be pulled forward as the horse jerks his head down. Fortunately, very few thorough-bred horses buck violently, their movement being more of a plunge. The horses of the Russian steppes, and the bronchos and ponies of our far Western country, are apt to have the vicious, genuine buck in perfection.

REARING.— With the young horse, rearing is the last frantic effort to unseat his rider; an old rogue will sometimes resort to it, having found his rider timid and much alarmed at the movement. A lady should never ride a horse that has once reared dangerously, unless the action was occasioned by the injudicious use of too severe a curb-bit. A horse that has once reared without provocation will be very apt to do so again. The danger of this vice is, that the horse may fall backward and upon his rider. This accident will be especially liable to occur when, in rearing suddenly and very high, he bends his fore-legs under his body. While he is in this position, should the rider feel him sinking down upon his hind-quarters, she must instantly leap from the saddle, at the same time giving, if possible, a vigorous push to the horse with both hands, as near his shoulder as she can readily reach without endangering herself. This is done that he may be made to fall to the right, and the impetus of the push will also convey her to a safe distance, should he fall to the left.

When a horse, after rearing, paws in the air with his fore-feet, he is then employing them for the same purpose that a tight-rope dancer uses his balancing pole, namely, to keep his equilibrium. In this case, there will not be much danger of his falling backward, unless his rider should pull him over by holding too tight a rein, or by using the reins to aid her in keeping her balance.

The first act of the horse, when he intends to rear, will be to free himself from the influence of the bit, and he will attempt to accomplish this by bending his neck in so as to slacken the tension on the reins; at the same time he will come to a stand by a peculiar cringing movement, which will make his rider feel as if the animal had collapsed, or were falling to pieces. This "nowhere" feeling will hardly be realized before the horse will stiffen his hind-legs and neck, and rise with his fore-feet in the air, bidding defiance to all control.

Under these circumstances, as the horse rears his rider must quickly yield the reins and incline her body well forward, firmly supporting herself by the second and third pommels; as she values her life, she must not strike her steed nor pull upon the reins, but must patiently wait until his fore-feet come to the ground, when the time for action will have arrived.

Although she may be taken by surprise when the horse first rears, she can anticipate his second attempt, which will generally be not far off, by taking a snaffle-rein in each hand, holding her hands low, and the instant she perceives that he is going to rise, loosening the left rein and tightening the right, so as to bend his head to the right. He cannot now complete the rear, because her action will compel him to move a hind-leg, and he will then be unable to rest his weight upon both hind-legs, which he must do in order to rear. As a punishment, he should then be turned around a few times, from right to left; this turning will also be very apt to prevent him from again rearing. Sometimes a severe stroke with the whip upon the horse's hind-quarters as his fore-feet are descending to the ground will prevent the second rear; as he plunges forward from the whip, the rider must be careful to prevent her body from being thrown forward by the plunge.

RUNNING AWAY.— The most dangerous runaway horse is the one that starts off from excessive fear, as terror will make a horse act as if he were blind, and he may then rush over a precipice, or violently collide with some object in his way. Terrified horses have been known almost to dash out their brains by violent collision with a stone wall, and even to impale themselves upon an iron fence. The least dangerous runaway steed is the practiced one, which runs because he has vicious propensities; for as he knows what he is about, he generally takes good care of himself, and thus, in a measure, protects his rider, of whose mishaps, however, he is entirely regardless. Some horses, when urged to do something that is beyond their ability, or when goaded by pain from any cause, will run, imagining that by so doing they can escape the evil. With these, the "bolt" or runaway is more the last furious effort of despair than real viciousness. A heavy-handed rider may cause a horse to run away, the horse, taking advantage of the constant pull upon the reins, is liable to make the hand of his rider a point of support, and then dash wildly onward.

When, from restlessness, a horse endeavors to break away, the curb-reins should be taken, one in each hand, and every time he attempts to run, a sharp pull should be made upon his mouth by means of these reins; he will thus be checked and prevented from starting upon a run. Should he once get fairly started, it will be very difficult to stop him promptly. In such a case, care should be taken not to make a "dead pull" upon the reins, but instead, a succession of pulls at short intervals, and these efforts should be continued until he comes to a stand; should the horse manifest any disposition to stop, the rider should, as he slackens his speed, make a continued pull on the reins as if reining him in from the walk, and this will gradually check him.

When a horse runs away from fear or pain, nothing will stop him except te voice of the rider in whom he has confidence, and for whom he entertains affection. In his terror, he will rely entirely upon her for aid and support, and if she fail him, the most severe bit will not stop him. An old offender may sometimes be controlled by a severe bit, or may be cured of his propensity for running by being placed in the hands of a good horseman who will allow him to run away, and when the animal wishes to stop, will then, by means of whip and spur, make him run still farther, and allow him to stop only when the rider pleases.

The management of a horse when he attempts to "bolt" has been described in the chapter on the Hand Gallop. A horse that has once fairly run away and met with some catastrophe, or that has thrown his rider, will never be a safe one to ride subsequently.

UNSTEADINESS WHILE BEING MOUNTED.— It is very annoying, as well as dangerous, to have a horse moving about unsteadily while the rider is attempting to mount; this restlessness is sometimes occasioned by his impatience and eagerness to start, and may then be remedied by having him held by the bit, with his right side placed against a wall, fence, or other firm barrier, where he can be kept until the lady has mounted. The horse must not be allowed to start immediately after the rider has become seated, but must be restrained until he is perfectly quiet, and must be chidden every time he commences to prance. A few lessons of this kind will teach him to stand still while being mounted.

When the horse from viciousness, or from dislike to carrying a rider, attempts to evade being mounted, he had better be disposed of; for should the lady succeed in mounting she will receive but little benefit from the ride, as the bad temper and unwillingness of her steed will not only make it unpleasant, but even dangerous for her.

Sometimes the restiveness of the horse may be the fault of the person holding him, who, perhaps, either takes too heavy a hold of the snaffle-rein, thus pressing the sides of the snaffle-bit against the animal's mouth, and pinching him, or pulls upon the curb-reins, which should not be touched. Either of these mistakes will cause the horse to move backward. Not unfrequently a horse will violently plunge and kick from the pain of some injury in his side or back, which, though not painful when the rider is seated, becomes so when she bears upon the stirrup. Such a horse is unsound and not suitable for a side-saddle.

STUMBLING.— When a horse, not naturally indolent, and having his ears well placed, allows the latter to project out and to fall loosely on each side of his head, he is then fatigued, and must be kept well supported by the bridle, for he may stumble, or even fall. Whenever a horse is felt to trip or stumble, the rider's body must instantly be inclined backward, her hands be lifted, and her horse be steadied and supported by sufficient tension on the reins. Should the tired horse be walking down a hill, he must always be well balanced by pressure of both leg and whip; this will keep him light upon his fore-legs, and he will not be so apt to fall.

A horse should never be whipped for stumbling, as it is not likely that he would do so of his own accord, and it would be cruel to punish the poor animal for what he could not help. It may be the fault of the blacksmith in not shoeing him properly.

Should an indolent horse fail to raise his feet sufficiently to escape tripping, the proper course to pursue will be to keep him collected and make him move at rather a rapid gait, because, when he is animated, he will lift his feet more briskly and to better advantage.

A straight-shouldered horse, when carrying a woman, will be apt to stumble, to bear upon the reins, and to move heavily on his fore-feet, and will therefore require an expert horsewoman to keep him moving in good form.

When the rider hears a metallic clinking sound at each step of her horse, it will be an indication that the shoes of his hind-feet are striking against those of his fore-feet; this is very dangerous, as in the trot, or gallop, he may "overreach" and strike one of his fore-legs with one of his hind-shoes in such a manner as to injure himself severely, or he may catch the toe of a hind-shoe in the heel of a fore-shoe so that they will become locked together, when the fore-shoe will have to give way and come off, or a terrific fall will ensue. Some horses overreach on account of their natural conformation, others only when fatigued; again, some will be free from this defect when fat, but will manifest it when they become lean from overwork, deficiency of food, or other cause. Young horses will occasionally move in this manner before they are taught their paces, but as soon as they are thoroughly trained this dangerous annoyance ceases.

When a horse falls to the ground, or merely falls on his knees, if the rider be not thrown off by the violence of the shock it will be better for her to keep to the saddle, as the horse will rise very quickly, and if she attempts to jump off he may step upon her as he is in the act of rising, or her habit may catch upon the pommel and add to the peril of the situation by causing her to be dragged along should the horse move on, or become frightened and run away. She must not attempt to assist the horse by pulling upon the bridle, but must allow him to get upon his feet in his own way. Should she be thrown off as he falls, she must free her skirt from the saddle as promptly as possible and quickly get away from him in order to escape being stepped upon as he rises. The fall of a horse upon his right side is much less dangerous than upon his left, because in the latter case the rider's left leg may be caught beneath him, perhaps injured, and she would then be unable to extricate herself without assistance.

WHIP AND SPUR.— A lady's whip is employed as a substitute for the right leg of the horseman in collecting and guiding the horse. For this reason, it must always be firm, strong, and well made. It is also used both to give light taps to the horse in order to increase his speed, and likewise, when necessary, to chastise him moderately and thus make him more obedient. If it can possibly be avoided, a lady should never whip her horse; but when it is required, one quick, sharp stroke, given at the right time, and with judgment, will subdue him and bring him to his senses. Deliberately to give stroke after stroke, or to flog him, will always do more harm than good, for it will make him wild, vicious, and unmanageable, and the lady will gain nothing by it except the reputation of being a *virago*.

When a horse has committed a fault requiring the whip, he knows that the first stroke given is for this fault, and submits; but he does not understand why the succeeding blows are given, and resents them accordingly. An expert rider will rarely whip her horse, and will never become angry at even the most obstinate resistance on his part, but will, instead, manage him intelligently, and subdue him in a subtle way that he cannot comprehend. She will turn his disobedient acts against himself in a manner that is mysterious to him, and which will make them appear to him to be the will of his rider. The horse will find himself foiled at every turn, in a way against which he can present no permanent defense, and there will be nothing left for him but submission.

When a horse fails in his attempts to gain the ascendency, and yields to her skill and authority, she should be generous and forgiving, and treat the vanquished one with kindness and consideration, letting him know that there is no resentment harbored against him. He will quickly appreciate this forbearance, and it will have a lasting effect. But while accepting the olive branch, she should not give him his usual pats and caresses for some little while afterward, as these acts might be misinterpreted by him as a weakening on the part of his rider, or lead him to imagine that he has been doing right instead of wrong.

A lady's horse should never be trained with the spur. The horse that requires a spur is unsuited for the side-saddle; even the dullest animal will soon learn that he is spurred only on one side, and will shrink from the attack by a shy or a jump to the right, knowing there is no spur on this side. An indifferent rider may place herself in danger by unconsciously spurring her horse, thus goading him to madness, and to such a frenzy of despair that the only alternative left for him will be to unseat his fair rider in order to escape the pain thus unconsciously inflicted upon him.

The novice in riding must not be dismayed nor discouraged by all the instructions in regard to defending one's self against restive and vicious horses, as she may ride for years, or even for a life-time, and never be in any serious danger. But a time might possibly come, when she would suddenly and unexpectedly be called upon to exert herself in order to exact obedience from her steed, or to extricate herself from a perilous situation, and then a knowledge of what should be done will be of great use to her. Being armed at all points, and understanding the means required for any emergency, she will not depend for safety altogether upon the caprice or the gentleness of her horse, but chiefly upon her own knowledge and skill; this will give her a confidence and sense of security that will greatly add to the pleasure of her ride.

EXPLANATION

1. The lips.
2. Tip of the nose. Figs. 1 and 2 form the muzzle.
3. Chanfrin, or face; the parts that correspond to the bones of the nose, and that extend from the brow to the nostrils.
4. The brow, or forehead.
5. The eye-pits; cavities more or less deeply situated above the eyes.
6. Forelock; hairs between the ears that fall upon the forehead.
7. The ears.
8. The lower jaw and channel, or space comprised between the two lower jaws. Cheek. Jowl.
9. The jaws: nether jaws.
10. The nostril.
11. The throat.
12. Region of parotid glands, at the posterior and internal part of each of the lower-jaw bones.
13. The crest.
13′. The mane.
14. Windpipe and groove of the jugular veins.
15. The chest, thorax.
16. The withers, or the sharp, projecting part at the inferior extremity of the crest and of the mane. It is formed by the projection of the first dorsal vertebra.
17. The back, or part upon which the saddle is placed.
18. The ribs.
19. The passage for the girths.
20. The loins.
21. The croup; the most elevated part of the posterior extremity of the body.
22. The tail.
24. The flank.
25. The abdomen.
27. The saphena vein.
28. The shoulder and arm.
28′. The point of the shoulder.
29. The elbow.
30. The fore-arm.
32. The knee.
33. The cannon bone, shank.
34. The large pastern joint.
35. The small pastern joint.
36. The coronet.
37. The front foot and hoof.
38. The fetlock and ergot. The fetlock consists of hairs, and the ergot of a horny-like substance constantly found at the back and lower part of the large pastern joints.
39. The haunch.
40. The thigh, gaskin, or femur.
41. The stifle joint.
42. The buttock.
43. The tibia, or leg proper (lower thigh); a small bone lies behind it, the fibula.
44. The hock (curb place).
44′. The point of the hock.
46. The cannon bone.
47. The large pastern joint.
48. The fetlock and ergot.
49. The small pastern joint.
50. The coronet.
51. Hind-foot and hoof.

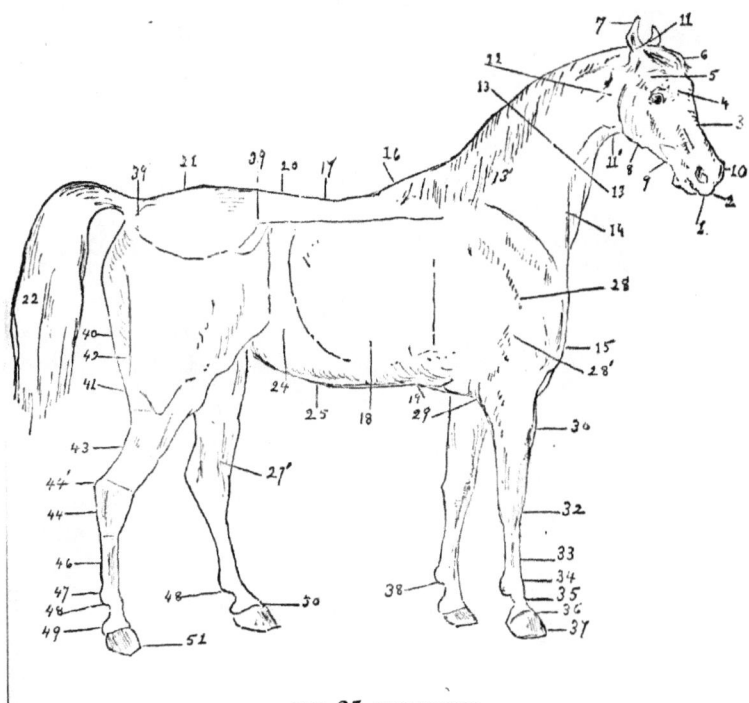

FIG. 35—THE HORSE

ADDENDA
GOOD RULES TO BE REMEMBERED

(1.) WHEN IN COMPANY with a gentleman, an accomplished horsewoman will prefer to have him ride at the right side of her horse, because, being thoroughly able to control her steed, she will require little or no assistance from the cavalier. On the contrary, if she be an inexperienced rider, it will be better for the gentleman to ride at the left side, because, in this position, his right hand will be free to render any assistance she may require, and he will also be placed between her and any approaching object.

(2.) A FINISHED HORSEMAN, when riding at the left side of a lady's horse, will not allow his spurs to catch in her dress, nor will he permit his steed to press so closely against this left side as to injure or interfere with the action of her left foot and leg.

(3.) IN THE PARK, or in any public place, a gentleman should always approach a lady on the off-side of her horse.

(4.) WHEN IN COMPANY with two ladies, a gentleman should ride on the off-side of them, and never between the two, unless they request it.

(5.) WHEN OBLIGED TO pass or meet a lady who is riding without an escort, always do so at a moderate gait; this is an act of politeness and consideration which may prevent her steed from becoming fractious.

(6.) WHEN PASSING BY a horseman who is leading another horse, never ride by him on the side of the led animal, for if you do the latter will be apt to kick or plunge, and become unruly. This precaution is essential for the safety of the horsewoman, as well as for the better management of the led horse by the horseman. In a crowded place it will be better to wait until there is sufficient room to pass without hindrance.

(7.) GIVE ASSISTANCE TO a companion, or other lady rider, when it is indispensable for her safety, but do not give advice unless directly requested. And if, when you are riding a fractious horse, assistance be politely offered, do not decline it.

(8.) In city, town, or village, always ride at a moderate gait.

(9.) Be extremely careful never to ask for a friend's horse to ride, but always wait until the animal is freely offered, and when accepted, do not follow the advice contained in the horseman's proverb,—"With spurs of one's own and the horse of a friend, one can go where he pleases."

(10.) Before setting out for a ride, in company with other lady riders, the equestrienne, after having mounted, should move a short distance away from the others, and then keep her horse perfectly quiet and steady; by this course the neighboring horses will not be apt to become uneasy and restive while her companions are mounting.

(11.) Always, when with others, begin the ride at a moderate gait. A number of horses, fresh from the stable, when assembled together, are apt, if started on a gallop, to become too highly excited; and it will always be better to have them start slowly.

(12.) Should a lady be a better horsewoman than her companions, and be riding a horse superior to theirs, she should restrain him, and not allow him to be constantly in advance of the others. It will be more courteous for her to follow the lead of her companions, and to consult with them as to the kind and rapidity of gait most agreeable to them. The preceding rules of politeness and propriety will be readily understood and appreciated. A lady under no circumstances will forget her tact and consideration for others.

(13.) In riding up hill the body should be inclined forward, and the bridle-hand be advanced, in order to give the horse space to extend his head and neck, as it is natural for him to do under such circumstances. In case the ascent be very steep, the rider may support herself by holding, with her right hand, to her horse's mane, but never to the off-pommel, because her weight may cause the saddle to slip backward.

(14.) In riding down hill the body must be inclined more or less backward, in proportion to the steepness of the hill, and as the horse lowers his head upon the commencement of the descent, the rider must advance her bridle-hand just enough barely to feel his mouth. Timid and awkward riders, on descending a hill, are apt to confine the horse's head too much, thus keeping it too high, and preventing him from freely stepping out, as well as from placing his feet firmly upon the ground. By doing this, they are likely to bring about the very catastrophe they are trying to avoid, namely, a stumble and a fall. Never ride at a rapid gait when going down hill.

(15.) IT IS ALWAYS customary to keep to the left when passing by others on horseback or in vehicles, who are going in the same direction as the rider; and in passing those who are approaching, to keep to the right. But, in the latter instance, should anything be present that might cause the horse to shy, and a declivity, ditch, or other source of danger be on the right, while none exists on the left, it will then be safer for the rider to take the left side.

(16.) WHEN CROSSING A stream, or when allowing one's horse to drink from it, a watchful eye should be kept upon him, especially in warm weather, lest he attempt to take an impromptu bath. If he begins to paw the water, or bend his knees, the rider must raise his head, give him a sharp stroke with the whip, and hurry him on.

(17.) AFTER SEVERE EXERCISE, or when the horse is very warm, he should neither be fed nor be allowed to drink until a sufficient time has passed to enable him to become composed, rested, and cool. Many a valuable steed has been lost because his mistress did not know this simple, but highly important rule. Again, a horse should never be ridden at a fast gait just after he has eaten a meal, or taken a good drink; he should be allowed at least an hour in which to have his meal digested.

(18.) A HORSE SHOULD never be allowed to drink from a public trough, if it can possibly be avoided; and when he is permitted to do so, the trough should first be emptied and then filled anew. Horses often contract serious diseases from these public drinking-places.

(19.) WHEN RIDING OVER a rough road, the horse's mouth should only be lightly felt, and he should be allowed to have his own way in selecting the safest places upon which to step.

(20.) WHEN IT IS observed that the horse is moving uneasily, at the same time violently twitching his tail, or giving a kick outward or under him, the rider may be certain that something is hurting him, and should immediately dismount, loosen the saddle-girths, and carefully inspect the girths, the saddle, and parts touched by them to ascertain whether a nail be loosened from the saddle, the skin be pinched or abraded, the hair be pulled upon by the girths, or whether some hard object has become placed beneath the saddle, etc.; she should also care-fully examine the head stall and bit, to see that all is right about the horse's head; after having removed or diminished the irritating cause, she should carefully readjust both saddle and girths.

(21.) IF, WHEN RIDING rapidly, it be observed that the horse is breathing with difficulty and with a strange noise, or that his head and ears are drooping, the rider should immediately stop him, as he has been driven too hard, and is on the point of falling.

(22.) A LADY'S HORSE should never be placed in harness, because in order to pull a load he will be obliged to throw his weight forward, thus spoiling the lightness of his saddle gaits.

(23.) WHEN TURNING A corner the horse should not be drawn around by the reins; these should merely indicate the desired direc-tion for the turn, and should never be drawn upon more than will bring that eye of the animal which is toward the direction of the turn into view of the rider.

(24.) SHOULD A HORSE which is usually spirited move languidly, and, during warm, or moderately cold weather, have his hair stand out and appear rough, particularly about the head and neck, or should he frequently cough, it would be better to relinquish the ride, have him returned to the stable, and a warm bran-mash given to him as quickly as possible. It may be that he has contracted only a cold that can be checked by prompt measures. But should he continue to grow worse, a veterinary surgeon should be speedily summoned. Be very firm and decided in not permitting the groom to administer his favorite patent medicines, because such nostrums are as liable to occasion injury to animals as similar preparations are to human beings.

(25.) A FEW OBSERVATIONS with regard to shoeing a horse may not be amiss. It may happen when riding on a country road, that one of the horse's shoes will come off, and the rider be obliged to resort to the nearest rural blacksmith to have it replaced. In such case she will find that some knowledge on her part of the manner in which a shoe should be fitted to a horse's foot will prove very useful. The blacksmith should not be permitted to cut the frog (the soft and elastic substance in the middle of the foot) of the foot, but should leave it entirely alone, and pare around the margin of the hoof just enough to adjust the shoe evenly and firmly. Country blacksmiths, as well as many in cities, are very fond of paring and rasping the horse's hoof, as they think they can make a neater fit of the shoe by such a course. An eminent writer on the subject of shoeing states that, except in case of disease, undue paring and rasping are never indulged in by persons who understand how to fit a shoe to the horse's feet properly; he also observes: "This is paring and rasping the horse's foot till it be small enough to fit the shoe, rather than kindle a fire and forge a new set which shall just suit the feet of the animal. It may to some readers seem like a jest, to write seriously about the horse's shoes being too tight; but it is, indeed, no joke to the quadruped which has to move in such articles. The walk is strange, as though the poor creature were trying to progress, but could obtain no bearing for its tread. The legs are all abroad, and the hoofs no sooner touch the ground than they are snatched up again. The head is carried high, and the countenance denotes suffering. It is months before the horse is restored to its normal condition."

(26.) THERE IS NOT the least necessity for stables being the foul smelling places they so frequently are, for if the hostler and his assistants perform their duties properly all offensive odors will be banished. A foul atmosphere in a stable, besides being repulsive to visitors, is, not unfrequently, the cause of blindness and other diseases of the horse, who will also carry the odor in his hair and communicate it to the clothing of his rider as well as to her saddle. For these reasons, a lady should always positively insist that the stable as well as the horse should be kept perfectly clean and free from obnoxious exhalations. Attention to cleanliness, and a free use of disinfectants will bring about this highly desirable result.

(27.) AFTER A RIDE, the saddle should always be aired, and placed where the sun's rays can fall upon its under surface. After exercise that causes the horse to perspire freely, the saddle should not be removed until he has become cool; this will prevent him from having a sore back, from which he often suffers when this precaution is neglected.

(28.) WHEN A LADY stops in her ride to visit a friend, she should always attend to her horse herself—be sure that he is properly hitched; that in warm weather he is fastened in a shady place, and that in cold weather he is protected, as far as possible, from the cold, as well as from wind, rain, or snow. It will sometimes happen, especially in the country, that, instead of being hitched, the horse will be allowed to remain free, but within some inclosure, that he may nibble the grass; in this instance, the saddle should always be removed, as otherwise he may roll upon it. A city horse, when ridden into the country, should not be allowed to eat grass, from a mistaken idea that it will be a good treat for him, for, as he is not accustomed to it, it will be very apt to injure him.

(29.) AFTER A GOOD seat and attitude in the saddle have been obtained, more freedom is allowable; should the rider have occasion to speak or to look aside, she should never move her shoulders, but only her head, and this momentarily, because it is required that a good lookout in front be kept up, to discover and avoid obstacles.

(30.) DELICATE PERSONS WHO desire to derive benefit from horseback riding in the country should select suitable hours in which to pursue this exercise. The intense heat of a summer noon should be avoided, as well as the evening dew, the imperceptible dampness of which will penetrate the clothing and, perhaps, implant the germ of some serious malady. Riding upon a country road in the noon heat of a summer day, where there is little or no shade, will tan and roughen the finest complexion, will overheat the blood, and will occasion fatigue instead of pleasure. An hour or two after sunrise or before sunset will be found the more pleasant and healthful periods of the day for this exercise. Riding in the country, when enjoyed at proper hours, is a sure brightener of the complexion, aerates and purifies the blood, and imparts wonderful tone to the nervous and muscular systems. Yet, in their great fondness for this exercise, ladies frequently carry it to excess, making their rides far too long.

(31.) WHAT TO DO with the whip, when making a call, has puzzled many a lady rider. Shall it be left outside, where it may be lost, or shall it be taken into the parlor, where its belligerent appearance will be entirely out of place? This much mooted question can soon be settled by the gentleman who assists the lady to dismount; he will usually understand what is required, and take charge of it himself. Or, in the absence of a cavalier, the whip may be handed to the groom who attends to the horse, or to the porter who waits upon the door. But should no groom or porter be present, it may be placed in some convenient and secure spot, as would be done with a valuable umbrella.

(32.) BEFORE MOUNTING HER horse, a lady should always pat his head and speak kindly to him, and, after the ride, should express her satisfaction in the same manner. The horse will fully appreciate these manifestations. Many persons consider a horse a mere living, working machine, yet it has been satisfactorily ascertained, by those who have investigated the matter, that this machine has feeling, affection, and a remarkable memory; that it appreciates favors, has a high sense of gratitude, and never forgets an injury.

(33.) THE SECRET OF secure and graceful riding is a correctly balanced seat in the saddle, one perfectly independent of reins or stirrup, and without exaggerations of any kind, whether the carelessness or indifference of the instinctive rider, or the affected, pedantic stiffness of the antiquated *haut école*. While maintaining a free, easy, yet elegant attitude, the rider should present to the spectator such an appearance of security and perfect equilibrium that it will seem as if no conflicting movements of the horse could throw her from the saddle. Carelessness and indifference cause the rider to look indolent and slovenly, while an affected, exaggerated stiffness and preciseness give her a ridiculous appearance, and destroy the pleasing effect of an otherwise correct seat.

(34.) GO QUICKLY IN the walk, quickly and regularly in the trot, and gently in the gallop. And bear well in mind the following supplication of the horse:—

> "In going up hill, trot me not;
> In going down hill, gallop me not;
> On level ground, spare me not;
> In the stable, forget me not."

ALL WOMEN ARE capable of enjoying the healthful exercise of horseback riding excepting those who may be suffering from disease. Every lady who has the means, whether young or advanced in years, should learn riding, for its sociability, healthfulness, and pleasure, without regard to her bodily conformation. It is folly to deprive one's self of this high enjoyment and captivating exercise, simply because one is no longer young, has only an ordinary figure, or because some persons appear to better advantage in the saddle, and ride with more ease and grace. According to such reasoning, one might as well cease to exist. If a lady cannot attain perfection, she can strive to come as near to it as possible, and if she secures a correct seat in the saddle, and a suitable horse, she will present a decidedly better appearance than one who, although having the slender, elegant figure so well adapted to the saddle, yet rides in a crooked, awkward attitude, or on a rough moving horse.

To become a complete horsewoman it is not necessary to begin the exercise in childhood. The first lessons may be taken in the twelfth year, though many of our best horsewomen did not begin to practice until they were eighteen years old, and some not until after they were married. Riding-teachers state that persons past their first youth who have never ridden learn much more readily, and become better riders than those who, though younger, have been riding without instruction, and in an incorrect manner, and, consequently, have contracted habits very difficult to eradicate.

Before closing this part of the work, there is one subject to which the author would earnestly invite attention. When a lady possesses a horse which has been long in her service, and been treated with the kindest and most loving care, and she finds that this faithful servant is becoming old and stiff, or that, from some accident, he has become almost useless to her, she should not part with him by selling him, for the ones to buy him will be those who have no sympathy for a horse and do not know how to treat him properly, but purchase him for hard and severe labor; their poverty compelling them to this course, as they cannot afford to buy any but old and maimed horses of very little value. To a well-treated and trained animal, the change from caresses to harsh treatment, from the pleasant task of carrying the light form of his mistress to the hardest of drudgery, must be acutely felt. The horse which has been kindly and intelligently managed is one of the most sensitive of living creatures, and has been known to refuse all feed and die from starvation, when placed under the charge of a cruel and ignorant master.

When the lady finds her favorite steed permanently useless, and cannot afford him an asylum in which to pass the remainder of his days in rest and freedom from labor, she should have some merciful hand end the life that it would be cruel to prolong in the hands of a hard master, simply for the few dollars that might be obtained for him. To thus destroy the animal may appear heartless, but, in reality, is an act of mercy; as it is much better for him to die a quick, painless death, than to be sold to a life of toil, pain, and cruelty, in which, perhaps, he may pass mouths, if not years, of a living death.

In terminating the present volume, the writer ventures to express the hope that her appeal to American women to seek health, beauty, and enjoyment in the saddle will not be passed by with indifference, and that the lady rider, after a careful perusal and due consideration of the instructions herein laid down for her benefit, may be awakened to a spirit of enthusiasm, and an endeavor "to well do that which is worth doing at all." To gain a knowledge of horsewomanship is by no means a mysterious matter confined to only a favored few, but is, on the contrary, within the reach of all. The requirements necessary to manage the horse are soon learned, but, as is the case with every other accomplishment, it is practice that makes perfect. Practice alone, however, without study or instruction, will never produce a finished rider; and study without practice will rarely accomplish anything. But when study and practice are judiciously combined, they will enable one to reach the goal of success, which every earnest rider will strive to attain.

In the endeavor to render the instructions and explanations in this work as clear and comprehensible as possible, many repetitions have unavoidably occurred; but as the book was more especially designed to instruct beginners, as well as those self-taught riders who have not had the advantage of a teacher, it was thought advisable not to leave any point in doubt, but as far as possible to render each subject independent of the others, and strongly to impress many essential points upon the mind of the reader.

To a majority of my countrywomen, with their natural tact and grace, it was only deemed necessary to point out their errors in riding; attention once called to them would, it was believed, undoubtedly lead to their prompt correction, and these riders would then cease to be victims of ignorance, constantly upon the verge of danger from incorrect methods of riding, and soon be able to excel in that most desirable and fascinating of all womanly accomplishments, secure and graceful horseback riding.

This has been the principal object of the author, who would not only have women ride well and elegantly, but with the confidence and enjoyment that true knowledge always imparts. Having spent so many happy hours in the saddle herself, she wishes others to experience a similar happiness, and if a perusal of these unpretending pages will create a zeal among her countrywomen for this delightful and invigorating exercise, and enable them to enjoy it in its highest sense, it will prove a source of much gratification to her, and she will rest satisfied that her efforts have not been in vain.

GLOSSARY
OF TERMS USED IN HORSEMANSHIP

Aids: The various methods employed by a rider to command the horse, and urge him to move forward, backward, etc., and in such gaits as may be desired. The superior aids are the hands acting through the medium of the reins; the inferior aids are the leg and whip. See *Effects*.

Appui, Fr. *Support*: The "give and take" movements, by which the horse is supported in his gait, called "appui of the hand." The sensation of the pressure of the bit upon the bars of the horse's mouth, experienced by the rider's hand. *Appui of the Collar*: The slope or talus presented in front at the union of the crest of the neck with the shoulders.

Attacks: Methods for urging or inducing the horse to enter upon any gait or motion required. See *Aids*.

Bars: The upper part of the gums (in a horse) that bears no teeth, and which is located on each side of the lower jaw. This part lies between the grinders (back double teeth) and the tusks; or, in mares and in horses deprived of tusks, between the grinders and the incisors (front cutting teeth). It is against this part, the bars, that the curb-bit rests. See *Cheek of the Bit*.

Bear to the right: To keep the right leg, from hip to knee, as stationary as possible, by downward pressure upon the right side of the saddle seat, and between the first and second pommels, at the same time keeping a firm knee-grasp upon the second pommel without hanging upon it; by this means, the rider guards against inclining to the left, a movement very apt to be produced by her position in the saddle and the motion of her

239

horse. The body of the rider must be maintained in an erect position all the time she is bearing to the right. See *Incline to the Right*.

Boot: A term sometimes applied to that part of the saddle-girths or flaps back of the rider's leg, and at which the horse may attempt to kick; also applied to the inferior portion of the rider's leg.

Bridle-hand: The left hand. When both hands hold the reins they are called the *bridle-hands*.

Bridoon: The snaffle-bit and rein, when used in connection with the curb-bit, but acting independently of it. The two bits together in the horse's mouth are called "the bit and bridoon," or "the curb and bridoon."

Bringing up to the bridle, also *Kept well up to the bridle*: To place the horse's head up and in position, so that when proper tension or pressure is made upon his mouth he will readily obey the reins. Some horses require stronger pressure than others, as stated under *Correspondence*.

Cannon bone, also *Shank*: The long bone situated between the knee and the fetlock joint on the front part of each fore-leg of the horse.

Canon: That part of a bit, on each side, that rests upon the bars of a horse's mouth when the bit is correctly placed.

Cantle: The somewhat elevated ridge at the back part of the saddle-seat.

Cheek of the Bit, also *Bars of the Bit*: The external straight or curved rods (levers) forming the sides of a curb-bit, and which, when the bit is in the horse's mouth, are applied along the outer sides of his mouth, the reins being attached to their lower extremities. That part of these rods situated below the bit in the month is called "the lower bar," or "cheek," and that portion above the bit, "the upper bar," or "cheek."

Chin-groove: The transverse furrow in which the curb-chain rests, on the under surface of a horse's lower jaw, at the back part of the lower lip. Also called "curb-groove."

Collected canter: A canter in good form.

Correspondence: The degree of rein-tension made by the hand of the rider upon her horse's mouth, which, when properly established, creates a correspondence between her hand and the animal's mouth, so that the slightest movement of the one is immediately felt by the other; in all cases this correspondence must first be had before any utility can be obtained from the "give and take" movements. Some horses require a greater degree of tension for this purpose than others, according to their training and the range of sensibility of their mouths.

Croup: The hind-quarters of the horse, from and including the loins to the commencement of the tail. This term is also applied by some to the upper part of the animal's back, where the haunches and body come in contact.

Curb-bit, also *Lever-bit*: A bit with a straight or curved lever or rod attached on each side, designed for the purpose of restraining the horse.

Curb-chain: A chain attached to the upper bar or cheek of thecurb-bit, and passed along the chin-groove, from one side of the bit to the other.

Curb-hook: A hook attached to the curb-chain, and designed to fasten it to the upper bar of the curb-bit; there are two of these hooks, one on each side of the bit.

Decompounded: Taken to pieces; each act, movement, or part of a whole or group, by or of itself.

Defend: A horse is said to defend himself when he refuses to obey, or attempts to bite, kick, etc.; he resists, contends.

Defenses: The resistances made by a horse when required to do anything, or when he is ignorant of the acts or movements demanded of him; he becomes alarmed, injured, or malicious, and employs his defenses.

Double bridle: The reins of the curb-bit and bridoon, when both bits are placed together in the horse's mouth.

Dumb-jockey: A couple of stout sticks or poles, crossed in the form of the letter x, and fastened upon the saddle; the reins are attached to the upper ends of these, and a hat may be placed upon one of them. Used in training colts.

Effects: Movements made by the hands, often aided by the leg or whip, which serve to urge the horse forward, backward, to the right, or left; indications.

Equestrian: A gentleman rider on horseback.

Equestrienne: A lady rider on horseback.

Equine: From *equus*, Lat. A horse; pertaining to a horse.

Equitation: Horseback riding.

False pannels: Pannels are stuffed pads or flaps, attached to and beneath certain parts of the saddle, in order to prevent these from injuring the horse; when these stuffed pads can be fastened to, or removed from the saddle at pleasure, they are termed "false pannels."

Fetlock: The tuft of hair that grows upon the back part of the fetlock joints of many horses' legs, and which hides the ergot or stub of soft horn that lies behind and below the pastern joint.

Fetlock joint: The joint between the cannon and the upper pastern bone of each foot.

Force the hands: The hands are said to be forced when the horse throws his head downward, pulling upon the reins so as to cause the rider to support the weight of the animal's head; sometimes this is effected so suddenly as to jerk the reins out of her hands.

Forehand: All that part of the horse in front of the rider.

Get out of condition: A horse is said to be in "good condition" when he is well, fresh, and sound; the reverse of this is termed "out of condition."

Girths: Stout straps or bands passed from one side of the saddle and underneath the horse's abdomen to the other side, where they are buckled tight and fast; they are designed to keep the saddle securely upon the horse's back.

Give and take: The traction and relaxation of the reins made by the fingers, and which must correspond with the movements of the horse's head; this action keeps up a correspondence with the horse's mouth, and at the same time supports him in his gait.

Hand: The height of a horse is usually measured by hands, four inches being equal to one hand. A rider is said to "have hands" when she knows how to use her hands correctly in controlling the horse by means of the reins.

Haunches: When a horse is made to throw his weight chiefly upon his hind-quarters, he is said to be "well placed on his haunches," and will then move more lightly upon his fore-legs. The haunch-bones are three in number, the superior one of which is firmly united to the spinal column (backbone) near its posterior extremity; the lower one on each side forms a joint with the thigh bone, passing downward in a more or less oblique direction. The obliquity of these bones enables the horse to place the muscles of the part in a position to act with greater advantage and power, and the degree of this obliquity serves to distinguish the thorough from the low bred, it being greater in the former. Wide haunches and broad loins are indications of strength and speed.

Hippic: Of, belonging to, or relating to the horse.

Hock, also *Tarsus*: The part or joint between the cannon or shank bone and the lower thigh or gaskin of the hind-leg: it consists of six bones; the part at this joint that projects backward and somewhat inward is called the "point of the hock." The hock is an important part of a horse, as any unhealthy or diseased condition of it will prevent him from resting on his haunches, and will thereby interfere with his free action in the canter and gallop.

Immobility: A disease in which the horse becomes unable to move, probably referable to the nervous system.

Incline to the right, or *to the left*: This differs from "bearing to the right," which see. It means, to incline the body, from the hips upward, to the right (or to the left), either when turning or riding in a circle.

In confidence: A horse is confident, or in confidence, when he completely surrenders his own will, and implicitly trusts to his rider without dreaming of resistance.

Inward rein: In turning or circling, the "inward rein," as well as the "inward leg," is the one on the same side as that toward which the horse turns, or the one toward the centre of the circle of which the turn forms an arc.

Legs well bent: See "*Well-bent hind-legs.*"

Lip-strap, or *Curb-strap*: Two small straps stitched to the curb-bit, designed to prevent a horse from taking the cheek of this bit into his mouth; an unnecessary appendage when the cheek is curved.

Lunge-line: A long strap or cord attached to the nose-band of the cavesson or head-stall of a horse in training, by means of which the trainer exercises and instructs him while he is moving around in circles.

Near-side: The left side. *Near-pommel*: The second pommel, on the left side of the side saddle; the second pommel of the old-fashioned saddle was called the "near-pommel," and the name still attaches to it. The "third pommel" is variously called the "leaping head" and the "hunting-horn," and is located on the left side of the saddle and below the second pommel.

Off-side: The right side. *Off-pommel*: The pommel on the right side of the saddle.

Outward rein: In turning or circling, the "outward rein," as well as the "outward leg," is the one opposite to the direction toward which the horse turns.

Overreaching, also *Forging, Clinking*: Is when a horse in moving forward strikes the heel or back part of a fore-foot with the toe or front part of the shoe of the hind-foot. When the stride of the hind-legs is carried so far forward as to strike the coronet or upper part of the hoof, it is then termed a "tread."

Pirouette: A movement in which a horse turns around without changing his place, the hind-leg of the side toward which he moves forming the pivot upon which he supports himself.

Port of the bit: The arched part in the centre of the curb-bit.

Resistances: See *Defenses*.

Retroacting: A horse retroacts when, in his volts, he steps aside, bearing his croup to the centre,—also when he backs toward an obstacle and fixedly remains there, against the will of his rider; and also when he suddenly throws himself upon his hocks at the moment his rider checks or stops him.

Ring-bar of the saddle: A bar attached beneath the saddle-flap on the left side and at its upper part, over which the stirrup-leather rolls.

Saddle-tree: The skeleton or solid frame of a saddle, upon which the pommels, leather, padding, etc., are properly disposed.

Snaffle-bit: Is the mildest bit used in driving a horse: there are two kinds, the plain snaffle and the twisted, and the latter form may be made to act very severely.

Surcingle: A wide band of cloth or leather, of sufficient length to pass around the body of a horse, and employed either to keep a blanket upon him, or to keep down the flaps of the saddle or the shabrack.

Thrown forward upon his shoulders: A horse is said to be thrown in this manner when, in moving, he throws his weight chiefly upon his shoulders and fore-legs instead of upon his hind quarters; he is then also said to "go heavy on his fore-legs."

Turn upon the shoulders: A horse is said to "turn upon his shoulders" when he throws his weight upon his fore-legs during the act of turning; it is a disunited movement.

Tusks, also *Tushes*: These are the canine teeth, two in each jaw, which grow between the grinders (back double teeth) and the incisors (front cutting teeth), being closer to the latter than to the former. They are frequently missing. Their uses are not well known.

Volt: The movement of a horse while going sidewise in a circle, his croup being toward the centre. There are several varieties of volt. An inverted or reversed volt is when the head of the horse is kept toward the centre of the circle.

Well-bent hind-legs: A horse with straight hind-legs does not possess good and easy movements; but if these limbs be well bent, he can be well placed on his haunches, and be easily collected, so that his action will be true and pleasant. See *Haunches*.

Yield the hands: Is to give the horse more rein by advancing the hands without allowing the reins to slip. To *give a free rein* is to allow the animal all the length of rein he requires without any traction or opposition.

HORSEMANSHIP
FOR WOMEN

HORSEMANSHIP FOR WOMEN

BY
THEODORE H. MEAD

WITH ILLUSTRATIONS BY GRAY PARKER

NEW YORK
HARPER & BROTHERS, FRANKLIN SQUARE
1887

EDITOR'S REPLICATION OF ORIGINAL TITLE PAGE

HORSEMANSHIP FOR WOMEN

CONTENTS

PART I

251

PART II

PART III

PART IV

ILLUSTRATIONS

PART I

AMATEUR HORSE-TRAINING

"MY DEAR," said my wife, "you don't mean to say you have *bought that* horse?"

"Why, yes, indeed," replied I; "and very cheap, too. And why not?"

"You will never get your money back," said she, "no matter how cheap you have bought him. Don't keep him. Send him back before it is too late."

It was a sultry July morning, and my wife stood on the farmhouse porch, in provokingly fresh attire, while I held my new acquisition by the bridle in the scorching sun; and just recovering as I was from illness, this conversation struck me as really anything but *tonic* in its character. However, bracing myself up, I replied, "But I don't want to get my money back; I intend to train him for my own use under the saddle."

"Oh, you can never do anything with that great horse. Why, he is the awkwardest brute I ever saw. Just look at him now!"

In fact, his appearance was anything but beautiful at that moment. His Roman nose, carried a long way forward and a little on one side, gave him somewhat the air of a camel; his coat showed no recent acquaintance with the brush; and as he stood there sleepily in the sun, with one hind-leg hitched up, he did not present at all a picture to charm a lady's eye. Nevertheless, he was, in fact, a reasonably well-made horse, a full black, fifteen and three-quarter hands high, sound, kind, and seven years old.

"He's just horrid," said my wife.

"Oh, that's nothing," said I; "that's only a bad habit he has. We will soon cure him of such slovenly tricks. Just see what good points he has. His legs are a little long, to be sure, but they are broad, and have excellent hoofs; his breast is narrow, but then it is deep; and that large nostril was not given him for nothing. You will see he will run like a race-horse."

"If you once get him started you can never stop him," said my wife. "You know how he pulls, and how nervous he is. He will go till he drops. You are not strong enough to ride such a horse."

"Oh, nonsense," said I; "you can see that there is no mischief in him. Look what a kind eye he has! The fact is, horses are often very sensitive; and while this one may never have been cruelly treated, yet he has been misunderstood, and his feelings hurt a great many times a day. Human beings are the only things he seems afraid of. As for his awkward carriage, it is no worse than that of the farm hand who has made such a failure of trying to use him, and who is, nevertheless, when he stands up straight, a well-made, good-looking fellow. A little careful handling will make that animal as different from his present self as a dandified English sergeant is from the raw recruit he once was. What do you think of his name? It is Sambo."

But my wife was not to be led off on any side question, and after intimating that such a plebeian appellation struck her as quite suitable, she continued; "Now you know that Mr. ——" (the farmer of whom I purchased) "knows a great deal more about horses than you do; you must admit that, for he has been buying and selling and driving them all his life, and he doesn't like him, or he wouldn't sell so cheap; and as for training him, for my part I don't believe horse-training can be learned out of books, as a woman would learn a receipt for making cake. Do get him to take the horse back!"

Now I have a great respect for my wife's opinion in general, and in this particular case all her points seemed well taken.

The horse was tall, and I was short; he was excitable, and I hadn't the strength of a boy; he was very awkward, and I had never trained a horse in my life. However, I had been reading up a little on the subject, and feeling the confidence in myself which a very little knowledge is apt to impart, I was determined to try my hand.

I had remarked that there was a certain French system which was, in the several works I had consulted, always spoken of with respect as a complete and original method, so I obtained a copy of the book, in which is set forth the *Méthode d'Équitation basée sur de nouveaux*

Principes, par F. Baucher, and having disentangled (no easy task) what was really practical from the enveloping mass of conceited sham scientific nonsense, I had numbered the margin so as to make a series of simple progressive lessons of half an hour each. The volume in question, which was not, by-the-bye, the present improved edition, I now produced in a somewhat dog-eared condition from under my arm. My wife, seeing that remonstrance was of no avail, took a seat on the veranda, so as to be ready to advise and assist, while my excellent friends, the farmer and his wife, came out "to see the circus," as they said, and established themselves in suitable midsummer attitudes, with countenances of amused expectation.

"The first few lessons must be given on foot," said I, and spreading my Baucher open upon the "horse-block," I proceeded to carry out its first injunction by placing myself, with riding-whip under my arm, in front of the horse, which was already saddled and bridled, and "looking him kindly in the face." He bore my gaze with equanimity, but when the riding-whip was produced he started violently; and when I raised my hand to pat his neck reassuringly he threw up his head and ran back. This evidently was not temper, but alarm. Clearly, moral suasion was not the kind that had been used with him hitherto. In plain English, he had been beaten on the head; and it was some time before he got over the impression made by such ill-treatment and ceased dodging at every sudden motion on my part.

However, a lump of sugar gave the poor fellow more confidence, and, avoiding all brusque movements, I went on to give him the first lesson of the Baucher series, viz., *To Come to the Whip.*

It is encouraging for beginners that this lesson, while producing conspicuous results, is in most cases very easy. In less than half an hour my audience was not a little surprised to see Sambo come to me at the slightest motion of the whip, and follow me about with neck arched, ears pricked up, and eyes lustrous with the unwonted pleasure of comprehending and voluntarily carrying out his master's wishes.

"Well, that's very pretty," said the farmer; "but what's the good of it?"

This criticism, it may be remarked, he continued to repeat at every step in the horse's education. He did not "see the good" of a double bridle with two bits. He did not see the good of teaching the horse to relax the muscles of his jaw and to hold the bit lightly in the mouth. He did not see the good of suppling the various muscles of the neck, on which, nevertheless, depend to a surprising degree the balance of the whole body and the easy motion of the limbs. In fact, he maintained his attitude of amused and good-natured incredulity until one day, after about three weeks, I rode Sambo into the lawn, his neck arched and tail displayed, and, with the reins hanging on my little finger, made him cut circles and figure eights of all sizes at a spanking trot.

COMING TO THE WHIP

Then my good farmer gave up, and said he really would hardly have believed it could be the same horse. What is more, he took off his own driving horses "the overdrawn check-reins" by which he had been hauling their noses up into as near a horizontal line as possible, and allowed them to carry their heads in a more natural manner.

The afternoon of his first lesson Sambo was put in double harness for a drive of ten or twelve miles, during which he annoyed me excessively by his restless dancing and fretting, so that next morning I expected to have to begin all over again; but, to my satisfaction, he had forgotten nothing, and came towards me at the first motion of the whip, so that I passed on to the *Flexions de la Mâchoire*, which we translate as the *suppling of the muscles of the jaw*. Here I came upon my first difficulty, and it lasted me several days. It was, however, the only serious one in my whole course, and from subsequent experience I am satisfied that my own awkwardness and disposition to compel obedience by main force were the principal causes of it.

However, success soon rewarded my perseverance, and I had the satisfaction of feeling the iron grip of the bit relax, and seeing the nose brought in and the face assume a perpendicular position.

Without at present going further into detail, I will simply say that at the expiration of a month, during which Sambo had been driven double almost daily, his education for the saddle had so far advanced that his head was admirably carried, his trot was greatly improved—his walk always had been light and swift—he could trot sideways to the right or left, could pirouette to the right or to the left on the hind-feet or on the fore-feet, responding to the pressure of the rein upon his neck or of the leg against his side, while he had become so steady that I could fire at a mark with a pistol from his back.

All this was very satisfactory progress, especially in view of my total inexperience, poor health, and the heat of the weather; but there is no doubt that any active young girl of sixteen or eighteen can do the like, for it was accomplished not by any mysterious or difficult process, nor by any exertion of physical strength, but by patiently following out, step by step, the processes which I am about to describe, and which are substantially those of Baucher, adapted to the use of a person of total inexperience, and that person a lady.

If any such, having accompanied me thus far, feels the impulse to try to improve her own mount, I will confide to her the fact that the incidents narrated really occurred within the last few years not a hundred miles from New York; and I hope that the following propositions, which are literally true, will help to encourage her to an undertaking in which she will find amusement, exercise, and a discipline as useful to herself as to her horse:

1. If, as is very likely, you feel a little afraid of your horse, you may be assured that your horse is a great deal more afraid of you.

2. If you can only make clear to him what you wish him to do, he will try his best to do it, and will feel amply repaid for his efforts by a few kind words and caresses.

3. His narrow brain can entertain only one idea at once, and therefore only one problem, and that a simple one, must be given him at a time.

4. Once the problem is mastered, a very little practice makes the performance of the task instinctive, so that it will be performed at the proper signal, even against his own will, provided his mind is occupied with something else.

This course of lessons is prepared with these facts in view.

"But is horse-breaking a fitting amusement for young ladies?" a mother asks, and with an air indicating that to her, at least, a reply seems quite unnecessary. My dear madam, it is not horse-breaking we are talking of, but horse-training, which is a very different thing. There are, doubtless, many women who could break a colt if they chose, but it is an undertaking which we certainly do not recommend. In the "breaking to harness" of an untamed horse there is naturally included more or less of training, but the essential lesson to be taught is that it is useless to resist the will of man, for sooner or later the horse will test the question, and put forth every effort to throw off control. When, however, panting and exhausted, he finally submits, he has learned the necessary lesson; and whether it be after a long fight with a brutal rough-rider, or a physically painless struggle with an adroit Rarey, he has learned it for life. Henceforth he accepts the supremacy of the human race, and, unless under the goad of maddening pain or terror, will never, save in rare instances, really rebel; obeying not men only, but women, children, and even the very tools and implements of man, so that a dog may lead him by the bridle. Like a spoiled child, however, a horse will sometimes presume upon indulgence, and, to use a mother's phrase, will try to see how far he can go.

At such times he is best opposed not by violence, but by firmness, reinforced, perhaps, now and then by a sharp cut with the whip, which, given unexpectedly at the precise moment of disobedience, will have the settling effect ascribed to the time-honored nursery "spank," and will bring him to his senses. Generally, however, what seems insubordination is in reality nervousness, which requires soothing, not punishment, and which you will be careful not to increase by fidgeting or by brusque movements of the reins. Even when severity is needed, a reproof in a cold, stern tone is often more effective than the lash.

Thousands of young girls, who for various reasons cannot ride in winter, have every summer within reach horses quite as good as the average of those at city riding-schools, but which they are never allowed to mount.

They look wistfully at the honest animals, longing for the exercise which would be so beneficial to their health and to their physical development, while so delightfully exhilarating to their spirits; but one horse is pronounced "skittish," another "hard-mouthed," and so on to the end. Nevertheless, some enterprising damsel manages to overcome all opposition, and, skirted, hatted, gloved, sets off in fine spirits. The horse, accustomed to the resistance of a heavy vehicle, moves forward with slow and heavy strides. Urged to greater speed, he rolls his shoulders so that it is almost impossible to rise to his trot. When put to the canter he pounds along the road, his hind-feet kept far in the rear and his head swaying up and down, while, missing the customary support of the bearing-rein, he all the time leans his heavy head on his rider's delicate arm, till it seems as if she would be pulled out of the saddle. However, the fresh open air is there, and the scenery; exercise, too, in plenty, and the pleasure of independent movement, so that our heroine is half inclined

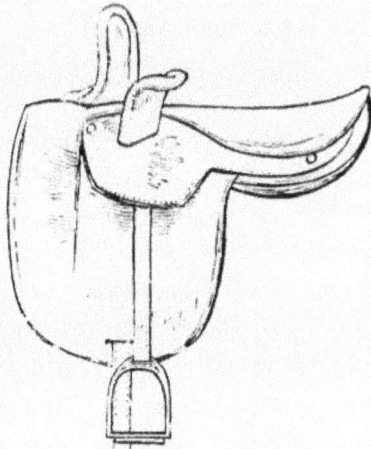

A GOOD SADDLE

to persevere. But, alas! an equestrian party on well-bitted, light-stepping horses sweeps by, casting a pitying glance at her rustic mount and helpless plight. Mortified and discouraged, she goes home and dismounts, determined not to try again. Nevertheless, her horse is very likely quite as good as theirs, and all he wants is a little "handling," as the horsemen say. For twenty-five dollars a riding-master will turn him over to her as docile and supple as any of them, and, with a little time and trouble, she can do it herself for nothing.

As for the proficiency in riding requisite, it is only necessary that you should not depend upon the reins for your balance—a common habit, but one destructive of all delicacy of the horse's mouth.

As the first half-dozen lessons of this course are to be given on foot, a riding-habit would only be in the way; so go to your first *tête-à-tête* with your new scholar in a stout walking-dress, easy in the waist, short of skirt, and of stuff that will bear scouring, for frothy lips will certainly be wiped on it. Let the hat be trim, the gloves strong and old, and the boots heavy with low heels.

The saddle should, if possible, be of the safe and easy modern pattern, with hunting-horn and low pommel on the right side—but of course any one which does not gall the horse can be made to do. It should have at least two strong girths, and must be so padded with wool as not to touch the backbone. Make sure, before putting it on, that there are no tacks loose or likely to become so in the lining.

The bridle should be a double one, with one "snaffle" or jointed bit, and one curb-bit, each having, of course, separate reins and headstalls. By-and-by you can use a single bridle, if you prefer, with whichever bit you think best suited to your hand and your horse's mouth.

The whip should be elastic and capable of giving a sharp cut (though you may never need to administer one with it), and it is convenient to have a loop of cord or ribbon by which it may be hung to the wrist. A good birch switch is better for your present purpose than the usual flimsy "lady's whip;" and if you are in the country, it makes a good whip to begin with, as you will probably soon wish to substitute a crop.

The place of instruction should be as retired as possible, so that there may be nothing to distract the horse's attention.

For the first few lessons it will be well, if you are not thoroughly at home with horses, to have a man—some friend or attendant—near at hand to give you confidence by his presence, and to come to your aid in case of necessity.

LESSON I
COMING TO THE WHIP

HAVE THE HORSE brought saddled and bridled. Walk quietly up in front of him, with your riding-whip under your arm, and look him kindly in the face. See that the bridle fits properly, as a careless groom may have neglected to adjust it to the length of the head.

The *throat-latch* should be loose enough to permit the chin to come easily to the breast; the bits should lie in their proper place on the *bars*, and the curb-chain should lie flat in the *chin groove*, just tight enough to allow your fore-finger to pass under it. The *bars* are that part of the gum between the *grinders*, or back teeth, and the *nippers*, or front teeth, which in the mare is destitute of teeth, and in the horse has a tusk called the *bridle-tooth*.

It is upon these bars, of course, that the bits should lie, and the curb-bit, according to military rule, at an inch above the tusk. By general usage they are placed too high, the proper place of the curb-bit being not up in the corner of the lips, but opposite or nearly opposite the chin groove, which is just above the swell of the lower lip. If the curb-chain is too loose the bit will "fall through," or turn around in the mouth. If it is too tight, or is ill adjusted, or if, from the bits being too high, it slips up where the skin is thinner and the bones sharper, it will give such pain that, to avoid it, the nose will be thrust out instead of being brought in. The chain should press below the snaffle, or the latter will unhook it. Adjust and settle the various straps with your hand, speaking kindly to your horse at the same time; but when you have begun to teach him, reserve all praises and caresses to reward him when he has done well. It is a good plan to give him a lump of sugar before you begin and after you finish each lesson.

Now, standing in front of the horse, take both curb-reins in the left hand at six inches below the bit, and, with the whip held tip downward in the right hand, strike him a light blow on the breast; in about a second give him another, and continue striking at the same interval, looking calmly at him the while, and following him if he steps backward or sideways.

A PROPERLY FITTED CURB-CHAIN

Sooner or later, and usually very soon, he will come straight towards you; then instantly relax his head, say "Bravo! bravo!" and stroke him on the face and neck. You will very likely hear him give a deep sigh of relief, like a frightened child. Give him half a minute or more, according to circumstances, to look about and recover from his nervousness—for you will find that his nerves work a good deal like your own—and then begin again, allowing him after every trial a half-minute or so of rest.

It will not be long before he discovers that the way to avoid the whip is to come straight to you, and he will do so at the least motion of it. Take advantage of this to make him curve his neck, put his head in the proper perpendicular position, and bring his haunches under him, by holding him back with the curb-reins as he presses towards you. This lesson, to a careless observer, looks rather pretty than useful, but is indispensable for your purpose, for it gives you the means of preventing the horse from backing while you are teaching him the flexions of the jaw and of the neck. It shows him, also, that the whip is only to be dreaded when he disobeys, so that later on it will become in your hands, strange as it may now seem to you, a powerful means of calming his ardor and soothing his impatience, and thus sparing your bridle-hand the sometimes excessive fatigue of restraining his impetuosity.

In practice it is not necessary to carry this instruction to the point where the horse will come to you from so great a distance as shown in the accompanying cut, though there is no difficulty in so doing.

A certain English nobleman used to say that a man was as much above his ordinary self on horseback as he was at other times above the brutes. Possibly more than one young equestrian, remembering the exhilaration of some morning ride, the quickened appreciation, the redoubled enjoyment of the beauties of nature, and of the charm of congenial companionship, will be ready to echo the sentiment. It is only true, however, even approximately, *when the rider controls all the forces of the horse*, and it is the object of the present article to put this perfect control within the reach of every one willing to take the time and trouble to acquire it, for not daring, but calmness, not strength, but perseverance, are the qualities requisite.

Both time and trouble undoubtedly will be required, for while, by even a careless use of this method, your horse may be made vastly more comfortable under the saddle, yet only by tact and patience can you win that mastery over his every volition by which his splendid strength, courage, and endurance will seem to be added to your own. You will find him, however, no tiresome pupil. On the contrary, every day will increase your pleasure both in his progress and in his companionship, for he will soon become attached to you, and will now and then turn his head and look at you with such an expression in his eyes that you will think the old belief in the transmigration of souls not so very wonderful after all. You will, besides, find in your lessons no contemptible discipline of character, for you will have to conquer your natural timidity in feeling your weakness opposed to his strength, to suppress your impatience when he is slow of apprehension, to remain calm when he is restive, and to award him your caresses, not because his neck is sleek and beautiful, but because he has done exactly as you directed. You will find also that they will have a tendency to improve your seat, by taking your attention from yourself, and with it some of the involuntary stiffness always born of self-consciousness.

A different, but equally practical, result of knowing something of horse-training is that wherever you may be you will have no difficulty in getting a mount—no small advantage either, as many an enthusiastic young girl can testify as she remembers the stony look which came over some comfortable farmer's countenance when she confidingly asked to ride one of his round-bellied horses. Many an owner of a trained saddle-horse would gladly have him ridden carefully by one capable of keeping him "in good form," while every horse-owner, no matter how poor his nags, dreads an ignorant rider as he does the epizooty. Probably scores of country stable-keepers and thousands of farmers, after a season's experience with ordinary city riders, have vowed never to let a woman mount one of their horses again. One of the former, at a popular summer resort, said to the writer, "Two ladies hurt my hosses more last summer than all the rest of the work. They ain't no more saddles to be found in my stable!" A neighboring farmer, who had at first thought to reap a golden harvest from his five excellent horses at a dollar a ride, hereupon remarked, "They hain't no sense. They think a horse will go like a machine, and all they've got to do is to turn steam on with the whip." Very different would have been the verdict had the riders but possessed even a slight experience in training, for the horses would have come from their hands improved in mouth and gait, and almost certainly uninjured by bad usage.

LESSON II

TO HOLD THE BIT LIGHTLY (*FLEXION DE LA MÂCHOIRE*),
USING THE CURB

B EGIN BY ASSURING yourself that the horse has forgotten nothing
of the previous lesson. Do not allow him to sidle up to you
upon your movement of the whip towards him, nor to twist his
nose towards you, but make him advance in a straight line.

Now, standing at the left of the horse's head, with your feet firmly
planted a little way apart, take the left snaffle-rein in the left hand, and
the left curb-rein in the right, at five or six inches from their respective bits, and having brought the head into the proper perpendicular
position, pull the two hands apart with gentle but steady force. Hold
your whip, meanwhile, tip downward in the right hand, to prevent him
from running back, which can be done without relaxing your pull by
tapping him with it upon the breast.

The object of this lesson, as well as of those which follow, is to
overcome involuntary muscular contraction. In some cases, as probably in the present one, the contractions are simply nervous, and will
cease with the mental cause; in others the muscles have grown into
improper positions, so that time will be required to set them right.

Your object at present is to get the jaw relaxed, so that you can
move it at pleasure without resistance, and this may take time and patience, for you must not be satisfied with anything less than complete
success, or you will repent it later. At first, however, seize the slightest
involuntary opening of the horse's mouth as an excuse to relax your
hold, caress and praise him, then let him stand a half-minute with his
head free, and begin again.

When he is submissive, and pleased with you, he will almost always show it by gently champing his bit; but do not be deceived by a

nervous simulation which you will probably detect, and which consists in opening the mouth a very little and immediately gripping the bit again. You will have been completely successful when, by simply drawing on the curb-reins, the head is brought to the proper perpendicular position, and the bit, instead of being gripped, is held lightly in the mouth, or, to use the school term, when the horse is "light in hand."

FLEXION OF THE JAW—USING THE CURB

This is the only lesson in the series in which it is possible (though not probable) that your unaided strength may be insufficient; if so, get some one to help you over the first resistance of the horse. With care and tact, however, you will in all probability require no assistance.

LESSON III

TO HOLD THE BIT LIGHTLY, USING THE SNAFFLE

B EGIN BY REPEATING in proper order all that has been done at the previous lessons. Now, having got the horse "light in hand" with the curb, relax the curb-rein and try to keep him light with the snaffle.

He will probably begin to bear on it. If so, restrain him by successive tugs, punishing him a little with the curb, if necessary, and always rewarding him with praises and caresses when he does well. Avoid any violent use of the curb, or the horse, in his efforts to escape the pain, may get his tongue over the bit, and thus acquire a very troublesome habit. It must be remembered that the bit being the principal channel of communication between his mind and yours, his whole attention is concentrated upon it, and he is almost as much disconcerted by a sudden harsh movement of it as you would be by an unexpected shout in your ear.

By this time your groom is perhaps watching you with interest, and may be trusted to repeat your handling, thus saving you some time and trouble; but, as a general thing, two lessons a day of from half to three-quarters of an hour each, are as much as a horse can receive with profit.

LESSON IV

TO LOWER THE HEAD

ALWAYS LOOK OVER your horse before beginning your instruction, to see that he has not met with any mishap. Observe that his eye is bright and that he feels in good spirits; run your eye over his limbs to detect any cut, bruise, or swelling; see that the hoofs are not cracked.

Assure yourself that he is properly groomed—one good test being the absence of scurf at the roots of the mane; that his mouth has been sponged out before putting in the bit, his hoofs wiped off clean—never, however, blacked—and that he is properly saddled and bridled. With a little practice you will do all this in half a minute,

LOWERING THE HEAD

271

while you are buttoning your gloves. About once a week ask after his food and appetite, and make the groom show you his shoes; and when the time comes for him to be re-shod (which should be at least once a month) positively forbid any trimming of the frog or of the inside of the hoof—any "cleaning up of the foot," as farriers are pleased to call it. The only part to be touched with the knife is the bottom of the outer, horny shell, which is not half an inch thick; and even this must be cut with moderation, never burned by fitting the shoe to it hot—the common makeshift of lazy farriers—nor filed on the outside, as both these operations not only weaken the hoof but impair Nature's arrangement for oiling and lubricating it. Should the

PUNISHMENT IN CASE OF RESISTANCE

horse not bear equal weight on all four legs, move him a step to see if the faulty posture may not have been accidental; and if it is repeated, examine the "favored" leg, carefully laying your bare hand on the hoof and joints to detect inflammation, feeling along the bones for lumps, comparing any suspicious spot with the same part of the corresponding leg, observing whether it is warmer or more sensitive than its fellow.

Having assured yourself that your horse is in perfect order, and that he has forgotten nothing of your previous instruction, you will now proceed to the lesson of the day. Place yourself on his left, or "near," side, take the snaffle-reins at a few inches from the bit, and pull his head downward. Should he not yield, cross the reins, by taking the right rein in the left hand and *vice versa*, which will pinch his jaw sharply, and pull again till he drops his head, when you will hold it down a few seconds, praising him the while; then raise it up, and allow him a little time to rest.

For our young readers we give below a few of the more usual technical terms, of which it will be found convenient to have a knowledge in the course of these lessons:

Amble.—A gait like pacing, but slower, in which the two legs on the same side are moved together.

Appel.—The gentle tug on the rein given by the horse at each step.

Arrière-main.—That part of the horse back of the saddle, called, not quite correctly, in this article, the croup.

Avant-main.—That part of the horse forward of the saddle—the forehand.

Bore.—To lean on the bit.

Bridle-tooth.—Tusk found in the horse's mouth, though not in the mare's, between nippers and grinders.

Bucking.—Leaping vertically into the air with all four feet at once.

Chin Groove.—That part of underjaw next the swell of lower lip in which curb-chain rests.

Curb.—Bit without joint, with levers at side and chain, which, passing under jaw, serves as a fulcrum to communicate pressure of bit to bars of mouth.

Deux Pistes.—To go on *deux pistes* is to advance with the body placed obliquely, so that the hind feet move on a different line or *piste* from the fore.

Elbow.—Joint of fore-leg next above knee, lying next horse's side.

Fetlock.—Joint next below knee.

Forearm.—That part of leg between elbow and knee.

Forge.—To strike the toe of the fore-foot with the toe of the hind-foot—usually the result of bad shoeing.

Frog.—Triangular piece of spongy horn in middle of sole of foot, forming a cushion for the navicular bone.

Grinders.—Back teeth.

Hand.—Four inches (one-third of a foot).

Hand-gallop.—A slow gallop.

Haute École—Haut Manége.—The complete course of training given in the French military riding-schools. To translate this by "high-school," as is sometimes done, produces a ludicrous impression.

Hock.—Joint of hind-leg between thigh and shank.

Interfere.—To strike the fetlock with the foot—often caused by bad shoeing.

Manége.—Horse-training, also the training-school itself.

Nippers.—Front teeth.

Pace.—A rapid gait, in which the fore and hind foot on same side move at same time and strike the ground together.

Pastern.—Bones between fetlock and foot.

Passage.—Moving sideways, as to close up or open the ranks, as in cavalry exercises.

Pirouette.—Wheeling on the hind-legs.

Pirouette renversée.—Wheeling on the fore-legs.

Piaffer.—A slow and cadenced trot, in which the horse balances a certain time on each pair of feet.

Piste.—The imaginary circle (usually, however, a well-beaten track) three feet from the wall of the *manége.*

Poll.—Top of head between the ears.

Rack.—A gait somewhat similar to *single-foot.*

Ramener.—To bring the head to the perpendicular.

Rassembler.—To get the horse together, with his legs well under him and his head perpendicular.

Shank.—Parts of fore-leg between knee and fetlock, and parts of hind-leg between hock and fetlock.

Single-foot.—A very rapid gait, taught principally in the Western States of America, in which one foot is put down at a time.

Snaffle.—Bit jointed in middle, without side levers or chin-chain.

Spavins and *Splints.*—Excrescences on bones of legs, usually caused by strain. When they occur on the fore-shanks they are called splints, and may do no harm. If on the hind-legs they are called spavins, and usually result in permanent lameness.

Stifle.—Joint of hind-leg between hip and hock, lying against horse's side.

Surcingle.—A girth extending entirely around the horse.

Thigh.—Popularly speaking, it comprises the two upper joints of hind-leg from hip to hock.

Throat-latch.—That strap of the bridle which passes under the throat.

Withers.—Highest point of shoulder between neck and saddle.

LESSON V

TO BEND THE NECK TO THE RIGHT AND LEFT, WITH THE REINS
HELD BELOW THE BIT (*FLEXIONS DE L'ENCOLURE*)

B EFORE BEGINNING EACH lesson it is well, as has been already
recommended, to review hastily the instruction previously
given.

Now place yourself on the left side of your horse, with your riding-whip tip downward in your right hand, and with your feet firmly
planted a little apart. Take the right curb-rein in your right hand at
about six inches from the lever of the bit, and the left curb-rein in your
left at three inches from the lever, and having brought the horse's head
to a perpendicular position, pull the two hands steadily apart, moving
the right hand to the right and the left hand to the left, so as to pry the
horse's head around to the right by means of the twist of the bit in his

"PULLING THE HANDS STEADILY APART"

277

mouth. If he offers to back, stop him by tapping his breast with the whip; if he tries to pull away his head, hold on tight, until presently he will turn his head to the right, when you will instantly say, "Bravo! bravo!" and after holding it so a few seconds, bring it back to its original position. Very soon he will take the idea, and you will bring his head around until it faces backward, being careful to keep it always exactly perpendicular, and not to allow the horse to move it of his own accord in any direction.

Now try to obtain this flexion with the right-hand rein alone, only using the left hand to assist it if he fails to understand or to obey, and also to bring back the head to its original position.

To bend the neck to the left requires simply a reversal of the process just described, and will give you probably no trouble. Do not be satisfied with anything else than an easy, graceful, and patient obedience on the part of the horse. Should he back or fidget out of his place, bring him

TO BEND THE NECK TO RIGHT OR LEFT, WITH THE REINS BELOW THE BITS

back to it before going on, as you will find that his associations (unconscious, doubtless) with place are remarkable, and that any fault is likely to be repeated on the spot where it was first committed.

When he will look backward on either side, and remain looking so upon your drawing upon the proper rein, the lesson is perfect. The utility of it may not appear at first, but will be evident at a later stage of your instructions.

LESSON VI

TO BEND THE NECK TO THE RIGHT AND LEFT, WITH THE REINS
THROWN OVER THE NECK

TAKE THE LEFT snaffle-rein in the left hand at about a foot from the bit, and with the right hand draw the right snaffle-rein over the horse's neck just in front of the shoulder, until both sides pull equally on the bit and the horse is "light in hand." Then, by drawing upon the right rein gradually, bend his head around to the right, gently feeling the left rein so as to keep the bit straight in the mouth and prevent him from moving faster than you wish; for in this, as in all other cases, while he is to do exactly what you direct, he is to do nothing more.

To bend the neck to the left, you will, of course, reverse the operation above described, standing on the other side of the horse, taking the right snaffle-rein in the right hand at a foot from the bit, and drawing the left rein over the shoulder with the left hand. Keep the horse "light in hand" all the time, and his head perfectly perpendicular, as any twisting of the nose to one side has a ludicrous appearance. Now repeat with the curb.

LESSON VII

TO MOVE THE CROUP TO RIGHT AND LEFT WITH THE WHIP

I T IS UNFORTUNATE that we have not in English a vocabulary of definite terms relating to the training and riding of horses. We will for convenience call all that part of the horse in front of the saddle the *forehand*, and all that part back of the saddle the *croup*.

Take both snaffle-reins in the left hand at a few inches from the bit, and standing near the horse's left shoulder, get him "light in hand" with the bit; and if his hind-legs are not well under him, make him bring them forward by tapping him gently on the rump with your extended whip, keeping the forehand motionless by your hold on the bit.

GETTING THE HORSE "LIGHT IN HAND"

Now, holding his head so that he will not move his left fore-foot, tap him lightly on the left flank near the hip until he moves the croup one step to the right.

281

Then pat and praise him, and if he has not moved his right fore-foot, tap his right leg with the whip to make him bring it forward even with the left. After a little rest begin again, asking and allowing only one step at a time, and persevering until he will move the croup one step over to each tap of the whip, pivoting on the left fore-foot and walking the right foot by little steps around it.

PULLING ON THE RIGHT REIN

When he is perfect with the snaffle, repeat the process with the curb, keeping his hind-legs well under him, and holding him "light in hand," while maintaining his left fore-foot immovable, with a delicate touch, to resemble as much as possible the action of the rein when drawn from the saddle.

Now repeat the process to the left, taking your stand near the right shoulder, and, with both snaffle-reins in your right hand and the whip in your left, proceed as before until the horse will walk one step at each tap of the whip around the right fore-foot, which should in its turn be kept so firmly in place as to bore a hole in the ground. Repeat with the curb.

This lesson, which will last, very likely, two or three days, may appear to some of no practical utility, but it is indispensable alike to your comfort when mounted, to the safety of those who accompany or meet you, and to the continued education of your horse. Who has not seen an untrained animal force his rider to dismount to lift some gate-latch which was really within easy reach, or prancing about in a crowd, to the terror and vexation of his neighbors, or in momentary danger of hooking his legs into the wheels of passing vehicles?

Now, if you trample on any one, or upset a light vehicle, though you risk, and perhaps break, your own bones, yet you are liable for damages; and this fact is so well known that a suit will be promptly begun against you. Besides, for your own sake you must have it in your power to get your horse's haunches, and with them your own person, out of danger from careless or mischievous drivers—just as a cavalry-man has to save his horse from a slash or thrust.

MOVING THE CROUP ONE STEP TO THE RIGHT

LESSON VIII
MOUNTED

*T*O ADVANCE AT *Touch of Heel and Stop at Touch of Whip on Back.*—Your horse's education must now be carried on from the saddle, and should he never have been ridden, it will be prudent to have a man mount him first upon a man's saddle, and afterwards upon your side-saddle, with a blanket wrapped around the legs to simulate a skirt. If the previous lessons have been carefully given, you will have no trouble in making him stand wherever you please while you mount, nor in getting him "light in hand" afterwards. First, however, see that the saddle fits snugly in its place, and that the girths are good and in order. If there are more than two, let the third be loose while the others are tight. The writer once saw a powerful horse burst

GETTING A HORSE ACCUSTOMED TO SKIRTS

285

two good English girths by a sudden bound and throw off his rider, saddle and all. If the girths and saddle are not very strong, put a broad, thin strap—a surcingle will do—over all.

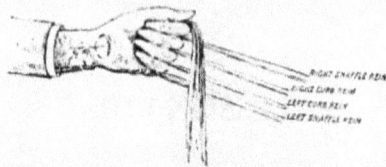

SHOWING REINS IN LEFT HAND

Being mounted, gather the reins all into the left hand in the following manner: Draw the right snaffle-rein between the fore and middle fingers, and the left snaffle rein under the little finger into the palm, throwing the ends forward together over the first finger, to be held by the thumb; in like manner draw the curb-reins into the palm on each side of the ring-finger, the left rein, of course, below, and the right above it, throwing the ends, like those of the snaffle, forward over the fore-finger and under the thumb. Now taking the curb-rein by the seam, draw it through your fingers till both reins fall equally on the bit; then do the same by the snaffle, but draw it so much tighter than the curb that the latter will hang loose, and any movement of your hand will be felt through the snaffle. Grasp all the reins firmly, your hand back upward, with wrist a little bent and elbow near your side, so that if the horse, stumbling, thrust his nose suddenly out, you will not be jerked from the saddle.

All this you will quickly get the knack of, and do as easily as you would thread a needle. You will observe that, having the width of three

ADVANCING AT TOUCH OF HEEL

fingers between the two snaffle-reins, you can, by bending your wrist to right or left, guide the horse as easily as with the reins in both hands. Get the horse "light in hand" by the usual play of the bit, first the curb, then the snaffle, tapping him on the right side, just forward of the girth, if he fails to respond or offers to back.

Now press him just back of the girth with your left heel, at the same time relaxing the rein a little. If he steps forward, pat and praise him, but if not, press him more firmly, at the same time touching him as before with the whip. When he moves forward praise him, and after a few seconds stop him, leaning back a little and laying your whip by a turn of the wrist on his back just behind the saddle. Then recommence, and persevere until he will start promptly forward at the touch of the heel, and stop at the touch of the whip on his back, keeping "light in hand" the while. If he is very sluggish you may have to strike him smartly for not answering instantly to the heel, but he will soon learn not to wait for the blow. Let the heel act close to the girth, as you will soon wish to move the croup over by the same means applied farther back. It is well not to start with the whip, nor by chirping or clucking, which is as likely

STOPPING AT TOUCH OF WHIP ON BACK

to excite your companion's horse as your own, and is annoying to most people.

Accustom your horse to stop short, whether at the pull on the reins, the touch of the whip, or the word "Whoa."

After riding have the saddle removed, and should a puffy spot appear on the back where it has pressed, take the hint at once and have the padding eased over the place, or a tedious and vexatious "saddle-gall" may result. There is no better treatment for such a spot than bathing with very hot water. As a preventive, however, it is an excellent plan to bathe the back with cold water, afterwards carefully rubbing dry.

THE WALK (COLT IN TRAINING)

The several instruments of torture represented in the above cut are the *dumb-jockey* upon the horse's back, the cavesson around his nose, and the *lunging-cord* in the hands of the groom—to whom the artist has very properly given the countenance of one who, had he lived in old times, would have lent a hand at the rack or the iron boot without wincing. The dumb-jockey has elastic reins, which are adjusted so as to hold the head in the proper position. The cavesson is a broad leather band, stiffened with iron, which is fastened around the nose just where the cartilage joins the bone, so that a tug upon it causes great pain, and will bring anything but determined vice to submission. These appliances are usually only the resort of laziness or ignorance, for none of them can for a moment compare with the human hand; and in fact they effect no saving in time, for it is not safe to leave a horse a minute alone with a dumb-jockey on his back, as he may rear and fall over backward at the risk of his life. The writer knew of an accident of this kind which ended the victim's usefulness in the saddle, and he has seen a strong and proud horse sweat profusely, with the thermometer at ten degrees below the freezing point, while being *lunged, i.e.*, driven in a ring, with a dumb-jockey on.

LESSON IX

MOUNTED

*T*o BEND THE *Neck to Right and Left.*—You can now, if you please, substitute a stiff *crop* for the flexible whip you have so far made use of. Having taken your place in the saddle and got your horse light in hand review the previous lesson; then, having your horse still carefully light in hand and light on foot—that is, with hind-feet well under him—draw gently upon the left snaffle-rein. When the horse's head has come around to your knee, keep it in that position an instant, and then put it straight again by drawing upon the right rein, insisting that his face remains perpendicular during the whole operation. Now go through the same process with the right snaffle-rein, and then repeat the whole operation with the curb. These flexions of the neck may now seem to you of doubtful utility, but as the education of the horse advances, your opinion will change. It is as rare for horses as for people to have a noble and graceful carriage; and while you cannot, of course, really change the shape of your mount, yet you can, by care, entirely change his appearance. His various gaits you can indeed improve, but for his *style* he depends, nine times out of ten, entirely upon you, and if you are indifferent he will be careless and probably clumsy.

BENDING THE NECK TO RIGHT AND LEFT

LESSON X

THE WALK

THIS GAIT IS apt to be hardly appreciated by youthful equestrians, whose love of excitement leads them often to prefer rapidity to grace of motion; but it can, with a little painstaking, be made swift and agreeable; and certainly, when light and animated, it shows off both horse and rider to better advantage than any other. It is, besides, an indispensable stage in the bitting of the horse; for until he will continue "light" while starting, stopping, and turning at a walk, he should not be put to a faster pace.

Your chief difficulty will be his propensity to drop into a jog-trot as soon as you try to quicken his steps; but this must be overcome by stopping him immediately and then recommencing the walk, urging him forward with the heel and encouraging him to lift his feet quickly by a delicate play of the bit, but leaving his head as free as possible. This will give you occupation, probably, for several days. Do not forget to praise him when he does well.

LESSON XI

TO MOVE THE CROUP WITH HEEL AND WHIP
(*PIROUETTE RENVERSÉE*)

HAVING YOUR HORSE light in hand and light on foot (that is to say, as we have before explained, with his face perpendicular, the bit held lightly, and his weight well supported on his hind-legs), tap him on the right flank with your whip or "crop" till he moves the croup one step to the left. Your great difficulty will be to prevent him from moving his right fore-foot, which by careful play of the bit you must endeavor to keep fixed to the ground, while at each tap of the whip the other three feet move one step around it. When this lesson has been satisfactorily learned, proceed to teach in like manner the movement of croup to the right, pivoting on the left fore-foot, substituting, however, for the tap of the whip a pressure with the left heel, applied as far behind the girth as possible.

Should he not understand this pressure, interpret it to him with the whip. As long as there seems to be any mental effort required on his part, pause after each step to caress and praise him. Be careful to keep him calm while learning, or he may tread one foot upon the other, possibly inflicting a severe wound, and after dismounting inspect his feet carefully to make sure that this has not happened.

MOVING THE CROUP WITH THE HEEL AND WHIP

LESSON XII

TO GUIDE "BRIDLEWISE"

UP TO THIS time your horse has been guided as in driving, by a pull upon one side of the bit, that is to say, upon one corner of the mouth, and it is time now to substitute a simple pressure of the rein upon his neck. The chief difficulty to be encountered is in the fact that, as the rein is attached to the bit, the tension of it against one side of the neck pulls the bit on that side, consequently conveying to the horse an impression exactly opposite to that intended. This difficulty must be overcome by patience, for this instruction cannot be completed in a single lesson, but will have to be carried on simultaneously with other work for a week or more. It is given by carrying your hand over, whenever you turn, to the side towards which you wish to go, so that the reins will press against the neck. Thus, if you wish to turn to the left, draw on the left snaffle-rein, and as the horse answers to it, carry your hand to the left, so that the right reins press against the right side of the neck. This must be done with judgment, or the bit, being pulled too hard on the right side by the tension of the rein on the neck, will stop him in his turn. Of course you will seek as many occasions as possible for turning, choosing, in preference, places where your intention cannot be misunderstood, as at a corner, for instance. There is no better spot than some old orchard, for the horse instantly takes the idea of going around a tree, and there will be more or less shade, and probably good turf. While he is learning this lesson do not distract his attention by other instruction; but as soon as he has mastered it, see that his head is always turned in the direction towards which he is to go, for it is a habit with horses, as awkward as it is common, to turn one way and look the other. At the same time always lean in your saddle towards the centre of the curve you are describing, and at an angle increasing in proportion to your speed.

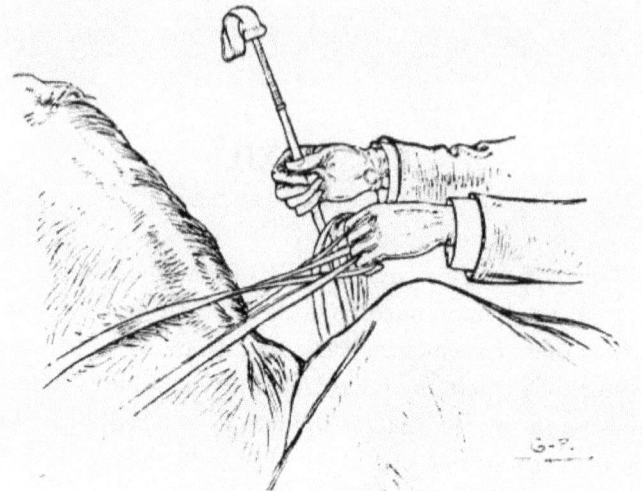

GUIDING BRIDLEWISE (TURNING TO THE RIGHT)

Some English writers depreciate the above method of guiding the horse, preferring to use the bit exclusively, but it is almost universal in the United States, and its advantages for ordinary riders are numerous and evident. Indeed, Stonehenge, a well-known English authority, says that in "this way a horse can be turned with a much greater degree of nicety and smoothness than by acting on the corner of his mouth."

LESSON XIII

THE TROT

WRITERS ON THE horse distinguish three kinds of trot, *viz.*, the "jog" trot, the "true" trot, and the "flying" or "American" trot. In the first the feet remain longer on the ground than in the air, and lazy animals are naturally fond of it, while spirited horses sometimes drop into it from impatience of walking. It is, however, apt to be a slovenly gait, which, though easy to the rider, should hardly be permitted.

In the flying trot the horse leaps a considerable distance through the air at each stride—evidently a mode of progression unsuited for ladies, who must attain speed in trotting by quickening the step without undue lengthening of the stride.

Your first care will be to prevent your horse from losing his "lightness," as he will be inclined to do at every change of gait or increase of speed—and this, while often by no means easy, is yet a task to be thoroughly accomplished if you wish for comfort or style in the future. You will observe in trotting, as in all other gaits, at each step a slight tug on the rein, called by some writers the *appel*, and this you will ordinarily yield your hand to, so as to keep a steady feeling of the mouth.

If, however, the horse begins to bear on the bit, hold your hand firmly, with the rein just so tight that at every step he will himself thrust his jaw against the curb. This will very likely bring him to his senses and restore his lightness, and if so, pat and praise him; but if not, tap him on the side with your whip, at the same time pulling on the curb for a second or two. If he does not yield to this, repeated two or three times, stop him short; and when, by the same method, you have got him to relax his gripe of the bit and arch his neck, allow him to go on again. He will dislike excessively to be stopped and started in this way, and when he finds that he will not be permitted to go in any way but the right one he will give up the attempt.

Do not try to succeed by giving a long, steady pull, nor by using force, as it will do no good, and may cause the tongue to be put over the bit—a very troublesome trick. Remember, in stopping, to lean back, and lay your whip, by a movement of the wrist, on the horse's back.

You will next turn your attention to your horse's gait. As the trot is rarely so easy that a lady can sit down to it with comfort, it is advisable to rise in the stirrup.

This is difficult and fatiguing if the stride is too long, and you will therefore prevent its extending too much by giving a little tug on the rein just as each step is made, at the same time with the heel keeping up speed and animation.

If your bitting has been thoroughly done, and your horse's mouth is fine and sensitive, you will probably find the snaffle best for trotting, and you will give a steady support with it.

Keep the step quick, elastic, perfectly cadenced, and without any rolling of the shoulders.

Should you happen to be mounted upon a horse which, from bad handling or his own faulty conformation, is disposed to "bore," or bear on his bit, you will ride with the curb, taking its reins in one hand, but in the other hand taking the snaffle, with the left rein drawn much tighter than the right. This will have an effect quite different from what one might expect, and will put a stop to this most fatiguing and annoying trick.

This recipe is not found in Baucher's book, but is said to have been given by him verbally to his pupils, and it is really "a trick worth knowing." If it does not have the desired effect, however, when practised with the left snaffle-rein, try it with the right, as the mouth—for instance, from the effect of double harness—may not be equally sensitive on both sides.

If you observe that the step of one foot is shorter than that of the other, making the horse appear lame, you may be almost sure you have fallen into the too common feminine practice of bearing too much of your weight on one side. An even balance in the saddle is of capital importance, and a rough-and-ready test is to observe whether the buttons of your habit are in the same plane as the horse's backbone, and your shoulders nearly equidistant from his ears—points of which you can judge as well as any one.

In the matter of the horse's gait you must be equally exacting, not resting so long as you can perceive the slightest irregularity or difference between the strides. It is desirable to cultivate such a sensitiveness to all the horse's movements as will enable you to know where his feet are at all times without looking, and the first step towards this is to learn to "sit close to the saddle." This firm and easy seat, coveted by every rider, is attained by some with much greater difficulty than by others. Many riders will bump about on their saddles for thousands of miles without being "shaken into their seat," because they neither abandon themselves to the instinct which correctly guides a child, nor, on the other hand, seek out and remove the cause, in the muscular contractions of the body and limbs.

A loose sack of grain set upright on horseback does not jump up and down, and, while it is not desirable to be quite so inert as a bag of grain, yet a lesson may be learned from it—which is, that the lower part of the person, from the hips to the knees, should be kept firmly and steadily, though not stiffly, in place, while the waist, with the back bent slightly inward, should be as flexible as possible, and the whole upper part of the person pliant and supple, so as to yield with a certain *nonchalance* to every movement.

Nervous riders, like nervous horses, are those in whom involuntary muscular contractions persist the most obstinately.

As both of the horse's strides are equal when the trot is true, it seems nonsense to talk, as some writers do, about the "leading foot" in trotting; and except that few horses are so perfectly symmetrical that both strides are equally elastic, there should be no difference to a man on which one he "rises," and he will therefore spare that foot and leg which, for any cause, he may suppose to be the weaker. A lady will without effort find the stride best suited to her.

Horses are often trained in our Western States to trot when the rider touches the back of their neck, and to single-foot or pace when he makes play gently with the curb-bit. These signals are injudicious, because in harness a slight movement of the bit sets the horse so trained to single-footing, and there is no way to communicate to him your wish that he should trot. It is better, therefore, to give the signal to trot by taking a firm hold of the snaffle, and laying your whip gently on his hind-quarter while you incite to speed with your heel.

After dismounting, observe whether your horse has *interfered*— that is, struck one or more of his fetlock joints with his hoofs; should the skin be knocked off, apply some healing ointment; and if the joint swells, bathe with water as hot as the hand will bear. This is the best remedy for all ordinary bruises and sprains.

LESSON XIV

THE GALLOP, HAND-GALLOP, AND CANTER

THESE ARE TREATED of by some writers as distinct, the canter being called "purely artificial;" but it will be convenient and sufficiently accurate for our purpose to take them up together and to consider the canter as what it in fact is—an *improved*, and not an "artificial," gait. Horses undoubtedly often canter in a rude way without being taught, as may be seen often in the field, and not seldom in harness, and you will probably have little trouble in getting your horse to do the same. It is this natural canter which is called by country people the "lope." It is of importance, however, that your horse should not change his gait without orders, no matter how hard pressed, this being especially true if he is to be driven as well as ridden. The signal to canter should, therefore, be such as can be given only from the saddle. It is well not to use the whip for the purpose, but to try by raising the bridle to lift the forehand, while stimulating at the same time with the heel. Should he persist in trotting, do not get vexed or discouraged, for he is only resisting temptation to do what he has expressly been taught not to do; but continue your incitements, raising the bridle-hand firmly at every stride till you have got him fairly off his feet into a gallop, when you will soothe his nerves by patting and praising him, and gradually calm him down into a canter, lifting your hand at every stride to prevent his relapsing into a trot. When he will canter promptly at the signal, you will get him "light in hand" before giving it; then make him start without thrusting out his nose, and keep him light by the means already detailed in the lesson on the trot. Next you will bring his haunches forward under him, which is the great point, and increase the brilliancy of his action by stimulating him with heel and whip, while at each step you restrain him by a gentle pull, so that he will not spring forward so far as he intended. Persevere until he will canter as slowly as he would walk. Your best guide will be to observe the action of some well-trained and well-ridden horse, and to endeavor to obtain the same in yours.

THE CANTER

To *change the leading foot* in cantering is, however, a more difficult matter, and we will postpone the consideration of it until his education is a little farther advanced. In the mean time you will avoid turning a sharp corner at a canter.

The hand-gallop is simply a moderate gallop in which the ear observes three beats,

as in the canter, but swifter; while in the extended gallop it hears but two,

though given with a sort of rattle, which shows that neither the fore nor the hind feet strike the ground exactly together, as they do in leaping.

Keep to the left, as the law directs, is an admonition on bridges and other thoroughfares in England which has often excited the surprise of Americans, very likely eliciting some such comment as "How stupid!" "How perfectly ridiculous!" Yet for many centuries it was really the only safe way to turn, whether on foot or on horseback, and as all our fashions of riding and driving are based upon it, it is hard to see why the custom should have changed in this country. In the olden time, when people went about principally on horseback, when roads were lonely and footpads plenty, it would have been "perfectly ridiculous" for a man to turn to the right and expose his defenceless bridle-arm to a blow from a bludgeon or slash from a hanger. Much more would it have been so had he a lady under his care, who would thus be left in the very front of danger, whether it might be of robbery from highwaymen, of insult from roistering riders, or of simple injury from passing vehicles. At the present day and in this country the danger last mentioned is the only one really to be feared, and it is so considerable that the question is often raised whether a lady be not safer at the right of her cavalier; but the still greater danger in this case of her being crushed between the horses, in case of either one springing suddenly towards the other, has caused it thus far to be decided in the negative. There is also always a possibility—slight, doubtless—of a lady's getting kicked or bitten when on the right; and it might be difficult for her companion, without risk to her limbs, to seize her horse by the head should he become refractory. In case of its becoming absolutely necessary to take a terrified or exhausted rider off of an unmanageable horse, there would probably be time for her escort to cross behind her and place himself at her left hand.

Now that we are on the subject, we may give a word of caution as to some other dangers of the road. Among those to the rider, the most common is *shying*; but vigilance—and perpetual vigilance will be necessary—will reduce this to the rank of simple annoyance. Get your horse past the alarming object somehow, even if he has to be led; get him up to it if you can, and then pat and praise him; never let him hurry off after passing it; never whip him afterwards.

Rearing is less common than shying, but more dangerous from the risk of pulling the horse over backward. To rear he must, of course, spring up with the fore-legs, and if his intention can be divined in time it may perhaps be frustrated by a smart stroke down the shoulder; but an active animal is usually up before his rider has had time to think, and the question is how to come safe down again. To this end, on no account pull on the bit, but, without letting go the rein, grasp a thick lock of the mane and hold yourself with it as close to the neck as possible—which will throw your weight in the best place, and prepare you to leap down, should it be necessary. If you have kept perfectly calm, so that the horse has not suspected that you were frightened, he will doubtless come down on his feet, and very likely may not rear again. If, however, you feel his hind-legs sink under him, he will be intending to throw himself down, and you must jump down instantly to avoid getting caught under the saddle.

Kicking, when coming unexpectedly, is more likely than rearing to unseat the rider. If you withstand the first assault, however, get the horse's head up by an energetic use of the bit, and look out that he does not get it down again. It is needless to say that should either of the last two tricks become a habit, it will make the horse quite unfit for a lady's use.

If your horse is restless and disposed to jump, or perhaps run, when horses or vehicles rapidly approach him from behind, occupy his attention by moving the bit a little from side to side in his mouth.

Running away is undoubtedly serious business, but all authorities agree that the safest plan is to let the horse run, if there is room, and that the best lesson for him is to make him continue running after he wishes to stop. A steady pull on the bit is quite useless, and so is any cry of "Whoa! whoa!" at first. But after a little the bit should be vigorously *sawed*, so as to sway the head from side to side if possible, and thus confuse him, while you speak to him in a commanding tone.

The dangers to the horse upon the road, however, are greater and more numerous than to yourself, but they may almost all be averted by care and watchfulness on your part. Beware of a fast pace on hard macadam; beware of loose stones, which may bruise the frog or cause a tedious sprain; beware of food, water, above all, of currents of air when he is warm.

LESSON XV

THE PIROUETTE, DEUX PISTES, PASSAGE

I N THE *PIROUETTE ordinaire* of the French *manége* the horse turns upon one of his hind-legs, walking on the other three around it, just as in the *pirouette renversée* of Lesson XI. he turned upon one of the fore-legs, around which he walked upon the other three; and now, as then, the chief difficulty is to keep him from moving the leg which is to serve as a pivot. The means for accomplishing this you have already acquired, and a pressure of the heel on the one side, or of the crop on the other, will prevent an intended movement of the croup, while by the rein against the neck you move the forehand to the one side or to the other. In wheeling to the left it is the left hind-foot, and

ORDINARY PIROUETTE

to the right the right hind-foot, which serves as a pivot. If your horse is stiff and clumsy in this exercise it will probably be because you have not got him together, with his hind-legs well under him, but at best you will probably find him less supple on one side than the other. Begin by moving the forehand but one step at a time, keeping your horse calm, so that he may not wound one foot with the other, holding your own person motionless, and gradually accustoming him to slight and delicate effects of hand, heel, and whip, so that he may to a by-stander appear to move of his own volition.

GOING ON "DEUX PISTES"

The *piste* (literally "trail" or "track") in the French *manége* is an imaginary circle lying three feet distant from the wall; which imaginary line, however, becomes in practice a well-defined path, which the horse soon learns to follow with little guidance from his rider. To go, then, "on two *pistes*" is to cause the horse to advance with his body placed obliquely, so that the hind-feet move on a different line from the fore-feet. In the cut the horse is shown directly across the *piste*.

The *passage* is a side movement without advancing. By it the cavalry close up their ranks, and to a civilian it is useful in many ways. Both of these movements you are now able to execute at pleasure.

THE PASSAGE

LESSON XVI

BACKING

THIS LESSON HAS been deferred thus far because, while it is one of the most practically and frequently useful, yet it is also the method which the horse naturally takes to escape from the unwonted constraint put upon the muscles of his neck and jaw in the course of the preceding lessons. You have had, therefore, to be on your guard hitherto against it; and had you taught it earlier you would have found your horse cunning enough to pretend to believe every play of the bit to be a signal to step back, and thus protract the instruction.

BACKING

Having, then, got your horse, as usual, well in hand, lean back and give a pull on the reins. If he steps back, well; if not, touch him with the heel or tap his side with the crop, and when he lifts his foot to step forward repeat the pull on the reins, when the foot will be replaced farther back; then pat and praise him, and persevere until he will, at each tug of the reins, move backward one step and no more.

Should he swerve to right or left, straighten him by a tap or pressure of the crop on his right side, or by the pressure of the heel on the left, as the case may require.

Your horse having learned to obey the pressure of the rein upon the neck, you may now, if you choose, adopt another method of holding the reins. It differs from that described in Lesson XIII. in that the two snaffle reins, instead of being separated by three fingers, have only one—the middle finger—between them; while the curb-reins, instead of coming into the hand between the snaffle-reins,

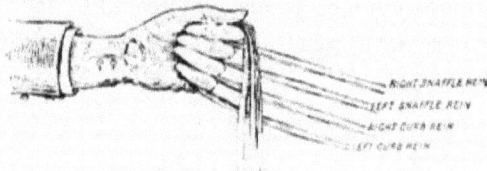

REINS IN HAND

come in below, having the little finger inserted between them.

This method, though formerly the one usually taught, being that adopted by the English cavalry, has not, on the whole, as many advantages as the other for a civilian.

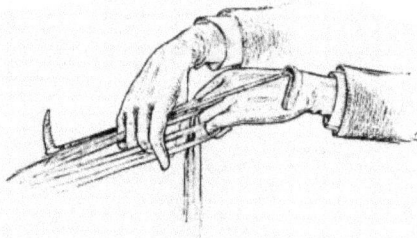

ACT OF CHANGING REINS

If you have occasion to use the left hand, or wish to rest it, change the reins into the right hand by placing the right, still holding the whip, over and in front of the left, both palms downward, inserting the right fore-finger between the reins separated by the left little finger, and so on, then grasping all together with the whip, and allowing the ends to pass out to the right.

This does not disarrange the reins, but makes it possible for you to take them back into the left hand in an instant by passing the left hand in like manner over the right.

LESSON XVII

RIDING IN CIRCLES—CHANGE OF LEADING FOOT

Y OU ARE NOW prepared to practise with profit a simple exercise, which you will find interesting to yourself, and, if carefully done, very improving to your horse. It is the riding in circles of small diameter. Mark out a number of rings of various sizes in some pasture-field with white pebbles or beans or small scraps of white paper, which may be scattered at intervals of two or three feet, so that the figures may not be remarked by the horse, but that he may receive his instruction from you only. Let the circles touch one another, so that you may change from one into the other, and thus turn to the right and left alternately. Begin at a walk, then proceed to a trot, practising first on the large circles, and then taking the smaller ones. Keep your horse "light in hand," and do not let him place his body across the line, but make him follow it accurately, with his neck and body bent around to the curve which it describes. When he is perfect in this exercise on level ground, move to some hill-side and begin again. When he can do figure 8's of a small size accurately at a smart trot on a pretty steep slope, you may congratulate your self on having made good progress, and may begin to do the large circles on level ground at a canter. Here comes in the troublesome matter of the "leading foot," and if you do not understand it, you must not be discouraged, for many persons ride "hit or miss" their whole lives long without thinking or knowing anything about it. The expression, besides, is misleading, and you will do well to study up the subject first on straight lines. Get a friend to canter beside you, and observe the motion of his horse's feet. You will see that the two fore-feet and the two hind-feet strike the ground not only one later than the other, but one in advance of the other, and that the one which leaves the ground last steps past the other and is planted farthest forward. It is this foot taking the long stride which is called, although it moves last, the "leading foot."

LEADING WITH THE RIGHT FORE-FOOT

It ought not to make any difference to the horse with which foot he leads, nor to his rider, if a man, so long as he follows a straight line; but whenever he has to turn, it becomes both to horse and rider of importance—if the curve is sharp, of very great importance—that he should lead on the side towards which he is to turn.

A little observation of your companion's horse when turning will make the reason clear to you. A woman's seat being on the left side of the horse, it is easier for her that the shoulder having the most motion should be on the right side, and ladies' saddle-horses are consequently trained to lead with the right foot; the result, we may remark, often being that the fore-foot which does most work gives out before the others.

The horse so trained, however, is in this way always ready to wheel to the right; but when he turns to the left, whether carrying man or woman, he must change and lead with the left foot; and if he has not sense enough to do so himself, you must teach him.

This, really, is not an easy task for an amateur, especially for the amateur feminine, who has not the efficient masculine resource of a pair of spurred heels. Even with their aid a man is often so embarrassed to make his horse comprehend that he gives up the attempt, and contents himself with "slowing down" before turning, his failure usually resulting from the insufficient previous training of the horse, coupled with his own ignorance of the successive short steps by which the latter may be led up to the performance of the wished-for act.

LEADING WITH THE LEFT FORE-FOOT

If you have been exact in the instruction hitherto given—if your bitting has been so thorough that your horse remains "light in hand" during all the manœuvres described in the foregoing lessons; if he responds instantly to the pressure of the rein upon the neck, and to the touch of the heel and of the whip upon the flank, so that you can move the forehand and the croup separately or at the same time in the same or in opposite directions; if he will rise from a walk into a canter without trotting; and if, finally, your drilling in the flexions of the neck permits you to bend his head to right or left when at rest or in motion without affecting the position of the forehand—then your horse is thoroughly prepared for the present lesson; and the same tact and patience which have brought you on thus far will assuredly carry you triumphantly through it.

First, however, you should learn to tell with which foot you are leading, and you can do so by leaning forward in the saddle while cantering, when you will see that the knee of the leading leg is thrown up higher than its fellow, and by bending still farther you may see this foot planted in advance upon the ground. If your horse has never been trained, it is as likely to be one foot as the other. Now, the first step to be taken is to put your horse in such a position that it will be easy and natural for him to lead off with the desired foot, and awkward to lead off with the other. This position is with the head turned in the direction you wish to go, and with the croup advanced a little in the same direction, so that the body is placed obliquely across the line of advance. Thus, if you wish to lead with the right foot, you keep his head turned in the direction you wish to go, while with the heel you move the croup over two steps to the right; then, touching him with the heel and raising the hand, you give the signal to canter, and he will probably lead off with the right foot. If not, stop him and try again, giving him a sharp cut with your whip just behind the right shoulder. To lead with the left the process is reversed, the croup being moved two steps to the left before the signal to canter is given, a sudden dig with the heel behind the shoulder conveying to the horse the hint to hurry forward his left leg. You can now begin to canter on the circles you have marked out; you will, however, at first come down to a walk before changing from one circle to an adjoining one—which change, of course, reverses the curve, and makes it necessary to change the leading foot.

This figure eight riding, thus, ∞, is most useful both for horse and rider when it is carefully done. Keep the horse "light in hand," and above all, *collected—viz.*, with his haunches well under him, and always with his feet exactly in the circle and his neck and body bent to the curve. As soon as he will lead off correctly from a walk, begin to teach him to do so from the trot; and when this lesson has been learned, practise him on the double circles, or figure 8's, beginning at a trot, and lifting him into a canter just as you pass from one circle to the other. This will accustom him to the idea of a change of movement at the time of a change in direction. Having got him to canter, continue on the same circle many times around and around, then bring him to a trot, and pass to the adjoining circle, lifting him to a canter just as you turn into it, as before, but of course leading with the opposite foot. Make your circles smaller and smaller, and continue till he has had time to appreciate the importance of leading correctly; then try to make him change at a canter, choosing for the purpose one of your smallest figure 8's, and indicating to him the change of foot on the same spot and in the same way as when you began by trotting, and you will no doubt be immediately successful.

If the horse in changing the lead of the fore-feet does not make the corresponding change with the hind-feet, he is said to be *disunited*. This fault must be corrected immediately, as it renders his gait not only uncomfortable to the rider, but very insecure.

PART II

THERE IS A large class of excellent people who feel a decided impatience at the very name of etiquette. "It is all nonsense," they say, and they will give you various infallible receipts for getting on without such an objectionable article. One admonishes you to be "natural," and your manners will leave nothing to be desired. Another sagaciously defines politeness to be "kindness kindly expressed," and intimates that if your heart is right your deportment cannot fail to be so too. All these philosophizings, however, give little comfort to the bashful young person just venturing into society, for unfortunately few of us are so happily constituted as always to think, much less to say and do, exactly the right thing at the right time, and the most unobservant presently discovers, very likely at the cost of no small mortification, that the usages of society, even when apparently arbitrary, cannot be disregarded with impunity. In the etiquette of the saddle, however, common-sense takes so decidedly precedence of the arbitrary and conventional that no courageous, kind-hearted, and sensible young girl, however inexperienced, need be afraid of committing any fatal solecism. The reason of this is that the element of danger is never entirely absent, and that the importance of assuring the safety and comfort of yourself and companions, to say nothing of lookers-on and passers-by, or of the noble and valuable animal you ride, far transcends that of observing any mere forms and ceremonies.

DRESS

Fashion at present, both in this country and in England, requires that the whole riding costume be as simple as possible, and entirely without ornament. Formerly much more latitude was allowed, and very pretty effects were produced with braid trimming across the breast, a little color at the neck, and a slouched hat with long feather or floating veil—witness the picture of the Empress Eugénie when Countess Montijo, and many a charming family portrait besides—but now fashion pronounces all that sort of thing "bad form," and a word to the wise is sufficient. The habit itself must be quite dark, or even black, perfectly plain in the waist, with black buttons up to the neck, and with a scant, short skirt only just long enough to cover the feet. The cuffs and collar must be of plain linen, no color or flutter of ribbon being anywhere permissible. The handkerchief must not be thrust in the breast, but kept in the saddle pocket, and if a veil is worn, it must be short and black. The hair should be so securely put up that it will not shake down, and that the hair-pins will not work out. In the matter of the hat more freedom of choice is allowed, and in the country almost anything may be worn, but wherever there is any pretence of dressing, the only correct thing is the regulation silk "cylinder," which, by-the-bye, usually looks better rather low in the crown, and which is every way a pleasanter and more serviceable hat than ladies who have never worn one are apt to imagine. About the cutting of a riding-habit, it may be remarked, there is nothing mysterious, although one might think so from the way it is often talked about, especially in the advertisements of fashionable tailors, and there is no reason in the world why any clever young girl should not make one for herself if she chooses. The only eccentricity about it, from the dress-making point of view, is the shaping out of a place for the right knee, so that the skirt may hang straight and not ruck up, and this can easily be managed at home by improvising a horse with a couple of chairs and a rolled-up rug, putting the saddle on it, and trying the effect in place. Be careful to leave plenty of room across the breast. A couple of straps should be sewn inside in the proper place, so that the toe or heel of each foot may be inserted to prevent the skirt from rising and exposing the feet; and these straps should not be strong, but, on the contrary, like all other parts of the skirt, and particularly the facing, should be made so as certainly to tear loose instantly in case of getting caught in a fall. Before leaving the habit, we may remark that the wearer should practise gathering it up, holding it in one hand, and walking in it at home, and if possible before a mirror. No petticoats ought to be worn, but merino drawers, and easy trousers of the same stuff as the rest of the habit. Beware of badly made seams, which have a vexatious way, as many a masculine wearer can testify, of pinching out a bit of skin at some inopportune moment. The trousers should be cut away a little over the instep, and fastened down under the sole with straps, which may be either sewed on or attached by buttons inside the band, in which case india-rubber is the best material, being easy alike on buttons, stuff, and fingers. Corsets should be worn as usual, but never laced tight, and it would be better that they should not have steel clasps or steel springs, which might be dangerous in case of a fall. The boots should be easy, broad-soled, low-heeled, and rather laced than buttoned, as less likely on the one hand to catch in the stirrup, and on the other to bruise the foot by chafing against the saddle. The gloves should be strong, but supple and easy, as it is important that every finger should have free and independent movement. Tight gloves not only benumb the hands in cold weather, but always cause an awkward handling of the reins, and may be positively dangerous with a fresh horse. As to the relative merits of crop and whip, there is room for difference of opinion. By many persons the former is looked upon as a senseless affectation of English ways, but the fact is that with a horse regularly trained to the saddle it is more useful than a whip, as by its aid a lady can "collect" her horse—that is, can make him bring his hind-legs under him, in the same way that a man does by the pressure of his calves. If, however, the horse has never been trained, and is sluggish or wilful, a whip may be more useful. Whichever of the two produces the better results will have the more "workmanlike" look and be in the "better form."

THE MOUNT

It is undoubtedly much pleasanter and more exhilarating to ride a good and handsome horse than a poor and ugly one, a horse adapted to one's size and weight than one too large or too small, too heavy or too light; but none of these points are matters of etiquette. On this whole subject etiquette makes only one demand, but that one is inexorable—it is *perfect neatness*. A lady's mount must be immaculate from ear to hoof, in coat and mane and entire equipment. It is in a great degree their exquisite neatness that gives such an air of style not only to English horsewomen, but to English turn-outs of all kinds, which, nevertheless, have not usually the "spick and span new" look of fashionable American equipages. On coming out, therefore, prepared for a ride, take time to look your horse over swiftly, but keenly, noting first that his eye and general appearance indicate good health and spirits; secondly, that he has been thoroughly groomed, his mane freed from dandruff, his hoofs washed, but not blacked; thirdly, that the saddle and bridle are perfectly clean and properly put on. Every buckle should have been undone and cleansed, the leather suppled, and the bright metal polished; the girths, three in number—never fewer than two—should be snug, but not tight enough to impede free breathing; the bits in their proper place, that is to say, the snaffle just high enough up not to wrinkle the corners of the mouth, and the curb considerably lower, with its chain, which should pass below the snaffle, lying flat and smooth against the skin in the chin groove; finally, the throat-latch loose. While it is not always wise to reprimand carelessness on the part of your groom on the spot, it is well never to let it pass unnoticed, while, on the other hand, it is a good plan always to show appreciation of especial attention to your wishes by a kind word or a smile.

MOUNTING

It is rather a trying ordeal for an inexperienced rider to mount a tall horse from the ground, even when there are no lookers-on, and many a one remains in bondage to chairs and horse-blocks all her life long rather than undertake it. The feat, however, is really so much easier than it looks, and when well performed makes the rider appear so agile and graceful, giving such an air of style and *savoir-faire* to the departure, that it is well worth every lady's while to acquire it. The first requisite is that the horse should stand still, and for this purpose the attendant should have given him some preliminary exercise, as the fresh air and bright light are so exhilarating to a high-strung horse that he cannot at first restrain his impulse to caper about. This preparatory airing should be entered upon invariably as calmly as possible, and begun at a walk, for a flurry at starting, and especially the use of the whip, will often disturb a horse's nerves for hours, making him unpleasant if not dangerous to ride. When the horse is brought to the

door, let the groom stand directly in front of him, holding the bridle
not by the rein, but with both hands by each cheek, just above the bit.
If he is a proud and sensitive animal, do not rush up to him excitedly
with a slamming of doors and gates, nor allow any one else to do so,
but approach with gentle steadiness. Stand a moment and look him

READY TO MOUNT

over, give your orders quietly, and pat his neck for a moment, speaking
pleasantly to him the while, so that he may get accustomed to your voice.

Now standing with your right side a few inches from the saddle,
facing the same way as the horse, and with your left shoulder slightly
thrown back, place the right hand on the second pommel, holding in it
the whip, and the reins drawn just tight enough to give a feeling of the
bit. Your attendant will stand facing you, and as close as convenient,
and will now stoop forward, with his hands clasped and with his right
forearm firmly supported on his right thigh. Now with your left hand
lift your riding-skirt in front, and place your left foot in his hands. Let
go the skirt, rest your left hand on his shoulder, and giving him the cue
by bending the right knee, spring up erect on the left foot, and, seating
yourself sideways on the saddle, place the right knee over the horn.

If your attendant is unused to rendering such service, you had better make your first essays in some secluded place, in which you can
instruct him where to stand, just how high to lift your foot, and caution

him to put forth strength enough to support you steadily, without lifting too violently. Do not be deterred by awkwardness on his part or on your own from learning to mount from the ground, for the more awkward, the better practice for you. Your attendant will now lift your skirt above the knee, so that it will hang properly without dragging, and then disengaging the stirrup from beneath the skirt, will place your left foot in it.

"ONE, TWO, THREE"

Too much care cannot be taken with the position in the saddle, which should be exactly as shown in the following cut. The left leg should invariably hang perpendicularly from the knee, with the heel depressed, and with the foot parallel with the horse's side. The length of the stirrup-strap should be such that the knee thus is out of contact with the hunting-horn, but near enough to be brought firmly up against it by raising the heel. The right knee should rest easily but snugly over the pommel, so as to grasp it in case the horse springs. Neither foot should be allowed to sway about nor to project so as to be seen awkwardly poking out the skirt. If your clothing does not feel quite comfortable, rise in your stirrup and shake it down, resting your hand, if necessary, on your attendant's shoulder, for it will be very awkward should it become disarranged on the road. Now put your handkerchief in the saddle pocket, take the reins in the left hand, or in both hands, as you prefer, and start the horse by a touch with the heel.

PLACING THE FOOT IN THE STIRRUP

It is, of course, the correct thing to mount from the ground, if possible, but here again common-sense comes so decidedly to the front that it is not too much to say that the sole indispensable requirement of an enlightened etiquette is *good-nature*. Certain it is that the eye masculine will follow with pleasure, and perhaps with some emotion, the movements of the young girl who comes out bright and fresh, gives her horse a pat or two, with a lump of sugar, as she glances him quickly over, looks kindly at her stable-boy, and then skips gayly into the saddle from a chair brought out by a maid, while the same eye will rest quite unmoved, except by a spirit of criticism, on the self-conscious and selfish damsel, though she be put on in the most approved manner by the smartest groom who ever wore top-boots. Mount, then, from the ground, if you have some one to put you on and some one to hold your horse; or, if the horse will stand without holding, cautioning your escort—if you are not sure of his expertness in such services—to be sure to raise your foot straight up, and to give you warning by counting one, two, so that you may be certain to have the leg straightened before he begins to lift, as otherwise the result may be the reverse of graceful. When in the saddle, rise in your stirrup, as already suggested, and

smooth down your dress, meantime thanking your escort and telling
him how well he did it. This smoothing down of the skirt it is a good
plan to practise frequently, first standing, then at a walk, then at a trot,
till you can do it deftly, almost without thought, for there is no telling
at what inopportune moment it may become necessary.

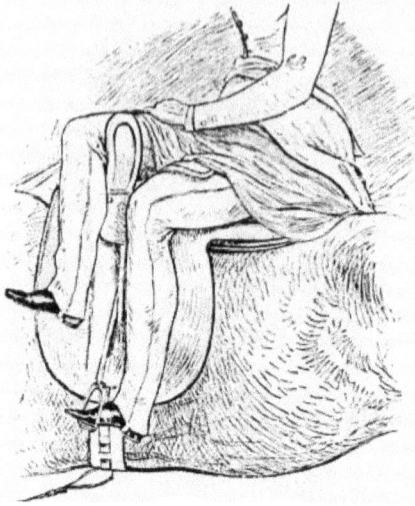

POSITION IN SADDLE

To mount from the ground without assistance is a feat which few
ladies would voluntarily undertake. It may be accomplished in an
emergency, however, if the horse is quiet and not too tall, by lowering
the stirrup sufficiently to reach it with the left foot, and springing up
with the aid of the hands, the left of which should grasp the mane and
the right the cantle of the saddle.

THE START

Do not put your horse in motion by a cut with the whip, which
would be trying to his nerves, nor by chirping or clucking, which
would be equally trying to the nerves of your companions, but by a
touch with the heel, or a pressure between your heel on the left side
and your crop on the right. If other ladies are to be mounted, move
on so far that they will be in no danger, either real or imaginary, from
your horse's heels, and never at any time put him in such a position
that he can kick any one, or that you can get kicked yourself by any

other horse. If you have to turn about on starting, try to do so by making your horse step around with his hind-legs (in the technical phrase, *pirouette renversée*), so as to avoid turning your back and presenting his haunches towards any one with whom you may be talking or from whom you are to take leave. To be able to do this easily and gracefully you must have him well "collected" and "light in hand."

ON WHICH SIDE TO RIDE

The next question that arises is on which side of her escort a lady should ride. This point, so much discussed and disputed in this country, is scarcely raised in England, where the universal habit of turning to the left makes it, under almost all circumstances, safer for her to be on his left, in which position he finds himself always interposed between his charge and any passing vehicle, whether it come from before or from behind. In this country, however, we have adopted—nobody knows why, unless it is because the French do so—the rule of keeping to the right, and yet without changing our manner of riding and driving, so that the result is often awkward and even dangerous. The teamster who used to walk on the left of his horses, so as to lead them out of the way when occasion required, still walks on the left, which now puts him in the middle of the road; the coachman still sits on the right, though the probability of contact has changed over to the other side; the lady's seat is still on the left side of the horse, which obliges her to choose between the danger of being caught by passing wheels or crushed by the horse of her escort. As there is no reason in the world, whether in the conformation of the female form or of the horse itself, or in the exigencies of equestrianism, that makes it inherently more proper to sit on one side of the horse rather than on the other, it seems strange that none of our independent American ladies should have undertaken to set the fashion of sitting on the right side. The Princess of Wales always does so, for some special reason. The Empress of Austria, who is well known as one of the boldest and most graceful riders as well as one of the most beautiful women in Europe, is said to have saddles made in both ways, using them alternately, and this plan is adopted by more than one of the noble ladies of England who hunt regularly in the season, with a view of preventing too constant a strain on the same set of nerves, and possibly causing an unequal development of the two sides of the person. However, accepting the present feminine seat as a thing not to be changed, the advantages in this country of riding on the one hand of the escort or on the other are so equally divided that the balance may incline to either side, and a lady is always free to do about it as she pleases without exciting remark. When riding on the right side, the lady is protected from passing vehicles, and the gentleman has his right hand free to assist her in any way, even to taking her off her horse in case of necessity; but if either horse were to shy towards the other, she might get bruised, and she is always liable to an occasional contact with her companion's person, which may not be pleasant. Children should certainly be kept on the right, and so should any inexperienced or very timid person; and at all times a gentleman should interpose himself between the lady under his charge and danger of any kind—as, for instance, reckless drivers, rude strollers, or a drove of cattle. When riding on the left, the lady is undoubtedly in a more exposed position, especially if her horse is disposed to dance or shy at rattling wagons and the like; but her escort, being able to ride closer to her, is enabled more quickly and safely to take the animal by the head, if necessary, and under all circumstances he should hold his reins and whip in his right hand, and in case of danger keep his horse well "collected," so as to be ready to act promptly and without any show of excitement.

THE SEAT

Position.—The lady's position on horseback is so conspicuous that the fact ought to stimulate the most indifferent so to place and carry herself as to show her figure to the best advantage, and this graceful carriage of the person will be found to be the first step towards achieving a firm and easy seat. The posture should be erect, the back slightly hollowed, the breast thrown forward, the chin drawn in so that the neck will be nearly vertical. The lower limbs should rest easily but firmly in their respective places, the left leg hanging perpendicularly from the knee downward, with heel slightly depressed, and foot parallel with the horse's side, the right toe raised a little above the horizontal, but not carried far enough forward to poke up the riding habit. The seat should be in the middle of the saddle, not on the right side of it with the body inclined to the left, which is excessively awkward, nor on the left side with an inclination to the right, which is equally awkward, and with the additional disadvantage of being sure to cause saddle galls. When the body is consciously *balanced* on the horse's back, when the shoulders are equidistant from his ears, and when the eyes, looking between said ears (an excellent habit), look straight along the road, and not off obliquely to one side of it, then the seat, whatever else it may not be, is at least in the middle of the saddle.

A SQUARE AND PROPER SEAT

The Hand.—As to the manner of carrying the arms, Colonel Hayes remarks that he has seen of late (in England) some ladies sticking out their elbows, but that he, for his part, decidedly approves of the old rule which forbade that daylight should be seen between a lady's arms and body. The sight which annoyed Colonel Hayes is not unknown in America, but probably most observers correctly attribute it either to ignorance or affectation. Certainly there is no reason for it, whether practical or æsthetic, as the raising of the elbow in which the reins act less correctly on the horse's mouth, while substituting angles for curves in the outline of the figure, and quite destroying the air of well-bred repose which is one of the great charms of a finished horsewoman. The arms should hang naturally by the sides, with the hands, a few inches apart, just above the knee, and as low as possible without resting on it, the nails turned down, the knuckles at an angle of forty-five degrees with the horizon, the wrists bent inward so as to permit of a little play of the wrist joint at each tug of the horse on the reins.

The Poise.—All this is not very difficult so long as the horse keeps quiet, or even when he merely walks; but how is this much-admired statuesque repose to be preserved at the trot, the canter, the gallop, to say nothing of incidental shying and capering? There is only one answer to this question, and that is—*practice.* But even practice is usually not sufficient without an accompaniment, infrequent and not always pleasant, *viz.,* frank and unflattering criticism; and every one who really wishes to excel, and to merit the praises which as woman she is certain to receive, will see to it that this wholesome corrective is often at hand. Practice itself, to be profitable, must be intelligent, and the cause of any discomfort from the motion of the horse should be sought out and removed. It will be found almost always to result from involuntary muscular contractions, especially of the waist, which should invariably be kept supple, as it is to a slight play of loin and thigh that the rider must look to prevent being thrown up by each spring of the hind-legs in cantering or galloping.

In rising to the trot, bear outwardly with the left heel, which will keep the knee close against the saddle, and prevent the leg from swaying about. At the same time be careful not to rise towards the left—an awkward but very common habit, which can be detected by the plan already suggested of sighting between the horse's ears. Mr. Sidney says, "The ideal of a fine horsewoman is to be erect without being rigid, square to the front, and until quite at home in the saddle, looking religiously between her horse's ears. The shoulders must therefore be square, but thrown back a little, so as to expand the chest and make a hollow waist, such as is observed in waltzing, but always flexible. On the flexibility of the person above the waist, and on the firmness below, all the grace of equestrianism, all the safety, depend. Nervousness makes both men and women poke their heads forward—a stupid trick in a man, unpardonable in a woman. A lady should bend like a willow in a storm, always returning to an easy and nearly upright position. Nothing but practice—frequent, but not too long continued—can establish the all-important balance. Practice, and practice only, enables the rider instinctively to bear to the proper side, or lean back, as a horse turns, bounds, or leaps." It is evidently not simply pounding along the high-road in a straight line on a steady nag which is here meant. The following advice, given by a lady who is herself an accomplished horsewoman, will furnish a clew to the sort of exercise which will be really profitable. She says, "Let the pupil practise riding in circles to the right, sitting upright, but bending a little to the horse's motion, following his nose with her eye; beginning with a walk, proceed to a slow trot, increasing the action as she gains firmness in the saddle. When in a smart trot on a circle to the right she can, leaning as she should to the right, see the feet of the horse on the right side, it may be assumed that she has arrived at a firm seat." Another excellent exercise is to lean over, now to one side, now to the other, now in front, far enough to observe the horse's action, the motion of his feet, and the regularity of his step.

ON THE ROAD

If good-nature is the quality most essential to *mounting* in a pleasing manner, that which will cause a lady to shine most *on the road* is kindness. Such a statement will perhaps bring a smile to the lips of some dashing girl who thinks that she has other means of pleasing, once mounted on a spirited horse, than the practice of any of the Christian virtues; but the writer, after many years' experience with *amazones* both young and old, believes it to be literally true. A lady who, without weakness, is gentle and thoughtful, will have, other things being equal, more sympathetic obedience from her horse, a finer hand, a more supple seat, and will bring him back fresher and her whole party home in better spirits than one who is not. To begin with, there is almost always one of the horses which is not equal to the others, but keeps up with difficulty, and as it is precisely that horse which should set the pace for the rest, it is well to observe the capacity of the different animals, and spare the feelings of any one of the party who may be poorly mounted. One might hardly suppose it necessary to mention so elementary a rule of politeness as that which bids us, when we ride in company, not to keep always in the best part of the road; but horses are sometimes selfish as well as human beings, and the selfish horse, like the selfish man, unless he is prevented, will imperceptibly crowd his patient companion into the ruts, when the rider will get the credit or discredit of the action. Another too common piece of thoughtlessness is the splashing at full speed through mud puddles, the result of which is naturally more apparent to one's neighbors than to one's self. If to an equestrian, however, being splashed or spattered is annoying, to a pedestrian it is nothing less than exasperating, and such a one will look after the person guilty of the rudeness with eyes of anything but admiration. One cannot be too careful, indeed, when riding near pedestrians, as they are decidedly susceptible under such circumstances, and likely to take offence; and especially is caution required where women and children are concerned, for it is impossible to conjecture what they will do if suddenly startled by the rapid approach of horses. The writer saw, one afternoon, a nursery-maid crossing Rotten Row with a baby-carriage (*Anglice, perambulator*), and two children holding to her skirts. When half-way over, a lady and three gentlemen came galloping down, followed by two grooms. The children scattered, the riders could not pull up, and for an instant it seemed as if the little party were doomed to destruction, as the horses appeared to pass right over some of them. The English rule, not only for country riding, but for the Park or other public places (and an excellent one it is), requires a gentleman to pull up and pass a lady, if alone, at a walk, whether she be on foot or on horseback, and though more latitude may be allowed a lady, yet she should not gallop up suddenly behind another lady who is alone, as a nervous horse might be so excited as to cause great uneasiness to a timid rider. If you should unfortunately produce such a result, by all means pause and express regret, and if your horse is quiet, offer to ride for a few minutes beside the sufferer—for so she may be called. In passing on the road, the rule is, when meeting, to keep to the right, but when overtaking, to pass to the left, and in like manner, when overtaken, to keep to the right, so as to leave the road free at your left. The only exception to this rule is in the case of led-horses, which, as they are often inclined to kick, should be avoided by passing next to the one ridden. When approaching a lady in a public place a gentleman should always do so on the off or right side.

It is sometimes rather a nice point to decide when assistance ought to be offered by a gentleman to a lady with whom he is not acquainted, and, if offered, whether it ought to be accepted. The following incident, recounted by Sir Joseph Arnould in his "Life of Lord Chief-justice Denman," is interesting as showing how such a question was discussed in what may certainly be considered as among the very best society in England. He says that on occasion of a visit which the Lord Chief-justice paid to Walmer Castle, three years before the Duke of Wellington's death, in a conversation about riding, the duke said, "When I meet a lady on horseback I always stop, and if her horse seems troublesome, offer to ride alongside her in the Row till it is quiet. The other day I met a lady on a fresh, violent horse, so I took off my hat and said, 'Shall I ride with you? My horse is perfectly quiet.' She knew me, for she replied, 'No, your Grace; I think I can get on very well.' After she was gone, I felt sure it was Jenny Lind." "We all agreed," adds Lord Denman, "that the great singer should have accepted the services of the great duke, whether she wanted them or not."

It is better not to fight a restive horse unless you have reason to be sure of victory, but rather get some one to lead him past the object or into the road which he may have taken it into his foolish head to object to. If he is in "that state of nervous irritability known as *freshness*" do not jerk the bit, but keep a steady, patient bearing on it, speaking soothingly to him in a low though steady voice, for his acute hearing will enable him to perceive distinctly tones which are almost or quite inaudible to your companions. Try not to have an anxious expression of countenance, no matter what he may do, but to look serene and smiling, as it will not only be more becoming, but will undoubtedly react upon your own feelings. If he pulls, it is well to take the slack of

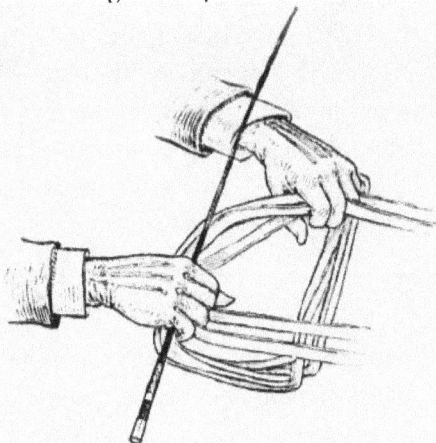

METHOD OF HOLDING THE REINS IN BOTH HANDS

the right reins in the spare fingers of the left, and *vice versa*, as this will give a firmer hold, and enable you to shorten the reins without relaxing their tension.

Always speak to your horse on approaching and on leaving him, and also whenever he has tried especially to please you, as your voice will soon come to have a great influence over him. There is a story told of two keepers in a zoological garden, one of whom was a favorite with the animals, while the other, though a more conscientious man, was disliked by them. The authorities, curious to learn the reason, had them watched, and it was found that the former always talked to the animals, while the latter served them silently. Too much conversation with one's horse, however, is apt to get to be a bore to one's companions.

THE PACE

This should vary with the nature of the ground, as it is dangerous to the horse, and consequently very bad form, to ride fast on a very rough or hard road. If slippery, a smart trot is safer than a slow trot or walk; but if walking, by all means let the horse have his head. If a steep place is to be descended, attack it at right angles, and not obliquely, for, when going down straight, a slip is likely to have no worse result than a momentary sitting down on the haunches, whereas, if going diagonally, it would probably bring the horse down flat. The canter, which is peculiarly the lady's pace, is much harder than the trot on the horse's feet and legs, especially on the leading foot and leg, and it should be reserved for comparatively soft ground. The lead with the right foot is easier for a lady, owing to her one-sided seat, than that with the left, and it would be considered awkward or ignorant for her not to start off with the right, although during a long ride it is well to change, so as to bring the strain upon a new set of muscles.

TURNING

Of course in turning you must always lead towards the turn, that is, with the right foot in turning to the right, and with the left in turning to the left. For instance, if you have to round a corner to the right, and are leading with the right foot, as will probably be the case, you have

nothing to do but to go on around, being careful to choose good footing for your horse, and avoiding particularly loose stones. If, however,
you are leading with the left, you must change, and you can best do so
in the following manner. As you approach the critical spot, *collect* your
horse with the curb, and bring him to a trot; then, just as you reach the
corner, make him swerve slightly to the left and instantly give the signal
to canter, at the same time turning him sharply to the right, pressing
your heel against his side back of the girth, and lifting the right snaffle-rein. It is well to draw back the right shoulder also, so as to throw
your weight on his left side, and leave his right leg free to make the long
stride. As this is by no means an easy operation for an unskilled rider,
except on a perfectly trained horse, I will give the directions also in detail for the reverse process of wheeling to the left. If your horse should
be leading with the left foot, you have, of course, no change to make.
If, however, you are, as usual, leading with the right, you must "change
the leg" to the left. As you draw near the corner, moderate your speed
and collect your horse with the curb, bringing him to a trot. Then, just
at the moment of turning, sway his shoulders a very little to the right,
give the signal to canter by raising your hand, and wheel sharply to the
left, at the same time pressing your crop against his right side back of
the girth, and raising the left snaffle-rein. While doing so, draw back
your left shoulder so as to throw your weight on the right side. If he
does not take the hint at once, do not be discouraged, but practise him
in some quiet place, choosing, if possible, a corner where the turn is
uphill; and when he does well, pat him and make much of him, for you
will find that no one of your admirers is more sensitive to your praises
than he. This matter of turning is well worth all the trouble it may cost
you, as it will give you a lively pleasure to find your horse's powerful limbs moving sympathetically to the gentle impulses of a woman's
hand, and, besides, it lends an air of style and *savoir-faire* which will
be fully appreciated by every looker-on who knows anything whatever
about riding. Be particular to lean over towards the centre of the curve
you are describing at an angle proportionate to the speed, just as the
horse does himself, that is, leaning to the right side as he wheels to the
right, and to the left when he wheels to the left. It is well not to let him
cut off his corners, but to preserve the same distance from the centre
of the road, just as if you were riding in company, and when this last is

the case be careful to keep exactly abreast both on the straight road and on the turns, for there is nothing that looks more countrified than to see riders straggling along irregularly like a party of mechanics out for a stroll on a Sunday afternoon.

It is well never to canter a carriage-horse unless you know him well, and are sure he will not thus be rendered unsteady in harness, and in like manner you should be considerate of your escort or companions, and not urge their horses beyond their proper gait. A good way to do, if you are much the best mounted of the party, is now and then, when the road is suitable, to gallop on and return again. It looks well to see a lady cantering beside a gentleman who is trotting; but the reverse never seems quite good form, and especially when it is evident that the gentleman's horse is galloping because he has been pushed off his legs.

A borrowed horse is an article which is looked upon with very different eyes by the elderly people who generally are the lenders, and the youthful riders that are usually the borrowers, and many a man, and perhaps many a woman too, remembers with shame and regret how little were appreciated or deserved the favors of this sort received in youthful days. A borrowed horse should be scrupulously ridden exactly as the owner wishes, and moreover the owner's desires ought to be respectfully ascertained in advance.

For cross-country riding the stirrups should be taken up at least one hole, and the same is advisable in mounting a strange horse. Another safe precaution, in the latter case, is a running martingale, which will prevent him from throwing up his head, as some horses have the habit of doing, to the great annoyance of the rider.

There are two or three more practical suggestions which may not be out of place here. The first and most important is that it is exceedingly dangerous to let a horse stand in a draught of air, or in a cool place, or eat or drink, when heated. In ten minutes he may be so crippled that he will never take a free step again. Ferry-boats are notoriously bad places, and a horse should never be taken on to them till quite cool. It is not well to let your horse crop the leaves or grass, as kind-hearted riders permit him to do sometimes, for it soils his lips and bits, giving him a slovenly air, and you run the risk besides of his wiping them on your habit before you part from him. Avoid letting your horse drink unless he really would be better for the refreshment, as he can hardly do so without wetting the curb-reins, making them stiff and dirty-looking.

THE GROOM

The costume of the groom is too well known to require remark further than that it should be scrupulously neat. In the country, top-boots, etc., are by no means *de rigueur*, and under many circumstances would savor more of pretence than of real gentility. The groom ought to be mounted on a strong and able horse, which, if unused to the saddle, he should train at least so far that he can with one hand, by the aid of his legs, force it to take and keep any position. When accompanying inexperienced riders his horse should be able to overtake theirs easily. The distance at which he should ride behind his mistress varies with circumstances—in a crowded street his place being close behind her, while in the Park or in the country he naturally falls farther back, though never beyond easy call. If he is mounted on a good saddle-horse, he should keep in his place, that is, always at the same distance, galloping if necessary; but if riding a carriage-horse, as is often convenient, he should not, unless absolutely necessary, force the animal beyond the fastest trot at which it looks well in harness. He should never canter any horse unless instructed expressly to do so, but should trot in a business-like way, rising in his stirrups, or, if necessary, should gallop, sitting straight, with hands low and feet thrust home in the stirrups. In all cases he should look straight forward, without appearing to notice what goes on around him. Nothing looks in worse form than a groom sitting lazily back on a cantering horse, and casting glances at the admiring nursery-maids along the way. When summoned to his mistress, he should touch his hat to acknowledge receipt of the command, and should ride quickly up on the off side, where he should listen in a respectful attitude with eyes cast down, then, touching his hat again, depart to carry out her orders.

PART III

LEAPING

ONE PLEASANT WINTER afternoon a fashionably dressed young man, crop in hand, spur on heel, and mounted on a tall horse, was seen to emerge briskly from a little grove in a gentleman's place, and come to a sudden halt in the level field across which he had intended to gallop. The cause was a new ditch, deep though narrow, stretching across from fence to fence before him. He looked at the obstacle a moment, then up and down the field, and remarked to a gardener, an old Scotchman, who stood looking on, spade in hand, "Well, I suppose I must go back." "I suppose so," said the old fellow, dryly, looking up out of the corner of his eye with an almost imperceptible smile. The young man reddened, hesitated, and then turned away, saying, as if the other's thoughts had been spoken out, "To tell the truth, I don't know whether my horse would if he could, nor whether he

APPROACHING A FENCE

could if he would." "An' the same o' yourself," muttered the old man in his grizzled beard. The sarcasm was not to be wondered at, as the speaker remembered what he had many a time seen, and very likely himself done in his younger days in some hunting field of the old country, for the ditch before him could have been cleared by an active boy, on his own legs, with a good run. Moreover, it is not improbable that the reader is ready to agree with the old satirist in thinking the young man a "muff." Nevertheless, both horse and rider might easily have come to grief, for the steep banks were crumbly, and while the rider's seat was not of the firmest, his mount was straight in the shoulder and a little stiff in the pastern. However, they were both as well fitted to overcome such a difficulty as nine-tenths of American horses and riders, and a very little previous practice would have enabled them to spring over without bestowing a second thought upon it. The total indifference on this subject of leaping among our people is really quite remarkable, for one can hardly take a ride anywhere in the country without there arising some occasions when even a little knowledge of the art would have added to one's pleasure. How often, for instance, an easy fence separates the dusty road, too hard as well as too hot for fast riding, from some cool wood with its shaded turf, where a gallop would be delightful and would do the horse good instead of harm. The reason of this indifference is not only the fear of getting shaken off, but a doubt as to the horse's ability to leap, and a dread of doing him some harm by such an unusual exertion. All these apprehensions are very likely well-founded, for if you have never done any leaping your first essay will, in all probability, give you a severe shock. Then if your horse is green at this sort of work, and the fence is at all difficult, he will not improbably refuse altogether, or jump so unwillingly and clumsily as to risk your bones as well as his own; and if he does not really fall, he may cause such a strain upon unaccustomed muscles as to set up a "splint" or "spavin," producing at least temporary lameness. Nevertheless, all these excellent reasons for not trying to leap can gradually, but rapidly and with perfect safety, be removed by practice, and practice of a kind very pleasant and interesting, while at the same time improving to your seat, giving it a firmness under all circumstances which no amount of riding on the highway could ever do.

Some horses are exceedingly fond of leaping, but the majority are indifferent, though on the whole rather averse to it, while a few positively will not try at all. The first thing to be done is to get your horse

A WATER JUMP

to take low and easy leaps without repugnance. For this purpose lay the bar you intend to use on the ground, and lead him over it without looking back at him or giving him any reason to suppose that you have any particular object in so doing. Should he object to stepping over it, be patient though firm, and when he has finally done so, pat and praise him; but if he has been bred in this country, and is used to bar places, he will probably give no trouble at this stage of his education. Now mount him and repeat the operation; then, having the bar raised a few inches, do so again, and continue doing so, always at a walk, until it is so high that he can no longer step over it. American horses are famous for their excellent tempers; nevertheless, at this point, unless you manage with care and with a judicious reference to equine peculiarities of mind and temper, you may meet with a refusal to proceed. In this event you must not use force or severity, or you may disgust the horse, perhaps forever, with the very exercise you wish him to learn to enjoy, but must content yourself with preventing him from sheering off and keeping him facing his task till, sooner or later, he will go over. Now praise him and make much of him, and ask no more jumping till the next lesson. It is not a good plan to put the bar up in an open place, for the horse will think it nonsense, and unless he is unusually docile will

resent what will seem to him to be an imposition in forcing him to
jump over it when he could easily go around it. A bar place or gate-
way is much better, as it cannot be "flanked," and he will not wonder
at being asked to go through it, but he should never be ridden backward and forward over the bar, nor allowed to see it raised, but should
be brought around to it by a circuit which, if possible, should be large
enough to make him forget the leaping, or think of it only as an accidental episode in the ride. The ground also should be no harder
than good firm turf. Let him jump towards his stable or towards
home by preference, and it will be well to let your assistant hold some
little article of food which he is especially fond of in view just beyond
the bar, so that his attention may be distracted from the effort, while
an agreeable association is given him with it, and he is prevented
from thinking that the obstacle is one of your making. Bear in mind
that your object at present is threefold: to induce him to take a liking
for the new exercise; to give him ease and confidence in the performance of it; and to train and strengthen by use the muscles brought
into play, so that none of the unpleasant results mentioned above
may follow. Therefore do not for a considerable time set the bar more
than two feet high, but practise him at it several times a day; first, as
already said, at a walk, then at a slow trot, and then at a canter, making him lead first with one foot, then with the other, until he not only
springs over without touching and without apparently thinking anything about it, but shows by his lengthening or shortening his stride
on approaching, so as to "take off" at the right distance, that his eye
is becoming educated; and, finally, until a careful daily inspection of
his feet and legs has proved that no soreness or tenderness anywhere
is caused by this exercise. If he does not jump clean, but knocks the
bar with his feet, it may be because he underestimates the height, as
not only horses but men too are apt to do in the case of open fences
made with posts and rails; therefore have a broad piece of board, two
feet long, stood up against the bar like a post, and make him leap over
it. If he still strikes, it will be well to try the plan which M. Baucher
so enthusiastically recommends for all horses, and which consists in
raising the bar a little just as the horse is in the act of springing.

It will be interesting to hear exactly what so great an authority
has to say on this subject. After remarking that the bar should not

be covered with anything to diminish its hardness, he proceeds: "I let two men hold the bare bar at six inches above the ground. The rider advances towards it at a walk, and at the moment when the horse, aided by the rider, takes the leap, the two men *raise the bar six inches*." The horse naturally strikes his feet against it. "I make him begin again, until he clears the bar without touching, notwithstanding the repeated raising of it at each leap. Then I have the bar held at a foot above the ground, and, as before, it will be raised six inches at the moment of the leap. When the horse is accustomed to clear this new elevation, I have the bar gradually held six inches higher, still continuing to raise it six inches at each leap, and I thus succeed, after a few lessons given with the regular progression above described, in making all horses jump obstacles of a height that they would otherwise never have been able to clear. This simple proceeding, well applied, will be useful even to exceptional horses, such as steeple-chasers, by teaching them to come more carefully to the point of 'taking off,' and will render falls less frequent." The idea of M. Baucher is to get the horse in the habit of jumping a little higher than he thinks necessary, so as to be on the safe side, and a very good idea it is. It is a practice among experienced riders to hounds in England, instead of leaping a post-and-rail fence midway between the posts, to leap as close to a post as possible, or directly over it when it is not much higher than the rail.

To return to our equine scholar, having practised him for a month or so at an elevation of two feet, his muscles will have adapted themselves to the new strain put upon them, and it will be safe to begin to raise the bar higher, and gradually to go up nearly to the limit of his ability. It is well, however, never to ask too much, as even a willing leaper will be sometimes so disgusted at what he thinks tyrannical exactions as to refuse obstinately ever to try again. The horse should never be allowed to rush at the bar, but should always, if approaching at a gallop, be collected, as much as a hundred feet away, so as to be under perfect control. The higher the leap, the slower the pace at which it should be taken, for the very momentum acquired by a rush, which would be useful in a water leap, would carry the animal against the bar instead of over it. The reins should be held in both hands, and after the horse has been collected with the curb, as may very likely be necessary, the curb should be relaxed, so that on approaching the leap he may feel only the

gentle pressure of the snaffle, which will not make him fear to thrust
forward his head, a fear which would possibly result in bringing him
down on all fours at once, or even with the hind-feet first. As he rises to
his leap, keep a steady but very gentle tension on the reins, being ready
to support him firmly as his fore-feet touch the earth.

It is now time to experiment with low stone walls and with
brooks, being always on your guard against those concealed man-
traps in the shape of loose stones, which form one of the chief
dangers of leaping in this country.

All this while we have been assuming the rider to be an accomplished horsewoman, and quite *au fait* at her fences. If, however, the
business is entirely new to her, let her not be at all disheartened, for her

RISING TO THE LEAP

own education can be carried on simultaneously with that of the horse, and without the least detriment to it. In this case, keep to the standing leap—that is, the leap taken from a walk—although it is really the most difficult to sit, until you can support the unusual motion without being in the least loosened in the saddle, and do not try the higher ones till you are perfect in the lower. The hands should be held as low as possible above the right knee, and pretty close to the body, so that they may have room to yield, and that the sudden thrusting out of the horse's head may not jerk you forward in the saddle, in which case the powerful impulsion of the hind-legs might pitch you out altogether. The advice is often given in books to lean forward and then backward in the leap, but the fact is that beginners, if they lean forward

COMING DOWN

intentionally, seldom get back in time to avoid the shock above alluded to, and teachers, therefore, as well as friendly *coaches*, often call out "lean back" as a lady nears the bar, which results in giving the learner an awkward though perhaps not unsafe manner. The fact is that there is no necessity to try to lean forward, as the rising of the horse will bring you involuntarily into a position perpendicular to the ground, while the play of thigh and waist to prevent being tossed up is of the same kind as that in the gallop, only proportionately increased, and it will become instinctive if leaping is begun moderately and carried on progressively as already recommended. In coming down you can hardly lean too far back. The left foot should not be thrust forward, but kept straight, or drawn a very little back and held close against the horse's side; the stirrup, into which the foot is pushed to the instep, being one or two holes shorter than for ordinary riding. On approaching the fence, be particular to do nothing to distract the animal's attention, as, for instance, by ejaculations or nervous movements of the reins and person; and after the leap do not fail to reward him by praises and caresses, for it cannot be too deeply impressed on the mind that he is exceedingly sensitive to them, and will consider them an ample reward for his exertion.

The object of these instructions being to enable a lady to master the art of leaping without a regular instructor, it will not be amiss to sum up the advice already given at length, in the words of two competent authorities, "Vieille Moustache" and Mr. Sidney. The former says:

"She should take a firm hold of the upper crutch of the saddle with the right knee, sit well into the saddle—not back of it, because the farther back the greater the concussion when the horse alights—put her left foot well home in the stirrup, and press her left thigh firmly against the third crutch, while keeping the left knee flexible; lean slightly forward, avoid stiffening her waist, in order to throw the upper part of her figure backward at the right moment to preserve her balance. The hands must not move except with the body, and above all no attempt to enliven the horse by jagging his mouth as he is about to rise—a pernicious habit, practised by riders of both sexes who ought to know better. Reins too short, head too forward, and pace too violent are the ordinary faults of beginners. Women have on their saddles a firmer seat for leaping than men."

Mr. Sidney remarks: "A sheep hurdle is quite high enough and the trunk of a tree is quite wide enough for the first steps in leaping. Balance, gripe of the pommels, and support of the stirrup must be combined; the seat as near the centre of the horse's back as the pommels will permit; the figure erect, not rigid, with the shoulders back, ready to bend gently backward as the horse rises in the air—not leaning forward, twisted over on the near side, like a popular spirited and absurd picture ("First at the Fence"), which really shows 'how not to do it;' the snaffle-reins held in both hands, at a length that will enable the horse fully to extend himself, and the rider to bear on his mouth as she bends back over his croup when he is landing. All this time her eyes should be looking between the horse's ears, so as to keep perfectly square in the saddle."

If the reader carries out the instruction already given with care, and exercises good sense and judgment, it is very unlikely that she will have a fall. Should this happen, however, there are two things to be remembered, first to get instantly away from the horse by scrambling or rolling, and secondly to keep hold of the reins. In any event, the timid may be reassured by reflecting that a fall is usually without any serious result, it being by no means as dangerous to come down with the horse as to be thrown from him.

PART IV

BUYING A SADDLE-HORSE

THE OPENING OF the horse-market is not announced to ladies by cards of invitation, though such an innovation on the old-fashioned methods might prove a great success in the hands of a skilful dealer. Nevertheless, as soon as spring opens, all over the United States, ladies are "shopping" for horses, but by no means in their usual jaunty and self-confident way, for their eyes, which do them such good service at the silk or lace counter, take on a timid and hesitating expression in the presence of this unwonted problem. The acquisition of a saddle-horse by a young girl is usually a long and complicated operation, in the course of which her hopes are alternately raised and depressed day by day, to be at last very likely disappointed altogether. It often begins at breakfast-time, somewhat in the following fashion: "Dear papa, don't you think I might have a saddle-horse this season? Eleanor B——'s uncle has given her a beauty, and we could ride together; and you know that is just the sort of exercise the doctor said would be good for me." The father hesitates, and few fathers there are who do not in their hearts long to grant the request; but he is a very busy man, and does not feel as if he could take any more cares upon his shoulders; and very likely he knows little about horses, and really has not the slightest idea how to set about such a purchase; and his mind misgives him as he remembers what he has heard of the tricks of dealers. So he says, "Oh, my dear, I don't see how we can manage it. We should be cheated, to begin with, and pay twice as much as he is worth, and he would run away and throw you off; and then he would be always sick, and finally fall lame, and would have to be given away before the season is over." This is the critical point of this part of the little family transaction, and if the daughter has nothing more convincing to offer in reply than some vague statement that she is sure she

351

sees plenty of good horses in the street, and that she does not see why her horse should be sick any more than any one else's, and that there must be plenty of good men to take care of him to be had at low wages, then probably her case is lost. But suppose that she replies: "Oh yes, papa, I *know* a horse that will do *nicely* and can't be sickly for he has worked all summer and not lost *a day* and he is eight years old and so has eaten all his wild oats by this time and he isn't a very pretty color but then we can buy him cheaper for that reason and I don't care so much for color as I do for *shape* and he is *very* well formed indeed his legs and feet are excellent and he has a broad shoulder and a pretty neck and head and we gave him a long drive the other day and he never missed *a step* and he isn't afraid of anything and I drove him fast up a steep hill and jumped out at the top to give him a bunch of clover and took the opportunity to listen to his breathing and to feel his pulse and there is nothing the matter with *his* heart or wind I assure you and I will promise to go to the stable once a day to see him." Then the chances are that, after laughing at the long sentence without a stop, and telling her she is a runaway filly herself, papa will say, "Well, suppose we take a look at this wonderful animal; we are not obliged to buy him, you know, unless we please, and I don't say what I may decide finally," and her case is won. To be able, however, to make the reply above supposed, simple as it sounds, indicates a very unusual amount of observation for a young girl.

There are many ladies who can at a glance tell real point lace from artificial, be the imitation never so good; but there are comparatively few who know the points of a horse, or can detect any but the most glaring defects or blemishes. The reason is simply want of practice, for the difference between the well-made and the ill-made horse, or between the sound animal and the spavined or foundered one, is far greater than that between the two pieces of lace above mentioned, which to most masculine eyes would appear exactly alike. With her superior delicacy of observation and quickness of perception, a woman ought to be, other things supposed equal, a better judge of horses than a man, and there must surely be a great many who, if they really believed this, would think it worth their while to master the small vocabulary of technical terms in which the information they require is always couched, and such would speedily find their reward in the opening of a new and interesting field of research. To begin with, how few ladies so much as know the names of the different parts of the animal! Head, legs, and body, eyes, ears, and tail, are about all the words in the feminine dictionary of horse lore, and whether the pasterns are not a disease of colts, the coronet a part of a bridle, and the frog a swelling in the throat, my lady knoweth not. A half-hour, however, given to the illustration on the following page, will remove once for all this preliminary difficulty, and will open the way to a consideration of the proper form and motion of the parts of which the names are here given:

PARTS AND "POINTS" OF THE HORSE, ALPHABETICALLY ARRANGED

Arm, or *True Arm* (8, 8).—Extends from the point of the shoulder (29) to the elbow (10). It should be long.

Back.—This is one of the four parts which, according to Arab saying, should be short.

Back Sinew.—The powerful muscle back of the cannon-bone. It should be free from contact with the bone.

Barrel, or *Chest.*—Should be roomy, as not only the lungs, but all the organs of digestion, are contained in it.

Belly.—This is one of the four parts which the Arab proverb says must be long.

Breast, or *Bosom.*—Should be deep, but not too broad, or speed will be diminished.

Cannon-bone (11).—The strong oval bone stretching between the knee and fetlock-joint in the fore-leg, and between the hock and fetlock-joint in the hind-leg.

Chin Groove.—The place just above the swell of the lower lip, in which the curb-chain should lie.

Coronet (14).—A cartilaginous band encircling the top of the hoof.

Crest.—The upper part of the back of the neck.

Croup (18).—Strictly speaking, the upper part of hind-quarters between hip and tail, but in a general way taken for that part of the body back of the saddle.

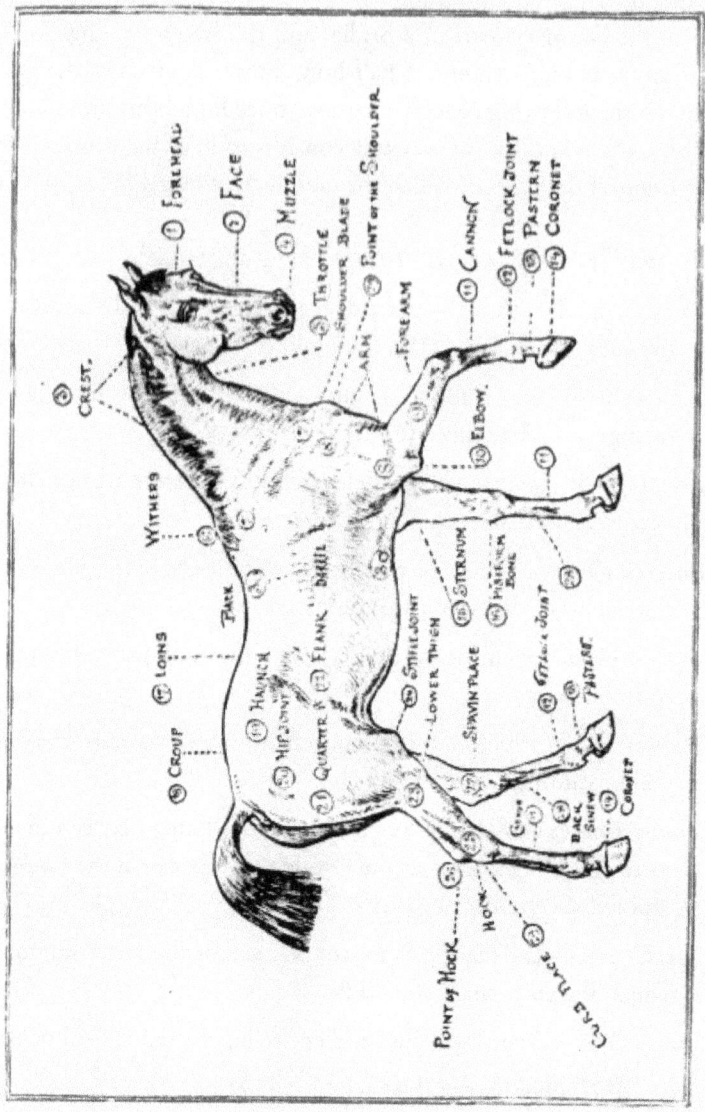

PARTS AND "POINTS"

Curb-place (29).—A part of the hind-leg, six or eight inches below the point of the hock, where "curbs," or enlargement of
the back sinew resulting from strain, are to be looked for.

Ear.—Neither too long nor very short.

Elbow (10).—Should not be nearly under the point of the shoulder, but considerably back of it, and should neither be turned
out nor pressed against the ribs.

Eye.—Should be clear and full, and of a gentle expression.

Fetlock.—The tuft of hair at the back of the pastern-joint. When
thick and coarse it indicates common blood.

Fetlock-joint (12).—Is between the shank and the pastern, and is
the same as pastern-joint.

Flank (22).

Forearm (9).—Should be long and muscular.

Forehead.—The broader, the more sense and courage. The average of six thorough-bred English horses was nine and a half
inches.

Frog.—The triangular piece in centre of bottom of hoof.

Gaskin, or *Lower Thigh* (23).—Should be strong and long, reaching well down. Measured from the stifle-joint to the point of
hock should be twenty-eight inches in a well-bred horse of
fifteen hands and three-quarters.

Girth (30, 30).—Gives approximately the capacity of the lungs.

Heel.—Should not to be too high or contracted, that is, drawn
together.

Hip.—Should be broad, with powerful muscles.

Hip-joint (20).—Is not always easily discovered by an amateur.

Hock (25).—One of the most important of the points of the
horse; should be large, clean—that is, without any rough
protuberances on the bone—flat, and "with a good clean
point standing clear of the rest of the joint."

Hoof.—Deep, like a cup; not flat, like a saucer.

Jaw.—Should be wide up toward the socket, to give room for windpipe, and permit of a graceful carriage of head.

Knee.—Can hardly be too large. Looked at from in front, should appear much wider than the leg, and should stretch out backward into a sharp edge, called the pisiform-bone.

Loins (17).—Broad, muscular, and arched slightly upward.

Lower Thigh.—See "Gaskin" (23).

Mane.—When thick and coarse, indicates inferior blood.

Muzzle (4).—Should be small, but with large nostril. A coarse muzzle indicates low breeding.

Nostril.—Open and prominent.

Pastern (13).—The short oblique bone between the fetlock and hoof. Should not be straighter than sixty, nor lower than forty-five degrees to the ground.

Pastern-joint (12).—Same as fetlock-joint.

Pisiform-bone (16).—At the back of the knee.

Point of the Hock (26).

Point of the Shoulder (29).—The lower end of the shoulder-blade, to which is jointed the true arm.

Poll.—The top of the head.

Quarters (21).—Should be muscular.

Ribs.—Should be well arched, and come up close to the hip.

Shoulder (7, 7).—Should be long and oblique.

Spavin Place (27).—Should be free from bony enlargement.

Stifle-joint (24).—Corresponds to the human knee.

Tail.—Not set on too high, but yet carried gracefully.

Thigh, or *True Thigh.*—Reaches from hip-joint to stifle. Should be long to give speed.

Thrapple, or *Throttle* (5).—Upper part of throat.

True Arm (8, 8).—See "Arm." To a careless observer it appears to form part of the shoulder.

Withers (6).—It is the height of the withers which gives the height of the horse.

To be a "good judge of a horse" is indeed an accomplishment as rare as it is desirable; but while it cannot be taught by word of mouth or pen, yet a few principles may be acquired which will be of great assistance in cultivating the eye. Even if the judgment be never so thoroughly formed as to be a safe guide unaided in purchasing, yet a great deal of pleasure may be derived from noting the comparative excellences of the really fine horses constantly to be seen in this country; and there is no reason in the world why a lady's opinion on this subject should continue to weigh as little as it has generally done hitherto. A graceful neck and an air of spirit usually win the feminine suffrages, yet often co-exist with a long back, spindle-shanks, and a chest both shallow and narrow. Nevertheless, a good neck is an excellent thing, and so is a small head, especially if it have a wide forehead; but next look to see if there is also (to use a horsey expression), "a short back and a long belly," a deep chest, a sloping shoulder, and legs broad and long above the knee and hock, but broad and short below.

The Arabs have a proverb that "there should be four points of a horse long, four short, and four broad." The long are the neck, the forearm, the thigh, and the belly; the short are the back, the pastern, the tail, and the ear; the broad are the forehead, the chest, the croup, and the limbs. The head should be small and bony; that of an English thorough-bred of fifteen and three-quarter hands will measure twenty-two to twenty-four inches in length, with the forehead eight to ten inches broad, the face dishing below the eyes. The withers should be high, the shoulder as broad as possible—not fleshy, but bony—and lying at an angle of about forty-five degrees. The chest should be broad and deep, to give room for lungs and heart. The knees should be broad, the hoofs large, and not flat, but deep.

The reasons for some of the above recommendations may be made clearer by a rough comparison between the frame of the horse and that of man. For instance, the shoulder of the former, from the withers to its forward point at the joint, is equivalent to the shoulder-blade and collar-bone of the latter, and a broad shoulder is as sure an indication of strength in the one as in the other. If the horse is "short above and long below," it gives him a carriage similar to that of a man with a full, broad chest, who holds his head high and his shoulders back.

The knee of the horse corresponds to the human wrist, and his *hock*, or "back knee," as the children call it, to our heel. The shank of the fore-leg, then, or the part between the knee and fetlock, corresponds to the hand, and the hoof and pastern to the fingers; while the shank of the hind-leg, or the part between hock and fetlock, corresponds to our foot, the hoof and pastern being the toes. The horse may thus be said to walk upon the tips of his fingers and toes, and it will readily be seen why the leg weakens in proportion as the pastern and shank lengthen. The arm proper of the horse is very short and almost concealed from view, reaching from the forward point of the shoulder to the elbow, which is close against the side.

The more oblique the shoulder, the greater the power of this arm to throw the forearm forward, so as to support the body in the gallop, and in coming down from a leap. A straight shoulder is adapted for pulling loads, but is not fit for the saddle, except upon level roads, becoming positively dangerous in broken ground. The two upper members of the hind-leg, reaching from the hip to the hock, are together commonly called the thigh, as the thigh proper, which stretches from the hip to the stifle-joint, is very short and almost concealed from observation. The stifle-joint, which corresponds to our knee, lies close against the flank. Read the description, to some extent traditional, of the wonderful mare Swallow, in Kingsley's "Hereward the Wake." She was evidently not from Arab stock, with her big ugly head; but horses—like men and women—of extraordinary strength, and beauty too, are sometimes happened upon in the most unlikely places. Indeed, in many an ungraceful form there is stored up an amount of vital energy which explains the saying that one can find "good horses of all shapes." Nevertheless, the presumption is always in favor of the well-shaped animal, and the acknowledged type of equine beauty is the English thorough-bred. This is of pure Arab blood, but so improved by many generations of careful breeding and training that it now excels not only all other European and Oriental races but the modern Arab himself, that is considered to be, weight for weight, twenty-five per cent. stronger than other breeds. One invariable mark of Arab blood, by-the-bye, is a high and graceful carriage of the tail. The eye should be kind and quiet, that of an Arab very gentle, even sleepy, when at rest, but full of fire and animation when in motion.

"The relative proportions of and exact shape desirable in each of the points described varies considerably in the several breeds. Thus, when speed and activity are essential, an oblique shoulder-blade is a *sine quâ non*, while for heavy harness it can hardly be too upright. *There are some elements, however, which are wanted in any horse, such as big hocks and knees, flat legs with large sinews, open jaws* (that is, with the lower jaw-bones wide apart), *and full nostrils.*"

It is well, after taking a general look at a horse and getting an impression of him as a whole, to divide him up mentally into sections, and examine these in detail one after the other. Taking first the head, which should be bony, not fleshy, remember that the more brain the more "horse sense." Next look at the neck, which should be neither too thick nor too long, but connecting head and shoulders by a graceful sweep. Then the forequarters, observing that the shoulder-blade and true arm are both long, well supplied though not loaded with muscle, and join each other at the point of the shoulder at a rather sharp angle. Then the "middle-piece," which should be rounded in the barrel, arched slightly in the loin, "short above and long below," and well ribbed up towards the hip. Next the hind-quarters, then the legs, knees, hocks, and feet, observing that the knees are firm, the cannon-bones and pastern are flat and strong, and that the back sinew is strong and stands free from the bone.

Now have the horse set in motion, and observe him first from one side, then from the other, and then from behind, noting the carriage and movements of the different parts in the order above given. This examination is practically the more important of the two.

Let no one suppose that mere verbal instruction, however judicious and elaborate, will, without practice, make a good judge of horse-flesh any more than it will of Brussels point-lace. All it is here intended to do is to aid in training the eye, which must be constantly exercised upon whatever specimens may come before it, comparing them mentally with one another, and noting their defects and

qualities whether of form or of motion. It will soon be found that
such observations, particularly when relating to the motions of the
horse, have a fascination peculiarly their own, and open a new and
wide field of amusement.

In examining a horse a lady cannot of course usually make the
thorough inspection personally which would be necessary to warrant
his limbs and wind perfectly sound, but she can, by taking a little time
to it, form an opinion which will be very nearly correct. She should
first master the vocabulary at the end of this chapter, which will give
her an idea what defects to be on the lookout for, and just where to seek
for them; and she should cultivate her eye at every opportunity by
scanning critically every horse she sees—or, to be more moderate, say
one or two a day—endeavoring to detect a "spavin" or "curb," or what
not, which the owner does not suspect or perhaps shuts his eyes to.
Then, when a horse is brought up for her approval, let her take her own
time, refuse to be hurried or humbugged, but, as already suggested,
look him over from all sides, at rest and in motion, and finally *get him
on trial for a week*. This last precaution is the most valuable of all, and
worth, as "Stonehenge" says, ten per cent. on the price of the animal,
and it can very often be obtained by the simple offer of paying for his
services in case he is not purchased; indeed, some of the most successful

THE SORT OF HORSE TO BUY

New York City dealers grant this privilege to any responsible cus-
tomer as a matter of course. To return to our inspection: First take
a side view from a little distance, observing that he stands perpendicularly on all four legs, bearing equal weight on each; any "pointing," or putting forward of a fore-foot to relieve it of its share of
weight, being indicative of tenderness if not lameness. Notice the
size, shape, and relative proportion of the different parts, and scru-
tinize them carefully for swellings, or for weakened or deformed
joints. Then do the same from before, then from behind. Now have
him led past you, first at a walk, then at a slow trot, insisting that
the groom shall not take him by the headstall, but by the end of the
halter, so as to leave him free to nod his head if he pleases. Now
have him saddled and bridled, and all his paces shown, finishing
with a smart gallop long enough to sweat him well, after which listen carefully to his breathing, which should be noiseless; observe
that the heaving of the flanks is regular and not spasmodic, and that
the beating of the heart is not violent or irregular. During your
week of trial take some disinterested person with you to serve as
witness in case of accident or misconduct, and work the horse hard
every day, so as to be sure that he does not lose his appetite when
fatigued, but being careful not to injure his feet by galloping on
hard roads, or to let him slip or strain himself in any way. Remember the oft-quoted words of the English stable-man: "It ain't the
speed that 'urts the 'orse; it's the 'ammer, 'ammer, 'ammer on the
'ard 'igh-road." After your first ride, leave the saddle on for twenty
minutes with the girths slackened, and next morning, before putting it on again, examine the back carefully for any soreness or puffy
spot, and if such exist, abstain from riding until it has quite disappeared, for a day of patience now is better than a week after a saddle-gall has become fairly established. The saddle, of course, should
fit the horse well, and there should always be a free space along
above the backbone and withers.

The cut on the preceding page shows a saddle-horse of the very
best form for a lady's use.

The color of a horse is an important factor in the price, except
in the case of animals of extraordinary qualities; and although different persons have their special preferences, yet probably the order

of the following list will give the average taste of the horse-buying public:

1. Blood bay with black points; that is, with mane, tail, and legs from the knee downward black.

2. Rich chestnut.

3. Rich brown.

4. Common bay with black points.

5. Common chestnut.

6. Dark dapple gray.

7. Full black.

8. Light bay with brown legs.

9. White.

10. Common gray.

11. Brownish-black.

12. Sorrel.

When your decision is finally made, obtain (from the person selling) a warranty, which had better be written upon the bill itself, giving the height, age, and color of the horse, and stating that he is sound, kind, goes well under the saddle and in single or double harness, and is afraid of nothing.

The vices which in the eye of the law make a horse returnable are Biting, Cribbing, Kicking, Rearing when dangerous, and Shying when dangerous.

In estimating the height of a horse it is convenient to remember that fifteen hands make exactly five feet—a "hand" being four inches, or a third of a foot.

To aid the inexperienced we give a cut showing a horse, originally of high spirit but faulty organization, broken down by ill usage, and also append a list of the various defects and ailments which every horse-owner ought to know something about.

LIST OF DISEASES AND DEFECTS

[Those printed in small capitals constitute UNSOUNDNESS in the eye of the law.]

Acclimation.—Horses removed from one part of the country to another have usually a period of indisposition, often of severe illness, and always for some time require more than ordinary care. It is well, therefore, not to buy a Western horse in the Atlantic States until he has been at least a month in his new surroundings.

Apoplexy.—Sometimes called "sleepy staggers." Begins with drowsiness, passing into insensibility, with snoring respiration, and ending in death.

BLINDNESS.—Often comes on gradually. Eyes of a bluish-black are thought suspicious, as is inflammation of ball or lid, or cloudiness of pupil.

BLIND STAGGERS.—See "Megrims" and "Staggers."

BOG-SPAVIN.—A soft swelling on the inner side of the hock-joint towards the front. It is caused by the formation of a sac containing synovial fluid which has oozed out of the joint. The result usually of brutality. Incurable.

BLOOD-SPAVIN.—A swelling in nearly the same place caused by an aneurism or sac of arterial blood. Incurable. Very rare.

BONE-SPAVIN.—A swelling caused by a bony growth on the inside of the hock-joint towards the front. It produces lameness, which sometimes passes off temporarily after a few minutes' work. Sometimes curable. This is what is usually meant by spavin.

Bots.—Caused by the larvæ of the bot-fly, which cling to the lining of the stomach by their two hooks till after several months they reach maturity and pass out with the droppings. They seem to do little harm, and should be left alone, as they cannot be destroyed by any medicine safe for a horse to take.

BREAKING DOWN.—A rupture of the tendons of the leg causing the fetlock-joint to give way downward. Incurable.

Broken Knee.—Indicated by white or bare spots, showing that the horse has been down, and is presumably a stumbler.

BROKEN WIND.—Accompanied by a husky cough, and indicated by heaving flanks and forcible double respiration after exercise. Incurable.

Capped Hock.—A soft movable swelling on point of hock, caused by a bruise, usually got in kicking.

CATARACT.—Opacity of the crystalline lens of the eye.

Chapped Heels.—Always the result of neglect. Often accompanied by fever and constitutional disturbance.

Cold.—Shown by dulness, rough coat, loss of appetite, tears and running at the nose. Give soft food and nurse well without exercise.

Colic.—Distinguished from inflammation of the bowels by intervals of quiet between the spasms, and by the fact that the horse will strike his belly violently in the hope of relief. Give first a warm injection, to remove any obstruction in lower bowel, and then administer stimulants.

Contracted Heels.—Often caused by improper shoeing, but often natural, and in this case producing no ill result.

CORNS.—Do not at all resemble human corns. A corn is a reddish and very sensitive spot in the sole of the foot under the shoe, caused by a rupture of the delicate blood-vessels, resulting in an abnormal fungoid growth.

Costiveness.—May bring on "blind staggers" in a horse inclined to this disease. No horse should be hurried when first taken out till his bowels have been moved.

COUGH.—Constitutes unsoundness while it lasts. Caused by foul air, dusty food, irregular work. Crush the oats, damp the hay, and give linseed tea for drink.

CRIBBING, or CRIB-BITING.—Is sometimes considered a vice, but is doubtless a result of indigestion. The horse lays hold of the manger with his teeth, straightens his neck, sucks wind into his stomach, and ejects gas. Probably some alkali, say lime-water or baking soda, would be beneficial.

CURB.—A soft, painful swelling on the back of the hind-leg six or eight inches below the hock. See illustration.

Cutting.—See "Interfering" and "Speedy Cut."

Discharge from Nostril.—Is usually caused by a simple cold, but may be a symptom of the contagious and incurable disease GLANDERS, and proximity to it should therefore be carefully avoided.

Distemper.—A disease of young horses, occurring once only. See "Strangles."

Ewe Neck.—Carries the head high and nearly in a horizontal position, so that the bit has not a proper bearing on the "bars," but is inclined to slip back towards the grinders.

FARCY.—An incurable and contagious disease, caused by blood-poisoning, and indicated by sores usually on inside of thigh, or on neck and hips. As it is communicable to human beings, every farcied horse should be immediately killed. It is well to avoid all approach to horses having sores of any kind. See "Glanders."

Filled Legs.—A swelled condition of the lower parts, usually caused by want of exercise, and relieved by bandaging and rubbing.

Fistula of the Withers.—An abscess among the muscles over the shoulder-blades, usually caused by pressure of saddle upon the bony ridge of back. Requires surgical operation.

Forging.—See "Overreaching."

FOUNDER, or FEVER IN THE FEET.—An inflammation of the parts between the crust of the foot and the pedal-bone, including the *laminæ*, which cease to secrete horn. It is caused sometimes by hard roads, and sometimes by eating or drinking or standing in a draught of air when heated. This name is commonly applied to any rheumatic lameness of the fore-feet or legs brought on as above, whether its seat be the feet, the tendons of the legs, or the muscles of the breast, in which last case it is called "chest-founder." The treatment, which is only palliative, is hot bathing and friction with liniments.

Gadfly Bites.—Often very annoying. May be prevented by washing legs and flanks with a strong tea of green elder bark.

Galls—from saddle.—Best prevented by leaving the saddle in place for twenty minutes after loosening the girths. When occurring, however, should receive prompt attention, as they are very tedious if neglected. Examine the back carefully after the first ride on a new horse, and also before putting on the saddle the next day.

GLANDERS.—A disgusting, contagious, and incurable disease, the chief symptom of which is a discharge from one nostril, at first transparent, then slightly sticky, then thick and yellow. As it is highly contagious to human beings, in whom it is equally dreadful and always fatal, *a glandered horse should be instantly killed, as the law requires.* It is well to avoid all horses having any discharge, however slight, from the nose. Glanders may be caught from "farcy," and *vice versa.*

GRAPES.—A filthy and incurable disease of heels and pastern, caused by gross neglect. It is the last stage of "grease."

GREASE.—An aggravated form of "chapped heels," accompanied by swelling, fever and a serous discharge. Wash clean frequently, and anoint with Dalley's salve.

Gripes.—See "Colic."

HEART DISEASE.—May be detected by auscultation. Incurable. Ends in sudden death.

HEAVES.—See "Broken Wind."

Hide-bound.—The skin appears too tight, and as if fast to the ribs. It is caused by a disordered stomach, and requires nourishing food.

Inflammation of Bowels.—The pain is continuous, and the horse is careful not actually to strike his belly with his feet. Requires, of course, very different treatment from colic, but an injection should be the first thing done.

Interfering.—Striking the fetlock-joint with the foot. Caused sometimes by weakness and fatigue, but usually by bad shoeing, and a good blacksmith is the best adviser.

Lampas.—A swelling of the gums, relieved by lancing.

KNEE-SPRUNG.—Incurable. Result of overwork.

KNUCKLED.—Same as "set over." A condition of the fetlock-joint corresponding to that of the "sprung" knee.

LAMINITIS.—The scientific name of "founder."

MAD STAGGERS.—Violent insanity, caused by inflammation of the brain. The last stage sometimes of sleepy staggers. Incurable.

Mallenders.—A scurvy patch at the back of the knee, caused by neglect, and not obstinate.

Mange.—An itch produced by a parasitic insect.

MERGRIMS.—A falling-sickness like epilepsy. It begins with a laying back of the ears and shaking of the head; is accompanied by convulsions; and passes off of itself in two or three minutes, the horse appearing to be none the worse. Often called "Blind Staggers."

NAVICULAR DISEASE.—An ulceration of the navicular-joint in the foot, causing lameness; incurable, except by extirpation of the nerve.

NERVED.—A nerved horse has had one of the nerves of the foot cut to remove the pain and lameness caused by the "navicular disease."

OPHTHALMIA.—A purulent inflammation of the eye. Epidemic.

ORGANIC DISEASE of the bony system anywhere constitutes unsoundness.

Overreaching.—Striking the toe of the front-foot with the toe of the hind-foot; sometimes called "clicking." Often remedied by shoeing.

Poll-evil.—An abscess in the top of the neck, near the head, caused by a blow.

PUMICE FOOT.—Bulging sole, weak crust, the result of "laminitis." Incurable.

Quarter Crack.—Occurs usually on the inside of fore-foot. A bad sign, as well as very slow and troublesome to cure.

QUIDDING.—Dropping the food half chewed from the mouth. Indicative of sore throat.

QUITTOR.—Burrowing abscess in the foot.

Rheumatism.—Cause, effect, and treatment the same as for human beings.

RING-BONE.—An enlargement of the bone by growth, a little above the coronet.

ROARING.—Caused by a contraction of windpipe. Incurable.

RUPTURES of all kinds constitute unsoundness.

Saddle-gall.—Swelling caused by chafing of saddle. If the skin is broken it is called a "sitfast;" if not, a "warble."

Sallenders.—Scurvy patch in front of hock-joint.

Sand Crack.—Occurs on the inside of fore-foot and on the toe of the hind-foot.

Scratches.—See "Chapped Heels."

Scouring.—Looseness of the bowels.

SEEDY TOE.—A separation of the crust of the hoof from the laminæ, the result of laminitis. Scarcely curable.

SIDE-BONE.—A bony growth just above the coronet, causing lameness. Incurable.

SPAVIN.—See "Bone, Blood, and Bog Spavin."

Speedy Cut.—A cut of the knee from the foot of opposite leg. Dangerous, because the pain often causes the horse to fall.

STAGGERS.—See "Apoplexy." "Sleepy," "Trotting," and "Mad" Staggers are different forms and stages of the same disease, caused usually by overfeeding.

Strangles, or *Colt Distemper.*—A severe swelling of the glands of the throat, which gathers and breaks.

STRING-HALT or SPRING-HALT.—A peculiar snatching up of the hind-leg, caused by some nervous disorder. Incurable.

Surfeit.—An eruption of round, blunt spots, caused by heating food.

THICK WIND.—Defective respiration without noise. Incurable.

THICKENING OF BACK SINEWS.—Result of strain.

THRUSH.—An offensive discharge from the frog, the result of inflammation, caused by want of cleanliness or overwork, etc.

THOROUGH-PIN.—A sac of synovial fluid formed between the bones of the hock from side to side.

Warble.—A saddle-gall when simply swollen but not broken.

Warts.—Should be removed, as they tend to spread.

WHIRLBONE LAMENESS.—Lameness of hip-joint.

Windgalls, or *Puffs.*—Little oval swellings just above the fetlock-joint between the back sinew and the bone.

Worms.—Sometimes troublesome, but less so than often supposed.

WHISTLING.—Caused by a contraction of windpipe. Incurable.

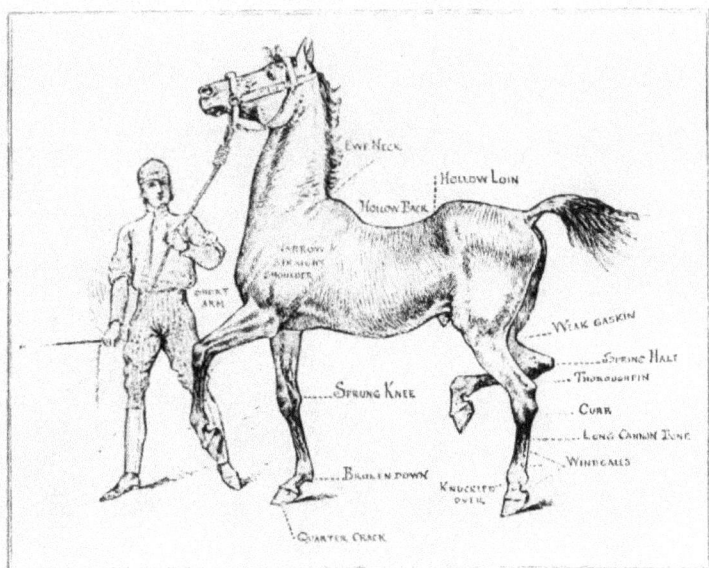

THE SORT OF HORSE NOT TO BUY

How Women
Should Ride

HOW WOMEN SHOULD RIDE

BY

"C. DE HURST"

ILLUSTRATED

NEW YORK
HARPER & BROTHERS, FRANKLIN SQUARE
1892

HOW WOMEN SHOULD RIDE

INTRODUCTION

I T HAS NOT been the intention of the author of this little volume to present the reader with elaborate chapters of technical essays.

Entire libraries have been written on the care and management of the horse from the date of its foaling; book upon book has been compiled on the best and proper method of acquiring some degree of skill in the saddle. The author has scarcely hoped, therefore, to exhaust in 248 pages a subject which, after having been handled on the presses of nearly every publisher in this country and England, yet contains unsettled points for the discussion of argumentative horsemen and horse-women.

But it happens with riding—as, indeed, it does with almost every other subject—that we ignore the simpler side for the more intricate. We delve into a masterpiece, suitable for a professional, on the training of a horse, when the chances are we do not know how to saddle him. We stumble through heavy articles on bitting, the technical terms of which we do not understand, when if our own horse picked up a stone we probably would be utterly at a loss what to do.

We, both men and women, are too much inclined to gallop over the fundamental lessons, which should be conned over again and again until thoroughly mastered. We are restive in our novitiate period, impatient to pose as past-masters in an art before we have acquired its first principles.

Beginning with a bit of advice to parents, of which they stand sorely in need, it is the purpose of this book to carry the girl along the bridle-path, from the time she puts on a habit for the first attempt, to that when she joins the Hunt for a run across country after the hounds.

There is no intention of wearying and confusing her by a formidable array of purely technical instruction.

The crying fault with nearly all those who have handled this subject at length has been that of distracting the uninformed reader by the most elaborate dissertation on all points down to the smallest details.

This author, on the contrary, has shorn the instruction of all hazy intricacies, with which the equestrienne has so often been asked to burden herself, and brought out instead only those points essential to safety, skill, and grace in the saddle.

No space has been wasted on unnecessary technicalities which the woman is not likely to either understand or care to digest, but everything has been written with a view of aiding her in obtaining a sound, practical knowledge of the horse, under the saddle and in harness.

CONTENTS

ILLUSTRATIONS

I
A WORD TO PARENTS

RIDING HAS BEEN taken up so generally in recent years by the mature members of society that its espousal by the younger element is quite in the. natural order of events. We can look upon the declaration of Young America for sport with supreme gratification, as it argues well for the generation to come, but we should not lose sight of the fact that its benefits may be more than counterbalanced by injudiciously forcing these tastes. That there is danger of this is shown by the tendency to put girls on horseback at an age much too tender to have other than harmful results.

It is marvellous that a mother who is usually most careful in guarding her child's safety should allow her little one to incur the risks attendant upon riding (which are great enough for a person endowed with strength, judgment, and decision) without proper consideration of the dangers she is exposed to at the time, or a realization of the possible evil effects in the future.

Surely parents do not appreciate what the results may be, or they would never trust a girl of eight years or thereabouts to the mercy of a horse, and at his mercy she is bound to be. No **Dangers of Early** child of that age, or several years older, has strength **Riding** sufficient to manage even an unruly pony, which, having once discovered his power, is pretty sure to take advantage of it at every opportunity; and no woman is worthy the responsibilities of motherhood who will permit her child to make the experiment.

Even if no accident occurs, the knowledge of her helplessness may so frighten the child that she will never recover from her timidity. It is nonsense to say she will outgrow it; early impressions are never entirely eradicated; and should she in after-life appear to regain her courage, it is almost certain at a critical moment to desert her, and early recollections reassert themselves.

The vagaries of her own mount are not the only dangers to which the unfortunate child is exposed.

Many accidents come from collisions caused by some one else's horse bolting; and it is not to be expected, when their elders often lose their wits completely, that shoulders so young should carry a head cool enough to make escape possible in such an emergency.

It is a common occurrence to hear parents inquiring for a "perfectly safe horse for a child."

Such a thing does not exist, and the idea that it does often betrays one into trusting implicitly an animal which needs perhaps constant watching. If fresh or startled, the capers of the most gentle horse will not infrequently create apprehension, because totally unexpected. On the other hand, if he is too sluggish to indulge in any expressions of liveliness, he is almost sure to require skilful handling and constant urging to prevent his acquiring a slouching gait to which it is difficult to rise.

A slouching horse means a stumbling one, and, with the inability of childish hands to help him recover his balance, he is likely to fall.

Supposing the perfect horse to be a possibility—a girl under sixteen has not the physique to endure without injury to her health such violent exercise as riding. From the side position she is forced to assume, there is danger of an injured spine, either from the unequal strain on it or from the constant concussion, or both.

If a mother can close her eyes to these dangers, insisting that her child shall ride, a reversible side-saddle is the best safeguard that I know of against a curved spine; but it only lessens the chances of injury, and is by no means a sure preventive, although it has the advantage of developing both sides equally.

Another evil result of beginning too young is that if she escapes misadventures and does well, a girl is sure to be praised to such an extent that she forms a most exaggerated idea of her prowess in the saddle. By the time she is sixteen she is convinced that there is no room for improvement, and becomes careless, lapsing into many of her earlier faults. Parents should guard against this. It is often their affection which permits them to see only the good points of their daughter's riding, and their pride in her skill leads to undue flattery, which she is only too willing to accept as her due.

Later I shall mention some of the principles a young rider should acquire, and it is the duty of those who have put her in the saddle when too young to judge for herself to see that she follows them correctly. The necessity of riding in good form cannot be too firmly impressed on her mind. One often hears: "Oh, I only want to ride a little in the Park; so don't bother me about form. I ride for pleasure and comfort, not work"—all of which is wrong; for, whether in the Park, on the road, in the country, or in the hunting-field, nothing is of more importance than to ride in good form. To do so is to ride easily, being in the best position to manage the horse, and therefore it is also to ride safely.

The desire to attract attention often induces women to ride. Young girls soon learn to do likewise, and their attempts at riding for the "gallery" by kicking the horse with the heel, jerking its mouth with the curb, that she may impress people with her **Vanity** dashing appearance, as the poor tormented animal plunges in his endeavors to avoid the pressure, are lamentable and frequent sights in many riding-schools.

Objectionable as this is in an older person, it is doubly so in a child, from whom one expects at least modesty instead of such boldness as this betokens. It is to be hoped that those in authority will discourage her attempts at circus riding, and teach her that a quiet, unobtrusive manner will secure her more admirers than an air of bravado.

II
GIRLS ON HORSEBACK

NOTWITHSTANDING THESE NUMEROUS reasons to the contrary, mothers will undoubtedly continue to imperil the life and welfare of children whom it is their mission to protect, and, such being the case, a few directions as **Hints to** to the best and least dangerous course to pursue **Mothers** may be of service to them.

Sixteen is the earliest age at which a girl should begin to ride, as she is then strong enough to control her mount, has more judgment, is better able to put instruction into practice, more amenable to reason, and more attentive to what is told her. If the parents' impatience will not admit of waiting until this desirable period, it is their duty to see that the child has every advantage that can facilitate her learning, and to assure her such safety as is within their power.

A common theory is that any old screw, if only quiet, will do for a beginner. Nothing could be more untrue. The horse for a novice should have a short but square and elastic trot, a good mouth, even disposi- **The Beginner's** tion, and be well-mannered; otherwise the rider's **Horse** progress will be greatly impeded. Even if the child is very young, I think it is a mistake to put her on a small pony for her first lessons, as its gaits are so often uneven, interfering with all attempts at regular rising to the trot.

Ponies are also more liable to be tricky than horses, and, from the rapidity of their movements, apt to unseat and frighten a beginner. They are very roguish, and will bolt across a road without any reason, or stand and kick or rear for their own amusement; and, being so quick on their feet, their various antics confuse a child so that she loses her self-possession and becomes terrified. It is just as bad to go to the other extreme, as a large, long-gaited horse will tire the muscles of the back, and, if combined with sluggish action, require twice the exertion needed for a free traveller. Furthermore, it destroys the rhythm of the movement by making the time of her rise only half as long as necessary, thus giving her a double jolt on reaching the saddle.

Having secured the right sort of horse, the saddle should be chosen with great care.

It is a shame that little girls are made to ride in the ill-fitting habits seen half the time. They must set properly, or the best riders will be

Costuming handicapped and appear at a disadvantage. A child's skirt should not wrinkle over the hips more than a woman's, nor should it ruck up over the right knee, exposing both feet, while the wind inflates the superfluous folds. Above all things, a girl should not lace nor wear her habit bodice tight, as no benefit can possibly be derived from riding with the lungs and ribs compressed.

It often happens that a child is put into the saddle before she has had the opportunity of becoming familiar with a horse, either by visiting it in its stall or going about it when in the stable. A more harmful mistake could not be made; the child is likely to be afraid of the animal the first time she is placed on its back, and nothing so interferes with tuition as terror. Many of the difficulties of instructing a little girl will be overcome if her familiarity with the horse she is

Preparatory Lessons to ride has given her confidence in him. She should frequently be taken to the stable, and encouraged to give him oats or sugar from her hand, and to make much of him. Meanwhile whoever is with her must watch the animal, and guard against anything which might startle the child. She may be lifted on to his back; and if he is suitable to carry her, he will stand quietly, thus assuring her of his trustworthiness and gaining her affection.

Before being trusted on a horse, a beginner should have the theory of its management explained to her; and here is another drawback to infantile equestrianism, as a young mind cannot readily grasp the knowledge. Nevertheless, she must be made to understand the necessity of riding from balance, instead of pulling herself up by the horse's mouth, and be shown the action of the curb chain on the chin, that she may realize why the snaffle should be used for ordinary purposes, so that in case of an emergency she may have the curb to fall back upon.

She must know that if she pulls against him, the horse will pull against her, and therefore she must not keep a dead bearing on his mouth. Unyielding hands are the almost invariable result of riding before realizing the delicate manipulation a horse's mouth requires. A light feeling on the curb and a light touch of the whip will show her how to keep the horse collected, instead of allowing him to go in a slovenly manner.

She must not try to make the horse trot by attempting to rise. Until the animal is trotting squarely she should sit close to the saddle, instead of bobbing up and down, as he jogs or goes unevenly at first.

When wishing to canter, in place of tugging at the reins, clucking, and digging the animal in the ribs with her heel, the child should be told to elevate her hands a trifle, and touch him on the shoulder with the whip.

No habit is more easily formed than that of clucking to a horse, and it is a difficult one to cure. It is provocative of great annoyance to any one who is near, and who may be riding a high-spirited animal, as it makes him nervous and anxious to go, for he cannot tell whether the signal is meant for him or not, and springs forward in response, when his owner has perhaps just succeeded in quieting him. Thus can one make one's self an annoyance to others near by, in a manner which might so easily have been avoided in the beginning.

After being familiarized with such rudimentary ideas of horsemanship, comes the time for putting them into practice.

It is a pity that there are not more competent instructors in the riding-schools, for it is of great importance to begin correctly; to find a teacher, however, who possesses thorough knowledge of the subject is, unfortunately, rare. Their inefficiency is amply demonstrated by the specimens of riding witnessed **Instructors** every day in the Park; and either their methods, if they pretend to have any, must be all wrong, or they are but careless and superficial mentors, as the results are so often far from satisfactory.

There are, to be sure, plenty of teachers who ride well themselves, but that is a very different matter from imparting the benefit of their knowledge and experience to others. With the best intentions in the world, they may fail to make their pupils show much skill in the saddle. Skill, and the power of creating it in the pupil, is an unusual combination.

If a young girl is to ride, she should be put in the saddle and not permitted to touch the reins. Her hands may rest in her lap, and the horse should be led at a walk, while the teacher shows her the position she must try to keep, and tells her what she must do when the pace is

Balance   increased. As she becomes used to the situation, and understands the instructions, the horse may be urged into a slow trot, she being made to sit close, without, at first, any attempt at rising. Then a quiet canter may be given her, but on no account should the child be allowed to clutch at anything to assist in preserving her balance. It is that she shall not rely on the horse's mouth for balance that I have advocated keeping the reins from her, and it is a plan which men and women would do well to adopt. Dependence on the reins is one of the commonest faults in riding, and every one should practise trotting (and even jumping, if the horse be tractable) with folded arms, while the reins are left hanging on the animal's neck, knotted so they will not fall too low. If the importance of riding from balance above the waist were more generally recognized, the seat would of necessity be firmer, the hands lighter, and horses less fretful.

Too much emphasis cannot be put on the importance of good hands. Good hands are hands made so by riding independently of the reins. Intuitive knowledge of the horse's intentions, sympathy and communication with him, which are conveyed through the reins in a manner too subtle for explanation, must accompany   **Hands** light hands to make them perfect. Such qualities are absolutely impossible with heavy hands, which are incapable of the necessary delicate manipulation of the horse's mouth. Light hands, therefore, should be cultivated first, and experience may bring the rest. A child, beginning as I have advised, will early hands when from experience she has learned their disadvantages.

After sitting close to the trot and the canter, the beginner must be told to rise to the trot. At first she will find it difficult to make her effort correspond to the action of the horse's fore-legs, but, having once caught the motion, she will soon have no trouble in rising regularly. When she rises correctly and without much effort, the reins may be given her. A snaffle will be the best to use until she is sure of not letting them slip through her fingers, or of not interfering with the horse's mouth. She should hold the reins in both hands, as this lessens the

CORRECT POSITION

probability of sitting askew, although as she becomes more certain of her seat she may transfer them to the left hand, and carry a whip or crop in the right.

If a double bridle has been substituted for the snaffle, the instructor must show the child that the left snaffle rein goes outside of her little finger, the left curb between the little and third fingers, the right curb between the second and third fingers, and the right snaffle between the first and second.

Now, as the child begins to have confidence in herself, is the time to guard against the formation of bad habits, which would later, if uncorrected, be difficult to eradicate.

If parents will take the trouble to make an impartial criticism of their daughter's riding, they can aid her by insisting upon her doing as she ought, which is beyond the authority of the riding-master.

They should see that her body is held erect, her shoulders squarely to the front and thrown back, head up, chin held back, arms hanging

Position straight to the elbows, hands low and close together, her right knee immovable, as from there she must rise. Her left leg must be held quiet, and the heel away from the horse, the ball of the foot resting on the stirrup; but she must be kept from placing too much reliance on that support, by practising without it every time she rides, taking care that, in relinquishing that aid, she does not instead take hold of the horse's mouth.

As the most trustworthy mount will at times be frisky or make a mistake, a child should be prepared for such a contingency, and know how to meet it. If a horse stumbles, she must sit well back and pull his head up. In rearing, the reins must be left loose and the body thrown forward. A tendency to back must be met with a sharp crack of the whip. In shying, she must try to sit **Management** close, and in case of a runaway she should understand that no good will come of throwing herself off. To stick close and try to direct him is all she can do, for she cannot hope to stop him when once started. If a horse falls with her, it is best to try and hold on to the reins, as then he cannot reach her with his heels; but if she cannot succeed in doing this, she must endeavor to get clear of him and as far away as possible, to avoid being rolled on or trampled upon as he makes his effort to get up.

INCORRECT POSITION

When I consider the trials and dangers she must pass through, a girl who is allowed to ride before she is sixteen has my sympathy, while I look with indignation on the mothers who thus thoughtlessly expose children to all the evils attendant upon a too early attempt at riding.

III
BEGINNING TO RIDE

THAT RIDING IS increasing in popularity is clearly attested by the crowded bridle-path of Central Park. It is greatly to be hoped, however, that with its growth in public favor a more than superficial knowledge of horsemanship will be sought for by those who desire to experience all the pleasure which may be derived from this sport. Women especially, laboring as they do under the disadvantages of a side-saddle and imperfectly developed muscles, should try to follow the most efficacious means of managing their horses, a result best attained by riding in good form.

Even those who consider themselves first-class horsewomen, and who are undoubtedly competent to manage an unruly animal, often have defects in form which destroy the grace and ease of their appearance, and prevent them, in case of an emer-   **Form** gency, from employing the full amount of power of which they are capable. Besides this, there are so many benefits to be derived from the exercise if one will take it in a common-sense manner that every endeavor should be made to extract from it the full amount of good.

This cannot be done with any undue strain on the muscles arising from either a poor saddle, a back bent almost double, the arms nearly pulled out by improper handling of the horse's mouth, or with that abomination a tight waist. Sense in dressing and attention to form are the two indispensable attributes by which women can make riding a means to improved health. Under such conditions all the organs are stimulated, and good digestion, an increased appetite, quieted nerves, better spirits, and sound sleep follow. With such advantages in sight, it is strange that more of an effort is not made to bring about these results by overcoming bad habits.

In most instances the faults come either from improper instruction, or vanity which will not permit or heed criticism. If her horse has

Insufficient been docile, and refrained from any attempt to throw
Training her, a woman is sometimes so impressed with her skill
that after a few lessons she no longer regards the ad-
vice of her instructor, and thinks she is beyond the necessity of heeding
his admonitions. Having acquired so little knowledge, she will soon
have numerous objectionable peculiarities in form, resulting from her
imperfect conception of horsemanship.

Occasionally, too, a woman considers herself "a born rider, with
a natural seat," and the result of this belief is a combination of pitiful
mistakes, when, had her taste for the sport been properly trained and
cultivated, instead of being allowed to run wild, she would probably
have become a rider. There might yet remain hope of her acquiring a
seat could she be convinced that there really is some knowledge on the
subject that she has not yet mastered.

In reference to those who have been taught by incompetent
masters, a great deal is to be said, both to enable them to adopt the
right way, and to prevent those who are desirous of learning from
falling into their mistakes.

Unfortunately it is almost impossible for a woman to mount without assistance, unless she be very tall and her horse small. In this case
she can reach the stirrup with her foot, and pull herself up by the saddle. Sometimes the stirrup can be let down and used **Mounting**
to mount with, then drawn up when seated in the
saddle. But this can only be done when the stirrup leather buckles over
the off flap, which is not usual. Another method is to lead the horse to
a fence or wall, climb that, and jump on to his back; but all these methods require a very quiet horse, and even then are not always practicable.

It is advisable to learn to mount from the ground as well as from a
block. This is done by placing the right hand containing whip and reins
on the upper pommel, the left foot, with the knee bent, in the clasped
hands of the attendant, the left hand on his shoulder, and, at a signal,
springing from the right foot and straightening the left leg.

Nine out of ten women, after mounting, first carefully adjust the
habit, and have the stirrup or girths tightened before putting the knee
over the pommel, while some even button their gloves before; and, as

a secondary consideration, when everything else has been seen to, they take up the reins, which have been loose on the horse's neck. He might easily wrench himself from the groom at his head, and without her hold on the pommel she would fall heavily to the ground; or if she were seated, but without reins, the horse might bolt into a tree, a wall, or another horse. She would probably grasp the first rein at hand, perhaps the curb, and then the horse might rear dangerously, and if she did not relax her hold on his mouth at once would be likely to fall backwards with her—the worst thing that can happen to a woman on a horse. All this may be avoided by taking the reins before mounting, and upon touching the saddle, instantly putting the right knee over the pommel. The reins should then be transferred to the left hand, with the snaffle on the outside, and the curb inside, but loose. It will then be the proper time to arrange the skirt and the stirrup.

To dismount she must transfer the reins to her right hand, take her left foot from the stirrup, and lift her right knee over the upper pommel, making sure that her skirt is not caught on any part of the saddle. She must then take a firm hold of the pommel with the hand containing the reins and the whip, the latter **Dismounting** held so that it will not touch the horse. If there is some one to assist her she may reach out her left arm, and by this she can be steadied as she dismounts. In jumping down she should keep hold of the pommel and turn slightly, so that as she lands she is facing the horse, ready to notice and guard against signs of kicking or bolting. Until she is fairly on the ground she must not let go of the reins or the pommel, for should the horse start she might be dragged with her head down, if her skirt or her foot caught, and without the reins she could not stop him.

It is well to discard the stirrup for some time during each ride, first at the canter, then at the trot, to make sure that too much weight is not **Stirrup** rested on this support, and that the rise is from the right knee. If too much dependence is placed on the stirrup the seat is sure to be too far to the left, unless the leather is too short, when the body will be as much too far to the right, instead of directly on top of the horse.

If these directions are observed, a very firm seat will be the result, which gives a confidence that enables one to be thoroughly flexible above the waist without fear of going off, and dispels a dread that often accounts for a stiff or crouching position. A test as to whether one is sitting sufficiently close in the canter is to put a handkerchief on the saddle, and note if the seat is firm enough to keep it there.

IV
IN THE SADDLE

THE FIRST IMPULSE of a novice is to grasp the horse with her left heel, while the leg is bent back from the knee so that it almost reaches his flank. Instead of this, the leg from **Below the** the knee, which should not be more than half an inch **Waist**

**INCORRECT
LEFT LEG
AND HEEL**

below the pommel, must hang naturally in a perpendicular line, and the foot parallel with the horse, the heel being held away from his side

**CORRECT
LEFT LEG
AND HEEL**

.and slightly depressed, the ball of the foot resting on the stirrup. This alters the grip entirely, and gives the greatest possible purchase, with the knee firmly in the angle between the pommel and the saddle flap, the thigh close to the saddle above, and the inside of the calf below, where one should be able to hold a piece of paper without having it fall out while trotting. The left foot will, of necessity, remain quiet a most desirable point often neglected.

Now for the right leg. The first direction usually given is to grasp the pommel with it. That is all very well, but it leads to a grievous error. In the endeavor to obey the order, the right knee is pressed hard to the left against the pommel, it is true, but in such a manner that there is considerable space between the leg and the saddle, extending from the knee half-way up the thigh.

Thus the rider rises, owing to her grip being too high, so that a person on the right can often see the pommel beneath her.

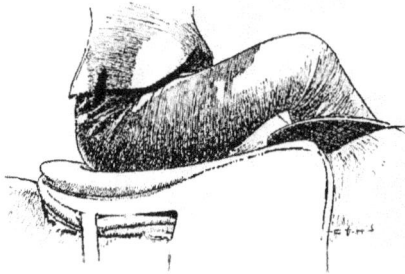

**INCORRECT
RIGHT THIGH
AND KNEE**

The first thing to do is to sit well back on the saddle, with the shoulders square to the front, and press down from the hip to the knee until as close to the saddle as possible. Then, when sure that the knee is down, taking care that it does not leave the saddle in the slightest degree, grasp the pommel. It is from this knee that one must rise, and the most essential point is to have it absolutely firm, with a secure hold on

**CORRECT
RIGHT THIGH
AND KNEE**

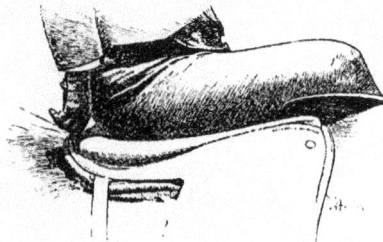

as extended a surface as possible. From the knee the leg hangs straight, kept close to the' horse, with the toe depressed just enough to avoid breaking the line of the skirt. It is seldom realized that the right leg below the knee should be held as firmly against the horse as the left, but such is the case.

The body should be held erect at all times, the back straight while rising, instead of appearing to collapse with each movement, or rising from right to left with a churnning motion instead of straight up and down; shoulders should be level the right one is inclined to be higher than the left, as well as farther forward well back and equidistant from the horse's ears, chest expanded, and chin held **Above the Waist** near the neck, as nothing is more unsightly than a protruding chin. The arms should fall naturally at the sides, bending inward from the elbow, but on no account to such an extent as to cause the elbows to leave the sides or form acute angles. All stiffness should be avoided. Some difficulty may be experienced at first, though, in attempting to relax the muscles above the waist while keeping the lower ones firm. A little practice will accomplish this, and, as a stiff carriage is most frequently the result of self-consciousness, it will be desirable to practice where there are no spectators. As the woman becomes more accustomed to riding she will lose some of her rigidity; but she must not go to the other extreme and be limp or careless in her way of holding herself. A woman's body should be at right angles to her horse's back, neither inclining backwards nor giving evidence of a tendency to stoop. Her anxiety to comply with these directions may render her conscious and awkward for a while; but if she will persevere, bearing

**CORRECT
KNUCKLES,
SIDE VIEW**

them all in mina, they will become as second nature, and she will follow them naturally and gracefully.

The hands should be held about two thirds of the way back between the right knee and hip, and as low as possible. They should be perfectly steady, and in rising never communicate the motion of the body to the horse's mouth. If the right knee is used to rise from, the **Hands and Wrists** seat will not need to be steadied by the reins. In the canter, however, the hands, as well as the body above the waist, should sway slightly with the horse's stride, but not more than is necessary; for that, and rising too high in the trot, give an appearance of exertion not compatible with grace.

The wrists should be bent so that the knuckles point straight ahead with the thumbs up, thus giving the horse's mouth play from the wrist, instead of, as is often the case, from the shoulder, the

**INCORRECT
POSITION OF HANDS**

former admitting of much greater delicacy of handling, and the give-and-take movement being not so easily observed. Most teachers instruct a pupil to keep her finger-nails down, but this also necessitates all movement coming from the shoulder, or else sticking out the elbows.

Many hold their reins in the left hand, allowing the right to hang at the side. This does not look well, and in case of an emergency, such as stumbling, the hand being so **Reins**

**HANDS
IN GOOD FORM,
FRONT VIEW**

far from the reins precludes the possibility of rendering the quick assistance required. The reins should be held in the left hand, but the right should be on them, lightly feeling the horse's mouth, thereby anticipating his movements.

The left snaffle- rein should go outside of the little finger, the left curb between the little and third fingers, the right curb between the third and middle fingers, and the right snaffle between the middle and

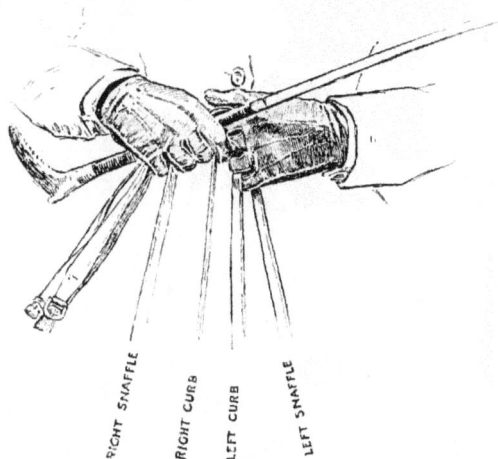

**SNAFFLE
OUTSIDE,
CURB INSIDE,
FRONT VIEW**

first fingers. They must all be brought through the hand, over the second joint of the first finger, where they must lie flat and in order, held there by the thumb. The third finger of the right hand should rest on the right snaffle, leaving the first and second free to use the curb if required, thus giving equal bearing on all four reins.

**SNAFFLE
OUTSIDE,
CURB INSIDE,
SIDE VIEW**

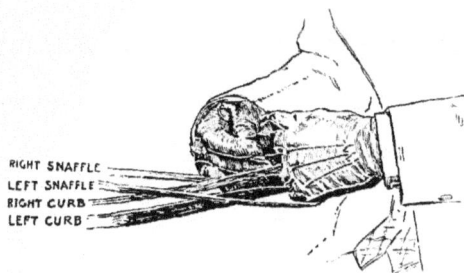

If the use of the curb alone is wanted, the third finger of the right should release the right snaffle, the first and second retaining their hold on the curb, and the desired result will be produced.

REINS IN TWO HANDS, SNAFFLE OUTSIDE, CURB INSIDE

If only the snaffle is desired, it may be brought to bear more strongly by keeping hold of the right rein with the third finger of the right hand, and reaching over on the left snaffle with the first finger.

When this method is pursued there is no necessity for shifting the reins or hauling at them, and constantly changing their position and length. When a rein has slipped through the fingers of the left hand, instead of pushing it back from in front it should be pulled to the proper length from back of the left hand.

It is quite correct, though inconvenient, to hold the reins in both hands; but the hands should be held close together, with the thumbs up, and always on the reins to prevent slipping. The little fingers then separate the reins, the left little finger, the left curb between the little

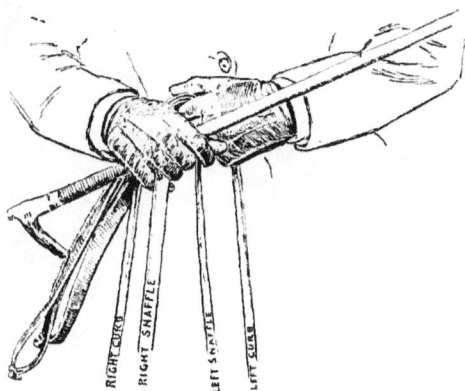

**POSITION OF
REINS AND HANDS
IN JUMPING,
CURB OUTSIDE,
SNAFFLE INSIDE**

and third fingers, with the reins drawn over the first finger; the right snaffle outside of the right little finger, the right curb between the little and third fingers, and these also drawn over the first finger, in both instances held by the thumbs. In this way the right reins may quickly be placed in the left hand by inserting the middle finger of the left hand between them without displacing the others. Sometimes the ends of the left reins are passed over the first finger of the right hand as well as of the left one, and carried on past the little finger, the same being done to the right reins, thus giving additional purchase should the horse pull.

It is well to know several ways of holding the reins, and to practise them all. For instance, the positions of the snaffle and curb may be reversed; indeed, many, expert riders always hold their reins with the curb outside and the snaffle inside, especially in jumping, where the curb is not used, and therefore requires a less prominent place in the hand.

Another position of the reins is to have the middle finger of the left hand separate the snaffle and the little finger the curb, both right reins being above the left ones. However, unless a horse is bridle-wise this plan is not a convenient one, because the right and left reins alternate. A horse so trained may be guided by a turn of the wrist. To turn him to the left the hand should be moved in that direction, pressing the right reins against his neck, and to go to the right the hand should be carried to that side, the thumb turned downward, thus pressing the left reins against the horse's neck.

REINS IN TWO HANDS, CURB OUTSIDE, SNAF-FLE INSIDE, SIDE VIEW

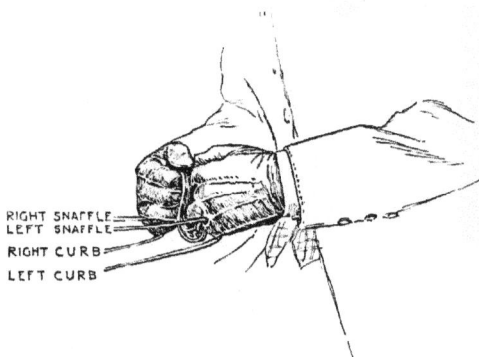

RIGHT SNAFFLE
LEFT SNAFFLE
RIGHT CURB
LEFT CURB

V
EMERGENCIES

Although she may ride in good form, and, when her horse goes quietly, feel at home in the saddle, no woman can be considered proficient until she is prepared for any emergency, and knows how to meet it.

Many horses show restlessness while being mounted, some carrying it to such an extent as to back and rear or swerve most unpleasantly. The groom at his head should hold him lightly but firmly by the snaffle, or, better still, the cheeks of the bridle; not lugging or jerking at him, but endeavoring to soothe him. If the **Eagerness to Start** horse swerves from her, he should be made to stand against a wall. The woman must get settled in the saddle as expeditiously as she can, not taking any unnecessary time in the arrangement of her skirt, which might augment the animal's uneasiness. Once mounted she must walk the horse quietly for a few minutes, using the snaffle only, as his restlessness may have come from expecting the spur on starting, as is customary with the horses of those who care for display rather than good manners. Before long she should dismount, and, at a different place, repeat the lesson without fighting him, even should he fail to show much progress at first. If he rears, the attendant should let go of his head until he comes down; then, before starting, try to make him stand a few moments. Each time the rider mounts she should increase the period of his standing, doing it firmly while talking to him, but without force or harshness, and presently he will obey as a matter of course and without an idea of resistance.

The most common fault of a horse is shying, and though no one **Shyers** who has a secure seat should be inconvenienced thereby, its treatment needs some discrimination. Shying often

405

HANDS AND SEAT IN REARING

arises from defective vision. If, however, the animal's eyes are in good condition, it may come from timidity, but in either case the horse should be soothed and coaxed up to the object of his aversion and shown its harmlessness. If it is merely a trick, then playing with his mouth and speaking in a warning tone when approaching anything likely to attract his notice will usually make him go straight. As a rule the whip should not be used, because the horse may learn to associate a blow with the object he has shied at, and the next time he sees it is likely to bolt in order to avoid the impending chastisement thus going from bad to worse.

For the same reason, I object to a horse being punished for stumbling. Disagreeable as it is, the fault usually comes from detective muscular action or conformation, or from not being kept **Stumblers** collected by his rider. It is not fair to punish the horse for these causes. The thing to do is to sit well back and give the reins a sharp pull to bring his head up, and then keep him going up to the bit, for if the rider is careless the horse will follow her example.

A rearing horse is not fit for a woman to ride. If she finds herself on one which attempts it, she must throw her weight forward and a little to the right, because she can lean farther forward on this than on the left side, to help the horse preserve his balance, as well as to prevent **Rearers** being struck by his head. If necessary she can clutch his mane, but on no account must she touch his mouth in the slightest degree. As he comes down, a vigorous kick with the heel, a shake of the snaffle, and a harsh exclamation may send him along. I cannot advocate a woman's striking him, for if he has a temper, it may arouse it to such an extent that he will throw himself back.

Those with a strong seat have no reason to fear a horse that plunges, if it does not develop into rearing or bucking. **Plungers** They should sit close and urge the horse to a faster pace, as it stands to reason that if he is kept going briskly he cannot so easily begin his antics as he could at a slower gait.

A woman is seldom if ever required to ride a horse which bucks, and if he is known to do it viciously she had better not try any experiments with him, as he will surely exhaust her in a fight. By bucking I **Buckers** do not mean the mild form of that vice which is usually found under that name in the East. Here an animal

that plunges persistently and comes down hard is said to buck; while if
his head is lowered, that settles the question in the minds of those ignorant of what a real bucking horse is capable. In encountering the
Eastern variety of this species, the woman must elevate the horse's
head, sit well back, and firmly too, for even the mild form of bucking
is not easy to sustain undisturbed.

The genuine article, the real Western bucker, is quite another matter. Newspapers have published instances of women who have managed to stay on one through all his various and blood-stirring antics;
but such cases are in fact unknown outside of Buffalo Bill's Wild West
Show, and there the animals have been taught to perform to order.
When the bronco bucks, he gives no preliminary warning by harmless plunging ; he simply throws his head down between his knees,
humps his back like a cat, and proceeds to business. He jumps into
the air, coming down to one side of where he started, with all four feet
bunched and legs stiffened, only to bound into space again. An occasional squeal adds to the general hilarity of the scene, and the alacrity
with which that meek-looking mustang can land and go into the air
again would astonish one not accustomed to the sight.

In riding a puller, his head must be kept in a correct position, neither low nor high, by lightly feeling his mouth until he gives to the
motion. Should he have his head up and nose out, elevating the hands

Pullers   and drawing the snaffle across the bars sometimes causes the bit to bear in such a manner that the horse will
drop his nose, and at that moment an effort must be made to keep it
there. This method is exceptional, however, and should be resorted to
only when other means fail, and the horse's head is so high, with the
nose protruding, that the bit affords no control. Ordinarily, the hands
should be low, one on each side of the withers, and quietly feeling the
snaffle until he obeys its signal.

If he pulls with his head down, almost between his knees, the
curb must not be touched, but the snaffle should be felt and the
hands held higher than usual and a little farther forward, playing
with his mouth. This may make him raise his head; but if not, then
several determined pulls, yielding the hand between them, given
without temper and with a few soothing words, may stop him. If he
has the bit between his teeth, quick give-and-take movements will

probably surprise him into releasing it. It is useless for a woman to try to subdue him by force.

It is well to have a horse's teeth examined for pulling, as one which has become displaced or sensitive causes excessive pain, and often results in this habit. When a horse shows a tendency to kick, by putting his ears back or a peculiar wriggle of the body, his head must instantly be pulled up and kept there, for in that position he will not attempt it.

A runaway nearly always frightens a woman so that she loses her head. Composure will best enable her to es- **Runaways** cape without accident. As the horse starts she must keep her heel well away from his side and her hands down, and instantly begin sawing his mouth with the reins; then a succession of sharp jerks and pulls should be resorted to never a dead pull and possibly he may be brought down.

Once well in his stride, no woman can stop a horse. She must then be governed by circumstances, and, if in a crowd or park, try to keep him clear of all objects, and not exhaust herself and excite the horse by screaming. Some one will try to catch him; and as a terrific jerk will be the result, she must brace herself for it. If the horse runs where there is open country, and she is sure his running is prompted by vice, not fright, she should urge him on when he tires and keep him going up-hill or over heavy ground if possible, using the whip freely, and not permit him to stop until he is completely done.

There are some good riders who advise pulling a horse into a fence to stop him, but there is always a chance of his attempting to jump it, while, as the rider tries to prevent this, the horse may be thrown out of his balance or stride and fall over the fence. If he is driven at a high wall or other insurmountable obstruction the horse will stop so suddenly that the rider is likely to be precipitated over the animal's head, even if she have a good seat. Again, the horse may miscalculate the distance and run into the object, perhaps seriously hurting himself and his rider. If this method is to be employed, a grassy or sandy embankment should be chosen, if possible, as there will then be fewer chances of injury.

Others believe in throwing the horse, which may be done by letting him have his head for a few strides, then suddenly giving a violent tug at the reins. If he can thus be made to cross his legs, he will go down. Another way is for a woman to put all her strength into pulling one rein, and if she can use enough force he may be twisted so that he will lose his balance and fall. Then the danger is that a woman will not get clear of him before he regains his footing and starts off, in which case she might better have remained on his back than risk being dragged at his heels. If some one else's horse is running instead of the one she is on, and it is coming towards her, a woman should instantly, but quietly, wheel her horse, and keep him as much to one side of the road as possible; and if she is sure of her control over him, a brisk canter will be the safest gait. Thus, if the runaway strikes her horse, it will not be with the same force as it would had they met from opposite directions. Besides, it is almost impossible to tell which way a frightened horse may turn, and in endeavoring to avoid him, if they are facing, a collision may result.

If a horse falls, from crossing his legs for instance, to keep hold of the reins must be the first thought, and then to get clear of him as quickly as possible and out of his way if he seems likely to roll. If the rider retains her hold on the reins, he cannot kick her, as his head will be towards her; nor can he get away, leaving her to walk home.

Punishment of a horse should never be begun without the certainty that what has given displeasure is really his fault, wilfully committed. Even then a battle should always be avoided, if possible, for it is better to spend a half-hour, or even much more, gently but firm-

Punishment   ly urging a horse to obedience than to fight him. It sometimes drives him to such a state of excitement and temper that the effects of it will be perceptible for days, sometimes weeks, in a nervous, highly strung animal, and he will, perhaps, prepare for a combat whenever the same circumstances again arise. That which comes from misconception on the part of the horse is often treated as though it were vice, and such unjust chastisement, without accomplishing its object, bewilders and frightens the unfortunate victim. Therefore one should know positively that it is obstinacy or vice, not dullness or timidity, which has made the horse apparently resist his rider's authority. A horse with much temper may only be made worse by the punishment he undoubtedly deserves; therefore, forbearance and ingenuity should be exercised to bring him into submission. Discipline must be administered at the time of insubordination, or it loses its meaning to the horse. It is folly to postpone punishing him, for then he fails to connect it with the act of resistance which has provoked it.

Another great mistake, and one to be strongly censured, is that of venting one's impatience or temper on the poor brute, which may be doing its best to understand the clumsy and imperfect commands of a cruel taskmaster.

Having calmly decided that the horse requires punishment, it should be given in a firm and temperate manner, no more severity being employed than is necessary. However, the whip should fall with force and decision, or it is worse than useless; and if a moderate amount of whipping or spurring does not result in victory, it must be increased, as, once begun, the fight must end in the conquest of the animal, or the woman on his back will thenceforth be unable to control him. It must be done dispassionately and continuously, and no time allowed him to become more obstinate by a cessation of hostilities when he might be about to give in. At the first sign of yielding, he should be encouraged, and the punishment cease, until he has had an opportunity to do what is desired of him.

While using the whip, the right hand should never be on the reins, as that necessitates jerking the horse's mouth and hitting from the wrist, a weak and ineffectual method. The blow should fall well back of the saddle and with the force given by the full swing of the arm. A woman usually expends her energy in hitting the saddle-flap, making some noise, to be sure, but not producing the desired effect.

If these suggestions are followed, there will be comparatively little trouble in learning to properly handle a horse that he may be kept up to the mark. Until having laid a solid foundation for one's self, it is useless to hope to obtain the best results from the horse, which will surely appreciate and take advantage of any incompetency on the part of the rider. Even if not aspiring to more than ordinary park riding, attention to these hints will add so materially to the comfort and safety of both horse and woman that it will be a subject of wonder to the latter how she could have found the wrong way pleasant enough to admit of any hesitation in giving the correct one at least a fair trial.

VI
CHOOSING A MOUNT

MUCH OF A woman's comfort will depend on the horse she chooses. She is too often inclined to procure a showy one, which pleases the eye, even though she cannot control his antics, rather than a trustworthy and less conspicuous mount.

In choosing a horse, she should not rely exclusively on her own judgment. Few women are aware of the artifices resorted to by dishonest dealers to render presentable some animal which in its natural condition she would at once reject; therefore she should **An Adviser** enlist the services of some man in whose knowledge of horse-flesh she has reason to place confidence, and of whose disinterestedness she is certain. When a horse is found which appears to fulfil her requirements, she should insist upon a trial of him herself; for, although he may go well and comfortably with her friend, a woman might not possess the qualities which had assured success in the former trial by the man. The horse would recognize the difference, take advantage of her inexperience or lack of skill, and act as he would not think of doing under an expert. Furthermore, gaits which would suit a man are often too hard for a woman, and a horse which he might think merely went well up to the bit would to her weaker arms seem a puller.

After being approved of by her friend, the woman should try the animal herself, outside, alone and in company. If he proves satisfactory, she should endeavor to have him in her stable for a few days, and during that time to have him examined by a veterinary surgeon, obtaining his certificate of the horse's soundness. An animal absolutely sound and without blemish is a rare sight; but there are many defects which do not lessen the horse's practical value, although their presence lower his price, and may enable her to secure something desirable which would otherwise have been beyond her means.

Such a horse should be accepted only after a thorough examination by the veterinary, and upon his advice. It is well to avoid purchasing a horse from a friend, unless one is perfectly familiar with the animal, as such transactions frequently lead to strained relations, each thinking bitterly of the other. Some, having pronounced their horse sound, would take offence should a veterinary be called; while if he were not consulted the horse might go wrong, and the purchaser would perhaps think the former owner had disposed of him with that expectation, or at least knowing the probability of it, yet their social relations would prevent accusation or explanation. Furthermore, a difference of opinion as to the price is awkward, and altogether it requires more tact, discretion, and liberality than most people possess to make a satisfactory horse-trade with a friend.

Having decided as to whose advice she will take, a woman should not be influenced by the comments and criticisms of others. If she waits until all her friends approve of her choice she will never buy a horse. However, by listening to what the best informed of them say, she may gain much instruction and knowledge. As a woman may wish to know what points are desirable in a horse, and what to look for, a general idea of this may be welcome. It is only by comparison that she will learn to distinguish whether certain parts are long or short, normal or excessive, therefore she should critically notice horses at every opportunity, and observe in what they differ from one another.

If a woman could have a Park hack made to order, the following points would be the most prominent: A horse should always be up to **Park Hack** more weight than he will have to carry; and as, in the Park, appearances are of importance, a woman should buy a horse on which she will look well. Much will depend upon her mount being of an appropriate size and build. A woman of medium size will look her best on a horse of about 15.2. No exact height can be fixed upon, as the present system of measurement is so incomplete.

A horse standing 15.2 at the withers, where it is always measured, may be much higher there than anywhere else, his quarters being disproportionately low. On the other hand, the **Measurement** withers might be low and the rump high, giving the strength, power, and stride to a horse of 15 hands which might be expected in one of several inches higher. In races and shows it enables low withered horses to run and compete against those which, although high at the withers, have not the posterior conformation to justify their being in the same class. The more common-sense and accurate method of measurement, if it would only be generally adopted, is to take the height at the withers and also at the rump, average it, and call that the size of the horse. For instance, a horse 15.3 at the withers and 15.2 at the rump should be registered as measuring 15.2½. The fashionably bred trotting horse often measures higher at the rump than at the withers, while the properly proportioned saddle horse should measure as high, or highest, at the withers.

In a saddle horse there are other points than height to be considered. If the woman is stout, the horse should be of substantial build, very compact, and like a cob. If she is slight, she will look best on a horse of light build and possessed of quality.

In my opinion, three quarters, or a trifle more, thoroughbred blood makes the pleasantest mount for a woman. Five to seven is a good age at which to buy a horse, as he will then have been through the early ailments of young horses and be just entering his prime.

As to his points, his head be small and clear-cut, with delicately pointed ears, prominent eyes, a fine muzzle, full nostrils, clean-cut angle at the throttle, and the head carried somewhat less than vertical to the ground; the crest curved, and the neck thin   **Conformation** and supple, but muscular and well set on to broad shoulders. These should be long and oblique, thus reducing the concussion and making the horse easier to ride as well as safer, because his forelegs are proportionately advanced, giving less weight in front of them to cause a fall should he trip. The true arms (commonly called lower bones of the shoulders), extend from the points of the shoulders to the elbows, and should be short, or the forelegs will be placed too far back. The forearms, extending from the elbows to the knees, should be large and muscular and rather long. Broad, flat knees are indicative of strength, and they should have considerably more width than the forearms or the shanks.

Below the knees and to the fetlocks the legs should be rather short, flat, deep, and fine, no swelling to prevent one from feeling distinctly, especially near the fetlocks, the tendons and ligaments quite separate from the shanks or cannons and the splint-bones. The fetlock-joints much developed give evidence of overwork, therefore any undue prominence is not desirable. Long, slanting pasterns give elasticity to a horse's gait and prevent disagreeable concussion; but if the length is excessive, there will be too much strain on the back tendons. The fetlocks reach to the coronet, below which are the feet, which must be of good shape and absolutely sound.

The thorax must be either broad or deep and full, so that the lungs and heart may have plenty of room to expand. It should be well supplied with muscle where the forelegs are joined to it, and these should be straight, with the feet pointing straight ahead. The toe should be under the point of the shoulder. High withers are preferred to low ones, but if they are too high they place a side-saddle at an uncomfortable angle, which needs an objectionable amount of padding at the back to rectify the fault. The back should not sink perceptibly, but it may be somewhat longer in a woman's horse than in a man's, as her saddle occupies so much more space; but the ribs should be long in front and short back of the girth, running well up to the hips. This conformation will prevent the saddle from working forward; a tendency to slip back may be checked by using a breast-plate.

A horse should be broad across the loins; if these are strong, and the horse well ribbed up, there will be no unsightly sinking of the flanks even in front of hips that are broad, as they should be. The thighs extend from the lower part of the haunches or hips to the stifle-joints, and these and the haunches are covered with powerful muscles, which, when well developed, form strong quarters. A well-placed tail, carried at a correct angle, adds greatly to a horse's appearance. From the stifles to the hocks are found the lower thighs, and these should be long and strong. The hocks should be prominent, clearly defined, and free from all puffiness or swelling. From the hocks to the fetlocks the leg should descend perpendicularly, neither bent under him nor back of him. The same rule applies to these fetlocks as to the fore ones; and the same may be said of the feet, but the latter are too important to dismiss without further comment.

The hoofs when on the ground should be at an angle of about forty-five degrees from the toe to the coronet. Any unevenness or protrusions on the wall of the hoofs, or a sinking-in at the quarters, should be viewed with suspicion. Breadth is desirable at the heels, and the bars should not be cut away. The frog should be nearly on a level with the shoes, and the soles should be slightly concave.

If a hunter is to be chosen, looks are not of so much importance, although I like him to be almost if not quite thoroughbred. However, if the animal can gallop and jump, has good staying **Hunter** qualities and a strong constitution, a kind disposition and a light mouth, good manners and plenty of power, he should not be discarded because he lacks beauty. A large head, ewe neck, ragged hips, rat-tail, poor coat, and other such ungainly points, are not bad enough to condemn him if he has the other qualities I have mentioned; and often a peculiarly shaped animal will out-jump a horse of the most correct conformation.

After carefully looking over the horse, a woman should have some one trot and canter him, to see that his action is what she wants. A Park hack should have free, easy gaits, with good knee and hock action, and **Gait** travel evenly and without brushing, cutting, inter- **and Manners** fering, dishing, or showing any such irregularities of gait. She should watch him from in front, from behind, and at the sides; and, after his trial by a man, the woman should ride him, and find out what his faults are under the saddle. His manners should be perfect: no sign of bolting, or rearing, or other vices; nor should he be a star-gazer, nor lug on the bit, as a good mouth is very essential to her comfort.

However, if he is green that is, unaccustomed to his surroundings and to being ridden he should not be rejected without a fair trial, to ascertain whether his cramped gait, shying, and other such failings are the result of inexperience under the saddle, or are established traits. The most desirable points are a light but not over-sensitive mouth, even gait, with swinging (not jerky or shuffling) action, a kind disposition with which quality considerable friskiness need not condemn him—good manners, and freedom from tricks and vices. He should be practically sound and of correct conformation—a more valuable attribute for safety and ease than high action.

VII
DRESS

SIMPLICITY IS THE rule for the habit. It should be of Thibet cloth—black, dark brown, or blue for winter, tan or a medium shade of gray for summer. All conspicuous colors and materials are to be avoided. It is well to have the skirt made of a heavy-weight cloth, which will help to make it set properly without the assistance of straps; while the bodice may be of a medium weight of the same cloth, that it may fit better and be less bulky. For very warm weather in the country a habit made of heavy gingham or white duck is cool and comfortable, and will wash. The skirt and bodice may be of the same material, or a silk or cheviot shirt and leather belt may be worn with the skirt. A straw sailor-hat completes this convenient innovation, but it should be reserved for use out of town.

The skirt should reach only far enough to cover the left foot, and be too narrow to admit of any flowing folds. Fashion and **Skirt** safety both demand this. A skittish horse is often frightened by a loose skirt flapping at his side.

I should be very glad to see the safety skirt, which is worn in the hunting-field, adopted in general riding. Its advantages are manifold. Although it appears the same, less cloth is used, therefore it is cooler; there is nothing between the pommel and the breeches, thus improving **Safety Skirt** the hold, and in case of accident it is impossible to be dragged. There are several kinds in use, but the less complicated the more desirable it is. The simplest is made like any other skirt, except that where the pommels come there is a large piece of the cloth cut out, extending in a circle at the top, and then straight down, at both sides, so that there is no cloth near the pommels or where it could catch in case of a fall. This leaves enough to extend under both legs when in the saddle, and looks like an ordinary one. Under the right knee, where the skirt is rounded out, a small strip of cloth buttons from this point on to the piece which is under the leg; this and an elastic strap on the foot keep it in place; but neither is strong enough to stand any strain, therefore would not be dangerous in a fall.

Another pattern has eyelet holes made on each side from where the cloth has been taken, and round silk elastic laced through them, thus preventing the possibility of disarrangement. Both of these skirts loop at the back, and can be kept from appearing unlike others if the wearer will immediately fasten them on dismounting. An ordinary skirt may be made safer by having no hem.

We hear a great deal now of the divided skirt, and the advisability **Divided Skirt** of women riding astride. The theory is good, as having a leg each side of the animal gives much greater control over his movements.

For most women, however, it is impracticable, since they cannot sit down in the saddle and grip with their knees as they should, owing to the fact that their thighs are rounded, instead of flat like a man's. It might be possible for a lean and muscular woman to acquire a secure seat, but not for the average one. Being short is another drawback to a strong seat against which most of them would have to contend. This is particularly trying, as so much of her weight is above the waist, making it difficult to ride from balance, which might otherwise replace the deficient leverage of the short thigh. Again, if on a large or broad horse, the constant strain on the muscles necessary when astride him must be injurious.

Aside from any physical reasons, the position for a woman is, in my opinion, most ungraceful and undignified, while few of them possess the strength to profit by the changed seat in forcing the horse up to his bridle or keeping him collected; and I cannot blame those who think it open to the charge of impropriety.

The bodice should be single-breasted, long over the hips, reaching almost to the saddle in the back, and cut away in front to show a waistcoat, the upper edge of which makes a finish between **Bodice** the collar and lapels of the waist and the white collar and Ascot or four-in-hand. The waistcoat gives more of an opportunity for the exercise of individual taste. The most desirable, I think, has a white background, on which is a black, brown, blue, or red check. It may be all tan or a hunting pink, plain, figured, or striped, so long as too many colors are not combined; but, as a rule, something quiet and simple will be the most desirable. In summer a pique **Waistcoat** waistcoat is worn, or something similar, that is light, cool, and will wash. A black or white cravat always looks well, or one which, without being glaring, harmonizes with the waistcoat.

Sense, health, and comfort all demand that the waist shall not be laced to the painful extent endured by many foolish and vain women. **Corsets** They would let out an inch or two if they could realize that the blood is forced from their waists to their faces, making them scarlet at any exertion, while they have difficulty in conversing except in gasps, and are compelled to walk their horses at frequent intervals to catch their breath.

It is so invigorating to feel the lungs expanded by a long, deep breath, and the blood, quickened by the motion of the horse, coursing unrestrained through all the veins, while the muscles of the back and abdomen are allowed full play, that those who go along panting and aching lose half the beneficial effects of riding, and more pleasure than they can possibly derive from trying to make people believe that they have small waists. The corsets are of great importance and must be of good quality and not very stiff, small bones being used instead of large ones or steels. They must be short in front and over the hips, that the movements may not be unnecessarily restricted, or the skin become raw from rubbing against the ends of the bones. A plain corset-cover should be worn over them, as the lining of the habit-waist sometimes discolors the corsets if this precaution is not taken.

Considerable latitude is permitted a woman in the choice of what she shall wear under her skirt. Boots and breeches are considered better form than shoes and trousers; but there is no reason **Boots,** why the latter should not be used, especially if the **Breeches,** shoes lace. Boots and tights, however, are the most **Tights** comfortable of all. Breeches are made of stockinette, re-enforced with chamois skin, and reach half-way down the calf, where they should button close to the leg the buttons being on the left side of each leg, that the right may not be bruised by the buttons pressing against the saddle. Chamois skin is sometimes used to make breeches, but it is not very satisfactory. At first they are soft and pliable, but after being worn a few times they become stiff and unyielding, and rain will render them hard as boards.

Tan box-cloth gaiters, extending from the instep almost to the knee, are sometimes worn with breeches and shoes. They are made exactly like those for men, and take the place of boots. Boots may be of calf-skin or patent leather, with wrinkled or stiff legs, the tops reaching a few inches above the bottom of the breeches. In warm weather tan boots are often worn; but, of whatever variety they may be, they should always be large, with broad, thick soles and low, square heels.

Trousers are of the same material as the skirt, and are also re-enforced. Elastic bands passing under the shoes keep the trousers down. Tights should be of the color of the habit, and fit smoothly without being stretched. They come in different weights, and either silk, cotton, or wool may be worn. They should have feet woven on them, thus doing away with the necessity for all underclothing below the waist.

When breeches or trousers are worn, tights may advantageously be substituted for the other usual garments worn under such conditions. If tights are not worn, whatever replaces them should fit snugly and be without starch or frills. The stockings should be kept up from the waist, as garters chafe the knee when it presses the pommel, and often interfere with the circulation. Some women wear union garments, which are practically tights extending from the neck to the feet, taking the place of shirts. However, when a shirt is worn it will be most comfortable if of a light weight wool. This absorbs the perspiration, and is therefore pleasanter to wear than silk, and more likely to protect from a cold. Outside of this should be the corset.

When it is cold a chamois-skin waist with long sleeves should be worn under the bodice, as this is much better than a fur cape, which is often used, and which confines the arms. A covert coat is the most convenient, but the former is more readily obtained. A wool shirt, short corsets, plain corset-cover, and tights are all the underclothing needed for riding. Some women wear a linen shirt, with collar and cuffs attached, like a man's, except that it is narrowed at the waist. With this the corset-cover is not needed.

Separate collars and cuffs are more generally used, and the scarf

Collars and Cuffs   should be pinned to the collar at the back, as these have a way of parting company that is most untidy. To make it more certain, a clasp or pin such as men use to hold a four-in-hand tie in place should fasten the ends of the scarf to the shirt-front or corset-cover, thus securing it against slipping.

The cuffs should not be pinned to the sleeve, as the lining of the coat will be torn, and the pin will catch on the habit and stretch and roughen it in places. A small elastic band put over a button at the wrist of the sleeve, and attached to the cuff-button, will answer every purpose.

Gauntlets should be discarded, and gloves worn large enough to admit of the muscles of the hand being used freely. Dogskin of a reddish shade of tan is the best material for gloves. The **Gloves** stitching is such as to form slight ridges of the glove itself on the back of the hand, the red stitches being scarcely perceptible at a little distance. It is difficult to find women's gloves broad enough for comfort in riding, and it is a good plan to buy boys' gloves, which give the desired freedom. They have only one button, an advantage over women's, which have two or three that are in the way under the cuff.

Should the wrists need more protection from the cold, wristlets may be worn, as they take up but little room. For cold weather, gloves come in a softer kid, like chevrette, and have a fleecy lining, very warm, but too soft and light to make the gloves clumsy. Flowers and jewelry are decidedly out of place on horseback, and a handkerchief should never be thrust into the front of the bodice. It should be put in the slit on the off saddle-flap, or in the pocket at the left side of the skirt where it opens.

The hair should be firmly coiled or braided on the neck, and not worn on top of the head. A top hat is correct, especially on formal occasions, but it should not be allowed to slip to the back of the head. **Hair and Hat** However, I prefer usually a derby, as being more comfortable and looking more business-like. It should be kept on by an elastic which fastens under the hair. Pins through the crown are an uncalled-for disfigurement, and a hat may be made just as secure without them. In fact, they will be of but little use if the hair is not done high. A large hair-pin on each side should pin the hair over the elastic; and if the wind or anything else causes the hat to become displaced, it will not come off entirely, forcing some one to dismount and restore it to the woman, who cannot get it alone. Hair-pins should be long and bent half-way up each prong, so that they will not easily slip out.

When a veil is worn, it should be of black net or gauze, never white or figured, and the ends should be neatly pinned out of sight, **Veil** instead of being allowed to float out behind, like smoke from a steam-engine. If a whip is carried for use, it should be a substantial stiff one, held point down, not a flimsy thing that a sound blow will break, nor should it be made absurd by a bow or tassel being tied to it. If for style, then a crop is the correct thing, with the lash-end held up. The handle should be of horn, rather than silver or gold, and the stick quite **Whip or** heavy and somewhat flexible. Short **Crop** bamboo sticks are in favor just now, and are often tipped with gold, and have a gold band a few inches from the end where it is held.

I do not approve of a spur for women, as it is difficult to use it just right, and its unintentional application often has disastrous results, while should she be **Spur** dragged by the foot, it will keep hitting the horse, urging him faster and faster. In mounting, the spur sometimes strikes the horse, making him shy just as the rider expects to reach the saddle, and a nasty fall is the consequence. Where a man would **CROP** use it advantageously, a woman cannot produce the same effect, having it only on one side. Moreover, a horse suitable for her to ride should not require more than her heel and her whip.

Some horses are very cunning, and will shirk their work if they discover that there is no spur to urge them, but such may be taught that

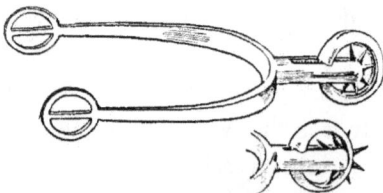

POSITION WHEN PRESSED AGAINST THE HORSE.

A GOOD SPUR

a whip in skilful hands is quite as effective. In a crowd a spur is of value, as it may be applied noiselessly, and without danger of startling other horses, as a whip will do. In leaping, a spur on one side of the horse and the whip on the other form a combination which will often compel him to jump when, from sulkiness or indolence, he has been refusing.

It requires some practice, however, to use it in the right place and at the right moment; a woman's skirt has an unhappy faculty of intercepting the spur when it should strike him, and her heel of hitting the horse when it should leave him alone. For these reasons I am in favor of women riding without a spur when it is possible, for, although it looks well as a finish to a boot, its adoption by inexpert riders may lead to sad results.

If a spur is to be worn, there are several kinds from which to choose. I prefer a box-spur with a rowel, such as men use, but having a guard, which prevents it from catching in the habit, and lessens the probabilities of its unintentionally punishing a horse. When it is applied with force, the rowel comes through the guard, which works on a spring, and upon releasing the pressure the guard again protects the sharp rowel. They may be of the kind that fit in a box which has been put in the heel of the boot, or they may have straps and buckle over the instep.

VIII
LEAPING

W HEN A WOMAN has attained some degree of proficiency in the saddle, she will probably desire to perfect herself in riding by learning to leap. Her equestrian education cannot be considered complete without this, but she should not attempt it until she has learned thoroughly how to ride cor- **Requirements** rectly on the road. A secure seat, light hands, a cool head, quick perception, judgment, and courage form a combination which will enable her in a short time to acquire skill in jumping. Few women possess all these qualities, but an effort should be made to obtain as many of them as possible before trying to jump.

The first lessons should be on a horse which has been well trained to this work and requires no assistance from his rider. He should inspire confidence, and jump easily and surely rather than brilliantly. I think it is well to begin in a school **In the Ring** over bars, as there the rider is not under the necessity of choosing a good take-off or landing, and is thus free to give undivided attention to herself.

Three feet is high enough to put the bars at the start; or they may be even lower should the rider feel timid. As she approaches the jump she must sit firmly in the middle of the saddle (not hanging either to the right or to the left, thereby upsetting the horse's **Approaching** balance), and she must look straight at the obstacle, **Jump** with her head up and her body thrown a trifle back.

The reins should at first be held in both hands, for several reasons. It lessens the chances of sitting crooked, and it prevents throwing up the right arm as the horse jumps a common and unsightly practice, calculated to frighten him and distract his attention from his work, and to jerk his mouth, while it has no redeeming features. In addition to this, when the horse lands, the reins are not so liable to slip through two hands as through one.

Approaching the jump, the horse should break into a moderate canter, and the only rule his rider will be likely to remember at the first trial will be to "lean back as he jumps arid give him his head." As she becomes accustomed to the action, her attention must be called to details. While nearing the jump, she must keep her hands low, and just feel her horse's mouth with the snaffle without interfering with it or shifting her hold on the reins. Quiet, steady hands are indispensable to success.

By watching his stride one can tell when he will take off. At that moment he will stretch out his neck; then she must, by instantly pushing them forward, let her hands yield to his mouth. This must be **Taking off** accurately calculated, for should the pressure on his mouth be varied too suddenly and at the wrong time, it would throw him out of his stride by letting go of his mouth when he needed steadying. Some advocate leaning forward before leaning back as the horse takes off, but the slight involuntary motion communicated to the body by thrusting the hands forward will be sufficient to precede the backward movement. Before he has finished his effort, she must lean back just enough (but no farther) to avoid being thrown forward by the action of his quarters or by the angle at which he comes down. Her left heel should not come in contact with him after he has taken off, although she may strike him with it to urge him on if he goes at the jump too slowly. Below the waist she must be firm and immovable; above, **Landing** yielding and flexible. As the horse lands, she regains her upright position, and should be careful that he does not pull the reins through her fingers. Under all circumstances she must have too firm a hold on the reins to admit of such an occurrence. If the horse stumbles at the moment of landing, he needs the support of her hands; or should he bolt, it must not be necessary to pull in the slack rein before being able to check him.

One of the most erroneous theories extant is that it is desirable to "lift" a horse at his fences. Doing so only necessitates carrying the weight of his rider's hands on his mouth, and risks pulling the horse into the jump, while he is hindered from stretching his neck, as he

TAKING OFF

must to land safely and correctly. Hanging on to his mouth is often the cause of a horse's landing on all four feet at once, or dropping too close

Lifting

to the jump. The pull on the reins holds him back, thus inducing these bad habits, and will often make him refuse or dread to jump, knowing that it entails a sharp jerk on his sensitive mouth. To a casual or ignorant observer it sometimes looks as though a good rider were "lifting" his horse; but it only appears so because, knowing intuitively at just what instant his hands must yield, he so accurately gives to the animal's mouth that the action of the horse's mouth and the rider's hands is simultaneous.

After some practice in the ring, a woman may try jumping out-of-doors, for inside there is not a sufficient variety of obstacles; and she should then have a breast-plate attached to her saddle. By this time she should, in jumping, hold her reins in one hand, the snaffle inside, curb outside, and quite loose. As she goes towards a

Out-of-Doors

jump, her right hand should be placed in front of the left on the snaffle to steady the horse. In this way she can remove it without leaving an uneven pressure on the horse's mouth, as would be the case if, as is customary, her hand had rested on the two right reins, then been suddenly withdrawn in order to urge the horse with the whip, or to protect the face from overhanging branches.

The most favorable conditions under which a woman may begin jumping in the country are when she can go across fields with a capable pilot to give her a lead over some easy timber or walls. She must never

Pilot

forget to see that the horse in front of her is well away from the fence before she jumps, or she will risk landing on top of him if he makes a mistake; or if he refuses, her horse, if too near, would be forced to do likewise. She should not allow herself to become dependent on the services of a pilot, or let her horse become accustomed to jumping only when he has a lead; therefore she must learn to choose a panel of the fence for herself.

Supposing the fences to be moderate, she must decide, as she canters towards the first, where she will jump, and there are a number of considerations by which she must be governed.

Selecting a Panel

First, to find a panel which is low, for in riding across country it is wise to save one's mount, as all his strength may be needed at a big place later on. Then the take-off

ABOUT TO LAND

must be looked to, sound level turf being chosen if possible; and if the landing is plainly visible, so much the better. A moderately thick top rail is often safer to put a horse at than a very thin round one, which is liable to be a sapling, that will not break if a horse tries to crash through it, as he is sometimes tempted to do by its fragile appearance.

It is well to send a horse at the middle of a panel; for, should he hit it, this, being the weakest spot, may break, while should he hit nearer the end, where it is strong, he may be thrown. Such details as these she will observe instinctively with a little practice. Having decided where she will jump, her horse's head must be pointed straight at the place, and her mind must not waver. If the rider is determined to go, and has no misgivings, the horse is sure to be inspired with the same confidence.

Having once put him at a panel, she should avoid changing her mind without good reason, as her uncertainty will be imparted to him. A fence such as described is jumped just as are the bars in the ring; safely over it, the next obstacle must be examined.

If it be a stone wall, it may often be taken in one of two places either where it is high and even, or where it is lower and wide, because of **Stone Wall** the stones which have fallen from the top. In the first instance it should be jumped in a collected manner, but at a slower pace than the second requires. At the latter some speed is necessary, as the horse must jump wide enough to avoid the rolling stones on both sides.

Few riders remember that it is as important to keep a horse collected when going fast as at any other time. When he **In Hand** is hurried along, no chance is given him to measure his stride or get his legs well under him, but he is nevertheless expected to take off correctly and clear the obstacle.

A good rider will always have her horse well in hand, and never hustle him at his fences, even if she goes at them with considerable speed.

If the take-off looks treacherous, or is ploughed or muddy, the **Trappy Ground** horse should be brought to it at a trot, well col-**and Drops** lected, and allowed to take his time at it.

When the ground approaching the jump is uphill, or descending, the same tactics should be pursued, and unlimited rein given the horse. On encountering a drop on the far side of a fence or wall, a woman must lean back as far as possible, leaving the reins long, but ready to support the horse's head as he lands. At a trappy place, where, for instance, there might be a broken-down fence among some trees, overgrown with vines and bushes, the horse must be taken quietly and slowly and made to crawl through the gap. His rider will even then have enough trouble in keeping her feet clear of the vines, and in preventing the branches from hitting her face, which she could not do if a jump were made with a rush. If her horse carries his head high, she can probably pass where it has been without injury by leaning forward over his withers, to the right, and raising her right arm to ward off the branches with her whip or crop.

Sometimes she will not notice a limb or other obstruction until almost under it, when it will be necessary for her to lean back, resting her shoulders on the horse's quarters. Under these circumstances it is most important that her right arm should guard her **In and Out** eyes from pieces of bark or other falling particles. Where two fences are within a few feet of each other, forming an "in-and-out," the pace needs to be carefully regulated. If the horse goes very fast, he will jump so wide that he will land too close to the second fence to take off as he should. Therefore if he is rushing, his stride must be shortened and his hind-legs brought well under him.

On the other hand, he must not go so slowly that all impetus for the second effort is lost, as he would then be likely to refuse. It is difficult to turn him in so short a space and get him into his stride before he is called upon to jump.

At a ditch or stream considerable speed is needed to gain the momentum necessary to cover the distance, and the horse must have plenty of rein given him.

A picket fence is usually regarded as a very formidable obstacle, but if negotiated properly it is no worse than others. It should be taken at a good rate of speed, for the danger is that the horse will get **Picket and Slat** hung up on it and be cut with the points by not **Fences** having enough impetus. It is not so dangerous to hit this fence in front, for it is frail and the top of the pickets will snap off at the binder if hit with force. A slat fence is more to be dreaded, on account of the ledge on the top of it formed by the binder. This should be taken with deliberation, as the thing to be guarded against is having the horse hit his knees on the ledge which protrudes a couple of inches beyond the fence. The lower slats give way easily if they are approached from the side where the posts are; if from the opposite direction, they are braced against the posts and offer great resistance.

Any fence that has wire on it should be avoided if possible, unless the horse has been trained to jump it. When it extends along the top of **Wire** a fence, the horse should be made to jump a post, as it is not safe to count on his seeing the wire. If the fence is made of strands of wire, with only a binder of timber, it should be taken slowly, so that the horse will not attempt to crash through it, under the impression that it is a single bar.

A stone wall having a rail on top must be taken in the horse's stride, for considerable swing is required, as there is **Combined** width as well as height to clear. When a ditch is on **Obstacles** the near side of a wall or fence, the horse should be allowed time to see it. When it is on the landing side, he should be sent at it fast enough to carry him safely over.

Thus far I have been supposing that the horse has gone without a mistake. Under these circumstances he should not be struck just to encourage him, as some maintain or he will grow to dislike jumping if associated with a blow.

No woman who rides much can expect to be always so perfectly mounted; therefore, a few suggestions as to what she should do in emergencies may be of practical value.

The most common fault of the jumper is refusing, and it must be dealt with according to its cause. If it arises from weakness in the hocks, the horse hesitating to propel himself by them, or from weak knees, or **Refusing** corns that cause him to dread the concussion of landing, he should not be forced to jump it is both cruel and unsafe. If he be sound and well, and the fence not beyond his capabilities, the rider must know whether the disinclina- **Timidity** tion to jump comes from timidity or from temper. She will soon learn to distinguish between the two, but it is difficult to lay down any rule for recognizing the difference. If she thinks it is for the former reason, the cause may be that he was not in his stride when he should have taken off, and was allowed to sprawl as he cantered. She should take him back and keep him well collected, making him take short, quick strides in the canter, measuring the distance, and giving him his head when he should take off. If he seems inclined to swerve or hesitate, the whip, applied just when he should rise, will often prevent his stopping. When over, a caress and a word of praise will greatly encourage him.

Temper is a very different and a very difficult thing to manage. Coaxing and ingenuity may accomplish something; turning him short at another place will often surprise him into jumping before he realizes it. The human voice has great power over animals, **Temper** and a few loud, sharp exclamations, with a quick use of the whip, may make him take off when otherwise he would have refused. A really obstinate horse, having made up his mind not to jump, needs such a thrashing as a woman is seldom able to give him. If she begins it, she must keep it up until she has conquered him, or he will try the same trick constantly.

As a horse almost invariably turns to the left when he refuses, a sharp crack on the near shoulder, being unusual and unexpected, sometimes prevents his turning. When, in one way or another, he finally has been forced to yield, he should be rewarded by a few words of approval. At the next fence a firm hold, keeping his head straight and his legs well under him, will be of more service than a whip, unless he refuses again, when the lesson must be repeated.

At least half of the refusals are the fault of the rider, and it is most unjust to punish a horse at such times. Unfortunately, conceit is such a common failing that few of us are willing to acknowledge ourselves in the wrong, therefore the poor horse suffers for our error. The timid rider sends the horse at an obstacle in such a **Rider at Fault** half-hearted way that he does not know whether he is expected to jump or not; or, feeling his rider waver, he imagines there must be unknown dangers connected with the place, and so hesitates to encounter them. One of a woman's frequent failings is shifting the reins as she nears a jump. This form of nervousness is very disconcerting to a horse, and takes his mind from the work in front of him.

Lack of skill makes one lug at a horse's mouth just as he is getting ready to jump, thus throwing him out of his stride and frustrating his effort. After one or two refusals, a woman often puts her horse at the place in a mechanical way, fully expecting the animal to stop, and doing nothing to guard against such an occurrence. If she would instead then summon all her courage, and determine to go either over or through the fence, and ride at it with resolution, the horse would be infected with her spirit and probably clear the obstacle, as he would have done at first had his rider's heart then been in the right place. In such cases it does not seem fair to punish a horse for our own want of nerve.

IX
LEAPING (continued)

O N A HORSE which rushes when put at a jump, the use of the whip will only make matters worse. This habit of rushing comes most frequently from the horse having **Rushers** been frightened while being taught to jump, either by extreme harshness and punishment or from having hurt himself severely. Even if it comes from viciousness, quiet, kind treatment will do more to eradicate the tendency than coercive measures.

Such a horse should be walked towards a fence until within half a dozen strides of it. This can best be achieved by not indicating that he will be expected to jump, but by approaching it as though by chance. Otherwise the restraint will make him the more unmanageable when he does start. He should be induced to stand a few moments, while his rider strokes him and talks to him in a soothing way. The snaffle should then be gradually and quietly shortened until there is a light but firm feeling on the reins, when a pressure of the leg (not of the heel, which might suggest a spur) will put him to a trot. If the hands be held low and steady and the voice be soft and pacifying, they will probably prevail upon him to trot all the way, although he may break into a canter a stride before the jump. When over it he should be gently, not sharply, pulled up, and coaxed to walk again, or, better still, to trot slowly. When he has learned to jump from the trot he will soon do so from a slow canter, which will be more trying for him, as it has a closer resemblance to the gait at which he has been in the habit of rushing, and he will therefore be inclined to return to his old failing.

Sometimes a horse will not go near a fence, and on being urged will back or rear. If he persists in backing, his head should be turned away from the jump, and when he finds his movements only bring him nearer the fence, he will stop. If then he is made to wheel suddenly, and can be kept going by whip or spur, he will be likely to jump. Should he,

Balkers instead, face the direction in which he should go, and rear whenever an attempt is made to urge him forward, the whip only inciting him to rear higher, the woman who hopes to triumph over him must resort to strategy; she must not whip him, at the risk of his falling back on her.

A ruse which may prove successful is to occupy his attention by playing with his mouth while he is allowed to go diagonally towards the fence. He will be apt to concede this point, in the hope of bolting alongside of it; but when he has been inveigled into a closer proximity to the jump, even if he be parallel to it, and before he has time to divine his rider's intention, he should be turned sharply to the fence. He must be ridden at it resolutely and with a firm hand, while a determined swing of the body, corresponding to his stride, conveys to his mind the impression that he will be forced to jump. If he can be kept moving forward, he cannot rear; therefore, should he attempt to swerve or bolt, a blow from the whip will keep him straight, and when he should take off, another will guard against a refusal.

A sluggish animal calls for constant watching, as he cannot be trusted at small places any more than at large ones. He is always liable to rap, or even fall, at his fences, because of the **Sluggards** careless, slovenly manner in which he moves. He should be forced up to the bit, and kept active by the whip, the noise of which is desirable in his case, as it will assist in rousing him. If his laziness or sulkiness is such that he will endeavor to crash through fences, he is not suitable for any woman to ride. He may miscalculate his power and come in contact with a rail which withstands his weight, when a fall will ensue.

In this case the lunging-rein should be resorted to, and, either in a ring or out-of-doors, the horse should be put over some stiff bars, that he may learn he will be hurt if he touches them. I do not approve of intentionally throwing him by pulling him in the jump; there are too many chances of his being injured, even though he has no weight to carry. The bars should be strong enough to sustain his weight, without breaking, so that if he hits them hard he will have a tumble and a lesson. The top bar should, if possible, be covered with straw, to protect the knees from sharp edges. Some forcible raps and a few tumbles will teach the horse the necessity of exerting himself, and how to bend his knees and lift his hind-legs over a jump.

A fall is, at the best, a dangerous and often a disastrous affair for a woman, whose very position on a horse lessens the chance of escape from such a predicament without injury. A safety skirt **Falls** will prevent her being dragged; but much harm may result from the fall, even though she be clear of the horse when he gets up. If she is not hurt, there is still danger that the shock to her nerves will weaken her pluck. Should such symptoms appear, she should remount at once; for the longer she waits the greater will be her apprehension, and it might end in her never regaining her nerve. She should make as light of the casualty as possible, and not regard it seriously if she has been only somewhat bruised or shaken up.

It is marvellous how many and what ugly falls one can encounter without being any the worse for them; nevertheless, no precaution should be neglected to prevent exposure to them. When a woman has experienced several, she will know instinctively what to do; but at first she should try to bear in mind some points which may help her on such occasions.

A rider not accustomed to jumping will probably lose her seat if the horse hits a fence with much force; as she feels herself going she should try to grasp the animal's neck, and not attempt to keep on by the aid of the reins, for by so doing she might throw him. Even if she has gone farther than the saddle, if she can fling her weight, above the waist, to the off side of the horse's neck, she will balance there for a moment, and that will give her time to grasp the saddle and pull herself back. Should she find herself beyond that, then as she slips off she can keep her head from the ground by seizing hold of the breast-plate with one hand, but without letting go of the reins.

These must always be retained, as their possession renders it impossible for the horse to reach her with his heels, and precludes the chance of his getting away.

If the horse bungles the jump, or comes down on his knees without disturbing his rider's equilibrium, and seems likely to fall, a woman cannot disentangle herself from him in time to get away. If he should go down, therefore, she must sit evenly, leaning back, that her weight may be taken from his fore-legs, while he is allowed plenty of rein. He may thus regain his balance or his footing after a scramble; but it will be impossible, in a slow fall like this, for a woman to be thrown clear of him. As he will not roll immediately, the closer she sits the better; so that if he tumbles on his near side, the force of the blow will be broken by the pommels, which, if she be sitting close, will hit the ground first, thus protecting her legs from the concussion. Moreover, if she were half out of the saddle, the pommels might strike her chest or crush a rib, and she would be more likely to be kicked.

As the horse makes an effort to get up, she must be ready to extricate herself from him and scramble as far away as possible, as the danger then is that he will not regain his feet, but will sink down a second time and thus roll over his prostrate rider.

If he should fall on his off side, a woman must strive to get clear on that side as he lands, and not where the horse's feet are.

Where a ditch has caused a fall, it is usually from unsound banks; therefore, in attempting to climb out, firmer ground should be chosen. If the woman has been thrown and the horse has landed on top of her, the ditch being deep or narrow, she must try to keep his head down until help arrives, so that he cannot strike her, as he might do, because of the limited space, in his struggles to get up.

In a stream, if she has preserved her seat, she must keep the horse moving, or he will be inclined to lie down.

If she has been thrown into the water, she must obtain a hold on the saddle and the reins, but use only the former to support herself until the horse reaches the shore.

In all of these events a cool head and presence of mind will be of the greatest assistance; but when a horse turns completely over at a fence, or falls heavily and without warning, to drop her stirrup, relax her muscles, and get clear of him as best she may is all a woman can do.

Occasionally, after a number of jumps, the girths become loosened and the saddle begins to turn. In such an emergency the horse's mane should be firmly grasped and the foot taken out of the stirrup. The horse should be quieted and stopped, if he is not too much startled by the turning saddle. With a breast-plate it will probably not turn all the way, and her hold of the mane will enable a woman to keep her head up until some one comes to the rescue.

It will probably be a long time before such a variety of contingencies as I have mentioned will happen to any one rider. A well-mounted woman may jump a great deal and escape with only a few tumbles. If she perseveres, there will be so many delightful experiences to counterbalance each mishap that she will gladly risk the consequences of indulging in a sport which, to so great an extent as leaping, develops her nerve, skill, and self-possession.

X
RIDING TO HOUNDS

WHETHER HOUNDS ARE running on the scent of a fox or a drag, a woman who is following them should always remember certain points to guide her in her conduct and in the management of her horse while in the field. **Courtesy**

Many a beginner renders herself objectionable by striving to take a place among the hard riders of the first flight.

It is not to be expected that a woman without experience in the hunting-field can keep up with those who have followed hounds for several seasons; and should she attempt it, the probable result would be a fall not only endangering herself and her horse, but compelling some man to come to her assistance, and thereby perhaps lose the remainder of the run. Even though too well mounted to have this occur, there are countless ways in which a novice, in endeavoring to keep on even terms with the leaders, may unwittingly call down anything but blessings on her head from those for whose good opinion she most cares. It is a mistake for her to suppose that people are watching her, ready to admire her pluck and dash, when she crashes through fences because her horse was not collected, or rides so close to the hounds as to risk hitting them. If she flatters herself that she is cutting out the work, it is pretty certain she has no business to be so far forward, and that she will add to the number of men who consider the hunting-field no place for women.

A beginner should be content to stay behind the first flight until, by experience and skill, she has earned the right to take a better place. **The Novice** At first she should find out which of the men go straight, yet ride cautiously and manage to keep the hounds in sight. Such a one she should choose as her pilot, rather than a reckless rider or one who shirks his fences. Unless she is very well acquainted with him, a woman should not let a man know that she is following him. It annoys him to think that some one is "tagging on behind," or that he is responsible for the jumps she takes. Above all things, she must invariably give him or any one in front of her time to get well away from a jump before she takes it. This is of the utmost importance, and is a point neglected by men and women alike in the excitement and impatience of a run.

If she desires to be looked upon otherwise than as a nuisance, she must be as unobtrusive and cool-headed as possible, always courteous to and considerate of others, patient when waiting for her turn at a narrow place, and not try to take jumps that well-mounted, hard-riding men deem impracticable.

Women seldom need to be urged on in the hunting-field; they require rather to be cautioned and restrained. If they are new at it, they do not know the dangers to which they are exposed, so go recklessly; if

Hard Riding they appreciate the chances they take, they grit their teeth and go desperately; if they are timid they nevertheless resolve not to be outdone, and, trusting all to their horse, go blindly, even closing their eyes at a critical moment. Therefore hard riding does not prove that a woman has either pluck or skill. She is an exception who goes straight and keeps with the hounds without taking foolish risks, unnecessarily tiring her mount, or interfering with others, for this requires judgment, discretion, skill, and nerve.

An undesirable trait observed in many instances is jealous riding. This cannot be too strongly condemned, not only for the unsportsmanlike spirit it betrays, but because it often threatens the safety of others than those who ride in that manner. A jealous rider crowds past people, jumps too close to them, and is constantly   **Jealous Riding** trying to be among the first, regardless of the consequences to those he or she hurries by. The motive that usually actuates a woman in such a case is vanity. She cannot bear to see another woman ahead of her, so she dashes along unmindful of the rules of etiquette and the hunting -field, until by pushing, crowding, and taking big chances for herself and against others, she reaches the object of her jealousy, thinking to wrest from her the admiration of the field. If the other woman is of the same mind and objects to being passed, a steeple-chase will ensue that may end in accidents, disabled hounds, and bad feelings. Admiration is far from the minds of the spectators, who do not fail to see that jealousy and vanity, not eagerness for sport, are the incentives to such hard riding.

When a woman begins riding to hounds, she should already have had some experience in larking a horse across country, **Desirable** and be acquainted with the way to take the different **Qualities** kinds of jumps she will encounter during a run. If she starts with a good seat and hands, pluck and nerve, a little time and practice will add composure, judgment, and discretion, and the experience necessary to cross a stiff country without mishap. She may then discard the services of a pilot and ride her own line.

When hounds are thrown in, she must watch them, and, although **Getting Away** not interfering with their work, be ready to get away on good terms with them when they begin to run.

Indecision at the first two jumps may cost one dearly, for during that moment of hesitation hounds slip away, horses crowd one another and begin to refuse, while the few who make the most of their opportunities ride on ahead with the hounds. Much hard galloping may retrieve the lost ground, but a stern chase is always disheartening to horse and rider. By getting away in front, both are encouraged, and start with mutual good-will and satisfaction relations which should always exist between a hunter and his rider.

If, after pointing her horse's head at a certain part of a jump, she thinks another place is more inviting, she must **Indecision** not change her course, unless certain that she can do so without inconveniencing some one else who may have been going straight at it.

It is inexcusable to turn from one place to another by cutting in ahead of following riders. It throws their horses out of their stride, and may force them to pull up in order to avoid a collision. Therefore, in suddenly changing her direction, a woman must assure herself that she is at least half a dozen lengths in front of her follower, who is going straight, or she must wait until she has been passed.

When a horse refuses, the rule is that the rider shall immediately pull out and give the next a chance to jump. This is so often overlooked in the **Right of Way** field, that a few words seem desirable to impress its importance upon the minds of those who hunt.

Women particularly seem to consider themselves privileged to keep their horse at a fence while he refuses at each trial, blocking the way, if there is no other place to jump, of those in their rear. Frequently, when her horse refuses, his rider thinks there is time to try it again before the next one reaches the place; she puts him at the fence, in her hurry turning him so short he could not jump if he wanted to, and the result is that he stops just as the other horse arrives, whose rider is thereby obliged to pull up.

Had the woman pulled to one side in the first place, and waited until her follower had given her horse a lead, which would probably have induced him to jump, both would have been in the next field much sooner than her impatience in the first instance eventually permitted.

A horse should not be ridden behind one that is likely to refuse, **Funk** or he may be inclined to imitate the misdoings of his predecessor.

In the same way, it is injudicious to take a horse to a place where others are refusing, either from their own or their riders' timidity. He is liable to be infected with their faint-heartedness; for it needs an unusually sensible, reliable horse to be the first to jump out from a crowd at a place that has stopped those in front of him.

It is far better for a woman to choose another way of reaching the hounds than to risk adding to the number of refusers, unless she be so well mounted as to be sure of giving the rest a lead.

A hot-headed, excitable horse will go more quietly if he can be made to think he is ahead of the others. Therefore his rider should choose a line for herself, apart from the others, **Excitable and** and if he is a good performer it will be safer to **Sluggish Horses** put him at a big jump where he can take it coolly than to trust him at a smaller place where other horses are crowding and goading him into a state of such impatience that in his anxiety to overtake any one in front of him he will jump without calculation, and endanger all in his vicinity by kicking, rearing, or rushing.

A sluggish horse, on the contrary, should be kept near others, that their lead and example may arouse his ambition and keep up his heart. It will not do to allow such a horse to fall far behind, as he will probably get discouraged and refuse to jump without a fight, at the end of which the hunt may have disappeared in the distance.

It is never wise to ride on the line of hounds, but rather to the right or left of them. Horses directly behind them **Proximity to** frighten the hounds and interfere with their hunt- **Hounds** ing. It also makes a few run very fast to keep from being galloped over, while many others sneak away or get behind the horses, of whose heels they stand in terror.

It is a nuisance to be obliged to stop and give some slow hound a chance to get by, or, if not considerate enough to do this, no rider likes to see a hound going through a fence with the probability of having a horse jump on him, should he pause for a moment on the other side.

A woman will escape these occurrences if she will keep to one side of the pack. In this position it is permissible to ride farther up than when so doing would bring her too near the pack; but the leading hounds must be watched closely, and should always be allowed plenty of room to turn sharp to the side where she is, without bringing them in contact with her horse. The instant they check, or even hover, for a moment, a woman must stop, and for two reasons:

In the first place, because she does not want to be in the way should it be necessary to cast the hounds in her direction; and, secondly, because she should seize every opportunity of giving her horse a few moments' respite, which she can afford to do if well enough up to notice what the hounds are doing.

She must be guided as to her course by the character of the country **Choosing a** over which she is riding. **Line**   If the hounds run over a succession of small hills, much unnecessary exertion may often be spared the horse by galloping around the base of them, instead of over their crest. But the hounds must not be lost sight of too long, or a sharp turn may hide them from view and conceal the line they have taken.

When a very steep hill is to be descended, it should be done by going down sideways in a zig-zag course, so that in case of a slip or stumble the horse will not roll over, as he might if attempting to make the descent in a straight line.

If the going is rough or through furze or some low growth of underbrush, a woman should sit well back in her saddle, and although guiding her horse, allow him plenty of rein to stretch his neck and see where he is putting his feet. Should he stumble or step into a hole, she will in this way have the best chance of keeping her seat, and he of regaining his balance.

If riding in a district where wire is extensively used for fencing, it will not do for a woman to go very far to one side of the hounds or to try to cut out a line for herself, unless she knows the country. Otherwise she may get pocketed by the wire, which few horses here are trained to jump, and which, therefore, should not be ridden at. In this case she would have to go back the way she came until she could get clear of it.

In jumping towards the sun, extra precautions should be taken. A horse is often quite blinded, and unable to accurately gauge the size of the jump he is to take, especially if it is timber. When the rays are directly in his eyes, the best thing to do is to walk him up to and alongside of the fence for a few yards, giving him a chance to measure it, then take him back and put him at it. This must not be done where it will interfere with any one else, but in any case such a jump must be approached slowly.

Wide ditches and streams are probably shirked as often as any kind of jump. Too much preparation for them excites the horse's suspicions and makes him hesitate, then refuse. A horse must be kept collected, yet sent along too fast to admit of any faltering on his part, and there must be no involuntary checking of his stride as the rider tries to see the depth or width of ditch or stream. When such are in sight, it is well to quicken the horse's pace, that he may reach the place before he sees any horse refusing, or before the banks have been made unsound by the jumping of the others. Each horse will probably widen the distance as the ground gives way beneath him, so a woman must use her own judgment in deciding where she will jump, instead of following some one else.

A bog or swamp is a most disagreeable place in which to be caught, and calls for calmness to get out without a wetting or fall. To quiet the horse is the first thing, and prevent his plunging into it deeper and deeper, as he will with every struggle. Should he be sinking, his rider must get off, keeping hold of the reins, for, although their combined weight would cause the bog to give beneath them, they might separately be able to keep on the surface, and quietly and gradually work their way to firm ground.

Whenever one comes upon something that cannot be seen at a distance, such as a hole, a drop, or a wire, the first person who discovers it should warn those behind by shouting back what it is, and, if possible, motioning where it is, that those in the rear may avoid it, each person cautioning the next one.

XI
SYMPATHY BETWEEN HORSE AND WOMAN

THE ADVANTAGES DERIVED from the existence of sympathy between horse and rider cannot be too highly estimated. When a woman gives her horse to understand that he will be ruled by kindness, he is very certain to serve her far more willingly and faithfully than if she tried to control him by force. If he has learned to be fond of her voice, it will calm and reassure him in moments of excitement which might otherwise result in a runaway; it will stimulate him to expend his best energies at her command, when force or punishment would fail, and will do more to establish a mutual understanding in a few weeks than would be gained in as many months of silent control.

A horse soon learns to distinguish the intonation of words of praise from those of censure, terms of endearment from admonition, and will often respond to them more readily than to severe discipline.

Few horses are so dull as not to be susceptible to kindness, or so vicious as not to be influenced by gentle treatment.

I do not approve of a woman, once she is in the saddle, entering upon a lengthy address of endearment to her horse if she is riding with friends. They may care for a little of her attention themselves; it is just as well not to show them the horse is the more interesting, even if she feels so. **Talking to Horse**

Moreover, incessant chatter becomes after a little time so familiar to the animal that the voice loses its power when intended to convey a definite meaning, and he fails to distinguish the difference between commands and idle pettings.

It is only necessary to reprove him, to give words of command, such as "walk," "trot," "canter," "whoa," which he may easily be taught to obey, and a few words accompanied by a caress to soothe, encourage, or command him when the occasion presents itself.

451

When living in the country, with a stable near the house, a woman is afforded the most favorable opportunity of making friends with her horse.

A good way to begin will be to dismount at the stable after a ride and take off the saddle and bridle.

It is very simple, for it is only to unbuckle the outside leather girth, stirrup leather, two inside girths, and perhaps a balance strap, and take off the saddle, unfasten the throat latch, lip strap, and curb chain on the bridle, throw the reins over his head, and take hold of the headstall, when he will withdraw his head.

She must have his halter ready to put on at once, or he might pull away.

This will give him a pleasant impression of her, which is an important point gained.

Should she through some mistake find no one in the stable, and the horse in a heat at the end of her ride, she should not hesitate to scrape him herself, brush the mud off his legs, put a light blanket on him, give him only a mouthful of water, and put him in his stall with a little hay. If she will rub his ears, and sponge out his mouth, it will be a great relief to him.

All this should be accomplished in a quiet manner, nothing done to alarm or excite him; and she may talk to him most of the time, and thus become quite friendly with him.

In the Stall When she visits him in the stall, she should always speak before touching him or entering, otherwise he might be startled and kick or plunge from fright.

If in a standing stall, entrance should always be made at the near side of the horse.

I greatly prefer a loose box in which the horse may turn at his pleasure. If he eats too much of his bedding, it is better to keep a leather muzzle on him than to tie his head up.

Before opening the door of the box, he should be induced to face it, to avoid the possibility of his kicking. This can be managed by offering him some sugar, carrots, or oats, which he will come for, held quietly on the palm of the hand, with the fingers out of his reach.

It is well for a woman, at first, to keep a light hold of the halter, so that he cannot crush her against the wall or hit her with his head.

She should never put her head above his, or a severe knock may be the result. She should pet him, avoiding all sudden movements, and accustom him to her voice ; when it has become familiar to him, he will listen for it, and neigh at her approach.

If he seems inclined to kick, the closer she keeps to him the better, as then she will receive only a shove, instead of the full force of the blow. If he shows a tendency to nip or bite, from play or mischief, he should be muzzled until, by coaxing and kindness, he has been made to give it up.

To strike him would be to turn his playful though dangerous prank into a vicious habit.

In petting him she should begin by stroking his neck, and gradually work down and backwards with a firm, light touch, until he does not resent being handled. He must be taught to let her lean on any part of him, and not to fear her skirts. This is often of value in case a woman is thrown and her habit catches on the saddle; for if the horse were accustomed to her weight and skirt being against him, he would not become frightened. Knowing her voice, he might be quieted by it, and had he learned the important lesson of stopping at the word "whoa," she might escape being dragged.

If in the course of a ride a woman dismounts at a house or stable, she should always be sure that a light blanket is immediately thrown over her horse. She should not start for a ride until **On the Road** some time after her horse has been fed, or his digestion will become impaired, as would hers under similar circumstances. After mounting, it is always well, by a light hold of the snaffle, to make a horse walk a short while; it is most annoying to have him start with a series of plunges or an inclination to bolt.

If he is so fresh that he will not walk without restraint likely to irritate him, perhaps spoiling his temper for the rest of the ride, it will be better to let him indulge in a brisk trot, after which he may be brought back to a walk. The next time, if having had more work, he will walk at first, while had his mouth been jerked the previous time, or a fight ensued, he would remember it, and prepare for a repetition of the performance.

A horse should not of his own will be allowed to change his gaits, but his rider must think to vary them; for if the horse is kept on one too long, it tires him unnecessarily and causes him to travel carelessly. Whatever gait she makes him adopt, it should be distinct and regular, and he should be kept collected and not urged beyond the pace at which he can comfortably travel.

A jog-trot, trotting in front and cantering behind, and other **Cautions** such eccentricities, should not be permitted in a park hack.

In turning a corner, the horse should always be somewhat supported, and have his hind-legs brought well under him, or he will be liable to slip. He should never be cantered around a corner unless leading with the foot towards which he will turn.

He should not be pulled up abruptly, unless to avoid sudden obstacles, but his pace should be gradually decreased until it is as required. A sharp stop entails considerable strain on the back tendons and hocks, and if done too often would be apt to make the horse throw a curb.

In going downhill, a walk is the gait which should be taken, or the horse's fore-legs will suffer. Should the ground be uneven and rough, or covered with rolling stones, the horse ought to be permitted to walk. His head should not be held too tightly, or he will be unable to see where he is going, while if the reins are slack he will appreciate that he must pick his way, and then will seldom put a foot wrong.

It is most undesirable to canter where there is a hard road; nothing will more quickly use up a horse than pounding along, each stride laying the foundation of windgalls and stiffness, if nothing more serious results from this ill-advised practice.

If a horse is at all warm, he must never be allowed to stand in a draught; five minutes of it might founder him, so that he would be ruined, or thrown into pneumonia. If, while on her ride, a woman should be forced to wait, she must keep her horse moving in a circle or any other way, keeping his chest from the wind as much as possible. Before reaching home, the horse should be walked for some time, so that he may enter the stable cool, and not be endangered by draughts if not attended to at once.

When riding with others, their horses should be regarded; and as the woman sets the pace, she should not make it faster than that which her companions' horses can easily maintain.

XII
PRACTICAL KNOWLEDGE OF THE STABLE

THE WOMAN SHOULD visit her horse in the stable, and there she cannot talk to him too much. If it be a private one, I assume that it is constructed on hygienic principles; but as horses are frequently boarded at livery-stables, a woman should not leave the choice of a stall to her groom. She should see that of **Stabling** those procurable it is the best drained and ventilated, though free from draughts, and well lighted. If these conditions are not obtained, sickness and incapacity may be looked for in the horse. She should notice the feed occasionally, and see that her horse is supplied with all he requires, and of the best quality, and that he has an abundance of good bedding. A frequent or indiscriminate use of physics is to be deprecated. Pure air, good food, careful grooming, and regular, moderate exercise are the best tonics.

She must learn to pick up her horse's feet, as she should examine his shoes personally, and ascertain that they have been made to fit the **Picking up Feet** feet, instead of the horn being rasped away to fit the shoes. The soles must be pared, but the frogs and bars should not be interfered with. She cannot expect to have the shoes on more than a month; although, if the horse has not had enough work to wear them down, they may be removed and put on again, for were they worn too long, corns and inflammation, causing lameness, would be the result. Another reason for knowing how to lift his feet is that he might pick up a stone on the road, and if alone she would be obliged to take it out, or run the risk of seriously laming him. While a woman is playing with him is an excellent opportunity for her to look at her horse's feet, which should be taken up in the following manner.

She must stand on his near side, a trifle back of his fore-legs, and facing his hind ones. She should run her left hand from his knee to his fetlock, behind, and inside of his near fore-leg, grasping just below his fetlock, with the fingers on the coronet and the thumb above on the pastern. A horse which has been broken will yield his foot, bending his knee at once, but sometimes with such force that she must keep her head held up, so that there be no chance of contact with his heel. With the right hand she can examine his foot, after which she may pass to his off fore-foot, and then to the near hind-leg.

For this she must stand close to his side, and stroke him firmly from the quarters to the hock. Passing her right hand under his hock to his fetlock, and grasping his foot as she did the fore one, she must raise it, letting the hock rest in the angle of her arm, while with her right hand she turns up the foot for inspection. She must not lean too far over or get back of the horse, or she is likely to be kicked if he offers any resistance.

Then, too, she may unfasten the roller and throw back his blanket, that she may be sure the saddle has not rubbed his back. A slight abrasion of the skin, if treated at once, will require only a day or two to heal; but if neglected for some days, the time will be greatly prolonged. If any soreness is detected, the saddle should be looked to immediately and the cause of the trouble remedied.

A shining coat is not positive proof that the horse is properly groomed. The hair should be rubbed the wrong way, and if the skin **Grooming** leaves a whitish deposit on the fingers, it will be well for the horse's owner to watch the groom the next time the horse is dressed, and to insist upon its being thoroughly done.

Much of what seems to be vice in a horse comes from his having been imperfectly bitted when young, or from subsequently having his mouth roughly handled. He should always be ridden in **Bitting** as easy a bit as possible, as some horses go well and quietly in a plain snaffle, and will pull, bolt, or run in a curb or any severe contrivance. No rule can be given as to what bit will best control certain tendencies. Experimenting with each kind will be the only means of finding out, but pulling is as likely to arise from an over-sensitive mouth as from a hard one, in which case a rubber snaffle might prove efficacious where a Chifney would fail.

Sometimes certain parts of the mouth become callous, and a bit bearing on a different place might produce the desired result. Most

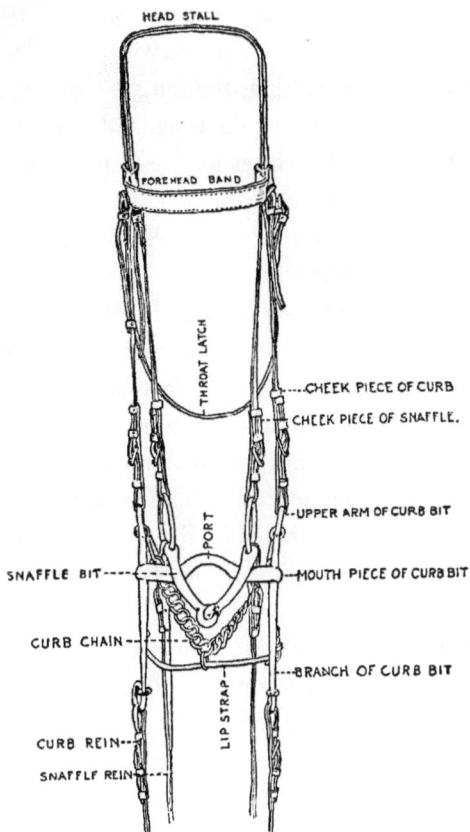

HEAD STALL

FOREHEAD BAND

THROAT LATCH

PORT

....CHEEK PIECE OF CURB

CHEEK PIECE OF SNAFFLE.

-UPPER ARM OF CURB BIT

SNAFFLE BIT----

--MOUTH PIECE OF CURB BIT

CURB CHAIN-

LIP STRAP

---BRANCH OF CURB BIT

CURB REIN--

SNAFFLE REIN----

DOUBLE BRIDLE FOR GENERAL USE

horses will go well in a bit and bridoon, varied to suit their peculiarities by the height of the port, the length of the branches, and the pressure of the curb-chain. There are certain points which should always be regarded. The mouth-piece must fit the horse's mouth exactly, being neither so narrow as to pinch him, nor so wide as to lose its power. The port should be the same width as the tongue-channel, and no higher than required to leave room for the tongue. The curb-chain must be sufficiently tight to furnish leverage for the branches, yet not so tight as to pinch the jaw when no force is applied.

Clipping horses in winter I have heard objected to on the ground of its being unsafe to deprive them of the thick coat which affords pro-

Clipping   tection from the cold. If their coat is thick and long, it is, in my opinion, much wiser to clip them, and for several very good reasons. Their work is rarely continuous, and the alternating of the heated with the cooling-off condition is very liable to work more or less injury. A heavy-coated horse which has been driven until very warm, and then left for half an hour to stand outside of a shop or house and become chilled by the wind striking the heavy wet coat, which frequently does not dry for hours, is likely to become a subject for the veterinary.

On the other hand, if the horse is clipped, he does not get so warm in the first place, and, in the second, would cool off more quickly and without danger of becoming chilled. In very cold weather quarter blankets will furnish all the protection necessary, and prevent the wind from striking the horse while standing.

With saddle horses, although not so important, it is an advantage to have them clipped, because a cold day is certain to make the rider go steadily to keep warm, and the horse, becoming overheated (if his coat is heavy), is in great danger of taking cold if permitted to stand for a moment in a draught.

No woman who rides should be without a practical knowledge of how to saddle and bridle her horse, as the groom often turns him out imperfectly bitted or girthed; and unless she knows how to do it herself, she will not perceive that anything is wrong   **Bridling** until too late to prevent mischief. She should learn to hold the bridle by the headstall, in her left hand, as with the right she slips off the horse's halter, and throws the reins over his head. Then

change it to the right hand, putting her left on the bits, which she gently inserts between his jaws. With the right she must pull his ears under the headstall, and then turn her attention to fitting the bridle.

She must see that the headstall fits, that the forehead-band is not too tight, and that there is plenty of room between the throat-latch and the throat. The snaffle-rein is fitted by the buckles of the cheek-piece, and should fall a trifle below the angle of the mouth. The curb needs careful adjustment, that the mouth-piece may rest exactly on the bars of the mouth. Then the chain must be hooked when quite flat on the chin -groove, but not tight enough, unless used vigorously, to inconvenience the horse. The lip-strap should pass through the small ring attached to the curb chain, thus keeping it in place. I like a bridle with buckles, or billets as they are called, rather than one which is stitched to the rings. In the first place, it is frequently desirable to change the bits, especially in a large stable, and being sewed would necessitate a bridle for each bit. Furthermore, when the bits are washed, the leather gets wet, and the stitching is apt to become rotten, and unexpectedly give way at a critical moment, when some unusual strain is put on it.

A noseband furnishes additional control over a **Noseband** horse; but it should not be attached to the bridle, or it may interfere with the action of the bit. It should have a headstall and cheek-pieces, and be buckled tight enough to prevent the horse from opening his mouth too wide, but it must not restrain his breathing.

If a martingale is used, I much prefer a running to a standing one. It is useful with star-gazers or horses that get their noses out too far. Some horses need one to steady them in hunting, but the running **Martingale** martingale is the only one which should be tolerated in jumping, and then not be used unless necessary. It is attached to a girth, and at the two upper ends are sewed rings through which the snaffle passes. With a running martingale there must be a stop on each snaffle, considerably larger than the rings of the martingale; otherwise there is danger of these rings getting caught in the bits, frightening the horse, and making him rear or back, as there is no way to release the pressure thus brought on his mouth. The length should be carefully regulated, so that it will keep the horse's head at the desired height. This admits of considerable play to the horse, but within control of the rider, while with a standing martingale no liberty is attainable.

Once mounted, the rider cannot influence its bearing; and should the horse trip, he cannot fling up his head, as he must to regain his balance.

For ordinary riding a breast-plate is not always used, but in hunting it is almost indispensable, and is always a safe-guard against a woman's saddle slipping back. It is **Breast-plate** put on over the horse's head with the reins, and one strap passes between his forelegs, through the loop of which one of the girths passes. Two other ends buckle, one on each side of the saddle, near the horse's withers, and it should be loose enough to admit of free movement in galloping and jumping.

CORRECT SADDLE

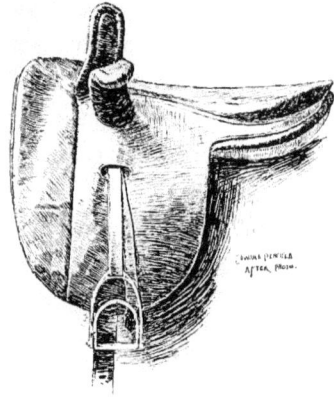

The saddle should be very plain in appearance. It must have a level seat, which can only be obtained in those having the tree cut away above the withers; otherwise, to clear them, the saddle must be so

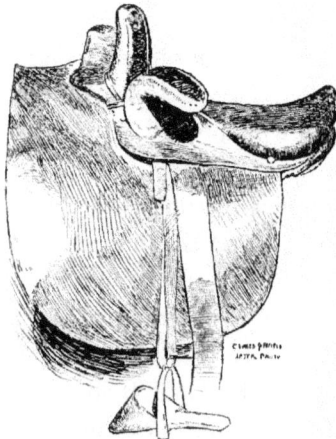

UNDESIRABLE SADDLE

elevated in front that it is sometimes six inches higher than the cantle, placing the knee in an awkward and fatiguing position, and

The Saddle   it is impossible to rise without an unusual amount of exertion, which will lead to arching the back, thrusting the head forward, and probably galling the horse's withers. There should be no third pommel, such as there formerly was on the right side of the saddle, bending to the left over the right leg.

The two pommels must fit the knees exactly, or the circulation will be impeded, and a cramp brought on which renders the muscles powerless to grip the pommels. The seat must extend about an inch beyond the line of the spine, and, although I usually object to it, for a child the seat should be covered with buckskin. No more padding should be used than is required to fit the horse's back, as it looks badly for the top of the saddle to be several inches above the horse. Moreover, the nearer one is to the animal's back, the greater will be the control. It enables one more readily to detect the stiffening of the muscles when mischief is contemplated, and to be prepared to thwart it. It should not have any superfluous straps, stitching, or attempts at ornamentation: the simpler the style the better; even the slit on the saddle-flap for the pocket is now frequently dispensed with. A safety pommel-band is sometimes fastened from the extreme upper forward end of the right saddle-flap to the top of the right pommel, thence to the left. This lessens the likelihood of a skirt becoming caught.

SAFETY STIRRUP, CLOSED

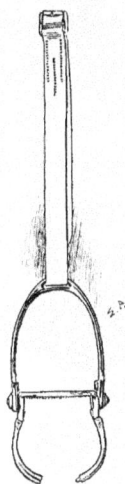

SAFETY STIRRUP, OPEN

On no account should a slipper stirrup be used, but a safety stirrup without any padding, and one which does not work by having the bottom drop out, as **Stirrup** these are apt to come to pieces when least desired, leaving the foot without any support. The best kind have the inner half-circle

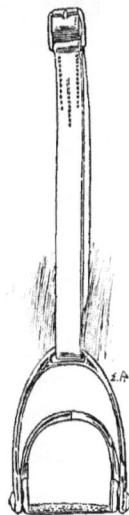

jointed in the middle and working on a hinge at both sides, so that it can open only on being pulled from below, as in case of a fall. Next to this in safety comes a plain, small racing stirrup.

The Fitz-William web girths are the best for a woman's saddle,
Girths   white being used in preference to darker shades.
There are braided raw-hide and also cord girths, the former being very serviceable, but they do not look so well as either of the others.

When the saddle is in position, free from the play of the shoulders, the first girth is taken up, then the back one, and kept clear of the horse's elbows, that his action may not be impeded. Although pulling the girths excessively tight is to be avoided, it will not **Saddling** do to leave them loose, as a woman's unevenly distrib- uted weight might cause the saddle to turn. Any wrinkles in the skin caused by the girthing should be smoothed away by passing the fingers between the girths and the horse. Then the stirrup-leather is buckled, after this the outside leather strap that keeps the saddle-flap in place, and finally the balance-strap, which must be fairly tight, assists in keep- ing the saddle in position. Before mounting she should always glance at the saddle and bridle, and be sure that they are properly put on; otherwise her ride may be rendered uncomfortable, if not dangerous.

A WELL-BALANCED CART

XIII
SOMETHING ON DRIVING

NINETY-NINE WOMEN OUT of every hundred are firmly convinced that instruction is by no means necessary to their driving instruction safely and in good form. Four men out of five labor under the same delusion. It is a sad error, **Desirability** that leads to numberless failures, and many acci- **of Instruction** dents which might so easily be avoided if the services of a competent teacher were employed at the beginning. Having seen others drive without any apparent difficulty, the novice conceives the notion that there is nothing to learn which cannot be mastered without assistance after one or two attempts. If such a one escapes a bill of damages, it should be credited to the ministering care of her guardian angel. She may indeed escape accident; she may learn to start without dislocating the neck of every one in the trap, and get around the corner without an upset; but she will never learn to *drive*. There is something more for her to know than that she must pull the off rein to turn to the right and the near one to go to the left, though this appears to be the extent of knowledge deemed necessary.

Women, even more than men, require a thorough understanding of what they are doing, for they lack the strength to rectify a miscalculation at the last moment. The ignorance, indecision, and weakness frequently displayed by women in driving are what so often render them objects of apprehension to experienced whips.

It is folly for any woman to flatter herself that she needs only a little practice, and that the rest "will come." If she has not begun correctly, practice will only wed her to the faults she must have acquired.

Assuming, however, for the sake of argument, that, after having discounted her call on an all-protecting Providence and stricken with terror her long-suffering friends, she manages to guide the family nag

465

along the turnpike without the aid of a civil escort to clear the road before her—what of it? She hasn't learned anything; her form is execrable; and in case of an emergency she is quite as unprepared as when she took up the reins weeks before, with the ill-conceived notion that she was not of the common clay, and that a whip, rather than a rattle, had been the insignia of her infantile days.

How much better, safer, and more sensible to acquire good form than by its neglect to become an object of ridicule to those who, by their knowledge of driving and exposition of superior horsemanship, are entitled to criticise others who have disregarded proper instruction, and, wise in their own conceit, relied on their ignorance for guidance.

Some women there are who drive only because they consider it the "proper thing." Absorbed in the opportunity for display, and ignorant of the fitness of things, they array themselves in the treasures of their

Vulgar Display wardrobe, more likely than not to be a gay silk, and, with every discordant ribbon and flounce of their *bizarre* costume loudly challenging the attention of the on-lookers, they sally forth perched on the box of a spider phaeton, Tilbury, or dog-cart, indifferent to, because ignorant of, the incongruity of their turnout, unconscious of the signal they have flung to the breeze, which unmistakably proclaims their lack of early instruction.

These are they who in the handling of their animals instantly call to mind the puppet-shows of our childhood days, and fill us with an almost irresistible desire to look under the box-seat and discover who is working the invisible wires. Every movement is spasmodic the arms work as though an alternating **Bad Form** electric current were constantly being turned through them the hands finger the reins nervously; and if the vehicle happens to be a two-wheeler, the unhappy driver looks as though every jolt of the poorly balanced cart would send her into the road from her very insecure seat.

Another harrowing spectacle is that of the woman leaning forward, a rein in each hand, with her arms dragged almost over the dash-board by her horse's mouth, a look of direful expectancy in her eyes, and a much be-flowered and be-ribboned hat occupying unmolested a rakish position over one ear, where it has fallen during her hopeless struggle with the reins.

It is strange women should not have a sufficiently clear idea of the fitness of things to realize that elaborate toilets of silks, **Costume** laces, and flowers, and large hats, although appropri- ate in a victoria, are inconvenient and totally out of place when driving a sporting-trap, such as a dog-cart.

A plain, neatly fitting, but not tight cloth suit, with a small hat, which will not catch the wind, is far more serviceable and in better taste. However, she should avoid the other extreme affected by the woman who desires to appear masculine and "sporty," and who, showing a large expanse of shirt front, wears a conspicuous plaid suggestive of a horse-blanket.

This specimen of feminine "horsy-ness" invariably drives with her hands held almost under her chin, and her whip in as vertical a posi- tion as herself. She is as powerless to control her animal as is the one who leans over the dash-board.

This is the sort of woman who compels her groom, if she have one, to wear a cockade in his hat, in ignorance of the fact that we in this **Cockade** country have no claim to its use. In Great Britain it is the distinguishing mark of either the royal family or the military, naval, or civil officers of the government; but used here it is only a meaningless affectation.

To achieve success, and to obtain a business-like appearance in driving, a woman must possess confidence in her **Confidence** power to control her horses, and it must be the con- fidence derived from knowledge and skill, and not that born of ignorance or foolhardiness.

She must know what to do, and how to do it promptly, under all circumstances, and this necessitates a thorough comprehension of the sport she is pursuing.

It is to be hoped she will gain this from competent instruction, and that she will embrace every opportunity of adding to her infor- mation on the subject.

A quiet, steady old horse, such as one might expect to see doing **The "Family-Horse" Fallacy** farm-work, cannot always be recommended even to a beginner, for he generally requires so little management that when he does occa- sionally become unruly it is so unusual that the woman is taken unawares.

Moreover, it makes one careless and slovenly always to drive a horse which goes along in a leisurely manner, without any display of life.

A woman who has been accustomed to such an animal will be at a loss to manage a spirited pair, should she be called upon to do so. If she begin with a horse which goes well into his collar and does his work generously, she will learn twice as much as she would in the same time with a lazy horse, and will sooner be able to drive a pair.

The position on the driving seat should be comfortable and firm,
On the Box   which cannot be the case when it is used merely to lean against, instead of to sit upon.

From the knee down, the leg should be but slightly bent, with the feet together and resting against the foot-rail.

The elbows should be held near the body, and the reins in the left hand, with the little finger down, and the knuckles pointing straight ahead, about on a line with or a trifle below the waist, and in the middle of the body.

Whether driving one or two horses, the manner of holding the reins is the same; but more strength and decision, as well as the judgment which, of course, experience will bring, are required for the pair.

The near rein belongs on top of the first finger,   **Position** held there firmly by the thumb, and the off rein should   **of Reins** be between the second and third fingers.

The gloves should be large, broad across the knuckles, and long in the fingers; otherwise cold, stiff hands will result from the impeded circulation.

The right hand, close to the left, should contain the whip, which must be held at an angle of a little less than forty- five degrees, and at the collar, about eight to ten inches from the butt, so that it balances properly.

When about to start, the reins should be tightened, to feel the horse's
Handling Reins   mouth, and a light touch of the whip will suffice to send him forward. The hand should then yield, so that as he straightens the traces there will be no jerk on his mouth.

In turning to the right or to the left, the reins must not be separated.

The right hand should be placed on the rein, indicating the desired direction, until the turn has been made; but a slight pressure on the opposite rein should keep the horse from going too near a corner.

The left hand must not relax its hold, so that when the right is removed the reins will be even, as they were before.

In stopping, the body is not to be bent backwards, suggestive of an expected shock, and the hands raised to the chin.

It cannot be too strongly impressed on the woman's mind that the less perceptible effort she makes, the more skilful will she appear. Therefore, if she take hold of the reins with her right hand as far in front of the left as she can handily reach, and then draw them back, she will have accomplished her purpose in a quiet and easy manner.

Driving a pair is much the same as driving one horse; but allowances should be made for the peculiarities of each, and **A Pair** they should not be treated as though machines of identical construction.

Frequently a woman driving a nervous horse with a quiet one will hit them both with the whip, when, should she touch the quiet one only, the sound of it would urge the other as much as the blow does the dull one.

Here is another objection to clucking to horses: one of them needs it much more than the other, yet they hear it with equal clearness, and simultaneously; therefore the high-mettled horse increases his pace sooner and more than his sluggish companion, and does more than his share of the work. Several noiseless touches of the whip, administered in quick succession to the laggard, will do more to equalize their pace than would a sharp, loud cut or any amount of clucking.

Sometimes a woman will experience great inconvenience from not having her horses properly bitted and harnessed. This should always be seen to, either by herself or some one who is competent to judge for her. When she has more than one horse to control, she will soon become tired if one of them pulls and the other will not go into his collar.

A judicious readjustment of the curb-chain and the coupling-rein will often make the difference between discomfort and ease.

POSITION IN TANDEM DRIVING

XIV
SOMETHING MORE ON DRIVING

WHILE A HORSE is doing his work in a satisfactory manner he should not be irritated by having his mouth jerked and the whip applied for the driver's amusement. It is a pity all women do not realize that a horse will accomplish, with less fatigue, much more work when taken quietly **Management** than he will if fretted and tormented by needless urging or restraint. Constant nagging affects an animal in the same way as it does a human being; and though a horse is usually subjected to such treatment through want of thought, it is none the less exasperating to him.

One result of this ordeal is that it prompts him to break into a canter as he becomes restless; and then he must be brought back to a trot by decreasing the speed and keeping the hands steady.

A stumbling horse must be kept awake and going at a medium **Stumbling** rate of speed. In either a very fast trot or a slow one he is likely to trip, and unless his driver is prepared for it, and ready to keep him up, he will probably fall, and she may be pulled over the dash-board.

A bearing-rein may assist in keeping him on his feet, but an habitual stumbler can never be considered safe. Such a horse must not be driven with loose reins, as a feeling on his mouth is necessary at all times.

When a horse persistently backs, there are two great dangers: first, he may upset the carriage, unless it cuts under; and, secondly, **Backing** he may back into something or over an embankment.

If the road be level, a woman must try to keep the horse from backing to one side, although in case of a steep declivity it may be necessary to pull him sideways, and risk an overturn rather than a fall over a bank. In all events, the whip should be vigorously applied, in the hope of starting the horse forward; if the woman have a groom with her, he should go to the horse's head at once and lead him.

Occasionally, backing may arise from sore shoulders caused by an ill-fitting collar; but if there is no such excuse for his action, and it should become a habit, the horse is not suitable for any woman to drive.

If desirous of making a turn in a narrow lane, it will often be necessary to back off the road, between trees or on to a foot-path, to obtain room. Some horses will not back under these circumstances, nor from a shed where they have been tied. In most instances all that will be required is to get out, take the horse by his bridle, and by lightly tapping one foot make him raise it, at the same time pushing him back by the bit. The other foot should be moved in the same way, and this repeated until he has gone far enough. After a few steps the woman may resume her seat, with the probability of the horse backing without further resistance.

If the horse is nervous, the pull at his mouth may make him back

Rearing and Kicking

so fast that in his excitement he will rear. In this event the reins should be loosened a moment and the animal quieted, after which the backing process may be continued.

If the rearing comes from temper, and takes place when he has been going forward, there should be no weight on his mouth while he seems in danger of falling backward, but a cut of the whip administered as he comes down may prevent his trying it again. It is important to feel his mouth at this juncture, as the whip will make him plunge forward, and the hold on his mouth must be firm enough to keep the traces loose as he lands; otherwise there would be a sudden strain on them, and consequently an unpleasant jerk, which might bring the carriage on to his hocks, as he stopped to gather himself for another effort, and, even if it did not make him kick or run, he would probably be bruised.

A determined kicker needs to have his head kept up, and for this purpose a bearing-rein will be found of great service. He should be driven with a kicking-strap, but it must not be too tight, or it will induce the habit it is intended to cure. He may kick if the crupper is too tight, so this also should be looked to.

When a rein gets under the tail of a horse, under no circumstances
should an attempt be made to pull it away. It   **Rein under Tail**
should be pushed forward, and the horse spoken
to in a reassuring manner.

If he does not then release it, a slight cut of the whip may divert
his attention; he will whisk his tail, and at this instant the rein must
be allowed to fall to one side, as were it pulled directly up, it would be
likely to be caught again. If these methods do not prove efficacious, a
woman must try to keep the horse straight, and prevail upon him to
walk until some one sees her predicament and comes to her assistance.
In some traps she might be able to reach forward and remedy the difficulty, meanwhile watching for any symptoms of kicking. But whether
she does it herself or directs some one else, she must see that the tail is
lifted, instead of an effort being made to pull the rein away.

Many mishaps come from this seemingly trivial occurrence, and a
horse frightened by improper treatment is liable to bolt or run.

It is always an excellent plan to have a horse trained to stop short at
the word "whoa!" This expression is usually misapplied, being made to
do duty for "steady" or "quiet," and it will be difficult to teach a horse
its true significance unless he is never driven without this end in view,
and the term employed only when it is meant.

In the event of a horse bolting, the chances are very great against

    Bolting   a woman's checking him. If she can do it at all,
and Running   it will be by sawing his mouth, and giving a suc-
                cession of sharp jerks, while endeavoring to
control his course.

The most dangerous and irrational thing she can do is to jump out
of the trap.

Severe injuries almost invariably attend such a proceeding; and if
it be possible to stay in, she should do so, never relinquishing her hold
on the reins. If from the swaying of the carriage she seems in danger
of being thrown out, a woman must make sure that her skirts are not
caught on anything, and that her feet are clear of the reins.

Men sometimes pull a runaway horse into a ditch or up a steep
bank, which stops him; but a smash or an overturn is inevitable ; and
should a woman attempt this, there is great danger of her being unable
to extricate herself from the tangle. She is handicapped by her skirts,

which are more than likely to cause her to be dragged should the horse manage to start off again. Besides this, after a struggle such as she will have had, a woman will seldom have enough strength left to force a horse from the direction he has chosen.

In whatever pranks horses indulge, the dangers are multiplied and **Crowded Driveways** intensified when encountered by a woman who ventures to drive in a crowded park or avenue during the afternoon.

Women of culture and refinement, realizing this, and wishing to avoid making themselves conspicuous on public highways, are content to be driven at this hour, reserving the mornings for the pleasure of handling the reins themselves.

Some women there are who drive better than most coachmen, and a few of these may desire to display their skill and their well-appointed traps when the spectators are most numerous. They may be competent to make their way through such a maze as one finds on popular carriage roads, but they do it in defiance of the condemnation they will receive from people of more refined ideas.

The majority of women who drive are unable to control their horses, and they need not flatter themselves that their immunity from accidents is the result of their skill. They owe their safety to the fact that men, appreciating the uncertainty of their movements, give them plenty of room, and keep as far as they can from anything driven by a woman.

Such women would be less objectionable if they were more considerate of others. For example, they should keep on their own side of the drive, and, if they are going **Road Courtesy** slowly, as much to the right of it as possible, that those who desire to pass may not have their way blocked.

Again, they should remember that some one is behind them, and that they should not endeavor to turn or stop abruptly without having intimated their intention to those in the rear.

Another heedless thing they do is, in passing a leading trap to turn in ahead of it so sharply that a more careful driver is forced to pull up rather than endanger his horses by having the wheels swing against them.

Women seem to forget now and then that they must always pass to the left of a vehicle in front of them, and not try to get through a small space on its right. If they would only take a few lessons in driving, pay attention to the instruction they receive, and cultivate consideration for others, their presence on the box might be welcomed more frequently and with greater warmth than it now is.

It would be well if equestrians rode with more regard for the convenience of those who are driving. When a bridle-path is provided for them, there is no reason why they should usurp any of the road intended for carriages. They would feel outraged, and justly so, if one vehicle should appear on their road; yet swarms of them daily use the drive, occupying much-needed space, and clattering and darting along, unmindful of startled horses and the narrow escapes of their own mounts from collisions with many wheels.

Comparatively few women are so fortunate as to have an opportunity to drive tandem or four-in-hand. If they are so situated that they would be likely to do so frequently, they should not hesitate to take lessons, as otherwise they would slowly learn from many dangerous and costly experiences **Tandems and Teams** what a trustworthy teacher could have shown them with safety and expedition. However, it is well to be prepared for all contingencies, and therefore many women may desire to know something about these branches of driving, in case they should in some unforeseen manner have an opportunity to essay them.

If, for instance, she were driving with a friend who offered to let her take the reins, a woman would not be expected to look to the harnessing and bitting, but there are a few points she might be glad to know.

The reins are held the same in tandem and team-driving. The first finger separates the leaders' reins, and the second those of the wheelers, with each near rein above the off one. Thus over the first **Reins** finger will be the near leader, under it the off leader, and between this rein and the second finger the near wheeler, with the off wheeler between the second and third fingers. The right hand must be free to hold the whip and to manipulate the reins.

The off-wheel rein will often need attention, as the third finger is not so strong as the other two used, and therefore this rein will more readily slip through.

In changing a rein it must always be done by pushing it back from in front of the hand, instead of pulling it through from behind.

The correct handling of the whip can be mastered only after much patience and constant practice, but its proper use is of paramount importance.

Women will find driving tandem easier than driving four, because, although it requires more skill to keep the horses straight, it does not call for the amount of muscle needed to manage four horses, the brake, and whip.

At first the weight alone of the reins would tire her, and of course there are more chances of mishaps with four horses than with two. In **Unruly Leader** the latter the leader has no horse at his side to steady him; but if well trained he will travel straight, and not attempt to turn around and join the wheeler. Should he do this and not respond to the reins, the whip should hit his neck with force sufficient to make him change his mind.

As a last resort, the wheeler must be turned to follow him, and then they must both be made to proceed in the direction desired by the driver. If the leader, instead of being exactly in front of the wheeler, gets too far to the right, his near rein should be shortened; but the wheeler must be made to meet him half-way by pulling his off rein at the same time. In the opposite case the off-lead and near-wheel reins must be shortened.

To turn a corner, say to the left, with a tandem or a four, the near-lead rein should be looped by taking up several inches, pushing it back of the forefinger, and holding it there in this shape with the thumb. The right hand must be placed on both off **Turning** reins, to guard against the turn being made too sharply, and the cart or coach being brought into contact with the corner. To turn to the right, the reverse tactics are employed, but it is more difficult to loop the off rein.

When the corner has been successfully rounded, the right hand should be taken away and the left thumb raised, thus leaving the horses in a position to go straight.

In going downhill all the reins should be shortened, and care taken that the leaders' traces particularly are loose, or they may pull the wheelers down when these should be holding back the coach.

The wheelers should always, if possible, start and stop the load.

In going uphill the leaders must do their full share, and on the level each horse must be kept up to his work.

An unnecessary nervous fingering of the reins should be avoided, as, besides being most unworkmanlike, it irritates the horses.

It is the height of folly for a woman to attempt to drive a tandem or a four-in-hand until she is thoroughly familiar with one horse and a pair. She may understand the theory of it, but until she has had some practice under proper instruction she should not take the reins, unless some one is near to assist her, or she will endanger not only her own safety, but jeopard that of those who may accompany her.

FINIS

SUGGESTED READING

BIOGRAPHIES AND MEMOIRS:

Brannaman, Buck, and William Reynolds. *The Faraway Horses*. The Lyons Press, 2001.

Camp, Joe. *The Soul of a Horse: Life Lessons from the Herd*. Three Rivers Press, 2008.

Carver, Sonora, and Elizabeth Land. *A Girl and Five Brave Horses*. 1961. Martino Fine Books, 2011

Eoff, Susan. *Seeing Through the Eyes of the Horse*. Selfseeds, 2015.

Golden, Flora. *Women in Sports: Horseback Riding*. Harvey House, 1978.

Martin, Ann. *The Equestrian Woman*. Paddington Press, 1979.

Resnick, Carolyn. *Naked Liberty*. The Carolyn Resnick Method, 2005.

Richards, Susan. *Chosen by a Horse*. Mariner Books, 2007.

Tierney, Maureen. *Horses a Better Way: My Journey with Horses*. CreateSpace Independent Publishing Platform, 2012.

COLLECTIONS OF ESSAYS:

Fox, Amy, editor. *Of Women and Horses*. BowTie Press, 2000.

HISTORY:

Bloodgood, Lida Fleitmann. *The Saddle of Queens: The Story of the Side-Saddle*. J. A. Allen and Company, 1959.

Gianoli, Luigi. *Horses and Horsemanship Through the Ages*. Crown Publishers, 1969.

NOVELS:

Bagnold, Enid. *National Velvet.* William Marrow and Company, 1935.

Gloss, Molly. *The Hearts of Horses.* Houghton Mifflin Harcourt Publishing Company, 2007.

Morpurgo, Michael. *War Horse.* Scholastic Incorporated, 1982.

RESEARCH STUDIES:

Adelman, Miriam, and Jorge Knijnik, editors. *Gender and Equestrian Sport: Riding Around the World.* Springer, 2013.

Dashper, Katherine. *Human-Animal Relationships in Equestrian Sport and Leisure.* Routledge, 2017.

TRAINING GUIDES:

Beach, Belle. *Riding and Driving for Women.* Charles Scribner's Sons, 1912.

Hayes, Alice M. T*he Horsewoman: A Practical Guide to Side-Saddle Riding.* 2nd ed.,Hurst and Blackett Limited, 1903

Hunt, Ray. *Think Harmony With Horses: An In-Depth Study of Horse/Man Relationship.* Pioneer Publishing Company, 1978.

O'Donoghue, Mrs. Power. *Ladies on Horseback.* W. H. Allen and Co., 1881.

Pony Boy, GaWaNi. *Horse, Follow Closely*: Native American Horsemanship. Lumina Media, 2006.

Slaughter, Jane R. *The Woman Equestrian.* Wish Publishing, 2003